A Catholic Cold War

A Catholic Cold War

*Edmund A. Walsh, S.J.,
and the Politics of American
Anticommunism*

PATRICK MCNAMARA

FORDHAM UNIVERSITY PRESS
New York • 2005

Library of Congress Cataloging-in-Publication Data

McNamara, Patrick H.
    A Catholic Cold War : Edmund A. Walsh, S.J., and the politics of American anticommunism / Patrick McNamara. — 1st ed.
      p.   cm.
    Includes bibliographical references and index.
    ISBN 0-8232-2459-7 (hardcover)
    1. Walsh, Edmund A. (Edmund Aloysius), 1885–1956—Political and social views. 2. Jesuits—United States—Biography. 3. Cold War—Religious aspects—Catholic Church. 4. Church and state—Catholic Church. I. Title.
    BX4705.W256M36   2005
    327.73′0092—dc22
    [B]

2005007329

Printed in the United States of America
07 06 05   5 4 3 2 1
First edition

CONTENTS

ACKNOWLEDGMENTS

I began the dissertation on which this study is based at the suggestion of my mentor, Professor Christopher J. Kauffman, but I could not have completed it without his expert guidance and unceasing support. Professor Kauffman's astute contextualization and his sensitive historical analysis make American Catholic history come alive, attributes that I hope will characterize my own historical work. I thank my readers, Monsignor Robert F. Trisco, editor of the *Catholic Historical Review* and professor emeritus of Church History, and Professor R. Emmett Curran, Department of History, Georgetown University, for their keen appraisals and suggestions. I am particularly grateful to Professor Curran for supplying me with archival materials pertaining to Walsh that he discovered while writing his history of Georgetown.

The archivists I encountered in the course of my research were models of efficient courtesy and service. They shared my enthusiasm, encouraged me in my research, and provided useful research tips along the way. I am particularly grateful to the staff of the Lauinger Library, Special Collections Division, Georgetown University, and to the staff of The Catholic University of America Archives. I also wish to acknowledge the influence of my former professors at Fordham University, particularly Professors Mark D. Naison, Paul A. Cimbala, and Reverend Mark S. Massa, S.J. They made me want to be a historian, and they continue to inspire me.

I would like to thank the following for the support they provided during the course of writing this book: Reverend Sean Ogle, Reverend Thomas Lynch, Reverend Peter Vaccari, Ed Wilkinson, Charles Morris, Alden Brown, Bob Armbruster, Jim Fisher, Reverend Gerald Fogarty, S.J., Vincent Tennariello, Charles Rabus, William Tarrant, Claudia Link, James Nolan, Nicholas Creary, Carmela O'Donnell, Ann Ford, Leonard Klie, and Joseph Coen. I have been very fortunate indeed to have a support network of such wonderful people.

This book is dedicated to my wife, Virginia, whose love makes all things possible.

ABBREVIATIONS

ADA	Americans for Democratic Action
AFL	American Federation of Labor
ARA	American Relief Administration
ASTP	Army Specialized Training Program
CAIP	Catholic Association for International Peace
CNEWA	Catholic Near East Welfare Association
CPUSA	Communist Party of the United States of America
DAR	Daughters of the American Revolution
ETO	European Theater of Operations
HUAC	House Un-American Activities Committee
NCWC	National Catholic War Council (1917–19); National Catholic Welfare Council (1919–22); National Catholic Welfare Conference (after 1922)
NRA	National Recovery Administration
OMGUS	Office of the Military Government of the United States
POAU	Protestants and Other Americans United for the Separation of Church and State
ROTC	Reserve Officers Training Corps
SATC	Student Army Training Corps
TWU	Transport Workers Union
UMT	Universal Military Training

INTRODUCTION

In the photo insert to Richard Gid Powers's 1995 history of American anticommunism, *Not without Honor*, two pages are devoted to images of significant Catholic anticommunists. At the top of the first page is a photograph of Patrick F. Scanlan, editor of the Brooklyn *Tablet* (1917–68), the preeminent anticommunist in the mid-twentieth century American Catholic press. Below Scanlan is the Reverend Edmund A. Walsh, S.J., founder of Georgetown University's School of Foreign Service. Because I had written my master's thesis on Scanlan's anticommunism and intended to focus on Walsh's anticommunism in my doctoral dissertation (and the study now before you), I found Powers's juxtaposition of these images compelling. As I further reflected on the particular photographic arrangement in Powers's book, I began to realize it might have significant implications for the historiography of American Catholic anticommunism.[1]

For the last fourteen years, my primary academic interest has been the history of American Catholic anticommunism. When I was an undergraduate at Fordham University, Professor Mark Naison suggested I write a seminar paper on the anticommunist component of the Brooklyn *Tablet*'s editorial policy. The topic intrigued me; even though my parents were longtime subscribers, I had never imagined the *Tablet* as a subject of scholarly interest. When I began my research, it appealed to me as a way of understanding my own background. As a child, I could remember the memorial Masses for Joseph McCarthy that the Catholic War Veterans held in nearby Forest Park, Queens, every Memorial Day weekend through the late 1970s.

Under the direction of Professor Thomas Curran at Saint John's University, I developed my paper into a master's thesis. By then, my interest in Catholic anticommunism had expanded beyond the nostalgic; I knew that this was a significant historical topic I wanted to further explore. In April 1997, Professor Christopher Kauffman suggested that I consider Edmund A. Walsh's anticommunism as a dissertation topic. As I looked into this option, I was surprised to discover that Walsh had not been the subject of a dissertation since 1970. An examination of the Walsh papers in the Special Collections Division at Georgetown University's Lauinger Library, however, soon showed that this was not due to a lack of material.[2]

Edmund A. Walsh is largely remembered today in connection with Senator Joseph McCarthy. Indeed, in March 1950, columnist Drew Pearson accused Walsh of prompting McCarthyism by suggesting that the senator emphasize communism in his 1952 reelection campaign. Pearson claimed that McCarthy's famous speech at Wheeling, West Virginia, in February 1950, in which he claimed to have a list of communists in the State Department, was the result of Walsh's advice. Because Walsh refused to publicly respond to the charges, the story gained credence, to the point where nearly every biography of McCarthy has cited Walsh as his mentor. As a result, Walsh's entire career has been overshadowed by his alleged association with the most infamous demagogue in twentieth-century American politics.

Long before 1950, however, Edmund A. Walsh was one of the best-known Catholic priests in the United States. In January 1919, at age thirty-three and a priest for less than three years, he founded the first school in the United States for diplomatic training, a major event in the history of American higher education. In 1922, the Holy See appointed Walsh to direct the Papal Relief Mission in famine-stricken Russia, the Church's first international relief project. In 1929, Pope Pius XI sent him to Mexico to aid the Church-state negotiations then under way; in 1931, he successfully negotiated with the Iraqi government to establish a Jesuit college in Baghdad. As an expert on geopolitics, he served as a consultant at the Nuremberg war crime trials. During the Truman administration, he was a highly respected adviser on Soviet strategies and goals in the early Cold War. Walsh's curriculum vitae is an impressive documentation of associations and accomplishments that extended far beyond the boundaries of the Catholic world before Vatican II. As a contemporary noted:

> Author, lecturer, diplomat, organizer and director of relief work, Father Walsh, in his multifarious activities, had to do with at least a hundred of the most prominent ecclesiastical, political, business, social and revolutionary personalities of his historical epoch.[3]

Quickly realizing what a formidable task it would be to consider Walsh's career as a whole, I chose instead to concentrate here on his anticommunism. After he retured from Russia in January 1924, Walsh spent the next four decades warning the American public about the moral and political threat that Soviet communism posed to the international community. By late 1952, when a stroke ended his public career, his anticommunist campaign amounted to four books and dozens of articles on the Soviet Union, as well as nearly two thousand lectures on this subject. No other Catholic anticommunist could claim such a record.[4]

What made Walsh unique among Catholic anticommunists was his being an expert on Soviet political theory and practice, something that Cardinal Francis Spellman, himself an impassioned anticommunist, patriot, and advocate of an aggressive American policy toward Russia, never professed to be. Although during the 1940s Father John F. Cronin, S.S., achieved a reputation as an expert on domestic communism, Walsh remained the leading American Catholic authority on its international aspect.

To date, there has been one biography of Walsh: Father Louis J. Gallagher's *Edmund A. Walsh, S.J.* Walsh's confrere and closest friend, Gallagher grew up with him in Boston and served as his assistant in Russia. While working on Walsh's biography, Gallagher served as the historian for Georgetown University's Jesuit community from 1954 to 1970. His extended obituary of Walsh in the Jesuit journal *Woodstock Letters* in 1957 appears to have been preparation for the larger work, which was published by the New York Catholic publishing house Benziger Brothers, in 1962.[5]

Although greeted with respectful reviews in the Catholic press, Gallagher's book otherwise received little attention. Writing in *America*, J. F. Gallagher noted that the book would "prove interesting and thought provoking not only to Fr. Walsh's wide circle of friends and associates but to anyone interested in the events of the past forty years." In *Emmanuel*, Thomas Sullivan praised Louis Gallagher for painting "an interesting picture of the humanity of an outstanding priest, educator and diplomat." In the *Homiletic and Pastoral Review*, Charles Dollen wrote that Walsh's story was "compelling" and deserved "wide attention," but he felt that Gallagher's own ability as an author, particularly his "sometimes pompous vocabulary," hindered the book's effectiveness. Nonetheless, he concluded, "the late Father Edmund A. Walsh, S.J., made as significant a contribution to American diplomacy as any Catholic priest since Bishop

Carroll," and this alone made Gallagher's book a "notable biography."[6]

Presenting a series of vignettes from various episodes in Walsh's life, rather than a comprehensive biography, Gallagher fails to place Walsh's accomplishments within a larger historical context, or to provide any critical analysis. He completely omits certain episodes in Walsh's life, particularly his connection with McCarthy. He draws freely on Walsh's letters in his text, but provides neither citations nor bibliography. In retrospect, it appears that Gallagher may have been too close to his subject to write a completely objective biography. The chief merit of his biography are the insights into Walsh's personality and character that only a close friend could provide.

Henry Hull's 1970 doctoral dissertation is a comprehensive study of Walsh's work in Russia with the Papal Relief Mission that is unlikely to be surpassed, yet both context and analysis are frequently lost in a forest of minutiae. Hull devotes little attention to the implications of Walsh's Russian sojourn for his subsequent anticommunist career. Although he makes excellent use of the Walsh papers at Georgetown, his primary sources are almost exclusively confined to that collection. Hull also overlooks certain negative aspects of Walsh's anticommunism, particularly the anti-Semitic implications that exist in some of Walsh's private writings and correspondence. Nonetheless, anyone wishing to study Walsh's Russian activity must begin with Hull.[7]

More recently, several scholars have ably discussed Walsh's career and its significance. In his history of the American Jesuits, Peter McDonough describes Walsh as "an entrepreneur" in the public square, "practically an institution by himself." In the most balanced and intelligent assessment of Walsh presently available, *Not without Honor,* Richard Gid Powers assesses Walsh as the "most influential Catholic anticommunist in the country," whose influence extended far beyond the bounds of the Catholic world. In his thorough analysis of Walsh's geopolitical thought, geographer Gearóid Ó Tuathail / Gerard Toal establishes Walsh's pioneer role in promoting geopolitics as an academic discipline during the early 1940s. These scholars have shown that there was a great deal more to Walsh's career than his alleged consultation with McCarthy.[8]

Based on my dissertation, the first extended treatment of Walsh's anticommunism, this study is divided into five chapters. Because

Walsh's anticommunism grew out of his work as an internationalist, Chapter 1 focuses on the founding of the School of Foreign Service. Although well within the larger Jesuit educational tradition of preparing students for public service, the school's founding was both a unique instance where a Catholic college anticipated rather than followed trends in American higher education and a significant, if overlooked, expression of American Catholic confidence in the interwar years. As the chapter makes clear, Walsh's particular contribution was as an activist, not as a scholar.

Patriot, internationalist, and Jesuit educator, Walsh sought to affirm the primacy of morality in the international realm. His interest in world affairs first developed during childhood in the 1890s, as America entered the world arena, and grew when he studied in Europe on the eve of the First World War. Boston Church leadership encouraged Catholics to be active participants in mainstream public life, which was a significant factor in Walsh's patriotism and his public Catholicism. A Catholic proponent of American exceptionalism in the tradition of Isaac Hecker and John Ireland, Walsh viewed the nation as a beacon of liberty and equality for the world. Like Hecker and Ireland, Walsh saw the Catholic Church as the bulwark of national life. If morality was the foundation of national life, religion was its source, and Catholicism was the truest form of religion. Neither Hecker nor Ireland, however, exercised the kind of influence on American public life that Walsh would exercise through the foreign service school.

Chapter 2 traces the development of Walsh's anticommunism during his stay in Russia, and his subsequent anticommunist activity in 1920s America. The religious persecution he witnessed in Russia led him to view the Soviet government as an international menace, the greatest threat to Christian and democratic ideals. The chapter goes on to show, however, that Walsh's own idealism was tainted—commingled with lower prejudices that privately linked communism with Judaism. When Walsh returned to the United States in 1924, communism was not a major public concern, American radicalism was still recovering from the Red Scare of 1919–20, and Catholics were more concerned with a resurgent anti-Catholicism. A study of Walsh's anticommunist activity during the 1920s thus helps to fill a gap in the history of American Catholic anticommunism.

Chapter 3 focuses on the Depression era (1929–41), when American communism experienced a resurgence, and anticommunism first manifested itself as a widespread impulse in American Catholic life. Catholic anticommunism assumed a variety of forms: the evangelical poverty of Dorothy Day, the demagogic populism of Charles Coughlin, and the popularized Thomism of Fulton Sheen, to name just a few. Walsh's unique contribution to Catholic anticommunism during the 1930s was as the Catholic expert on international communism, and as a leader of opposition to diplomatic recognition of the Soviet Union. During the 1930s, Walsh's conservatism became evident in his opposition to increased governmental spending on New Deal programs. At the same time, he began to formally articulate his anticommunism within the context of Ignatian spirituality. Using a key phrase from Ignatius, Walsh declared that the modern world faced a choice between "two standards," Christianity and communism.

Chapter 4 focuses on the war years. Most historians of anticommunism assume that American Catholics consciously repressed their anticommunism in the interest of the war effort. During this period, however, Walsh's geopolitical perspective allowed him to see communism and Nazism as two sides of the same coin. One of the first American educators to promote geopolitics as an academic discipline, Walsh became its leading Catholic interpreter. Through his work with the War Department as a lecturer on geopolitics during the war and as a geopolitical consultant at Nuremberg, his public reputation grew.

Chapter 5 addresses Walsh's role in the emerging anticommunist consensus at the start of the Cold War, when he became a valued consultant to the Truman administration and a leading Catholic supporter of an aggressive American policy toward the Soviet Union. Idealist Walsh publicly challenged realist George Kennan to debate American foreign policy. As the chapter shows, however, Walsh's idealism had its dark side. In endorsing a nuclear "first strike" on the basis that the Soviets were inherently immoral, it ignored the consequences for the enemy civilian population. Chapter 5 also reassesses Walsh's relationship with McCarthy, in the hope of demonstrating Walsh's real significance in the history of Catholic anticommunism from the 1920s through the early Cold War.

This study employs several archival sources that are indispensable for chronicling Walsh's anticommunist activity and interpreting its significance. The papers of Georgetown professor William Franklin Sands, located at the Philadelphia Archdiocesan Historical Research Center, provided valuable insights into Walsh's ability to recruit faculty for the foreign service school in its early years. The letters between Walsh and John J. Burke in the National Catholic Welfare Conference Archives at The Catholic University of America are essential for tracing the growth of Walsh's anticommunism during his Russian sojourn. The papers of William S. Culbertson, who headed the Geopolitical Section of Military Intelligence for the U.S. Army during the Second World War, located in the Manuscript Division of the Library of Congress, made it possible to survey Walsh's geopolitical work. The Joseph E. Davies Papers, also located at the Library of Congress, which contain the record of Walsh's participation on the presidential advisory commission that advocated peacetime conscription, help highlight his anticommunist activity during the early Cold War.[9]

When I began studying American anticommunism in the late 1980s, high on my assigned reading list were Daniel Bell's *The Radical Right* and David Caute's *The Great Fear*. Bell's anthology contains Richard Hoftsadter's highly influential essay "The Pseudo-Conservative Revolt," which portrayed anticommunism as motivated by irrational fears. For Hofstadter, anticommunism was an expression of insecurity he termed "status anxiety." Reflecting Hofstadter's influence, Caute's history of the McCarthy era describes anticommunism as an expression of "hysteria." "One of the appeals of McCarthyism," Caute writes, "was that it offered every American, however precarious his ancestry, the chance of being taken for a good American simply by demonstrating a gut hatred for Commies."[10]

When I examined Patrick Scanlan's editorial policy, I found these arguments easy to accept. To a large extent, Scanlan's anticommunism *was* motivated by the need to show that Catholics were as patriotic as their non-Catholic neighbors. His editorials seethed with the ethnic resentments that permeated Depression-era New York. Although I found it hard to disagree with Hofstadter and Caute, I felt that something was lacking in their treatment of anticommunism. It seemed as though they were still reacting to the McCarthy era, and they seemed unable—and possibly unwilling—to understand anticommunists as they understood themselves.

Richard Gid Powers's 1995 book *Not without Honor* went a long way toward filling this need. Despite his unconcealed conservative bias, Powers provides the most comprehensive history of American anticommunism presently available. Although he recognizes that insecurity was a significant factor for many anticommunists, Powers argues that not all anticommunists were so motivated. For Powers, the reductionist approach of Hofstadter and Caute does not do justice to a complex historical phenomenon that was a significant aspect of twentieth-century American politics and culture: "the myth of monolithic anticommunism" has obscured its complex and multifaceted nature.[11]

Powers characterizes American anticommunism as "a protest movement" against a system whose core tenets were "thoroughly alien to American values." Although he touches on the "irresponsible" anticommunism of Charles Coughlin and Joseph McCarthy, he argues that they were not the archetypes of the movement. What had been a largely white Anglo-Saxon Protestant movement during the "Red Scare" of 1919–20, he notes, expanded into a multifaceted movement that included African-American, Jewish, and Catholic anticommunists by the 1920s. The motivation for adopting anticommunism varied from community to community, as well as from individual to individual:

> There was no one thing that was American anticommunism; there were many American anticommunisms. All that anticommunists had in common was their hatred of communism, but each group hated it for different reasons.[12]

Powers's "many anticommunisms" thesis is a useful model for historians of Catholic anticommunism. Because every pontiff from Pius IX to Pius XII condemned communism and socialism, Catholic anticommunism had a doctrinal basis. In a broad sense, every Catholic was a de facto anticommunist. This does not imply, however, that all Catholic anticommunists had identical motives and emphases. Dorothy Day and Charles Coughlin, for example, both opposed communism, but Day's program of evangelical poverty had little in common with Coughlin's demagogic anti-Semitism. Their respective motives and emphases differed greatly, and the same might be said of other Catholic leaders, such as Patrick Scanlan and Monsignor John A. Ryan. It might well be argued, therefore, that there were many Catholic anticommunisms.

Catholic anticommunism has frequently been depicted in general terms as an attempt on the part of a minority group to prove its patriotism. Catholics were deeply affected, the argument goes, by the hostile anti-Catholicism of the 1920s, which culminated in the defeat of Alfred E. Smith in the 1928 presidential election. The rise of domestic radicalism during the 1930s and the specter of communist infiltration during the Cold War gave them the chance to attack an enemy who was even more un-American than they had been accused of being. This argument has its merits when one considers the case of Patrick Scanlan, though not so much in other cases.

During the interwar years, there was a growing confidence on the part of Catholics, who saw themselves as defending traditional American ideals in an age of increasing secularism. Chief among these ideals were the universality of moral values and their immutable nature. William M. Halsey writes that the lapse in Protestant idealism after the First World War allowed Catholics to assume the mantle of idealism. Among the secularizing trends in modern society that Catholics opposed were skepticism in postwar literature and relativism in law and morality.[13]

Catholic idealism manifested itself in a variety of ways in the interwar years. Walsh's anticommunism was one important expression of that idealism, growing out of his attempt to bring moral principles to bear in the field of international relations. Catholic anticommunism was a movement broad enough to include both the confidence of an Edmund A. Walsh and the minority consciousness of a Patrick Scanlan. Describing Walsh as an "idealist," however, is not to deny that his anticommunism contained an uneasy mixture of high principles and low prejudices. It is hoped, rather, that this study of his anticommunism will encourage scholars to further explore the complex and multilayered aspect of twentieth-century American Catholic anticommunism.

A Catholic Cold War

Edmund A. Walsh

Bostonian, Jesuit, Activist, and Educator

"New Occasions, New Duties"

Few historians would deny that 1919 was among the most tumultuous and eventful years in American history. Having emerged victorious from the First World War, the United States stood as a major power on the international scene. But when President Woodrow Wilson attempted at Versailles to establish a more equitable world order than had existed in 1914, America's allies, wanting revenge for four years of carnage and bloodshed, rejected his Fourteen Points in the treaty signed in Paris on June 28, and imposed heavy penalties on the German people. At home, Congress voted down American participation in the League of Nations. The majority of the American people, exhausted from the war effort, economic recession, and social unrest, desired a "return to normalcy."

By 1919, however, it was less feasible for the nation to ignore its international obligations. Economic growth, especially in foreign trade, had rapidly accelerated since 1865. The Spanish-American War led to overseas territorial expansion. Indeed, already in 1917, when Congress declared war on Germany, the die had been cast. Wilson's arrival in Paris in February 1919 signified the way of the future for the United States. America was on the world scene to stay and would have a significant role to play.

Both professionally and intellectually, Americans were ill prepared to assume such a role. The U.S. Foreign Service would not be established until 1924, with the Rogers Act. For most of the nation's history, diplomacy had not been considered a career that involved preparation. Important posts were often rewards for political support, and recent college graduates worked in lower-level positions before choosing a career elsewhere. Few colleges and universities offered courses on international law, and international relations had not yet emerged as an academic discipline.[1]

In the postwar period, the responsibilities of American diplomats expanded significantly. International trade, largely unsupervised by the government before the war, was afterward subjected to increased supervision. American businessmen abroad increasingly sought diplomatic assistance—to make contact with local officials, to advise on the wording of business contracts, and to familiarize themselves with the local culture. New responsibilities implied a need for training in several areas: international law, foreign trade, and foreign languages and cultures. Yet, before 1919, American higher education offered no programs for foreign service training.[2]

On November 25, 1919, however, an event took place on the campus of Georgetown University in Washington, D.C., that bore directly on filling the growing need for trained diplomats. Administrators, faculty, and students gathered in Gaston Hall for an event unique in the history of the 130-year-old Jesuit university. The audience was by no means typical for an academic gathering. In attendance were diplomats, representatives from the State and Commerce Departments, and members of the business community. The ceremony's purpose was to formally inaugurate the School of Foreign Service into the university.[3]

The seeds for the school's establishment were planted seventeen months earlier. In June 1918, newly appointed University President John B. Creeden, S.J., made the initial proposal to the Board of Regents. The proposal was accepted, but it was agreed that implementation could not begin until the war ended. The following February, the School of Foreign Service began a provisional semester in Healy Hall with sixty students. Over the next few months, the school received hundreds of inquiries and applications. The school's directors were able to recruit an impressive faculty from a wide variety of backgrounds, one unique among Catholic colleges and universities. By the time the inauguration took place, significant progress had been made toward a permanent endowment.[4]

The main speaker at the inauguration was the school's organizer and first regent, the Reverend Edmund A. Walsh, S.J. Ordained in 1916, Walsh had joined the Georgetown faculty in May 1918 at the age of thirty-two. That fall, he worked in the War Department as an inspector for the Student Army Training Corps, a program designed to mobilize higher education's resources for the war effort. Rejoining the faculty in December, Walsh established the foreign service school two months after his return.

He began his speech by denoting the most important lesson Americans had learned from the war, the realization that "the peoples of the world constitute one huge family, whose interests are in common and whose members are interdependent." The result was the "de-provincializing of the American mind." This shift, he emphasized, served to accentuate the need for training in the foreign service:

> Having entered upon the stage of world-politics and world-commerce we assume world-wide obligations. Our viewpoint can never be quite the same again. New occasions teach new duties, none more insistently than that of scientific education for those to whom shall be entrusted the good name and forwarding of the material interests of the United States.[5]

If a foreign service school was needed before the war, Walsh argued, it was "indispensable now." Diplomats and businessmen needed specialized training in foreign languages, law, and business. Furthermore, he insisted, they should study the social, economic, and political conditions of the countries where they worked. Doing so would promote a "wider and deeper sympathy" with the inhabitants, good will being essential to diplomatic and economic harmony.

At the same time, however, Walsh asserted that the school's true purpose was not mere vocational training. Graduates had a special mission; in their overseas work, they were to "be an effective and substantial agent in furthering the ideals of these United States." That is, part of their work was to exemplify democratic ideals in their daily activities, a very Wilsonian concept. The reasoning behind this argument, he believed, was summarized so well by Daniel Webster that Walsh could not "refrain from quoting [Webster's words] as the epitome of the ideals of the School of Foreign Service":

> It cannot be denied but by those who would dispute against the sun that with America and in America a new era commences in human affairs. And let the sacred obligations which have devolved on this generation and on us sink deep in our hearts.

The freshness of the American promise had not faded for Walsh in the eight decades since Webster's Bunker Hill address. America's entry into world affairs gave Webster's words a new sense of urgency. Like Webster, Walsh believed that a "beneficent Providence" had destined the United States to be a beacon of liberty to the world at large. The American people were endowed with "a great soul, a great heart, a great mind." Diplomats and businessmen had a key role in this work because they were the most prominent representatives of the United States abroad.[6]

Walsh's inaugural speech shows how much he endorsed the notion of American exceptionalism, a belief that extends back to John Winthrop's image of the "City on a Hill," giving American nationalism a quasi-religious fervor. According to this belief, what made the nation unique was its example of equality and liberty, making it the most complete expression of democracy in world history. Because America represented the highest standard of living ever seen, a result of Divine Providence, Americans had a mandate to bring the fruits of its blessings to the rest of the world. In such a framework of beliefs, those involved in overseas work assumed an almost missionary-like aspect.[7]

American exceptionalism had its Catholic proponents, especially Father Isaac Hecker and Archbishop John Ireland. Founder of the Paulist community in 1858, Hecker devoted himself to promoting harmony between Catholicism and Americanism. Insisting that, just as a soul needs guidance, so, too, does a polity, he believed America could not become a truly great nation unless it progressed spiritually at the same pace as materially. Only the Church was capable of strengthening the common American soul, thereby making unity a spiritual and political reality. "Hecker called for nothing less than a Catholic America," writes his most recent biographer, David O'Brien, "not for the sake of the Church but of the nation and its people."[8]

Archbishop John Ireland of Saint Paul, Minnesota, provided similar reasoning. His basic premise was that morality was the foundation of national life. Religion "gives life to morality," he wrote, and the "underlying religious spirit of the people is the surest hope of the republic." Of all the religions, insisted Ireland, no religion offered a surer hope to Americans than the Catholic Church. In Church teachings, the republic would find "the best safeguards for its life and prosperity, and the more the country acknowledges these teachings, the stronger and more durable its civil institutions will become."[9]

Walsh's underlying assumption was that Georgetown University and the Society of Jesus had key roles to play in the promotion of the American ideals of democracy. Throughout its history, the university prided itself on its religious contribution to the public sphere. The founding of the School of Foreign Service was both an extension and an expansion of that commitment. In elucidating the university's role, Walsh's inaugural speech reflects two major themes in his public career: patriotism and internationalism, so characteristic of his imprint on the school.

From the start, the school received high praise in both government circles and the press. Assistant Secretary of State William Phillips stated that everything about the school "points to success." Acting Secretary of Commerce Edwin F. Sweet hailed Georgetown as "entering upon a splendid career." One newspaper described the School of Foreign Service as

> the most important expression to date of the determination of the educational forces of the United States to not only meet the immediate demand, but to intelligently and efficiently train the youth of today to meet the responsibility of tomorrow and so equip the nation to achieve its destiny in the new American era which will be predominated by export business.

Another newspaper praised the school for meeting a "long felt need of American interests in foreign commerce." The Catholic press was especially enthusiastic. The *Philadelphia Catholic Standard-Times* saw the school as "evidence that the Catholic colleges are not only abreast of the times, but even anticipate conditions," for the new school had "no counterpart in any other American colleges."[10]

The school's curriculum was divided into four sections. The Language and Cultural section covered language training, rhetoric, and an obligatory course in moral philosophy. Languages included Japanese and Chinese, often unavailable in American colleges and universities at that time. In the Political Science section, students took "Elements of Diplomacy," "International Law," and "Consular Practice." The "Economic and Commercial" section offered "Tariffs and Treaties" and "Foreign Exchange." The fourth section was devoted entirely to the shipping industry.[11]

The faculty came from a wide variety of backgrounds: academia, State Department and other government agencies, and business.

William S. Culbertson of the U.S. Tariff Commission taught "Tariffs and Commercial Treaties"; Emory R. Johnson, dean of the Wharton School of Finance, "Ocean Transportation"; Manuel Torres of the Mexican Embassy, Spanish; and Boris Volynsky of the Russian Embassy, Russian. Wesley Frost of the State Department offered a course in "Consular Practice."[12]

As early as 1905, George Washington University founded a short-lived Department of Politics and Diplomacy, but the emphasis was on theory with little attention to practical training. Other colleges and universities offered courses on international relations and international law, but these were often electives. Harvard and Columbia had made plans for a foreign service school, but not realized them by 1919. Though not the first to conceive such a school, Georgetown was thus the first to bring it to life, offering both theory and practical training in a complete academic program specifically designed to prepare students for foreign service. Other programs followed, and by 1931 over seventy universities offered courses and programs applicable to foreign service careers.[13]

The founding of Georgetown's School of Foreign Service was a major event in the history of higher education in twentieth-century America. Unlike most Catholic colleges, which followed and adapted to educational trends, Georgetown was at the origin of a trend; the major universities followed suit, in some cases motivated less by the desire to be up to date than by what Philip Gleason calls "force of circumstance."[14]

It is ironic that the school's founder was a recently ordained priest with no diplomatic experience. Half of Edmund Walsh's life had been spent as a scholastic (unordained seminarian) in the confines of a Jesuit community, and he had been at Georgetown less than a year. Academically, he never progressed beyond the theology required for ordination, although he was awarded an honorary doctorate from Georgetown in 1919.[15] For the rest of his life, he signed himself "Edmund A. Walsh, S.J., Ph.D." and was known as "Dr. Walsh." Nothing could appear more unlikely than that such a person should found the first diplomatic training school in the United States. We need, therefore, to look at Walsh's background to determine the major influences on his career.

BOSTONIAN AND JESUIT

Edmund Aloysius Walsh was born on October 10, 1885, the last of six children born to John and Catherine Noonan Walsh. A second-generation American, John Walsh was a Boston police officer for nearly four decades. As a child, Catherine Noonan had emigrated from Ireland with her family. Their youngest son attended public grammar school and won a scholarship to the Jesuit-run Boston College High School in 1898. Graduating in 1902, Walsh entered the Jesuit novitiate in Frederick, Maryland. Not until 1918 did he visit Boston for any extended length.[16]

Walsh grew up at a time of unprecedented nationalistic posturing called "jingoism." John Higham has labeled the last decade of the nineteenth century the "nationalist nineties." Patriotic societies were widespread, the more prominent being the Sons and Daughters of the American Revolution and the Grand Army of the Republic. During the 1880s, American history textbooks first came into wide usage. Periodicals promoted veneration of the flag among American youth in the 1890s, when all schools were legally required to fly flags. Nationalist sentiment was especially strong in Boston. James Martin Gillis, future Paulist editor of the *Catholic World*, recalled of his childhood: "You see we were particularly patriotic in Boston; we were proud of possessing Faneuil Hall, 'The Cradle of Liberty,' the Old North Church, Bunker Hill, and a dozen other vivid reminders of the Revolution."[17]

Boston Catholicism encouraged patriotism, or what Philip Gleason calls "a sense of national belongingness." Between 1846 and 1907, Boston's episcopal leaders, Bishop John Fitzpatrick and Archbishop John Williams, faced with an influx of Catholic immigrants and a hostile native population, sought harmony by promoting peaceful assimilation. They believed that if Catholics faced discrimination in hospitals, schools, and social organizations, the answer was not to establish their own, but, rather, to fight prejudice within the existing system. Thus Catholic institutionalism did not assume the dimensions in Boston that it did in New York or Philadelphia; indeed, according to Boston historian Thomas H. O'Connor, "the eventual integration of immigrant Irish Catholics into the social and political life of the oldest Puritan community in America would take place in a gradual and non-violent manner."[18]

Louis Gallagher was a boyhood friend of Edmund Walsh in South Boston, followed him into the Jesuits, and accompanied him to Russia in 1922. But it was the Spanish-American War, Gallagher recalled in his 1962 biography of Walsh, that first aroused Walsh's interest in international relations. On the occasion of his fiftieth anniversary as a Jesuit, Walsh himself recalled the impact of that war:

> My generation, in 1898, quite naturally, was fascinated by the external-ities. We thrilled at the sight of uniforms on Boston Common as men enlisted. We paraded and we struck . . . belligerent postures on village greens and playgrounds in imitation of the indomitable Teddy Roose-velt. . . . We identified ourselves with Teddy Roosevelt as he charged up San Juan Hill at the head of his Rough Riders. . . .

When Admiral George Dewey's squadron entered Boston harbor at the end of the war, the thirteen-year-old Walsh and his friends rowed out to greet the victorious fleet.[19]

Walsh's patriotism expanded during the years 1909–12, when, as a Jesuit scholastic, he taught at Georgetown in the preparatory, or high school, division. No doubt the experience of living in Washington, D.C., was an important factor, but equally so was Georgetown itself. Opened in 1792, the university boasted a history nearly as old as the United States. Major events in its life often intersected with Ameri-can history at large, a fact duly noted at countless commencements and anniversaries. Speakers often pursued the connection between John Carroll, the university founder, his brother Daniel, and their cousin Charles Carroll, all of whom participated in the founding of the republic.[20]

In May 1912, an event took place on campus that made a great impression on the young scholastic: the dedication of John Carroll's statue, which bore the inscription "Priest-Patriot-Prelate," in front of Healy Hall. The main speaker at the dedication was Georgetown alumnus Chief Justice Edward D. White, who focused on Carroll's contributions to the early nation. Forty years later, Edmund Walsh said that he was able to recall it "vividly, indeed as if it were yes-terday."[21]

White's speech stressed the commonalties between John Carroll and his cousin Charles Carroll of Carrollton, signer of the Declaration of Independence. The college and the nation, the chief justice contended, were founded on identical principles. Georgetown's purpose was to reinforce the principles upon which the Founding Fathers operated. The school's graduates were to form "a great army of morality" that would be "the mainstay and prop of the institutions which the fathers founded." Georgetown, he concluded, was better equipped than any other institution for this task: the nation and the university were "one the complement of the other; to me they seem to be the one, the necessary resultant of the other, and when the work done here has failed and ceases to produce its effect, the work done there will pass away and our institutions will crumble."[22] The speech invokes two themes Walsh would pursue in his own public career—how Georgetown's and the nation's history intersected, and how democracy and religion mutually reinforce one another.

Study abroad over the next two years was an important factor in developing Walsh's interest in international relations. In September 1912, he was sent to Europe for graduate studies, still a relatively rare event for American scholastics at that time. Though archival sources offer no clue as to why he was sent, there is a possibility that his superiors felt he was not ready for ordination; or perhaps, on the contrary, the decision was a sign of their confidence in his maturity. Accompanying him was Vincent A. McCormick, a New Yorker who entered the novitiate a year behind Walsh, and a close friend who eventually served in Rome as the "American Assistant to the General of the Society of Jesus."[23]

Walsh began classes toward a graduate degree in classics at Dublin's University College, but withdrew in January when the academic senate refused to recognize his Georgetown bachelor's degree. In March 1913, he enrolled in a similar program at the University of London, which was interrupted when his provincial directed him to begin theology in the summer of 1913. He was assigned to the University of Innsbruck in September, where he remained until the outbreak of the First World War in August 1914.[24]

Academic interruptions notwithstanding, Walsh's travel abroad was an important factor in developing his future professional interests. He came to appreciate the international character of the Society of Jesus, describing one Jesuit house as a "veritable congress of nations." During this period, Walsh kept a diary, which revealed that international relations, not theology, was his true passion; his interest

grew stronger, the nearer that Europe drew to war. He did not talk
about his studies, but wrote extensively on lectures he attended, and
ruminated on the diplomatic and political situation.[25]

In England, Walsh attended lectures on a wide variety of subjects
at the London School of Economics and elsewhere. The topics that
fascinated him most were international law, the relationship between
economics and politics, and the future of Europe. In one diary entry,
he reflected on the nations that would be the "great empires of the
future," an indication of his future interest in geopolitics. He frequently attended court cases and sessions of Parliament, noting on
one occasion the differences between American and English legislative procedures.[26]

By the summer of 1914, Walsh's diary focused exclusively on the
approaching European conflict. He collected articles on current
events, adding brief reflections. In Austria, he had an opportunity to
see the approaching war up close. The following excerpt, written as
war broke out, reveals his real interests:

> Another week of thrills—a new declaration of war almost every day!
> . . . But the outlook is black indeed. That universal European confla-
> gration, long feared[,] seems at hand. *France is expected to attack Ger-
> many* or Austria at any moment—and then Italy must thro' [*sic*] her
> treaty, join Austria and Germany. But Italy is not trusted—she may
> fail her allies at last moment for her own interests, but if she does [she]
> sacrifice[s] the last remnant of her national honor. . .[27]

He had found his life's work.

The American theologians were sent home within a few weeks.
Walsh continued theology at Woodstock College, Maryland, and was
ordained with twenty-eight other men on June 28, 1916. The following year he did parish work in New York City, a postordination Jesuit
tradition, and returned to Woodstock to complete theology. In May
1918, he was once again assigned to Georgetown as prefect of studies
for the College, a post recently vacated by the newly appointed President, the Reverend John Berchmans Creeden, S.J.[28]

A "Continued Service to the Country"

At a special meeting of the regents shortly after his appointment,
President Creeden "sought advice about introducing next year spe-

cial courses by way of preparation for the consular service." The board's response was enthusiastic, and the president set about establishing what would become the School of Foreign Service.[29]

Recent research by Professor R. Emmett Curran shows that Georgetown had been interested in such a school for several years. On March 31, 1913, President Alphonsus J. Donlon brought before the consultors a proposal for a "School of Diplomacy." The proposal was accepted, and Donlon wrote a confrere in Rome's Jesuit Curia:

> We hope to develop a new course in connection with the Law School—a school of Political and Social Science, including a school of diplomacy. It is a course that is in great demand just now. . . . I have great hopes that we shall be able to accomplish our design[30]

Exactly why the 1913 proposal went unrealized is not clear, but circumstances were more propitious by 1918. The need for a foreign service school was evident, but why Georgetown felt called upon to start it is not obvious. The answer lies in two areas: first, the general wave of confidence that permeated the American Catholic community during and after the war; second, the traditional Jesuit approach to the relationship between religion and culture, one that may be traced to the original charism of the order.

Jay Dolan has written that the year 1917 witnessed the highest collective display of American Catholic confidence. Nowhere was this more evident than in the formation of the National Catholic War Council (NCWC) that fall. The NCWC's purpose was twofold. The immediate aim was to unify American Catholic resources to aid the war effort. In addition, the American hierarchy wanted an organization capable of asserting the Church's interests at the national level. Because of this, the NCWC remained in place after the war, as the "National Catholic Welfare Council" (after 1922, "Conference"), dedicated to lobbying for Catholic interests and being a central coordinating agency for Catholic action. The organizing genius behind this work was the Paulist John J. Burke, and it was largely through his efforts that the NCWC became an effective organization.[31]

Although Georgetown had no official connection to the NCWC , it was not immune to the general confidence pervading American Catholic life. During the war, Catholics felt they had an unprecedented opportunity to prove their Americanism, and they participated enthusiastically in the war effort. In the war's aftermath, their leadership felt confident enough to address larger social issues in the 1919 "Bishops' Program of Social Reconstruction," a document hailed by Upton Sinclair as a "Catholic miracle."[32] The founding of the foreign service school, though not a collective effort in the same sense, it was nonetheless a significant expression of postwar Catholic idealism. But where the NCWC's efforts concentrated mainly on the domestic scene, the School of Foreign Service sought to address America's role in the world at large.

In late 1918, John Creeden wrote to his provincial, Joseph H. Rockwell, about the plans for the school. He characterized the school's work as a "continued service to the country" that "would bring the Society into contact with the prominent men in finance and government." Later, in June 1919, he stressed to Rockwell that the school "will exert a wide and important influence." The university, he implied, could exert a wider influence on society by producing future statesmen and financiers imbued with a sense of moral responsibility. The end goal would be the desire to promote the common good.[33]

Creeden's rationale for the school denotes a distinctively Jesuit approach. Indeed, according to historian John O'Malley, public service has been a major goal of Jesuit schools from their beginning. Ignatian spirituality, notes theologian Michael Buckley, focuses on the widest possible good, and Jesuit colleges offered such an opportunity. Graduates carried into the public sphere the values they learned, spreading them on a wider scale. The humanistic ideal of Jesuit schools, Buckley writes, was "to prepare the individual for the 'active life' of service to the common good of society, and in a Christian context, to the Church."[34]

In the ongoing dialogue between religion and culture, the Jesuit apostolate has traditionally taken what might be termed a "permeationist" approach. In their educational ministry, the Jesuits operated within the bounds of the culture to achieve their desired end: the promotion of the common good. The Jesuit sense of public Catholicism may be expressed in the order's motto "Ad Maiorem Dei Gloriam" (To the Greater Glory of God).

The creation of the School of Foreign Service at Georgetown University remains a prime example of this approach. Unlike the traditional Jesuit college, the school offered only one course directly related to a religious curriculum. Moral philosophy was taught by

Father Thomas I. Gasson, dean of Georgetown's Graduate School. While the foreign service school's program was not overtly religious, it was geared toward a religious end. At a time of increasing relativism in higher education, the school's purpose was to train leaders inculcated with a sense of moral responsibility, leaders dedicated to influencing America's approach to international relations.[35]

ACTIVIST AND EDUCATOR

The year 1918 brought together three men whose common interests and respective talents would bring the School of Foreign Service to fruition: John Creeden, Edmund Walsh, and Constantine E. McGuire, U.S. secretary of the Inter-American High Commission, an agency charged with coordinating the financial policies toward Latin American countries. All three had been interested in Georgetown's influence in the context of America's growing international role.

On October 13, 1958, the School of Foreign Service was rededicated as the "Edmund A. Walsh School of Foreign Service." A month later, Jesuit Henri Wiesel, a contemporary of Walsh and a scholastic at Georgetown from 1916 to 1918, wrote to University Archivist William V. Repetti, S.J., and asked that his letter be placed on file for access to future scholars. Noting that the recent ceremony made him reflect on the school's founding, Wiesel asserted "that Edmund Walsh was *not* the founder of the Foreign Service School but that John B. Creeden, S.J., was the founder." According to Wiesel, who had worked with both men, Creeden had often discussed a prospective foreign service school, and, indeed, had conceived the entire plan while Walsh was still in theology. When Creeden became president of Georgetown in May 1918, the opportunity arose to establish such a school, but it was delayed by the war. Calling him a "man of visions," Wiesel maintained that Creeden had "no flair for publicity as did Walsh," that he needed Walsh to organize the school, attract benefactors, and recruit faculty. Wiesel was quick to insist, however, that Walsh's role should not be less appreciated; rather, it should be reevaluated to reflect more accurately the nature of his and Creeden's respective contributions.[36]

Other documents in the university archives suggest that Constantine McGuire may have played a greater role in the founding of the school than Wiesel or others realized at the time. McGuire shunned publicity to an extreme, even refusing to be listed in the university catalogue. Carroll Quigley, professor of history at Georgetown, characterized him as a behind-the-scenes man and contended that McGuire had developed the master plan for the foreign service school.[37]

Born in Boston in 1890, McGuire attended the Boston Latin School and Harvard, receiving a doctorate in history with a dissertation on medieval law. A trip to Europe in 1913–14 awakened his interest in international relations. He was particularly impressed by the Sorbonne's Ecole Nationale des Sciences Politiques, a school of diplomacy established in Paris after the Franco-Prussian War. His visit there led him to consider whether a similar school might flourish in the United States.

After receiving his doctorate, McGuire decided not to enter the teaching profession, opting instead to work for the Inter-American High Commission, where he befriended persons such as Leo S. Rowe, future chief of the State Department's Latin American Division, and the renowned Columbia law professor John Bassett Moore. Rowe and Moore were among the first foreign service school faculty members. During the war, McGuire worked for the State Department drafting international agreements. By 1918, he was well respected in government circles, and had established many important connections.[38]

According to Quigley, it was around this time that McGuire concretized a plan for the school and, through the help of a Jesuit friend, met with Creeden to present his ideas. In June, Creeden then brought the plan before the Board of Regents. If Creeden had not acted on his interest in a foreign service school before then, it may be that he did not have the details for a blueprint until he met with McGuire. Whether this is the case or not, it is certain that the two men needed each other to achieve their desired goal.[39]

Quigley's account is supported by the reminiscences of another faculty member. In 1960, J. DeSiqueira Coutinho, longtime professor of Portuguese, recalled meeting McGuire at Washington's prestigious Cosmos Club in May 1918. McGuire told him of his plans for meeting with Creeden, "a subject he had been contemplating for some time." McGuire's friend, Richard Tierney, S.J., editor of the Jesuit weekly *America*, arranged the meeting with Creeden, who accepted it enthusiastically.[40]

Georgetown's archival sources support, to a large extent, the Quigley and Coutinho accounts. In a May 1918 document entitled "Memorandum on a School for the Diplomatic Service," McGuire detailed a curriculum encompassing foreign languages, commerce, and international law. "The establishment of a school for the diplomatic and consular service," he wrote, "has been a favorite topic among those interested in the improvement of our foreign service for some years." Harvard and Columbia had been considering it, he noted, but had not yet taken any action. Georgetown's opportunity was ripe, concluded the memorandum, and the university could count on the help of both the State Department and the financial community.[41]

In December, Creeden wrote Rockwell that enthusiasm for the school among alumni and government officials was high. Washington, D.C., was an ideal location for the school, he insisted, because "we can call on the experts of the Government and Representatives of foreign countries." Creeden hoped to raise an endowment and felt he could "count on the assistance of men interested in foreign trade." He concluded:

> To carry out my plans of organization I need the help of Fr. Edmund Walsh. He will be mustered out of service and will be just the man to organize the new school. The work will bring him into contact with officials and the excellent impression he has already made will be continued.[42]

This letter is significant in elucidating Walsh's particular contribution to the school's founding. At the same time McGuire was working on the academic programs, Creeden needed an energetic young man who could interest donors and persuade prestigious scholars to join the faculty. In short, he needed an activist, and he found one in the confident and colorful young priest who had just joined the Georgetown faculty.

By all accounts, Walsh was a colorful character. As Wiesel observed, he had a flair for publicity. Since high school, he had been active in theater as a student player and later as a faculty moderator. Contemporaries agree that Walsh carried himself with an aura of drama. On campus, he wore a long black cape. For photographs he often posed in front of a map, or leaning on a globe. His entry into a lecture hall was accompanied with a dramatic flourish rivaling Bishop

Fulton J. Sheen on 1950s television screens. One alumnus recalled that Walsh was "an artist. What he did he did with style"; another described him as "a man of great personal charm, great tact [with] a delicate and mirthsome sense of humor. He was a diplomat to his fingertips."[43]

The late Father Joseph T. Durkin, who taught history at Georgetown for more than a half century, lived with Walsh in Georgetown's Jesuit community for two decades. An unabashed admirer, he described Walsh as a "superb lecturer" of great personal charm, although he admitted that Walsh was neither a scientific scholar nor an intellectual, at least not in the sense that Gustave Weigel and John Courtney Murray were. Instead, Durkin characterized Walsh as a "man of action," a model of the Jesuit rhetorician who uses eloquence to persuade others to a greater good. He agreed that Walsh did cultivate a dramatic presence, but insisted that he did so with a higher goal in mind. Walsh used these talents in the interests of the School of Foreign Service.[44]

Walsh and Creeden had discussed the possibility of a foreign service school before the June regents' meeting. In the fall of 1918, shortly after becoming dean of the College of Arts and Sciences, Walsh was called into service for the War Department. As a member of the Committee on Education and Special Training, he was appointed assistant educational director for the Student Army Training Corps (SATC), responsible for inspecting units in the New England region. His job was to inspect over thirty colleges and universities, assuring their compliance with SATC requirements.[45]

The First World War necessitated central direction of the economy by the federal government for the first time in American history. The War Industries Board was charged with mobilizing industrial production; the War Food Administration, with controlling production and consumption; the Capital Issues Committee, with regulating private investment; and the War Finance Corporation, with directing and financing industrial expansion. Furthermore, the federal government took over the railroad, telephone, and telegraph systems. Indeed, according to Arthur M. Schlesinger, Jr., the national government "had never gone so far in the operation and conduct of business."[46]

The SATC was part of a larger effort to mobilize American educational resources on behalf of the war effort. As of October 1, 1918, all able-bodied men on college campuses were inducted into the army as privates. In addition to their regular studies, they were given military instruction and required to take the "War Issues Course," outlining the war's causes. This grandiose program was cut short when Congress ordered demobilization in November 1918.[47]

Walsh's work with the SATC generally tended toward the routine and bureaucratic. Much of it dealt with questions about numbers: How many students on a given campus were enrolled in the SATC? How many were taking languages? How many were taking the War Issues Course? But the experience did give him an otherwise unaffordable view of the best universities in the country. Among the schools he inspected were Yale, Harvard, and M.I.T. In looking at their course catalogues, as part of his official duties, he saw that none had a program for diplomatic training.

Although Louis Gallagher contends that the idea of the foreign service school first came to him at this time,[48] the archival evidence, much of which may have been unavailable to Gallagher, proves otherwise. Walsh returned from New England in December 1918, and the school was started in February 1919. He could not possibly have gone to New England, returned to Georgetown, recruited faculty and donors, and started provisional classes all within two months. Creeden had already proposed the school in June. The SATC experience only served to enforce for Walsh the unique opportunity that Georgetown had already seized.

While he was in the Northeast, Walsh was also working to recruit donors for the future school. In November 1918, he wrote Creeden that he had recently visited Father Joseph Farrell, S.J., at Fordham. A close friend of Walsh, who had entered the novitiate with him in 1902, Father Farrell arranged for Walsh to meet his cousin James A. Farrell, president of the United States Steel Corporation and a longtime advocate of foreign trade. Walsh successfully presented the foreign service school plan to Farrell, who took a personal interest in Walsh's project, giving twenty thousand dollars toward a permanent endowment in 1919 and contributing regularly to the School of Foreign Service until his death in 1943.[49]

In Boston, Walsh met with Judge Charles A. DeCourcy, a Georgetown alumnus on the Massachusetts Supreme Court, who mentioned a number of financiers and government officials, including Labor Commissioner Charles Neal, that Walsh might approach for help on getting government lecturers for the school. Walsh wrote Creeden that renowned Catholic diplomat and writer Maurice Francis Egan had already volunteered to lecture; he concluded by asking how McGuire was coming along with the school's mission statement. The enthusiastic tone of his letter reveals that Walsh was most in his element as an activist, public relations expert, and principal fund raiser.[50]

William Franklin Sands, an attorney, Georgetown alumnus, and descendant of an old Maryland Catholic family, recalled in the 1930s how Walsh had recruited him to teach at the foreign service school. Sands's recollection provides an otherwise unavailable perspective on Walsh's activity at the origins of the school:

> I remember well when you came to see me in my office in New York sixteen or seventeen years ago and explained what the Foreign Service School was intended to be. You were founding it at a time when American business abroad seemed to be growing to dazzling proportions; when American diplomacy seemed to be about to enter a definite and understanding direction; when it seemed that the United States, firmly established at home, were about to exercise a powerful influence upon the rest of the world, and it seemed to be more necessary that this influence be exercised upon right principles and right methods. You had a great vision of such a school as you were founding, and you were right.[51]

Returning to Georgetown in December, Walsh met with Department of Commerce officials, who agreed to provide statisticians, economists, and trade experts as lecturers. Constantine McGuire worked on constructing the preliminary statement, and also helped to recruit faculty, including several associates in the Inter-American High Commission and the State Department.[52]

Only McGuire was sufficiently familiar with diplomacy and foreign trade to conceive and work on the details of the school's curriculum. Creeden had the interest, the most professional educational experience of the three, and, by May 1918, the authority to implement the plans. Walsh had long been interested in international relations, and employed his talents with singular interest as an activist to persuade academics, financiers, and government officials to join the faculty or lend their financial support to the project. The founding of Georgetown University's School of Foreign Service was thus a collaborative effort: McGuire was the expert, Walsh the activist, and Creeden the educator.

None of these revelations undermines Walsh's role in a great educational endeavor. Creeden's term as president of Georgetown ended in 1924; McGuire, who had envisioned the foreign service school as high-tech research institute, regarding the undergraduate program as a necessary evil, left the university in 1921. Walsh would remain with the school until his death; credit for the school's subsequent growth and success thus belongs to him. There "can be no doubt," Louis Gallagher writes, "as to who did the plow work, the irrigation, the harvesting, and the marketing of this new field of education, once the university decided to take it over." Indeed, for many alumni, "Father Walsh *was* Georgetown."[53]

Willard Beaulac, who entered the School of Foreign Service in 1921 after naval service, recalled that there was a real excitement among his peers: "Every student . . . was part of an exhilarating experiment and he knew it." Beaulac would serve as ambassador to several Latin American countries, including Chile, Colombia, and Argentina. Richard P. Butrick, a member of the first graduating class of 1921, recalled that as Regent, Walsh took a hands-on approach, forever patrolling the corridors, visiting classes and helping students. As Seth Tillman writes: "Father Walsh, anything but a remote eminence, was ubiquitous."[54]

Because the School of Foreign Service was a night school for its first seven years, Walsh was able to recruit prominent faculty from other schools to lecture in the evening during those years. The majority of the professors had full-time jobs elsewhere in government, academia, or business. Paul H. Coughlin, an early graduate, recalled Walsh's recruiting method: habitually checking the newspapers to see when "prominent names" were scheduled to come to Washington, Walsh would then contact them and arrange a lecture at the school.[55]

Late in the winter of 1920–21, Walsh arranged a series of lectures at Georgetown on international relations. The list of speakers was quite impressive for its day. Among them were historian Carlton J. H. Hayes of Columbia, former American Historical Association President J. Franklin Jameson, renowned constitutional law scholar James Brown Scott, Yale law professor Edwin M. Borchard, and James Laurence Laughlin of Harvard. In 1922, the lectures were published under the title *The History and Nature of International Relations*. Although Walsh's name appeared on a book cover for the first time, as editor, the book's significance lies not so much in Walsh's scholarship, as in his ability to recruit prominent scholars for his forum.[56]

Walsh possessed a lucid vision of both the school's educational mission and its larger moral purpose, a vision entirely his own, and one he expressed in a number of speeches and articles during the early years of the foreign service school. As William V. O'Brien, professor emeritus of Government at Georgetown and former president of the Catholic Association for International Peace, put it, "[Walsh's] mark was on that school."[57]

Walsh spoke on the need for "progressive statesmanship and sound commercial policy" in a May 1920 address to the National Foreign Trade Convention. There was a danger in the unprecedented economic growth attending the war that Americans might fall prey to an unbridled materialism. The question needed to be asked: "Have we been enriched intellectually and spiritually to the same degree?" The danger was that Americans might lose sight of their solemn obligation:

> Having entered upon the stage of world politics and world commerce, we assume world-wide obligations and should be errant to our high mission if, in ruinous conceit, we turn our backs on the wisdom streaming across the path from that beacon light in human progress, the history of past ages.

Speaking in Washington in 1921, Walsh delineated the School of Foreign Service's ultimate purpose: to produce "a trained body of men bred in a spirit of devotion to the institutions and idealism of the United States."[58] On the occasion of the school's fifth anniversary, he again made reference to the school's "high mission." The School of Foreign Service, he declared, promoted "true citizenship, the inculcation of pure patriotism, and intelligent service in the cause of world peace through mutual understanding among the peoples of the earth."[59]

In his introduction to the *History and Nature of International Relations*, Walsh wrote that the United States had indisputably "become the focal point of interest for the civilized world." Financially and politically, the nation was now a leader in world affairs. A school of foreign service, therefore, was never needed more urgently than now. Its raison d'être was to prepare leaders with a "right understanding of the origin of civil society." Walsh's underlying assumption was that the foreign policies of nations "will naturally be largely influenced by the philosophy underlying the decisions of those who direct the destinies of states."[60]

In Walsh's view, although the United States was essentially a moral nation with a duty to enlighten the rest of the world, it had experienced a dramatic increase in secularism during the 1920s:

> The material wealth and profits that have poured into our coffers during the past ten years stagger the imagination. But with them have come the insidious perils to moral life, even to spiritual well being, that usually accompanies swift ascent to power and affluence.

The antidote was "Knowledge. For Knowledge is Light which purifies and heals." Knowledge had a moral aspect, and morality was a clear objective reality based upon universal principles; the Foreign Service School aimed at training moral agents in what William Sands called "right principles and right methods."[61]

According to Henry F. May, in the years immediately before the war, there had been a "loss of American innocence," by which May means a set of core beliefs characterizing nineteenth-century American culture: the certainty and universality of moral values, as well as a belief in the inevitability of progress. When these beliefs came under attack, Protestant America lost confidence in its own ability to provide moral leadership for the nation. On the other hand, asserts William Halsey, perceiving this moral vacuum, Catholics wished to provide the missing leadership. They still believed in the values described by May, and held on to their innocence; they sought to bring their beliefs to bear on the larger culture.[62]

The creation of the NCWC was one expression of Catholic idealism, but the creation of the School of Foreign Service was an equally idealistic if overlooked contribution. Its creation was an exercise in innocence, the work of a Catholic idealist. As the idealist-realist debate emerged in American foreign policy, Walsh supported the idealists. He wanted to ensure that religious morality, not secular relativism, became the guiding principle. With prosperity came responsibility, and his school's task was to rekindle long-held ideals among America's future leaders.

The success of the foreign service school had, almost from the start, attracted the attention of the Jesuit Generalate in Rome. Although Father General Wlodimir Ledochowski initially disapproved of the school being established without his prior knowledge or approval, in February 1920, an American Jesuit in the Curia wrote Creeden that Ledochowski was nonetheless highly pleased at the school's scope and nature. Its stature would "enhance the prestige not only of Georgetown but of the Society and especially of the Church." One important result of the school's stature was that Edmund Walsh's name was increasingly recognized in ecclesiastical circles, particularly within his own order, as an authority on international relations.[63]

On November 5, 1920, Constantine McGuire wrote Walsh regarding what he perceived as the school's next big task: organizing a department of Russian studies. He suggested that such a department offer courses in Russian language, ethnography, economics, history, and social conditions. A conversation with a Russian emigré he met made him think "how important it is to develop the Russian market." He urged that the foreign service school move quickly:

> Five or ten years from now the demand for men who know Russian well will relatively far exceed the [number of] men who know the language; and those who are acquainted with Russian life and the conditions under which it is carried on, will find themselves in very great demand.[64]

Thus McGuire may have been the first to suggest Russia as a field of study to Walsh.

In February 1922, Walsh was called to Rome by Father Ledochowski to head the Papal Relief Mission to Russia. The mission required a Jesuit who understood diplomatic workings, and Walsh was known to the Curia for his work at Georgetown. For nearly two years, he worked in Russia, witnessing the Soviet experiment in its early stages. His experiences there formed the foundation for his anticommunist activity over the following three decades. But Walsh's anticommunism cannot be understood outside the context of his earlier experiences. He went to Russia as an already committed idealist, patriot, and internationalist, an activist who stressed the primacy of morality in the affairs of nations. How his Russian experience affected him and his work is the subject of chapter 2.

"What Think Ye of Russia?"

Walsh and Catholic Anticommunism in the 1920s

Edmund A. Walsh was absent from Georgetown during the 1921–22 academic year. He was completing his tertianship (the period of Jesuit spiritual formation following ordination, which concludes with the "fourth vow," a promise to undertake any mission, anywhere in the world, at the request of the Holy See) at the Jesuit community in Paray-le-Monial, France.[1]

In February 1922, Walsh was called to Rome by Father General Ledochowski at the behest of Pope Pius XI to organize and direct Vatican relief efforts in famine-stricken Soviet Russia. Between July 1922 and December 1923, he served as director of the Papal Relief Mission. He oversaw the distribution of food and clothing at relief centers from the Crimea to Moscow, which fed hundreds of thousands of starving Russians. The mission was the Catholic Church's first foray into international relief work, a project that paved the way for future ventures such as the Catholic Near East Welfare Association in 1926, of which Walsh was to be the first president, and Catholic Relief Services in 1943.

In addition, the Holy See empowered Walsh to negotiate for the release of clergy imprisoned by the Soviet government and for the reopening of Catholic churches closed in December 1922. "The special 4th vow," Walsh wrote John Creeden from Russia, "is something very tangible just now." The Holy See never established formal diplomatic relations with the Soviet Union in its seventy-four-year history, but during the time he was in Russia, Walsh functioned as the Vatican's unofficial chargé d'affaires.[2]

Historian Richard Gid Powers writes that Walsh's "experience in Russia turned him into an anticommunist for the rest of his life."[3] Indeed, as Louis Gallagher would observe in his obituary for Walsh, it "directly influenced every major project he conducted during the rest of his life."[4] By the end of the 1920s, Walsh was widely regarded as the premier Catholic spokesman on Soviet government and ideology. In verifying Powers's view, this chapter traces the development of Walsh's anticommunism during the years 1922–29. Soon after he returned to the United States in 1924, Walsh would begin a campaign to warn the public of the Soviet threat by means of lectures and articles; he would revise the foreign service school curriculum to include mandatory courses on Soviet political theory and practice.[5]

THE RUSSIAN FAMINE AND THE
AMERICAN RELIEF ADMINISTRATION

In early 1921, as the Soviet government attempted to consolidate power after the revolution and to bring the civil war that had raged from 1918 to an end, a drought set in. It would give rise to Russia's most devastating famine, claiming over five million lives by the end of 1922—in the words of historian Richard Pipes, "the greatest human disaster in European history, other than those caused by war, since the Black Death of the fourteenth century."[6]

Because famines were a frequent occurrence throughout Russian history, rural communities had traditionally protected themselves against them by reserving an "insurance" crop supply. During the civil war, however, the Soviet government, under a policy known as "War Communism," confiscated the reserve crops, leaving the peasants helpless. Almost one-half of all agricultural regions were affected, and one-fifth of these regions experienced total crop failure. The Soviet government was unprepared for such a disaster; much to its chagrin, it was forced to seek outside help.[7]

On July 13, 1921, at the request of his government, playwright Maxim Gorky issued a public appeal for international aid, to which Herbert Hoover, secretary of commerce and director of the American Relief Administration (ARA), responded with an offer of assistance. Negotiations between the Soviets and the ARA, the world's largest private relief organization, took place in Riga, Latvia, on August 10. According to the Riga Agreement, the ARA would oversee all relief work. On August 24, 1921, at a meeting of the European Relief Council in Washington, D.C., eight American religious and civic groups were granted the ARA affiliation they needed to participate in Russian famine relief. Each organization was allowed independent action, but all personnel appointments required the approval of the ARA's Russian relief director, Colonel William N. Haskell, U.S. Army. The National Catholic Welfare Council (NCWC), founded in 1917 as the central coordinating body for Catholic welfare activity in the United States, was among the eight, thus ensuring that Catholic relief work in Russia would be conducted under NCWC auspices.[8]

THE HOLY SEE AND THE RUSSIAN FAMINE

Ever since the October Revolution in 1917, the Holy See had watched events in Russia with keen interest and concern. In December 1921, Pope Benedict XV reacted to news of the growing famine by sending Monsignor Giuseppe Pizzardo, under-secretary of state for Extraordinary Affairs, to discuss a possible papal relief mission with Vaclav Vorofsky, the Soviet commercial representative in Rome. Unfortunately, Benedict died in early 1922, before any action could be taken.

On February 13, 1922, Cardinal Achille Ratti succeeded Benedict as Pope Pius XI. Having served as nuncio in Warsaw during the Russo-Polish War of 1918–20, and being as interested in Russian affairs as Benedict had been, the new pontiff allowed the negotiations to continue. He was assisted by the strongly anticommunist Jesuit Father General Wlodimir Ledochowski, whose brother was a general in the Polish Army. On March 12, 1922, Secretary of State Cardinal Pietro Gasparri signed an agreement with Vorofsky, providing for a relief mission to enter Russia under the auspices of the Holy See.[9]

In retrospect, given the Holy See's longtime anticommunist position, it may seem difficult to understand how the Vatican would attempt dialogue with the Soviets. It must be kept in mind, however, that in 1917 the failure of dialogue was not perceived as a foreordained conclusion. Because the revolution eliminated the Orthodox Church's monopoly, Vatican officials had reasons to hope for a potential Catholic revival in Russia, where they had formerly been excluded. Indeed, Russia's small Catholic community had actually welcomed the overthrow of the Romanovs.[10]

At the outset, the Soviet government did not adopt an explicitly antireligious policy, which led Vatican diplomats to regard relations with the new state as a strong possibility. Jesuit historian of Vatican diplomacy Robert Graham argues that the Holy See was not unwilling to deal with governments despite differences in religion or ideology. He notes, for example, that popes through the centuries had maintained relations with Protestant and Islamic governments; in the 1790s, the Holy See made strenuous efforts to preserve contact with France's revolutionary regime. Graham concludes: "The history of papal diplomacy belies the image of rigidity which many minds seem to attach to its relations with the Soviet Union." In 1922, then, a papal relief mission to Soviet Russia did not appear to Vatican diplomats to be a foreordained failure.[11]

THE ARA, THE NCWC, AND WALSH'S APPOINTMENT

According to the Riga Agreement, however, even a *papal* relief mission required ARA affiliation, which meant that the Holy See could only operate in Russia under the auspices of the National Catholic Welfare Conference. Although NCWC leaders had considered the possibility of participating in relief work, as of February 1922, they had not appointed a representative. In March, Paulist Father John J. Burke, the NCWC's general secretary, wrote Herbert Hoover that this was "principally owing to lack of information as to how our representative would serve." A more pressing reason was that the council was battling both internal and external foes. Its opponents in the American hierarchy, Cardinal William H. O'Connell of Boston and Cardinal Dennis Dougherty of Philadelphia, lobbied the Vatican for the suppression of the NCWC, arguing that it undermined episcopal authority. At the same time, anti-Catholicism was on the rise in 1920s America, and Burke was involved in the fight against the Oregon School Bill, a nativist measure, which, if passed, would have outlawed Catholic schools in that state.[12]

If the Holy See was to work in Russia, it needed the NCWC, a factor that may have helped the council during its battles with O'Connell and Dougherty. Because the August 1921 Washington meeting had stipulated U.S. citizenship as a requirement for relief directors, the Holy See would work in Russia on American terms, under American Catholic direction. Thus the Catholic Church's first foray into international relief work became, by necessity, an American operation. Colonel Haskell, the ARA's director for Russian relief, was well disposed toward the mission, and had already expressed his own preferences for a director.[13]

A regular army officer on detached duty, Haskell was a highly regarded administrator, having directed relief work in Armenia and Romania in 1919. Through his wife, Winifred, Haskell had strong connections to the Georgetown Jesuits. His brother-in-law Father Joseph Farrell, S.J., was Walsh's classmate and close friend, and thus a point of contact between Haskell and Walsh. Before leaving for Russia in 1921, Haskell informed his superiors at the ARA of his choice of Walsh, whose background and experiences made him an ideal candidate for director of Catholic relief work in Russia.[14]

According to Walsh, Haskell repeatedly cabled the NCWC from Moscow for a representative, but received no reply. He then contacted the Holy See (whether directly or through the apostolic delegate in Washington, D.C., is not known) to request Walsh's appointment; on February 13, 1922, he cabled Walsh at Paray-le-Monial, asking him to serve as the NCWC's Russian representative. In response, Walsh contacted John J. Burke and was authorized to act as the NCWC's representative for a three-month period (with later renewals); a week later, he received a cable from Father General Ledochowski summoning him to Rome.[15]

On February 26, 1922, Walsh arrived at the Jesuit Curia in Rome; over the next two weeks, he conferred with the Vatican's highest authorities: Pope Pius XI, Father General Ledochowski, Cardinal Pietro Gasparri, and Monsignor Giuseppe Pizzardo. As a result of the meetings, it was decided that Walsh would proceed to Russia to examine famine conditions, assess what needed to be done, and report back to the Vatican with his findings. Once the details of the mission were arranged, Walsh was to return to Washington, where he would finalize the arrangements for ARA affiliation.[16]

"THE MOST REACTIONARY AND SAVAGE SCHOOL OF THOUGHT KNOWN TO HISTORY": WALSH'S INITIAL ENCOUNTER WITH SOVIET RUSSIA

Walsh arrived in Moscow on March 23, 1922. After conferring with Colonel Haskell, he spent the next month visiting the famine-ravaged districts and closely observing ARA operations in preparation for his assignment. Walsh's arrival coincided with the start of the Soviet government's most extensive antireligious campaign. On February 26, the Soviets had issued a decree for the confiscation of all valuable objects from churches, ostensibly to raise money to feed the starving; in Moscow, Walsh witnessed troops confiscating liturgical vessels from a church.[17]

Although it may seem self-defeating for the Soviets to launch such a campaign in the middle of a famine just as many religious groups were sending food and supplies to Russia, Soviet historians agree that Trotsky and Lenin alike saw the famine as an opportunity to crush religion, the last vestige of the old order. By confiscating church valuables, in the name of relief work, he hoped to show the Soviets as the true friends of the people—and to depict the churches as unsympathetic toward the starving for refusing to part with their silver and gold.[18]

The year 1922, writes historian Arno Mayer, signaled "a hardening of the showdown with the Church."[19] Church confiscations were soon followed by the arrest and trials of Orthodox bishops, priests, and laity. Twenty-eight bishops and over 1,200 priests were either murdered or executed in that year alone. Antireligious processions lampooned Christian liturgies, and theater plays undermined religion's place in Russian life. Finally, a split occurred in the Orthodox Church, when government-sponsored reformists formed "The Living Church" in 1922.[20]

As historian Daniel Peris explains in his study of 1920s Soviet antireligious campaigns, however easy it may be to assume, "in the aftermath of the Soviet regime's decades-long opposition to religion," that the Bolsheviks held a consistent antireligious stance from the start, such was not the case. The Decree on the Separation of Church from State and School from Church, issued January 20, 1918, did not prohibit religious belief or practice; it privatized them. Indeed, William Husband describes the decree as "nonreligious rather than antireligious," suggesting that opposition to religion was not central factor to the Bolsheviks' ascent.[21]

Peris notes that Marx and Engels expected the masses to be completely alienated from religion by the time of the revolution. Bolshevik leaders had prepared themselves to deal with issues of class, politics, interest groups, and ethnic tensions, but they did not expect religion's grip over the people to be as strong as they found it in 1917. Religion, Peris asserts, remained a popular force in Russia; Orthodoxy remained a central component in Russian peasant culture. For the majority of Russians, even those whose religious observance was irregular, the Orthodox Church constituted "a consecrated order of earthly and heavenly affairs."[22]

In 1922, the Soviet government was not yet the all-powerful dictatorship it would become under Stalin; Soviet leaders were seeking to create an alternative culture with atheism at its center. Recent scholars have shown that this attempt was not merely a reaction to religion's continued vitality in Russian life, but an expression of strongly held ideals regarding the development of humankind's full potential. According to William Husband, the goal of Soviet antireligious legislation was to create an enlightened citizenry, what he terms the "New Soviet man,"[23] who was to understand life in materialistic and scientific terms, emancipated from inhibitions previously imposed by the supernatural. Husband notes that the Soviet government was the first modern government "to promote the rejection of all religious deities as a sustaining national ideal."[24]

In his Russian diary, Walsh indicates his awareness that a conflict of ideals was taking place. He expressed his "fear for the consequences in the economic, the political, the social, the religious, educational orders—of [the] *entire* world." Soviet communism, he wrote, had no precedent. It was "the most reactionary and savage school of thought known to history," inaugurating a "reign of terror that makes the French Revolution insignificant." Unlike the French Revolution, which was essentially a French affair, the Bolshevik revolution was "not national . . . but international," with a goal of

> World Revolution, or in other words, universal Socialism with its concomitants—no state, no government, no belief in God, no marriages, no religion or in a word, the total destruction of the present Christian civilization and the substitution of the Communistic state.

In a diary entry crucial to understanding how he became an anticommunist, Walsh wrote that Bolshevism was "bent upon the destruction of spiritual ideals." Soviet communism was thus not merely a political issue, but a direct challenge to his most deeply held beliefs and ideals.[25]

THE BEGINNINGS OF THE PAPAL RELIEF MISSION

Returning to Rome on May 3, 1922, Walsh was instructed by Cardinal Gasparri to proceed to Washington, D.C., where he was to present President Warren G. Harding a letter from the pope petitioning the Americans to continue relief work; he was also to meet with Hoover to arrange the Papal Relief Mission's ARA affiliation.[26] Before leaving for America on May 15, Walsh helped compose the letter to Harding. On May 27, he arrived in Washington, where Archbishop Giovanni Bonzano, the apostolic delegate, arranged the White House meeting. On May 31, Walsh presented the Holy See's letter to Harding, and the following day he conferred with Hoover, who approved the relief mission's ARA affiliation, with the NCWC operating as liaison between the two. In Russia, the mission was to purchase food and supplies from the ARA, which the mission's own personnel would distribute. The Holy See contributed $200,000 to the start of the mission.[27]

Walsh proceeded to New York and then to Rome on June 17. Father Louis Gallagher, S.J., his friend and future biographer, accompanied him as his assistant. In Rome, Walsh received an official papal declaration of his appointment as mission director and authorization "to direct the distribution of provisions sent into Russia by the Holy See [and] to treat, in the name of the Holy Father, with all competent authorities, of the affairs that the Holy See has entrusted to him."[28] According to historian Henry Hull, whose 1970 study of the Papal Relief Mission is the standard work on the subject, Walsh's appointment signified "the first time . . . the Holy See sent a representative invested with a diplomatic character to a Communist Government."[29]

Although the mission's director was American, its staff of ten priests and two brothers was international, coming from Greece, Yugoslavia, Czechoslovakia, Italy, Spain, and Germany (but not from Poland, in deference to the strong anti-Polish sentiment then prevailing in Russia). In addition to Jesuits, it included Salesians, Divine Word Missionaries, and members of the Spanish Congregation of the Immaculate Heart. Indeed, never before in the history of the American Jesuits had one of their own led such an international endeavor.[30]

Before their departure, Monsignor Pizzardo instructed the mission staff not to protest "even if Catholic Churches are plundered and native Catholic priests arrested."[31] Earlier in May, Pizzardo told Walsh that the "first thing" to do was to engage the "goodwill of present authority in order to work for souls later." If a conflict with Soviet authorities arose in a given situation, Pizzardo said it was better to sacrifice a "few trainloads of food rather than lose [the] good will of [the] Soviets."[32]

Vatican motives in Russia were subject to constant scrutiny, and the missionaries placed under continuous surveillance throughout their stay in Russia. In his unpublished 1931 memoir, Colonel Haskell offered the following explanation:

> In the beginning of the revolution the existence of the Communist Party was more precarious than now. It had with some reason a fear of counter-revolutions. They saw every organization, [especially] such a well-organized one as the Church, in the light of a possible nucleus of resistance, opposition and counter-revolution. This feeling of fear was justified as the revolution hung by a thread for several years. The fear has passed now but as late as 1921–1922, during the great famine, a suspicion existed in the Communist Party that relief organizations on missions of mercy were in reality the advance guards or smoke screens of a move to destroy them.[33]

Historians have also debated papal motives, and their interpretations fall into three schools. The first, exemplified by James J. Zatko's 1965 study *Descent into Darkness*, stresses the Holy See's humanitarian impulse and underplays its diplomatic motives, whereas the second, exemplified by Hansjakob Stehle's 1979 *The Eastern Politics of the Vatican*, overemphasizes the Vatican's political motives and implies that philanthropy was a cover-up for the secret "hope that the Catholic Church could still become the heir of the Orthodox in Russia."[34]

The third school, exemplified by Henry Hull's 1970 doctoral dissertation "The Holy See and the Soviet Union, 1918–1920," steers a middle course. Hull argues that, although the Vatican did indeed want to investigate the status of Catholicism in Russia, its relief work was motivated by sincere impulses of compassion and charity. The Holy See's philanthropic and political motives were thus not mutually exclusive but "intertwined," resulting in what Hull calls the "twofold character of the Papal Mission sent into Russia."[35]

On July 10, 1922, Pius XII issued the apostolic epistle *Annus fere iam est*, urging Catholics throughout the world to support Russian relief. One scholar has recently estimated that Catholics worldwide contributed approximately two million dollars to Russian relief work. In the United States, the American hierarchy designated October 29, 1922, as a collection day for relief work in Russia, Austria, and the Near East. The Administrative Committee of the NCWC sent out a letter to every bishop requesting support, and the appeal was highly successful.[36]

"THE THRESHOLD OF AN IMPORTANT WORK": WALSH'S RELIEF WORK IN RUSSIA, JULY 1922–MARCH 1923

At the end of July 1922, Edmund A. Walsh officially entered Russia as the director of the Papal Relief Mission. From the start, he found his dealings with local officials highly frustrating. He complained that supplies were not ready for his staff upon arrival; he found the housing inadequate and that Soviet officials wanted him to work in areas other than had been originally agreed upon. Nonetheless, he wrote John J. Burke in August: "We are, I think, on the threshold of an important work, and I feel myself in much the same position that you must have been in when the war came and you had to organize the N.C. War Council overnight."[37] On September 29, 1922, the first station opened at Eupatoria (Yevpatoriya), a former resort spot in the Crimea, with the papal insignia displayed over doors through which one thousand children passed.[38]

Walsh's relief work proved to be a great success. Applying the organizational skills he had demonstrated in 1919, he established relief stations in each of the famine districts, as the Soviets had requested. By November 1922, the Papal Relief Mission was operating four main relief stations: Moscow, Eupatoria, Rostov-on-Don, and Krasnodar. The thirteen members of the mission directed relief work at each station, assisted

> by a corps of Russian employees, clerks, interpreters, translators, typists, warehouse managers, chauffeurs and such indispensable adjuncts of an operation which must be conducted on business lines as it does the purchase, shipment by land and water, insurance, storage and wide distribution of thousands of tons of foodstuffs.[39]

In November, the mission and its 2,500 employees were feeding 35,000 Russians a day; by 1923, at the height of their activity, they fed 158,000. Walsh wrote John Creeden at Georgetown: "I do not believe history has recorded a more extensive relief operation than this present charity to the Russian people."[40]

In his 1962 biography, Louis Gallagher explains that Walsh "was in Russia on a dual capacity; as Director of the Papal Mission and as Vatican agent representing the interests of the Catholic Church." Shortly after he arrived in Russia, Walsh wrote John Burke that his duties were to "direct the field operations" and to "treat with the Soviet Government, an item requiring most of one's time."[41] By the end of the year, diplomatic issues came to consume more of his time at mission headquarters in Moscow.

"The question of Church interests," Gallagher observed in his unpublished memoirs, "created as much work and worry for Father Walsh as did the prime purpose for which he went into Russia, and it kept him resident in Moscow for almost the entire period he spent in the country." Walsh did not, indeed, could not, oversee everyday operations. In December 1922, Father Joseph Farrell, S.J., Walsh's classmate and Haskell's brother-in-law, arrived in Moscow to aid Walsh. Described by Gallagher as "an expert business manager," Farrell had been a newspaper editor before he joined the Jesuits. He assumed the daily administrative work, freeing Walsh to handle other pressing tasks.[42]

"The Great Closing": December 1922

In October 1922, Walsh had met with Archbishop Jan Baptist Cieplak, who had become administrator of the Archdiocese of Moghilev, with ecclesiastical jurisdiction over all of Russia, after the Soviets expelled Archbishop Edward von der Ropp in 1919. In June 1922, the Soviets had ordered Cieplak to relinquish all church property, but he refused on the grounds that canon law forbade its secular administration; he continued to refuse even when threatened with church closings. Because Cieplak's lines of communication were severely hampered, Walsh acted as his liaison with the Vatican.[43]

On December 5, 1922, in what historian of Russian Catholicism Father Christopher Zugger refers to as "the Great Closing," Soviet troops closed all of Petrograd's and three of Moscow's Catholic churches. Because Moghilev's see was located in Petrograd, the church closings paralyzed "the structural center of the Soviet Catholic Church." Walsh sent a letter of protest off to the Soviets, but received no response. Nonetheless, he continued to petition that the churches be reopened by Christmastime. "I have thus far avoided," he wrote Cardinal Gasparri,

> all semblance of interference on religious questions in order not to compromise the work of the Relief Mission. . . . I have taken no step that would tend to alienate the good will of the authorities, though I am persuaded that the work has expanded sufficiently to make representations that would bear considerable weight. I am awaiting, consequently, the expression of your wishes in the matter of strong protest to the Soviet Government.[44]

Throughout this period, Walsh's letters made frequent reference to what he called "abnormal and absolutely unprecedented conditions" surrounding the Church-state conflict in Russia. In January 1923, he wrote Burke that he was "trying to maintain the mental attitude of calm so essential in the face of the abnormal conditions facing us on every side." Asserting that the antireligious processions then occurring in Moscow had "no parallel in recent history," he warned Cardinal Gasparri that "it must never . . . be lost sight of that the avowed purpose of the [Soviet] Government is to *destroy every religion*," and that none of its officials "can have any other objective in his acts and negotiations."[45]

"THE BEGINNING OF A VERITABLE NERONIAN PERSECUTION": THE CATHOLIC CLERGY TRIALS OF 1923

After conferring with the Vatican in February 1923, Walsh advised Cieplak to sign the church property contracts, but, by then, it was too late. On March 3, troops in Petrograd arrested the archbishop and fourteen priests, as well as Exarch Leonid Feodorov, the leader of the Byzantine-Russian Catholics. Charged with obstructing Soviet law regarding church property, proselytizing minors, and counterrevolutionary activity, bishops and priests were shipped to Moscow to stand trial before the Supreme Revolutionary Tribunal. On March 20, Walsh wrote Gasparri that the antireligious climate in Russia had intensified after the arrests, and he soon expected "serious trouble." Walsh sent a formal protest to the Soviet Commissar for Foreign Affairs, Georgi Cicerin, but received no reply. On March 21, the last week of the Western Church's Lenten season, the trial began. Accompanied by an interpreter, Walsh attended the trial as the Holy See's official representative.[46]

Whereas the clergy trials of 1922 were directed against the Orthodox Church, those of 1923 were directed against Russia's Catholic leaders. When Walsh and other anticommunists complained about what they regarded as rigged trials, they did not exaggerate. Richard Pipes describes the trials as "spectacles that had more in common with 'agitational' theater than with judiciary proceedings."[47]

The March 21 trial gave Cieplak and his fellow clerics scant opportunity to mount an adequate defense. On March 25, the beginning of Holy Week in the Latin rite, the clergy were found guilty on all counts. Cieplak and his Polish vicar general, Monsignor Constantine Budkiewicz, were sentenced to death. In the wake of the Russo-Polish War, Budkiewicz was perhaps inevitably subject to a severe sentence. Exarch Feodorov was sentenced to ten years' solitary confinement and the remaining priests received extended prison sentences. The end result, writes Christopher Zugger, was to leave the Catholic Church in Russia "stunned and leaderless."[48]

Louis Gallagher recalled that the trial was "perhaps the most nerve racking week in Father Walsh's life." Walsh requested permission from the Soviets to administer last rites to Cieplak and Budkiewicz, but was refused. Using the German consul's office, Walsh cabled the news to the Vatican. As news of the trial's outcome spread, worldwide opposition arose against the sentences. The United States, Great Britain, France, and Germany sent formal protests, which influenced the Soviets to commute Cieplak's sentence to ten years' imprisonment.[49]

Monsignor Budkiewicz, however, was not so fortunate. On the evening of March 31, the monsignor was taken from his cell and executed on the steps of the Lubyanka prison. Walsh received a series of anonymous telephone calls in Russian, every half hour for nearly two hours, from someone who spoke coarsely amid laughter and commotion. Soon afterward, Walsh discovered that Budkiewicz had been executed by the Cheka, the Soviet secret police.[50]

WALSH'S REACTION AND RESPONSE TO THE TRIAL

The execution of Budkiewicz affected Walsh profoundly. Christian Herter, assistant to Herbert Hoover and future Massachusetts governor, saw Walsh shortly after the trial at a dinner in Moscow. Walsh "talked for three hours," Herter wrote to a colleague, "on his opinion of the whole Russian situation and on the murder of the Catholic priest. . . . Can you imagine anything more brutal? . . . Dr. W. is very jumpy and somewhat bitter [and] a bit too irritated to be sound at present."[51]

On April 5, Walsh wrote to John Burke:

> The week of the Passion is truly a week of the Passion in the Capital City of the Bolshevists. As the whole Christian world knows, this week signalled the beginning of a veritable Neronian persecution, prepared long before and now being actually carried out . . . that the communists and atheists might show their triumphant power, for they have constantly sought the destruction of all religion among the Russians.[52]

In May, Walsh was permitted to visit Archbishop Cieplak, who was under guard. The sight of the imprisoned prelate caused him great anguish, which he described to Cardinal Gasparri:

> The "Cheka" Agent who was appointed to listen took up his position right beside me and never was more than three feet away and heard every word. The appearance of an Archbishop of Holy Mother Church thus guarded and treated as a dangerous criminal in the hands of men who looked like the lowest types of criminals themselves, affected me very deeply, with an indignation and scorn that I had great difficulty in restraining.

At the end of the interview, Walsh knelt to kiss Cieplak's hand as if the prelate were still wearing his episcopal ring.[53]

Driven by an ideology that justified any means, including duplicity, lying, and murder, the Soviets were striving to eradicate Christianity, the basis of Western civilization. "The very existence of the Catholic Church in Russia," Walsh wrote Gasparri, "is at stake." To Monsignor Pizzardo, he asserted: "The issue here is clear enough; it is atheism against Christianity."[54]

AMERICAN PRESS REACTION TO THE TRIAL:
RELIGIOUS AND SECULAR

Not all Americans shared either Walsh's moral outrage or his opinions regarding the Soviets, however. In a May 1923 article for the *Nation*, the Reverend John Haynes Holmes, founder of the Community Church of New York and a board member of the American Civil Liberties Union, denied there was religious persecution in Russia. He had recently visited Russia and had "looked in vain for evidence of such atrocities" as were described in the religious press. The March trials, he asserted, were "purely political." The government was "refusing to allow the shadow of religion to hide conspiracy against the state," and to suggest otherwise was "ridiculous." In a *New York Times* interview, Percy Stickney Grant, Rector of New York's Methodist Church of the Ascension, insisted that the clergy were being prosecuted for political crimes.[55]

Holmes's and Grant's opinions did not go unnoticed in the Catholic press. James M. Gillis, the newly appointed Paulist editor of the *Catholic World*, attacked "the significant moral blindness or callousness of the radical weeklies in regard to the horrible news from Russia." Focusing on what he regarded as the indifferent reaction of the *Nation* and the *New Republic*, which did not have "the moral instinct to see how grievous a crime had been committed," Gillis argued that their indifference highlighted the hypocrisy of

> the liberal press, which pretends to admire martyrdom and to adore fidelity to principle, [but] couldn't recognize spiritual heroism, when face to face to it. It has no rebukes for the persecutors, and no word for the martyrs but insinuation, innuendo and false accusation.

He went on to harangue "our parlor and college Bolsheviki" who sympathized with the "Russian experiment."[56]

The Jesuit weekly *America* compared Soviet actions to anti-Catholic efforts in Oregon to outlaw private education. Editor Richard H. Tierney, S.J., declared that the "same spirit" that led to the outlawing of religion in Russia was at work in the United States. "Let us not be unmindful," he concluded, "that the philosophy which teaches the complete and absolute supremacy of the civil power, is now in high places, even in our own land."[57]

Considering that he would become the preeminent anticommunist in the 1930s Catholic press, Patrick F. Scanlan of the Brooklyn *Tablet* took a surprisingly balanced view of the events in Russia. Scanlan distinguished between the Soviet government, which had "branded itself as a blundering, vicious, atrocious tyranny," and the Russian people, who "should not be held responsible for the crimes of the few radicals, who have usurped the prerogatives of government."[58] Although the clergy trials and the reactions they engendered from Catholics and non-Catholics alike marked the first extended discussion of Soviet Russia in the American Catholic press, the issues raised were soon overshadowed by concerns over a growing anti-Catholicism. For many American Catholics, the Ku Klux Klan was the major issue of the 1920s. The concerns expressed for a brief time in 1923 would come to the fore again during the 1930s.[59]

"The World Should Know the Truth": Edmund A. Walsh, Soviet Russia, and the American Public

For one Catholic leader, however, communism was becoming, and would remain, the central issue. Walsh carefully followed how the American press covered news from Russia. When, in March 1923, the Reverend John Zelie, a Presbyterian minister who had worked with the Federal Council of Churches in Russia and who knew Walsh, claimed in the *New York Times* that the Papal Relief Mission distributed food only to Catholics, Walsh called his remarks as "a stab in the back," and asked John Burke to make a radio reply.[60]

After reading Holmes's May 1923 article in the *Nation*, Walsh suggested to Burke that someone "make a public offer of *$10,000* to the man who can prove that the murdered Monsignor [Budkiewicz] was *shown* (not *charged* or *accused*) to be guilty of 'treason, spying and treasonable activity in time of war.'" He sent Burke copies of his notes from the trial, which he claimed were the "only complete record of the trial now in U.S.A." He also supplied him with information on the mission and the state of the Church in Russia. Burke sent the notes to Catholic periodicals and ran the information on the NCWC News Service wire.[61]

Because of his diplomatic work, Walsh asked Burke not to use his name in connection with any published items, "beyond vouching

[for] their accuracy." During 1923, Walsh anonymously authored articles on Russia in *America*, the *Catholic World*, and the *Woodstock Letters*. The *Catholic World* article, for example, referred to him as "long resident in Russia . . . a scholar of world-wide reputation and unquestioned authority, who would be made liable to Bolshevist persecution, were his identity to be revealed." Walsh also corresponded with the secular press. For example, in the spring of 1923 he took photos of Russian antireligious posters with a pocket camera and sent them to the *New York Herald*.[62]

To Walsh, Holmes "and others of his kidney, as well as Dr. Percy Stickney Grant . . . deluded readers" by downplaying the plight of religion in Russia. Walsh dedicated himself to counteracting their strong influence on public opinion. "I believe the world," he wrote Burke, "should know the truth." The events of April 1923 intensified his conviction:

> With the last Catholic Bishop now in Boutirka prison in Moscow, with 22 Catholic priests in prison in Moscow *alone*, and [Budkiewicz] murdered, it seems to me that the time has now come to silence these "pinks" sitting at ease in N.Y. and elsewhere![63]

To appreciate the true significance of what was happening in Russia, Walsh proposed the following hypothesis to Burke:

> What would the clergy of the U.S. do if Congress should—in some impossible hypothesis—(1) Confiscate every church, school, priest's house and convent. (2) Forbid the teaching of religion to everybody under 19 years of age. (3) Require every priest to submit his sermon to the local Communist party leader. (4) Send anti-Christian propagandists into the schools to ridicule Christianity and destroy every vestige of supernatural religion. (5) Organize processions for the streets [and] burn in effigy God, the Blessed Mother, the Saints and all holy objects. Ask the Bishops and priests what we would do.

Furthermore, he wanted to see the bishops of the United States "come out in a ringing statement against Russia" because his diplomatic status prevented him from doing so.[64]

Walsh was particularly dismayed at the sympathy certain American Protestant leaders displayed for the Soviet government. In Moscow, during the week of April 29–May 5, 1923, the Living Church, the Soviet-sponsored wing of the Orthodox Church, held its Second Church Council, which proceeded to deny the existence of religious persecutions, express its support for the government, and abolish the patriarchate. As a result, Russian Orthodoxy split between the Patriarch Tikhon's followers and those supporting the Living Church. Among the council participants was an American, Bishop Edgar Blake of the Methodist Episcopal Church, who expressed his support for actions taken by the council. Walsh viewed Blake's attitude as clear evidence of American Protestantism's moral bankruptcy:

> As the heroic defense of their faith made by the Petrograd Catholic priests will ever remain the honor and glory of the Catholic Church, so it must remain forever the shame and scandal of the Protestant community that a Methodist Episcopal Bishop named Blake, of the American Church, participated in the Council and spoke against the Patriarch. He definitely associated himself with the group which declared the Patriarch "a traitor worthy of the death penalty."[65]

Historian Peter Filene notes that during the trials, American Protestant observers displayed "an ambivalent attitude" toward the proceedings. Filene further contends that Holmes was representative of what he terms a "precedent of Protestant sympathy for the Soviets." Convinced that America's Protestant leaders did not sufficiently appreciate the moral gravity of the conflict, Walsh concluded that Catholics had to assume the vanguard in the battle with communism.[66]

This viewpoint situates Walsh with the Catholic leaders described in William M. Halsey's *The Survival of American Innocence*. By the 1920s, according to Halsey, Catholics had come to see themselves as the defenders of traditional American values, chief among these being the certainty of moral values, their universality, and the inevitability of progress. Catholics saw these values threatened by a rising tide of secularist tendencies in modern society, such as skepticism in literature and relativism in law and morality. A lapse in Protestant idealism after the war, Halsey argued, gave Catholics the opportunity to see themselves as the defenders of values formerly espoused by writers such as William Dean Howells and now attacked by others such as H. L. Mencken.[67] Walsh was attempting to assert traditional values in the new field of international relations, in the face of what he perceived as a menace far worse than gradual secularization. In this sense, his battle might be understood as extending the domain of American Catholic idealism.

EDMUND A. WALSH AND THE "JEW AS REVOLUTIONARY"

Walsh's idealism coexisted with secretly harbored prejudices, however. In his diary, Walsh described Soviet communism as a "wholly Jewish movement." Although he conceded that Lenin and the upper echelons of leadership were not Jewish, he insisted that "at least 75%" of the leaders were. "If Lenin is the brain of the movement," he insisted, "the Jews provide the Executive Officers," listing Trotsky, Zinoviev, and Kamenev as examples. The main reasons for Jewish radicalism, he wrote, were "Jewish antagonism to Christianity [and] internationalism."[68]

Shortly before he left Russia in 1923, Walsh would openly express this opinion in a letter to Cardinal Gasparri, who had relayed Soviet complaints about Walsh's brusque manner and insensitivity to Slavic culture. Walsh responded that he employed "the formal language of International Relations [but it] was not strange . . . that they find my insistence on justice and the rights of religion irksome." Furthermore, he asserted, he "thoroughly understood" and appreciated the Slavic mindset, but that, in the Kremlin, "the 'mentalité slave' has been replaced by [that of] the Jewish Communist." He concluded:

> I beg therefore to assure the Holy See that the Slav is thoroughly understood and assisted in Russia. It is not the Slav mentality which the Mission does not understand, but rather the Jewish greed for gold and hatred of Christianity, which I have found it necessary to combat.[69]

The notion of "Jew as revolutionary" became a hallmark of modern anti-Semitism beginning in late nineteenth-century Europe. In his 2001 work on Catholic anti-Semitism, James Carroll traces its beginnings to the 1871 Paris Commune uprising. The murder of the archbishop of Paris by the Communards, along with Karl Marx's endorsement of the Commune, "solidified the image of Jew as revolutionary" for many Catholics. During the Dreyfus Affair in the1890s, several French Catholic leaders, notably the Assumptionist editors of the daily *La Croix*, accused French Jews of secretly masterminding the secularization policies that weakened the Church's influence.[70]

In 1898, the English Jesuit Provincial John Gerard, concerned that the failure of his confreres to condemn the rabid anti-Semitism sweeping France would have negative repercussions in England, sent Father Sydney Smith to France to investigate Jesuit involvement in the Dreyfus case. Smith found substantial support among Jesuits for the anti-Dreyfusard cause; he encountered one French Jesuit who claimed "it does not matter whether or not Dreyfus is innocent . . . the greatest possible condemnation must be brought against the Jews."[71] While the controversy raged in France, Father Herbert Thurston objected to an article on the ritual murder of Christian children in the Jesuit *La Civiltà Cattolica*, but was chided by Jesuit General Luis Martín, who stated that

> the efforts of Fr. Thurston and others to clear the Jews of such a ritual crime and other serious accusations down the ages . . . did not contend with the texts brought forth in the old *Civiltà* articles and the explicit and published confessions of Jewish converts.

A strident conservative, Martín further rebuked Thurston for "yielding to the liberal inspiration of the English press [and being] more inclined to what was convenient with the liberal Catholic party."[72]

Two decades later, in 1919, the English Jesuit *Month* would offer up its baldly anti-Semitic view of Jewish participation in the Russian Revolution:

> The authors of Russia's downfall and ruin are German Jews, and are doing what they can to identify Jewry with revolution. The international Jew is the backbone of the International, the fomenter of class war, the solvent of patriotism, the foe of institutional religion. He is a nuisance and a danger to Europe.[73]

Thus it becomes clear that, as was the case with many other institutions of the day, an undercurrent of anti-Semitic sentiment did run through Jesuit life when Walsh entered the Society of Jesus.

Larger influences at work in American society may have also played a part in influencing Walsh's attitude. John Higham argues that the notion of "Jew as radical" widened during the First World War era as Jewish Americans assumed key leadership roles in the Socialist Party, and that American Jewish support for the October Revolution "sharpened an emerging image of the Jew as a subversive radical." The postwar Red Scare and Henry Ford's publishing the *Protocols of Zion*, the infamous fabrication so fervently touted by twentieth-century anti-Semitism, in his *Dearborn Independent* further popularized this image, which may have been another influence on Walsh.[74]

In May 1922, however, Walsh referred in his diary to one specific source: *The World Revolution*, a 1921 book by Nesta Webster (1876–

1950), an Englishwoman whose works are still published by the right-wing John Birch Society. According to historian of American anticommunism Richard Gid Powers, Webster "had worked out a master conspiracy theory that all of world history since the revolutions of the eighteenth century had been masterminded by secret societies, with the Bolsheviks only the most recent." The conspirators Webster describes were motivated by the destruction of Christianity and the creation of an all-encompassing world state, themes employed in Walsh's own anticommunism.[75]

Thus, although Walsh was an idealist, he was a flawed one. In his campaign to preserve American democratic principles in the face of a deadly enemy, motives and sentiments that directly contravened these principles—and that did not just represent the "survival of American innocence"—played a central role in his anticommunism. Less than ideal motives and sentiments were also present in the form of a privately harbored anti-Semitism, which had its roots in the several influences described above. Indeed, one of the central incongruities of Walsh's anticommunism was its mixture of high principles and low prejudices.[76]

LAST MONTHS IN RUSSIA: JUNE–NOVEMBER 1923

By spring 1923, the Russian famine had significantly abated, which led the ARA to terminate operations in June. As the emergency diminished, Soviet hostility to American capitalists became more pronounced; indeed, ARA officials discovered that the Soviets were exporting grain even as relief agencies continued to send food shipments. "In the summer of 1923," Colonel Haskell wrote in his memoir, "when I took my departure with the last of the other Americans to leave Russia, Moscow and the other large cities had become active centers of trade, and there remained nothing to remind us of the conditions we had seen two years earlier."[77] From September 1921 to June 1923, total ARA expenditures reached seventy million dollars, with relief workers feeding nearly eleven million Russian men, women, and children.[78]

Four days after the ARA's departure, the Soviets terminated the Vorofsky-Gasparri Agreement of March 1922, which had served as the basis for the Papal Relief Mission. Walsh attempted to draw up a new contract, but the Soviets refused to cooperate, instructing him to make his petitions by mail rather than in person. The work was frustrating, he wrote Burke, and he was "infinitely weary of the continual battling." In June, Walsh conferred with the Congregation for Extraordinary Ecclesiastical Affairs in Rome about the mission's future. In a private meeting with Pius XI, Walsh asked the pontiff to appoint a bishop or apostolic delegate for Russia to continue the work, but, he wrote Creeden:

> they sent me back to Moscow with a new letter of credentials to [Chicherin] naming me again Vatican Representative, sort of chargé d'affaires for the time being. I did my best (and d——est) to have a Bishop or Apostolic Delegate appointed, but instead they sent me back with more power and authority than I ever had.[79]

On July 4, 1923, Cardinal Gasparri issued an official declaration of Walsh's diplomatic status, charging him "to treat with all competent Soviet authorities on the subject of the different questions, and upon which he might have the occasion to enter into negotiations."[80]

Despite the hampering of its relief work, Walsh remained with the Papal Relief Mission in Moscow for nearly six months after the ARA departed. In June, he closed several feeding stations after receiving instructions to cut spending by one-half. By that time, however, he informed Creeden that "relief work for the starving forms but a small fraction of my work . . . the chief occupation being rather those of an unofficial representative in dealings with the Soviet Government."[81]

When Walsh returned to Russia from Rome on July 12, the status of the imprisoned clergy became *the* priority. He advised the pope that the policy of prisoner exchanges was the best means of securing their release, adding that representatives of several eastern and central European nations holding Soviet prisoners were willing to participate. Walsh worked with diplomats from Lithuania, Poland, Hungary, and Germany. Although the Soviets released several of the priests, they refused to release Archbishop Cieplak. Walsh's attempts to reopen the churches in Petrograd and Moscow were similarly unsuccessful.[82]

Scholars agree that the Soviets allowed the Papal Relief Mission to remain because they hoped to gain diplomatic recognition from the Holy See, which they regarded as an important precedent. Walsh advised Gasparri against recognition; he warned him that the Soviets had no intention of mollifying their "anti-Christian policy." Insisting that the ideological bent of government officials prevented their dealing fairly with "foreigners, all of whom are considered 'Bourgeoisie' and 'Capitalist[s].'" He added:

> In all these matters I beg to warn Your Eminence that the duplicity of these people is unbelievable if not actually experienced on the spot. Lying is the ordinary refuge and it simply renders normal intercourse, whether diplomatic or commercial, almost impossible.

Indeed, their ideology impelled Russian leaders to lie and deceive: "I know the tactics."[83]

In August 1923, Walsh proposed to Gasparri that the mission be terminated. The famine had passed and conditions improved; sending further supplies "only releases equivalent sums of Soviet money for revolutionary propaganda for the overthrow of established governments in Europe and elsewhere."[84] At the same time he suggested an office be maintained in Moscow for future negotiations, he urged that relief be sent to Germany, which faced a pending famine: "If hunger becomes acute in Germany the possibilities of despair on the part of the population and some sort of Bolshevism are not to be disregarded."[85] When the negotiations with the Russian government became increasingly difficult, he ordered a halt to food distribution. Walsh purchased a house in Moscow, but was prevented from moving in when he refused to allow Soviet agents to share it. In September, Louis Gallagher and several staff members left Russia. By then the lone mission member in Moscow, Walsh wrote Creeden that "there is not another [Jesuit] within a thousand miles." In October, shortly after one last, unsuccessful attempt to secure a contract to continue relief work, he received word from the Vatican to close the mission. On November 16, 1923, Edmund A. Walsh left Russia, never to return.[86]

He arrived in Rome on December 3 and privately conferred with Pius XI two days later. Over the next month, Walsh was assigned to the Secretariat of State to serve "as a sort of a 'Russian Division.'" Soviet officials in Rome were lobbying for diplomatic recognition by the Holy See, he informed Creeden, adding that "some pretty deep politics are being played at this moment." While serving as Gasparri's Russian adviser, Walsh prepared a report on the Papal Relief Mission's activities. In January, he was sent to Germany to help the nuncio, Archbishop Eugenio Pacelli, who would become Pope Pius XII in 1939, establish German relief work. Walsh set up a warehouse for supplies in Hamburg, but "begged off" a permanent assignment. After receiving permission to return to the United States, Walsh sent his report on German relief to the Holy See. On January 26, he departed for home, arriving in Washington on February 7, 1924.[87]

THE AFTERMATH AND SIGNIFICANCE OF
THE PAPAL RELIEF MISSION

The work of the Papal Relief Mission formed an important chapter in the history of Vatican-Soviet relations during the years 1918–30, which Henry Hull characterizes as a "study in full-circle diplomacy," moving from mutual exclusivity in 1918 toward dialogue in 1921. The withdrawal of the mission in 1923, signaling the end of the Holy See's attempts at rapprochement with the Soviet government, marked a shift toward "absolute polarity and mutual repulsion." Although, in 1926, the Jesuit oriental scholar Michel d'Herbigny was consecrated a bishop in Berlin by Archbishop Pacelli and sent to Russia, where he secretly ordained bishops, d'Herbigny was expelled and the new bishops were imprisoned as soon as the Soviets discovered the nature of his mission, bringing Vatican-Soviet relations to a standstill.[88]

From a diplomatic viewpoint, the Papal Relief Mission appeared a failure: none of the Holy See's goals was achieved. When Walsh left Russia, the clergy were still in prison, the churches remained closed, and no diplomatic solutions had been reached. During 1922–23, Vatican-Soviet relations had neither advanced nor improved, and the famine relief experience only intensified previous animosities. Nonetheless, Hull writes, Walsh's mission was the Holy See's first attempt at dialogue with a communist state and "if only for the practical experience gained from this contact, it was worth the Church's effort."[89]

From a humanitarian viewpoint, however, the Church's first foray into international relief work was an astounding success. During the mission's twenty-month life span, Walsh administered seven feeding stations, employing 2,500 Russians. At the height of its activity, the mission fed 158,000 starving children. In March 1926, the Holy See enlisted Walsh's organizational genius to create the Catholic Near East Welfare Association (CNEWA), a permanent pontifical organization designed to centralize Catholic relief efforts in Russia and the Middle East under the supervision of Cardinal Patrick Hayes of New York. As the first president, Walsh oversaw the first annual fund drive in January 1927, which raised over one million dollars.[90] In her study of the CNEWA's formation, Margaret McGuinness writes that Walsh's appointment was a sign of favor from Pius XI. Louis Gallagher also stresses the confidence Pius had in Walsh: "The signal success of the Vatican Relief Mission to Russia . . . marked him as a diplomat held in reserve for emergencies."[91]

In the summer of 1928, Pius XI asked Walsh to visit Mexico in the capacity of an unofficial observer as Ambassador Dwight Morrow, with the help of John J. Burke, was attempting to negotiate a Church-state settlement.[92] Although communist-related issues were present in the Mexican controversy, and Walsh played a visible part in the concluding ceremonies in June 1929, the Mexican episode was a minor event in his career, one he seems to have been happy to have left to the NCWC, and one most notable as an expression of the confidence Pius had invested in him. Thus, for example, Walsh paid little attention to the resumption of Church-state conflict in Mexico during the 1930s. His main interest was and continued to be Russia.[93]

Walsh's experience in Russia, most especially the 1923 clergy trials, affirmed his commitment to anticommunism. His basic presuppositions regarding international order, the central part Western civilization had to play in maintaining it, and Christianity's role as the basis of that civilization were all directly challenged by what he saw in Russia. For Walsh, in their drive to replace morality with dialectical materialism, the Soviets constituted the most urgent threat to international life. Events in Russia, therefore, had international repercussions that no nation could afford to ignore. Because he viewed Protestant clergymen as forfeiting their prophetic role, he regarded it as his responsibility to warn the American public about what was happening in Russia. In 1928, Walsh summed up this viewpoint in his first book on Russia, *The Fall of the Russian Empire*:

> For the student of political variations, the World War spelled the end of national complacencies based on national isolation and ignorance of international organizations. That devastating conflict was fought in vain if it has not left men convinced that the nations of the earth constitute a huge, international family whose basic interests are common, and whose members are far more interdependent, acting and reacting

on one another far more seriously and directly, than we imagined prior to 1914. No mortal sickness, be it physical, spiritual, or intellectual, that attacks one member of this social organism can ever again be regarded with indifference even by the healthiest member of human society.[94]

While in Russia, Walsh had already devised the outline of his future anticommunist program, to consist of lectures, books, and articles—and reshaping the foreign service school's curriculum. From June through December 1923, he corresponded with Canadian journalist Francis McCullagh, the *New York Herald*'s Moscow correspondent who covered the clergy trials. At McCullagh's request, Walsh and his confrere at the Vatican, Michel d'Herbigny, had examined the proofs to McCullagh's book on the trials, which had already been rejected by several publishers, who found it "arid" and directed too much toward a Catholic audience. Walsh agreed to help McCullagh find an American publisher.

In a December 1923 letter to John Burke, he proposed that the NCWC appropriate funds to guarantee the purchase of one thousand copies of McCullagh's book, arguing that it had relevance for Burke's own work and would

> be a very valuable contribution against [those] who are clamoring for recognition of Soviet Russia. The book is an authentic and permanent record of the Bolshevik anti-religious campaign *and certainly should be put before the American people* . . . as the book shows in a convincing way the inevitable de-Christianizing results of Bolshevism. It could be used very effectively in your campaign against such tendencies as have been manifested, for example, in the Oregon Law.[95]

The following spring, the New York firm of E. P. Dutton and Company published the book. Even though the *New York Times* reviewer praised it as "virtually indispensable for anyone who wishes to reach correct conclusions" about Russia, the book quickly faded into obscurity, an indication of the weakness of anticommunist Catholic sentiment in the 1920s.[96]

While still in Moscow, Walsh had told Creeden he intended to reshape the foreign service school's curriculum, with a greater emphasis on Russian studies. Since 1919, there had been few Russian-related courses offered at the school. Former Russian artillery officer Serge Petrenko taught a language course from its inception, while

Czarist refugee Baron Serge Korff, formerly assistant governor of Finland and law professor at the University of Petrograd, offered courses on eastern Europe as well as diplomatic history. Writing from Moscow in September 1923, Walsh urged John Creeden to keep Korff on the faculty:

> He is good material and an ornament. Don't let Columbia [University] get him through unwillingness on our part to pay. Rather sacrifice some of the others. With my two years in Russia [we] shall, I think, be able to constitute a "Russian Department" of high class.[97]

COMMUNISM AND ANTICOMMUNISM IN 1920s AMERICA: AN OVERVIEW

When Walsh returned to Washington in 1924, Russia was not the burning issue it would become in the following decade. In a survey of 1920s daily periodicals, Peter Filene found that less than 9 percent of the articles covered foreign affairs. Of these, only 44 magazine articles during the years 1925–28 had Russia as their subject, compared to 86 during the years 1919–21. Moreover, only 5 books were published on Russia between 1921 and 1926. These numbers would increase, however, during Stalin's Five-Year Plan, the Great Crash, and the growing movement for the Soviet Union's diplomatic recognition, whose supporters argued that Russia would inevitably drop the revolutionary rhetoric and climb on the capitalist bandwagon.[98]

Beginning with the Wilson administration in November 1917, American policy toward the Soviet government had been strict non-recognition. Presidents Harding, Coolidge, and Hoover maintained what Filene terms the "abnormalcy of recognition." One study by Russian scholars states that during the 1920s "there were three main non-recognition doctrines in the political arsenal—hostile Soviet propaganda on United States territory, confiscation of American property, and non-payment of debts." At the same time, trade between the two nations did increase, and American intellectuals developed a strong interest in Russia. W. E. B. DuBois and Theodore Dreiser, for example, both visited the Soviet Union. During the late 1920s, American tourism to Russia greatly increased; of the twenty-one books on Russia published in 1928–29, seventeen were tourist guides.[99]

Postwar American radicalism was marked by division and decline. In March 1919, the Third International, or Comintern, a worldwide communist organization dedicated to promoting revolution abroad, was formed in Russia. The American Socialist Party divided over the question of affiliation, with founders Eugene V. Debs and Morris Hillquit opposing attempts to "Bolshevize" the party. In August 1919, the party's left wing seceded to form an American communist party, consisting of two divisions: the Communist Party of America for foreign-language groups, and the Communist Labor Party for the English-speaking members. The division proved a severe blow to the American Socialist Party, which never recovered its prewar strength.[100]

The Red Scare of 1919–20 was a continuation of the wartime "One Hundred Percent Americanism," whose main components, according to Robert K. Murray, were an enforced ideological conformity, right-wing nativism, and a "scare psychology," all of which continued to influence public opinion. Bolshevism's gains in Russia sparked an anticommunist hysteria that was manipulated by patriotic societies such as the American Protective League and the American Legion. Following widespread arrests and deportations, American communist and socialist party membership dropped to 7,500 by 1927. Moreover, as Arthur Schlesinger observes, 1920s America "seemed to be on the edge of a new abundance," a factor further depriving radicals of their earlier appeal.[101]

J. Edgar Hoover, who acquired renown as head of the Justice Department's "Radical Division," represented the WASP middle class that formed the core of the wartime antiradical movement. Despite Hoover's abuses of civil liberties, which served to discredit the anticommunist cause, the movement continued throughout the 1920s, when it began to assume a previously absent multicultural dimension. Ralph M. Easley, who headed the National Civic Federation, the premier anticommunist organization of the 1920s, belonged to the older group. Members of other religious and racial groups joined the movement, including Abraham Marshall, a Jewish lawyer from New York, and African-American George Schuyler, leading Powers to conclude that American anticommunism was a much more pluralistic movement than scholars have previously assumed. For Powers, there was "no one thing that was American anticommunism; there were many American anticommunisms."[102]

AMERICAN CATHOLICS AND "THE ANTICOMMUNIST IMPULSE"

"Roman Catholics," writes Patrick Allitt, "opposed Communism right from the beginning."[103] According to Jesuit scholar Donald F. Crosby, the first concrete expression of Catholic antiradicalism in the United States occurred in the 1880s during the Knights of Labor controversy. Archbishop Michael Corrigan of New York and Bishop Bernard McQuaid of Rochester opposed the Knights, whose constitution and customs they considered too similar to those of European radical movements, and they fought for its condemnation by the Vatican. The Knights, however, had episcopal supporters, led by Cardinal James Gibbons of Baltimore, who saw that a condemnation would weaken the American Church's popular support; these supporters successfully worked to prevent the condemnation. Crosby concludes: "The incident is important . . . because it shows the continued concern of the Church over Communist influence on Catholics in America."[104]

The first widespread organized antiradical movement among American Catholics occurred in the early twentieth century, reaching its high point in 1914. A large factor in its growth was the expansion of the American Socialist Party, founded in 1901 by Debs and Hillquit. During the 1912 presidential campaign, Debs drew nearly one million votes. Perhaps a more significant factor was the association many Catholics saw between socialism and a resurgent anti-Catholicism during the years 1910–14, as evidenced, notes John Higham, by the rise of anti-Catholic lectures and by the dissemination of the spurious Knights of Columbus's "bogus oath," allegedly exposing a secret promise to forcefully eradicate heresy. The most powerful expression of prewar anti-Catholicism, however, was in the pages of the Aurora, Missouri, newspaper *The Menace*, which was founded by the disgruntled progressive Wilbur Franklin Phelps in 1911, and whose circulation peaked at 1.5 million subscribers in 1915.[105]

Higham explains the prewar anti-Catholic movement as "an outlet for expectations which progressivism raised and then failed to fulfill." Anti-Catholic writers and lecturers came across as progressives with socialist sympathies, often decrying Catholicism as a religious "trust" cooperating with big business to oppress American workers. The anti-Catholic rhetoric of the period frequently referred to a "Roman Catholic Political Machine," whose aim was to "rule and dominate the American people." In addition, the anti-Catholic bias of many socialist speakers and writers led to a heightened Catholic perception of the connection between socialism and anti-Catholicism.[106]

During these years, antisocialist pamphlets by Catholic writers began to appear in large numbers. In addition, the Knights of Columbus sponsored antisocialist lecturers such as Peter W. Collins and David Goldstein. Perhaps the most significant response to prewar anti-Catholicism, however, was the creation of *Our Sunday Visitor*, whose first issue appeared May 5, 1912. Its editor, Father John F. Noll of Indiana, was concerned about the rise of radical movements such as socialism, which, Leon Hutton notes, he perceived as "masks of anti-Catholicism." As editor and later as bishop of Fort Wayne, Indiana, Noll emerged as one of the most consistent opponents of socialism in the prewar years. Noll's main interest was the continued presence of anti-Catholicism in American life, with domestic issues taking priority over foreign affairs.[107]

Like most Americans during the 1920s, Catholics lost interest in overseas news, particularly when domestic affairs assumed a greater urgency. These years saw the last powerful expression of organized anti-Catholicism with the resurgence of the Ku Klux Klan, the passage of the 1924 Johnson-Reed Immigration Act, attempts to outlaw Catholic schools in Oregon, and the opposition to New York governor Alfred E. Smith's 1928 presidential campaign. According to Higham, the Roman Catholic replaced the German and the Bolshevik as the worst subversive threat to the "American way of life." One Mississippi constituent typified this attitude in a letter to his senator, asking: "Are the Bolsheviks any worse than the Irish?"[108]

Patrick F. Scanlan, editor of the Brooklyn *Tablet* from 1917 to 1968, expressed an outlook typical of many Catholic leaders at the time. Although he would become the premier anticommunist in the Catholic press during the 1930s, Scanlan's earlier editorials paid little attention to communism. In 1918, he dismissed Russia's new rulers, stating that, because they "do not favor a nation under God, they will fail." Anti-Catholicism was the major concern of the 1920s *Tablet*: Scanlan viewed the Klan as a far greater threat than the "Bolshevists or the out and out anarchists." This widely shared outlook helps explain the McCullagh book's lukewarm reception in 1924.[109]

Spreading the Anticommunist Gospel in 1920s America

For Edmund A. Walsh, however, communism *was* the central issue. According to Louis Gallagher, in 1924, Walsh perceived that "the American general public, not excepting the professionals and the elected representatives of the people, were either ignorant of or indifferent to the menace of Communism." Shortly after his return from Russia, he was invited to confer with Secretary of State Charles Hughes and several other officials regarding "many questions about Russia—about politics, economics and religion."[110]

There is no doubt that Walsh was on a crusade to spread the gospel of anticommunism in 1920s America. He sought to do this, first, within the context of academia and, second, through lectures, books, and articles addressed to the general public. He was well prepared for these tasks. Gallagher writes that Walsh "returned from Russia with ample experience to supply him with material for writing and lecturing for the rest of his life."[111]

As regent of Georgetown's foreign service school, Walsh added courses on Soviet theory and practice to the curriculum. In 1923, he had expressed his hopes of starting a Russian department with Baron Serge Korff. When Korff died in 1924, Walsh continued with his plans for the department. The December 1924 catalogue listed a new course required for upperclassmen: "Russia in Revolution," taught by "Rev. Edmund A. Walsh, S.J., Ph.D." Its focus was communism's development from Marx through the October Revolution, and promised "a detailed study of the Soviet form of government as a unique experiment in political science." Walsh, according to the course description, had "spent the past several years in Soviet Russia and has had unusual opportunities to observe the cause and effect of Sovietism."[112]

The 1925 catalogue listed Walsh as the instructor for "American Institutions and Ideals," which proposed to trace "the spread of democratic ideals" in contrast to "the class legislation manifested in the structure of the Soviet State." Unlike other courses at the foreign service school, however, this one was open to the general public; it comprised ten lectures, from January through March, a series that became known as the "Winter Ten" and was popular in Washington circles until it was discontinued in 1942. As regent, Walsh was training moral agents to operate in the public arena, in the interest of the common good, a central component of the Jesuit charism.[113]

Another component of that charism is the tradition of the Jesuit rhetorician addressing a larger public audience, which is what Walsh aimed to do through his lectures, articles, and books on Russia. Walsh wrote one book and several articles on Russia during the years 1924–29, but he preferred to go on the lecture circuit. Indeed, Louis Gallagher estimates that Walsh delivered approximately 1,500 lectures on various aspects of Soviet Russia from 1924 to 1952, an average of one a week. In February 1924, he lectured on his relief work, predicting that a "distinct 'Papal Relief' organization of world-wide scope and similar in function to the Red Cross will be among the permanent agencies working for the success of mankind." He also berated visitors who returned from Russia with roseate impressions. By March, he wrote Cardinal Pizzardo that he had already given seven lectures and that he "had many more yet to give."[114]

Walsh was one of the first speakers, Catholic or non-Catholic, to warn American policy makers of the Soviet danger. According to his obituary in the *Washington Post*, when Walsh returned from Russia he was "probably the best-informed American on the origin and consequences of the Bolshevik Revolution." A February 1924 *Washington Star* article announcing a Walsh lecture on Russia stated that he was "regarded as one of the best-informed men on Russian affairs." A curriculum vitae that listed twenty months of relief and diplomatic work in Soviet Russia gave Walsh a credibility no other American Catholic leader could claim.[115]

Walsh spoke at all possible occasions in every state of the union: at communion breakfasts, trade conferences, commencement exercises, and Daughters of the American Revolution (DAR) conventions. He also served as a lecturer at military institutions, both at the Command and General Staff School, and at the War College. Dwight D. Eisenhower, who attended the War College in 1928 as a major, vividly recalled Walsh's presentation three decades later:

> The subject of the talk was the threat that an atheistic dictatorship posed to the free world, and the certainty that that threat would grow unless we—all of us—armed ourselves with the spiritual and intellectual capacities that we could develop so that we could get others to understand and so that we could oppose that threat practically and

effectively. . . . I remember that occasion if for nothing else than the excellence of the presentation.[116]

One Georgetown alumnus recalled that Walsh's lectures were popular with upper-class Washingtonians. "Ever since the first tent was pitched in 1703," writes journalist Roxanne Roberts, "Georgetown has attracted the rich and famous—or those who wanted to be near them." Walsh took advantage of his surroundings to become a part of the Washington social fabric. Carroll Quigley, a longtime faculty member, recalled that Walsh fit right in at Georgetown "high society":

> Our late Regent was a very sophisticated man, fully at home in very diverse social conditions and completely master of almost any situation. He was like some legendary old world prelate, tolerant, wise, and very sophisticated. . . . He was an entertaining conversationalist in any company, an excellent raconteur, and quick at repartee."[117]

Peter Filene writes that Stalin's 1927 victory over Trotsky and the launching of the Five-Year Plan persuaded many Americans that the Soviet Union was retreating from rigid collectivism and moving toward "acceptable" political and economic principles. One of the major themes that Walsh stressed in his speeches and writings, however, was that such was not the case. In his study of how American writers interpreted Stalinism during the years 1927–47, Eduard Mark places Walsh among those who "stressed the primacy of ideology in the USSR." To those who suggested the Soviets were moving toward greater moderation, Walsh replied that their revolutionary rhetoric was not just rhetoric.[118]

No one, Walsh declared at an August 1924 lecture in New York, "who knew the facts could doubt the basic and militant atheism of the Soviet program." In a 1926 debate with Professor Jerome Davis of the Yale Divinity School, Walsh asserted that Soviet revolutionary declarations were not "merely academic rhetoric," but an "avowed purpose." In an address to the DAR, he declared that the "Bolshevist purpose . . . is to impose the tenets of militant communism upon the entire world." Walsh warned DAR members that duplicity was central to the Soviet program. Russia's rulers, he asserted, "have two faces—one which they present to the League of Nations at Geneva and the other, their true countenance, which they reveal when gathered in council at Moscow."[119]

In March 1925, at New York's Economic Club, Walsh participated in a conference on recognition of the Soviet Union. Organized by Colonel Haskell, the conference consisted of recognition supporters, represented by President Henry N. MacCracken of Vassar College, and Professor Jerome Davis, and opponents, represented by Walsh, American Federation of Labor President William Green, and John Hays Hammond of the National Civic Federation.[120]

Describing himself as "an American citizen owing political allegiance to one supreme ideal, the Constitution of the United States," Walsh acknowledged the evils of the Czarist regime, "the outstanding political anachronism of modern times," whose "excesses justified a dozen revolutions." He made a distinction, however, between the October Revolution and the one preceding it, which actually deposed the Romanovs. Walsh pointed out that, in April 1917, the Wilson administration extended recognition to Alexander Kerensky's Provisional Government, which attempted to approximate democratic ideals. He further asserted that this recognition did not extend to the Bolshevik regime, which came to power in October 1917.[121]

The Soviet regime represented an "entirely new set of conditions in the economic, political, social and legal domains," Walsh contended, a fact that overrode all arguments for recognition. The Soviets had publicly repudiated international law by canceling Russia's wartime debts, their antireligious propaganda violated natural law— the basis of national life—and their revolutionary program aimed to destroy Western civilization. Walsh summed up the antirecognition platform:

> Hitherto the existence and inviolability of the Natural Law and the Law of Nations were among the preambles ordinarily assumed and reverentially acknowledged by the Power seeking recognition. . . . But in the present case we see the strange anomaly of a government seeking, officially, admission into the consortium of civilized nations and at the same time proclaiming publicly that not only does it repudiate the accepted usages that have made organized society possible among men, but that it intends to destroy the entire fabric of existing society, displacing all our cherished institutions, art, culture, laws, and the Constitution itself, in order to reconstruct all things on a socialistic basis![122]

To drive home his point, Walsh cited the Soviet constitution, "the authentic expression of Soviet ideals," which proclaimed "officially that the Soviet system begun in Russia is to spread to the entire world. . . . Nothing is clearer than this world-wide programme." Walsh explained that the Soviet diplomats intended to spread the revolution by "intensifying class consciousness among the dissatisfied natives of the countries to which they were accredited." Walsh then contrasted the American and Christian with the Soviet way of life:

> In American jurisprudence and Christian philosophy the State is bound to protect the interests of the individual having been created by the collective will of the individual members of civil society. That is reversed in Soviet Russia. There the Communist State is the be-all and the end-all of the entire system of jurisprudence, and the individual is important only as a means to an economic end. That is the direct antithesis of an individualistic concept of free democracy.

He ended by observing that Americans visiting Russia "encounter tyranny," whereas Russians visiting here "fall heir to a rich heritage of liberties."[123]

Throughout the 1920s, Walsh continued to stress the incompatibility of American democracy and Soviet communism. In a May 1925 lecture in Washington, he described the Soviet revolutionary as "diametrically and militantly opposed" to the U.S. Constitution. In 1929, Walsh stated that Russia was intent "upon the destruction of the Constitution, the home, and religion in this and other countries." In a 1927 article entitled "Some Observations on the Soviet Problem," Walsh confirmed that a struggle did exist between the United States and Russia, but that it was ideological rather than economic, and that the American government was justified in withholding recognition until Russia learned "mutual respect and confidence, respect for law, respect for international law, for the inalienable rights of law, and respect for divine law."[124]

Although Walsh had wanted to write a book on Russia from the time he returned to the United States, the CNEWA appointment temporarily sidetracked this plan. In preparation, he traveled to eastern Europe, he interviewed Kerensky and other participants in the February Revolution and the Provisional Government, and he corresponded with Sir Bernard Pares, director of London's School of Slavonic Studies and a highly respected Russian scholar. The book was finally published in 1928 under the title *The Fall of the Russian Empire: The Story of the Last of the Romanovs and the Coming of the*

Bolsheviki. In it, Walsh describes his Russian experience as follows: "Twenty months . . . I spent in Russia during the period of transition. . . . And for four years more I sought the opinions of many men in many lands, always asking, 'What think ye of Russia?' "[125]

The Fall of the Russian Empire traces the period from the fall of the Romanovs to the Bolshevik ascendancy. As a historical study, the book has more in common with nineteenth- than with twentieth-century methodologies. Emphasizing literature over science, its style tends to the melodramatic, as evident in its description of the Bolshevik rise to power:

> For eight weary months Russia had been on the auction block. Lenin, nearer to the soil from which armies and electors are recruited, offered an alluring programme of peace, land, bread, ownership of factories, and supreme political power for the proletariat. Kerensky's appeal for popular support was more nebulous, because less daring. His government, in the eyes of the impatient masses, stood for none of these fundamental necessities, despite the fact that a creditable array of basic reforms, civic, industrial and agrarian, had been sponsored and many of them actually introduced by the Provisional Government. But his intent could not be couched in the colorful language of his opponent. His rule suffered from the inevitable limitation which conscience and a sense of responsibility impose on dominant parties, but which a desperate minority ignores when unrestrained by moral or legal principles. As morality and legality are of "bourgeois origin," the pragmatic Bolshevik, rejecting both, enters every contest with an immense advantage over all comers.[126]

The book received mixed reviews. The *Catholic World* hailed it as "enormously interesting reading," and declared there was "no more valuable contribution to contemporary history." The *New York Times* praised Walsh's research and ability to depict the Russian Revolution "as an episode of the long tragedy of mankind, a tragedy whose recital should purge the soul through pity and terror." By contrast, the *Bookman* stated that Walsh's book made "no real contribution to our knowledge or understanding of the Russian Revolution."[127]

The *Nation*, for its part, was harshly critical. Reviewer Harold Kellock, the American adviser of the Soviet Information Bureau in Washington, D.C., berated Walsh for writing of Russia

> with the flaming innocence and wonder of a tabloid editor handling a Snyder murder or the misadventures of a Peaches Browning. Indeed,

he dwells upon scenes of murder and destruction with such voluptuous detail that the news editor of any tabloid might well consider putting his cub reporters in school at Georgetown University, where Father Walsh is Regent of the School of Foreign Service.

Kellock accused Walsh of "naïve disregard of his sources," of listing incorrect names and dates, and of having a poor command of geography. The *New Republic* was similarly critical, commenting that "stray facts float forlornly in a riot of fiction," and that Walsh seemed unable to decide whether "history be a science . . . or literature."[128]

But, as Henry Hull is quick to point out, *The Fall of the Russian Empire* was meant to persuade rather than inform. Walsh's books "were not written as historical treatises intended to be the ultimate word on the developments in Russia, but as persuasive accounts of a trained observer whose purpose was to awaken Western readers to the dangers of Soviet Communism."

Joseph T. Durkin, who as a Jesuit priest would teach history at Georgetown for nearly half a century beginning in the 1940s, asked Walsh in 1928 how he was preparing to write his book. Walsh replied that he was reading "a bit of Tolstoy, a bit of Dostoyevsky, some Russian history, to get a feel for the subject."[129]

Walsh wanted to make three main points in *The Fall of the Russian Empire*: first, that the fall of the Romanovs and Russia's successor government was "the most stupendous political event . . . since the break-up of the Roman Empire"; second, that the October Revolution

> was not merely a revolution in the accepted sense as historically understood—that is, a re-allocation of sovereignty—but revolution in the domain of economics, religion, art, literature, science, and all other human activities. . . . It was meant, and so proclaimed by its protagonists, to be a challenge to the modern State as constituted, not merely in Imperial Russia, but throughout the entire civilized world[;]

and, third, that "Bolshevism is an international reality which only the hopelessly intransigent can ignore." Though the term "totalitarianism" had not yet been coined in 1928, Walsh's description of the "collective man" here presages that "ism."[130]

Between 1924 and 1929, by focusing, not on domestic radicalism, but on international communism, with its headquarters in Moscow, Walsh had established himself as the premier Catholic exponent of anticommunism in the United States. Although many of his fellow Catholics were concerned about the domestic menace of anti-Catholicism, he continued to warn about the danger that lay overseas, a danger, he stressed, that would soon be impossible to ignore.

EDMUND A. WALSH AND AMERICAN FOREIGN POLICY

In *The Wilsonian Century*, diplomatic historian Frank Ninkovich brings a new perspective to the idealist-realist debate that has been central to twentieth-century American foreign policy. For Ninkovich, realism, or the objectivist school, is "the idea that external realities or structures of power in international society shape and determine the behavior of states," whereas idealism, or Wilsonianism, insists that morality and not mere objectivity govern the affairs of nations. Idealism has held sway in policy-making circles from Theodore Roosevelt to Bill Clinton

> not only because it seemed to make sense of a confusing modern world, but also because it successfully passed the test of experience. In the face of numerous crises, Wilsonianism maintained enough plausibility as an explanation of world politics—in fierce competition with realist doctrines, it should be remembered—to convince American statesmen of its rightness. And to an amazing degree, it succeeded through a pragmatic process of trial and error in structuring the world in accord with its own preconceptions.[131]

During the 1920s, Walsh established himself as the premier Catholic spokesperson for idealism in American foreign policy, a position he held for the next three decades. Other American Catholic leaders espoused this position as well, especially from the 1930s on, but what made Walsh unique was that he spoke on this topic as an "insider," namely, as director of the foreign service school, a member of the academic community, and as a prominent member of Washington society. He had an expertise on foreign affairs in general, and Russia in particular, that no other priest could dare to claim. When he spoke on Russia, he spoke as an expert who had worked there and knew his subject.

In his December 1929 speech to the Knights of Columbus at their Brooklyn chapter house, "The Holy See and International Peace," Walsh called for an international tribunal that would not "be controlled by political power, but which shall be of a purely moral character and therefore have the capacity to decide issues on an objective basis." In opposition to the "balance of power" realist notion,

> peace on earth can be maintained, international comity assured and the hard-won fruits of civilization preserved only if international relations rest on something more basic and permanent than the pragmatic sanction, increased armaments, the predominance of force or the fallacious argument of an accomplished fact. . . . International law based on purely utilitarian ethics, to the exclusion of natural and divine law, is a house builded on the sands of delusion, destined to crumble under the storms of human passion. History, with all its volumes, teaches nothing if not that.

This speech provides the rationale that connected Walsh's work at the foreign service school and his vigorous anticommunism. Walsh entered Russia convinced that events in one part of the world inevitably affected the rest for better or for worse. During the years 1922–23, he encountered a regime bent on toppling what he regarded as the basis of international life, and he devoted the last thirty years of his own life to combating that regime through a public awareness campaign that led to his becoming the most important and influential Catholic anticommunist in the United States.[132]

3

"The Two Standards"
Walsh and American Catholic Anticommunisms, 1929–41

During the 1920s, communism, whether domestic or international, failed to interest the American public. A complacent indifference toward foreign affairs permeated the decade. In the following decade, however, worldwide economic unrest, political shifts in Europe and Asia, along with the expansion of communism and fascism, the twin pillars of totalitarianism, forced Americans to pay closer attention to events abroad, whether they wanted to or not. At the same time, the rise of domestic radicalism, heightened by the Great Depression, became a greater concern than had previously been the case.[1]

For Catholics, the communist issue assumed a paramount importance. Communism had always been an ideological bête noire for Catholics, but its development as a social movement and political force increased Catholic concerns. From pope to the local parish priest, warnings against the "Red Menace" permeated Catholic life. Communists in politics, labor, schools, and popular movements were presented as manifestations of a worldwide malady. In a survey of American Catholic periodicals, historian Robert L. Frank discovered 838 entries on communism in the 1934–38 edition of the *Catholic Periodical Index*, a quadrupling of the entries contained in the 1930–33 edition.[2]

In the United States, Catholic anticommunism was manifested in various ways. On the Left, Dorothy Day counteracted communism's appeal with a radically evangelical poverty hitherto unseen in American Catholic life. On the Right, the obsessive anticommunism of Brooklyn *Tablet* editor Patrick F. Scanlan and Father Charles E. Coughlin, the "radio priest," devolved into a demagogic bigotry fueled by longtime urban ethnic rivalries. In the academic arena, expert on social justice John A. Ryan and philosopher Fulton J. Sheen addressed communism within the context of their respective spheres. At the local level, "labor priests" promoted Catholic social teaching while challenging communism in the labor movement.

Most scholars note that, because Catholic anticommunism found its roots in doctrine, Catholics of all persuasions embraced it. As David O'Brien explains:

> "Communism" became a slogan used to attack all policies seen as harmful to the Church and her teachings, from birth control to labor unions. Even the most socially conscious Catholics frequently defended their proposals as alternatives to communism, rather than as imperatives arising from Christian belief.[3]

Just as Richard Gid Powers has asserted that there were many American anticommunisms, so, too, it might be said that there were many *Catholic* anticommunisms.[4]

This chapter focuses on Edmund A. Walsh's career as an anticommunist from the start of the Depression through America's entry into the Second World War. Among Catholic anticommunists, Walsh was unique in that he addressed communism, not as a philosopher or theologian, but as a political scientist specializing in international relations, a position enhanced by his role as regent at Georgetown. In March 1930, the *New York Times* described him as "an authority on the contemporary history of Russia." "Walsh was *the* Jesuit expert on international communism," Steve Rosswurm writes, "and probably the order's most influential man in Washington, D.C." No other Catholic leader of the era could boast Walsh's expertise, which allowed him to operate as a quasi-political insider in American public life.[5]

Walsh attempted to persuade the American public and American policy makers that Soviet Russia was and continued to be ideologically driven, its goal being world domination. In his speeches and writings throughout the 1930s, particularly in his opposition to the diplomatic recognition of the Soviet Union, Walsh hammered his constant message home: communism was the greatest enemy facing American democracy, which was based on a morality rooted in Judeo-Christian values.

At the same time, Walsh's patriotism concealed a subtle jeremiad against what he perceived as the increasing secularization of American life. Indeed, Walsh's lectures at the FBI's National Police Academy from 1935 to 1952 focused, not on communism, but on the moral decline that abetted the era's lawlessness. As a nationally renowned educator, Walsh also exposed the secularizing forces he saw at work in academia. He argued that, with increasing specialization, American higher education was neglecting the moral formation of future leaders, thereby affording communism an opportunity to expand in the United States.

THE VIEW FROM ROME: PIUS XI, WLODIMIR LEDOCHOWSKI, AND COMMUNISM

The rise of totalitarianism on both the Left and the Right in 1930s Europe became a central concern for Pope Pius XI, who issued condemnations of both during his pontificate. Pius's anticommunist encyclicals included *Miserentissimus Redemptor* (1928), *Caritate Christi Compulsi* (1932), and *Divini Redemptoris* (1937). In *Non abbiamo bisogno* (1931), he condemned the fascist claims on Italian youth; in *Mit brennender Sorge* (1937), he declared Nazi race theories incompatible with Christian beliefs. Before his death on February 10, 1939, Pius planned to issue an encyclical condemning anti-Semitism, *Humani Generis Unitas*, for which he enlisted the aid of the American Jesuit John LaFarge.[6]

Historians have long debated whether Pius regarded communism or fascism as the greater threat. Citing the stronger language of *Divini Redemptoris*, as compared to *Mit brennender Sorge*, Eamon Duffy accuses the pontiff of "softness toward the Right," of being an authoritarian whose "social thinking was overshadowed by hatred and fear of communism." J. Derek Holmes suggests that, though Pius may first have been more concerned with communism, he eventually viewed both ideologies as equally threatening. Similarly, Roger Aubert contends that, as the 1930s progressed, Pius became increasingly disgusted with totalitarianism on both the Left and the Right.[7]

As Father General of the Society of Jesus, Wlodimir Ledochowski (1914–42) set a strong, but not strident, anticommunist tenor for the order. A staunch conservative elected during the pontificate of Pius X, Ledochowski was, according to Peter McDonough, a "reactionary" who "fitted the mold of antimodernist Catholicism." David Southern argues that Ledochowski, who helped write the 1931 social encyclical *Quadragesimo Anno,* "managed to inject a potent dose of anticommunism" into the document.[8]

In April 1934, Ledochowski issued a letter to the Jesuit Provincials in North America, the order's most rapidly growing segment, exhorting them to lead a "project of a worldwide systematic warfare against the common enemy of Christianity and civilization." He regarded communism as the "growing evil of our time," whose appeal to the workers posed a primary threat to "religion, morality and the social order." Calling for a greater coordination of anticommunist activities among American Jesuits, Ledochowski drew a comparison between the current situation and the Reformation era:

> The Society of Jesus came into existence at a period particularly critical for the Church, with the providential mission of stemming the tide of revolt initiated by the so-called Reformation. . . . Does it not look as if the present emergency entailed a fresh call on our zeal and generosity as soldiers of Christ and of His Church, a call to take up arms against the great heresy of our times, more dangerous perhaps than any enemy of the past?[9]

It is evident, then, that papal and Jesuit leadership were unreservedly anticommunist. Events in Soviet Russia in the late 1920s served to solidify their opposition. On April 8, 1929, the Soviet government issued the Law on Religious Associations, imposing extensive restrictions on religion in public and private life. The opportunities for religious ceremonies were narrowed considerably, and all church work with youth was banned. Property belonging to religious groups was nationalized: thousands of churches and synagogues were converted into clubs, meeting halls, and theaters. State-supported organizations such as the Bezbozhniki, "The League of the Militant Godless," founded in 1925, sponsored antireligious processions and distributed pro-atheist propaganda.[10]

As a result of the 1929 law, Henry Hull writes, relations between the Vatican and the Soviet Union shifted from attempts at coexistence to a pattern of mutual exclusiveness that lasted over sixty years. The Holy See formulated spiritual rather than diplomatic responses. For example, Pius XI placed the Russian people under the patronage of the recently canonized Saint Therese of Lisieux, gave spiritual indulgences for the prayer "Savior of the World, Save Russia," and in 1929 established the Russicum, the Pontifical Russian College of the Byzantine Rite. Students at the Russicum were prepared for future missionary work among the Russian people.[11]

Why Pope Pius XI Asked Prayers for Russia

In the Roman Catholic liturgical calendar, March 19th marks the feast of Saint Joseph, Patron of the Universal Church. Pius declared Sunday, March 19, 1930, a universal day of prayer for Russia. Setting March 19th as the appointed day provided some indication of the extent to which Pius regarded Soviet communism as a threat. "From that day on," Hull comments, "the total polarity of interests between the Holy See and Soviet Russia remained so apparent that overtures on either side were not again attempted." Until Vatican II, at the conclusion of the Mass, American Catholics prayed for the "conversion of Russia." Even before devotions to Our Lady of Fatima became popular in the Cold War era, notes Richard Gid Powers, anticommunism was well embedded in the liturgical weavings of everyday Catholic life.[12]

Archbishop Michael J. Curley of Baltimore chose Walsh to deliver the sermon at the March 19th Mass in the archbishop's Cathedral of the Assumption. Archdiocesan historian Thomas Spalding notes that during the 1930s, Curley had become "one of the most knowledgeable and certainly one of the most outspoken members of the hierarchy on the menace of communism." Before the March 19th Mass, Curley issued a letter to the archdiocese, the text of which clearly shows Walsh's influence:

> A Godless nation is aborning. Atheism is the recognized state religion.
> . . . Churches, temples and monasteries have been razed, or if left
> standing, have been handed over by the Government to Communistic
> uses and in cases employed for pornographic purposes. Mass execu-
> tions have been the order of the day in Soviet Russia. . . . It has re-
> sulted in death and exile worse than death to countless numbers of the
> Faithful, their priests and their bishops. No religion is spared. Only
> the negation of Atheism may flourish. We can scarcely visualize the
> moral conditions consequent on such a war against God.[13]

Under the auspices of the Catholic Near East Welfare Association (CNEWA), Walsh published a pamphlet entitled *Why Pope Pius XI Asked Prayers for Russia*, a copy of which was sent to every American priest and bishop. In a *New York Times* interview before the March 19th Mass, Walsh stated:

> Tomorrow, when in accordance with the proclamation of Pope Pius, Catholics in this country and throughout the world offer prayer for those who suffer religious persecution in Russia, all Catholic priests will have as supporting material for their supplications and sermons copies of a pamphlet entitled "Why Pope Pius XI Asked Prayers for Russia on March 19, 1930."[14]

Pius's request for prayers, Walsh wrote in the pamphlet, was not a "political action," but "a defense of one of the most fundamental, universal and inalienable human rights against an unjust aggressor." Walsh cited the work of Soviet-sponsored atheist organizations such as the League of the Militant Godless, provided statistics on murdered and imprisoned clergy, with copies of Soviet antireligious cartoons in the appendix. The Soviet Government, he argued, had enlarged its antireligious "domestic policy into an international menace which strikes at the very foundations of Christian civilization." Religious persecutions were no longer "a purely internal question," he insisted, but were part of a worldwide program. To declare otherwise, he stated, "is intellectual suicide for a man, whether he be a Prime Minister, a Senator or a paid propagandist."[15]

Before March 19th, Walsh sent a copy of *Why Pope Pius Asked Prayers* to *Time* magazine. When Walsh could not verify dates for the antireligious cartoons reproduced in the pamphlet's appendix, cartoons he had acquired in Russia, *Time* suggested that the persecutions may have abated since then: "In a word, the Walsh pamphlet is another presentation of the same out-of-date stories."[16]

Walsh replied that *Time*'s stance on this issue impugned its own credibility as an impartial reporter of current events: "This deliberate . . . distortion of evidence . . . will emphasize the extreme caution and reserve to be exercised hereafter in accepting the quips and pranks of *Time* as serious reporting." The Jesuit magazine *America* supported Walsh: "As chief counselor to Nero and similar worthies *Time* would have been invaluable. It could have informed them that Peter and Paul were put to death not because they preached the Gospel, but because they violated an imperial edict." This incident, although not a major event in Walsh's career, does confirm his self-imposed role as anticommunist watchdog.[17]

In promoting the March 19th Mass, Walsh played a central role in organizing and publicizing what may be termed "the first anticommunist awareness campaign" for American Catholics, making effective use of Catholic organizations such as the CNEWA and of non-Catholic organs such as the *New York Times*. As the Soviet antireligious campaigns intensified, domestic radicalism grew, and the recognition movement expanded, Walsh gained greater notoriety as an anticommunist activist. In addition to promoting public awareness campaigns, he sought to increase government awareness of the communist threat, and to berate any person or organization he regarded as minimizing Soviet religious persecutions.[18]

THE GREAT DEPRESSION AND THE RISE OF AMERICAN COMMUNISM: AN OVERVIEW

Few historians would deny that the Great Depression served as the primary catalyst for the growth of American radicalism. During the 1920s, Arthur M. Schlesinger, Jr., writes in the first volume of his trilogy *The Age of Roosevelt*, the United States appeared to be "on the edge of a new abundance." Increased industrial production throughout the decade, with its promise of increased wages for the American labor force, helped create a widely shared optimism in the American economic system. At the time of his inauguration, Hoover was, as one historian notes, "the most widely respected man in America."[19]

The decade's optimism ended on October 24, 1929, the day of the stock market crash, which paved the way for the Great Depression of the 1930s. Countless businesses closed their doors. In 1930, 4.3 million Americans, 8.7 percent of the entire population, were unemployed, and by 1932, that number would exceed 12 million. Financial turmoil in Europe compounded the American situation, as transatlantic depressions fed off one another. "The Crash," historian David M. Kennedy writes, "was unimagined and almost unimaginable. Nearly three decades of barely punctuated economic growth, capped by seven years of unprecedented prosperity, gave to the mood . . . in the entire country, an air of masterful confidence in the future."[20]

An inexperienced politician who held firm economic convictions on the relationship between government and private industry, Hoover saw increased federal aid as having long-term adverse implications for governmental power. For example, he believed direct federal payment for unemployment relief would weaken the nation's moral fiber. In struggles with Congress over the budget, he appeared "a peculiarly artless politician." Public relief measures in 1932 failed to save his reputation, when he "was the most loathed and scorned figure in the country." Labor strikes and hunger marches heightened fears of revolution. Indeed, by late 1932, according to Raymond Moley, "terror held the country in grip."[21]

"The 1930s," writes historian of American communism Harvey Klehr, "marked the height of Communist influence in America." American communists first organized unemployment rallies in New York and other cities in 1930. They became participants in the civil rights movement through the legal aid they provided in the Scottsboro Case, and their organizing work in Harlem. As the National Industrial Recovery Act protected the right of labor to organize in 1933, Communist Party members entered the unionization drive as successful organizers. Joshua B. Freeman, in his study of New York's Transport Workers Union, contends that their popularity was due to organizational ability rather than ideology.[22]

During the Depression, writes Richard Gid Powers, "Communists were winning a reputation as the oppressed's most courageous defenders." Between 1930 and 1935, notes Nathan Glaser, party membership increased nearly fivefold, reaching 55,000 at its high point in 1938, although, as Historian Albert Fried contends, the party exerted greater influence as participants in a larger movement for social and economic justice. By the middle of the decade, Klehr writes, American communists had blended into "the liberal mainstream."[23]

Over the last five decades, scholars have debated how strong ties were between Russia and the American Communist Party (CPUSA). During the 1950s, Theodore Draper contended that the CPUSA was "the American appendage of a Russian revolutionary power." A revisionist historiographical school, championed by scholars such as Ellen Schrecker, Mark Naison, and Fraser Ottanelli, minimizes the role of ideology, depicting members of the Communist Party as normal political participants in the American democratic process and suggesting that their ties to Russia were largely nominal. More recently, Harvey Klehr and John Earl Haynes, citing hitherto unavailable documents from the Soviet archives, argue that Russia did fund the CPUSA and that many American communists were involved in covert espionage work. Klehr and Haynes conclude that their findings make it impossible to ignore what they call "the dark side of American communism."[24]

THE FISH COMMITTEE AND THE
BEGINNINGS OF 1930s ANTICOMMUNISM

"In 1930," write Soviet historians Nikolai Svachev and Nikolai Yakovlev, "anti-communist hysteria revived in the United States, with Hamilton Fish as its standard-bearer." In that year, Ralph M. Easley of the antiradical National Civic Federation claimed to have discovered documents exposing a proposed May Day uprising, which he sent to New York Congressman Hamilton Fish. A committed anticommunist who had visited Russia with a congressional delegation in the early 1920s, Fish successfully pushed for a congressional committee to investigate communist activity in the United States. The Fish Committee was the first federal inquiry into Communist Party activities since Senator Lee Slater Overman's judiciary committee held hearings in the winter of 1918. The Fish Committee began hearings in June 1930 and continued through early 1931.[25]

For Fish, the best way to fight communism was to give the widest possible publicity to communist theory and practice. At its opening, the committee defined its purpose:

> to investigate Communist propaganda in the United States and particularly in our educational institutions; the activities and membership of the Communist Party of the United States; and all affiliated organizations and groups thereof; the ramification of the Communist International in the United States . . . and all entities, groups, or individuals who are alleged to advise, teach, or advocate the overthrow by force or violence of the Government of the United States, or attempt to undermine our republican form of government by inciting riots, sabotage, or revolutionary disorders.

Communists and anticommunists testified at the hearings, including Communist Party leader William Z. Foster, Easley, and members of both the American Legion and the Daughters of the American Revolution.[26]

Invited to testify on Soviet political theory and practice, Walsh first appeared before the committee on June 9, 1930, and returned on November 10. In his introductory overview of Soviet history, Walsh insisted that Russia's October Revolution "must be interpreted in an entirely different sense from every other revolution that the world has ever known . . . a revolution not only in the political form of government within Russia, but . . . a complete transformation of all existing society." The Soviet goal, he asserted, was "to create a new archetype of humanity entirely of the type called a collective man, as opposed to the soul-encumbered man . . . they want to blot out all individualism and erect what they call the collective man, the mass man." Moreover, the Soviets intended to extend this system through-out the world.[27]

According to Walsh, the Soviet government aimed "to overthrow every other form of government on the face of the earth . . . by every means at its disposal." In the Soviet mindset, the world was *divided only into two entities*, two groups. It seems to draw a line right through humanity, and you fall on one side or the other. The whole world, every government, every State, is either capitalistic or socialistic." He described the Third International as the instrument used for fomenting revolution abroad and binding national communist organizations "together with a solidarity of a common objective, with head-quarters in the city of Moscow, under the control and leadership of . . . the Soviet Government." William Z. Foster, Walsh declared, "gets his instructions" from Moscow, which in turn provided "all possible assistance to the Communist Party of America when they find it necessary." The Soviet government and the Third International, he concluded, are "the right and left arms ruled by the same brains."[28]

Communists strove to "profit" by the Depression, Walsh informed the committee, through "strikes, stirring up unrest, and so on." American communists promoted discontent among American workers, manipulated the race issue, and spread their doctrine in American higher education through pro-communist academics. Acknowledging that social abuses existed in industry, he insisted nonetheless that the communist organizer functioned as a "professional agitator," opposing what he called management's efforts at "real reform." Using agitation tactics learned from Moscow, communists in the labor movement promoted violence by provoking police and starting a riot "in the hope of causing bloodshed."[29]

Walsh also berated Americans who sympathized with the Soviet experiment. The Soviets, he contended, made a practice of inviting "certain types of American university professors and intellectuals, as the category is called," to Moscow. During their visits, "the advantages of communism are emphasized, but its political intent and the indefensible persecution of the individual are minimized and kept in the background." Walsh categorized such persons as "valuable propagandists" at American colleges and universities, who allowed communism to make significant inroads into "the colleges and educational circles."[30]

Regarding the race question, Walsh alleged that Communist Party spokesmen used this issue to their own advantage. Moscow, he informed the committee, saw "the possibilities of the Negro as a revolutionary center," viewing African-Americans as a "weak point of the industrial situation in the South [which] ought to be particularly cultivated." African-American communists were trained in Moscow "how to use that weakness in the Southern States." Walsh declared that African-Americans in the North were "more susceptible" to the communist appeal, "whereas, the large mass of Negroes, especially in the South, as I know rather well, are considered a conservative element, rather than an inflammatory element."[31]

Powers writes that the committee made Fish "the best known anticommunist in the country," but at a price. The May Day uprising papers Easley discovered, which had served as the committee's raison d'être, were proved a forgery in May 1930, much to the embarrassment of both men; indeed, they had "reduced anticommunism to a joke," discrediting the movement. According to Anthony Troncone, however, Fish's ultimate goal was not so much to expose a particular plot, as it was to promote an anticommunist public awareness campaign at a time when the pro-recognition movement was on the rise. Nor did the committee's work preclude future anticommunist investigations on the part of Congress, such as the House Un-American Activities Committee (HUAC), created in 1938.[32]

On January 10, 1931, when his committee's report was published, Fish held a giant rally in Madison Square Garden to announce the formation of the American Alliance, which he described as "a central organization in Washington, allied with various groups, opposed to communism, so as to unite all efforts to combat effectively the spread of communism in the United States." In 1932, Walsh would write Fish that he regarded the committee's report to be

> a most exhaustive and valuable contribution to a clear understanding of the incredible international program of the Soviet Government working through the Communist Party of the United States. That report should be in the hands of every student and patriotic organization.[33]

"THE SUBJECT OF ACRIMONIOUS DISCUSSION"

In early 1931, Walsh published his third book, *The Last Stand: An Interpretation of the Five-Year Plan*. Ratified in 1929, the Soviets' Five-Year Plan sought to expand the industrial base of what remained a largely agricultural nation through centralized management and increased production. As Richard Pipes notes: "It was a Marxist-Leninist axiom that a socialist society must rest on an industrial base." Many American business leaders, seeing in Russia the world's largest undeveloped market, welcomed this move during the Depression.[34]

The Last Stand was written when the plan's effects were still under debate. Walsh wanted to remind Americans about the ultimate purpose of the plan in the minds of the Soviet leaders, and on that basis to argue against diplomatic recognition of the Soviet government. "The motive underlying the Five-Year Plan," he began,

> has been the subject of acrimonious discussion. It has been variously defended, as pure philanthropy, economic idealism, heroic devotion to a bigger and better Russia, and an example of laudable modernity that proposes merely to assure Russia her rightful place as an independent economic unit in an industrialized world.

In response to these arguments, he countered: "The Five-Year Plan is a programme for the further extension of the great October Revolution . . . an elaborate plan for upbuilding a socialist economy and culture—a socialist society."[35]

Noting that "the French Revolution was a Sunday School picnic compared to the Russian Revolution," he argued: "there is hardly one of the principles underlying American tradition which Soviet jurisprudence does not deny . . . and is hopeful of denying elsewhere."

Walsh cited this point and the clandestine activity of Soviet ambassadors in fomenting discord abroad as compelling arguments against American recognition of the Soviet Union. The appendix of his book listed groups opposing recognition together with their statements.[36]

Although *The Last Stand* went through three printings in five months, it met with mixed reviews. The *Bookman* praised Walsh's writing style and lack of bias. *The New Republic* commended Walsh's dialectical ability, but criticized his defensiveness with regard to American capitalism. The *New York Times* went further, declaring that Walsh was "out to prove a case, and anything that is grist goes through the mill." Calling Walsh "the outstanding anti-Bolshevik Catholic in the United States," the *Nation* dismissed his latest work as containing "most of the usual anti-Communist arguments thrown, helter-skelter, into one basket and salted with ineffective invective." Even though *The Last Stand* did not leave a lasting mark either as history or political science, indeed was quickly forgotten by both academics and the general public, it must be noted that, as was the case with *The Fall of the Russian Empire*, Walsh wrote it as an activist and polemicist to make a point.[37]

WALSH AND THE FIGHT AGAINST DIPLOMATIC RECOGNITION OF RUSSIA, 1930–33

In the decade before the United States finally recognized the Soviet Union, in the first session of every Congress, and despite the continuing U.S. policy, begun by Woodrow Wilson, of shunning the Soviet government "as an outlaw," Utah Senator William E. Borah would introduce a resolution for the diplomatic recognition of Soviet Russia. During those ten years, many Americans would be persuaded that Soviet Russia was making the inevitable move toward capitalism. Historian Joan Hoff Wilson notes that, though the banking industry opposed recognition, industries exporting goods abroad that had done poorly during the 1920s economy did not. They favored opening new overseas markets and saw the Soviet Union as one such market. During the Depression, Wilson notes, the economic argument for recognition assumed a greater urgency.[38]

As the prorecognition movement gained strength between 1930 and 1933, Walsh became ever more actively opposed to it. By 1933, he was, according to historian Edward M. Bennett, "a leading spokes-man in the fight against recognition." Walsh helped organize rallies and lectured throughout the nation on what he regarded as a poten-tially grave diplomatic mistake. "Long before the Soviet satellite countries were subdued, and far in advance of the Yalta Conference," Gallagher writes, Walsh "endeavored to persuade the directors of American foreign policy that religion was the only safeguard of mo-rality, and that morality, in turn, had no substitute as a protection for national and international industrial and economic society."[39]

In addition to its far-ranging consequences, Walsh argued, recog-nition had more immediate political repercussions. As he told an au-dience at the New York Athletic Club in April 1930, Soviet diplomats were trained to "agitate for revolutions in all countries where they were admitted"; Soviet Russia had appropriated over one million dol-lars for that purpose. Even in countries where Soviet ambassadors were not officially received, local communists received instructions from Moscow "in the art of inciting riots as preliminary revolts."[40]

Walsh singled out three groups for special opprobrium: prore-cognition business leaders, politicians advocating recognition, and celebrities who praised the Soviet system. Business leaders were mo-tivated by mere commercial interests rather than patriotic considera-tions. In a May 1933 article, he wrote: "There are some in our midst who would sacrifice self-respect and public welfare in the sacred name of hypothetical trade and dubious export possibilities." Walsh singled out Senator Borah among the politicians for his "habitual disregard for the actualities." In response to Borah's argument that the United States had extended recognition to governments as di-verse as revolutionary France and fascist Italy, Walsh retorted:

> Recognitionists who press this argument are either uninformed or ma-licious. They suppress the vitally important fact that none of these for-eign powers has set up in its capital city an organization for the purpose of overthrowing foreign governments; their leaders launch no invitation to nationals of other countries to wage civil war against the authorities of their respective lands.[41]

In late 1931, Walsh had launched a radio attack on literary giant George Bernard Shaw, who praised the Soviet experiment after re-turning from a tour of Soviet Russia. On an NBC radio address, Shaw had chided Americans for their lack of appreciation for the Soviet system. On October 11, 1931, Walsh had made a radio reply, stating that Shaw's account of Soviet Russia lacked credibility because his trip had been "arranged by those skilled window-dressers in the Political Bureau of the Communist Party."[42]

Walsh contended that Shaw did not appreciate the fundamental difference between the American and Soviet systems: The former was based on the Declaration of Independence, a "broad charter of fundamental and inalienable rights universally applicable." In an exercise of rhetorical comparison, Walsh declared:

> Instead of unlimited freedom of the press, there has been created a State monopoly in absolute control of the printed word. Instead of liberty of speech, there is the eternal threat of the [Soviet Secret Police] and the haunting spectre of universal espionage. Instead of freedom of religion, there has been initiated an obscene war on God financed by the State itself and designed to suffocate the inalienable rights of conscience. . . . Instead of inviolability of person, home, and possessions, there have been thirteen unbroken years of terrorism, summary requisitions, domiciliary visits, and wholesale executions without trial before hidden tribunals.

Walsh's reply to Shaw took on a particular urgency at a time, Gallagher notes, when the Russian recognition issue "was at its apex."[43]

For Walsh, recognition was more than simply a political or economic issue, which explains the vehemence he employed in addressing it. In a February 1933 speech, he described the Soviet regime as "the most brutal, the most anti-social, the most anti-Christian and anti-American force on the face of the earth today." It was impossible, he declared, to "make a treaty with that evil trinity of negations." In a 1932 *Catholic Historical Review* article, Walsh had written that the Soviet Union was "no longer a geographic expression" but "an idea." Anyone who minimized the primacy of ideology merely "scratched the surface of the Communist mind [and] has not pierced the first of the seven veils of propaganda that obscure the basic issue between two clashing civilizations."[44]

Recognitionists, he argued at Georgetown in the spring of 1933, were either ignorant of communism's true nature or else deliberately distorted the truth to further their own ends:

> For a decade I have resisted both Soviet theory and practice within as well as outside the confines of Russia. I know it to be the most brutal,

most anti-social, anti-Christian and anti-American force on the face of the earth today. It has not changed its fundamental character nor modified its hostile international program one iota since I made my first acquaintance with it, all the Senator Borahs . . . to the contrary notwithstanding.[45]

Despite recognitionist protestations, he warned the public that "Moscow is not content to live and let live." At the heart of this issue were "two civilizations, diametrically opposed in their principles, their practices, and their objectives."[46]

The American Constitution's system of checks and balances provided an ideal balance point between what Walsh deemed "the autocratic and anarchic tendencies inherent in human nature." What distinguished the American democratic system from its English predecessor was that the English emphasized the rights of individuals as English *subjects*, whereas the American stressed their rights "as *men*, as rational *human beings*." The Constitution used "language applicable to all times" to distinguish between the state and the individual through the recognition of certain inalienable rights belonging "to every citizen by his very nature, not by grant of the state."[47]

Citing Cardinal Robert Bellarmine's attack on James I's "Divine Right of Kings" theory as a significant influence on Thomas Jefferson, Walsh viewed American democracy and Catholicism as mutually reinforcing. Along with Roger Williams and William Penn, one of the "pioneers in the field of religious freedom" was Lord Baltimore, who legislated religious tolerance in the Maryland colony. In a speech at the University of North Carolina in 1938, Walsh spoke on the Catholic jurist William Gaston (1778–1834), the first student to register at Georgetown in 1791. For Walsh, Gaston was the epitome of Catholic patriotism:

> If his contribution to the uplifting of the American democracy were analyzed, I think it would be found to spring from an amalgam of two cognate elements: a passionate but rational love of the United States, and a deep, philosophical faith in the religion he professed.[48]

For Walsh, patriotism meant defending both democracy and religion, a task that belonged, not just to Catholics, but to all believers. In this regard, at a dinner commemorating its fiftieth anniversary, Walsh praised the fraternal order of the Elks. Citing the order's four fundamental virtues: charity, justice, brotherly love, and fidelity, he asked, "Was there ever greater need for those four fundamental virtues of democracy?" The Elks' "ideals" were a bulwark against "the international claims of the Soviet Government which seeks to abolish both the American Constitution and belief in God."[49]

Walsh took pains to note that, in defending the "American way of life," he was not "blindly defending Capitalism." Indeed, he asserted that there was no "intrinsic sanctity" attached to this particular economic system, even though capitalism had evinced "reverence for Christian civilization whose very foundations [were] being attacked by the Soviet State," and "equal reverence and gratitude for the precious heritage of civil liberties to which American citizens fall heir." Whereas the Soviets regarded their own system as an "untouchable deposit of faith," Walsh insisted that capitalism's future depended on its own "public record of useful service."[50]

In short, communism was "a religion" intent on reshaping humanity "in an image and likeness determined by Moscow." Its revelation was found in the works of Marx, whose "interpreter and high priest" was Lenin, with party members as its missionaries. Walsh extended the comparison, noting that Red Square, where Lenin's embalmed corpse was "exposed for veneration outside the Kremlin walls, has become Mecca for the faithful." The Communist Party's ultimate goal was not heaven, but "a despiritualized humanity." This missionary zeal for an atheistic cause, Walsh stated, "differentiates the present Communist Party from every other political group."[51]

In an address to the Eastern Commercial Teachers' Association in April 1933, Walsh announced: "For the Soviet Statesman there is but one categoric imperative—*Thou shall Communize the world or else destroy it.*'" Although he conceded that Soviet communism had an appeal based on injustice, rather than correcting defects in the existing system, it attempted to overthrow that system:

> It has levelled [its] attack not only at the State and bourgeois civilization in general but at Divinity itself for whom it would substitute an extreme materialism which reduces mankind to ranks and files of mechanized martinets all indentured to the service of a brutal and dictatorial government geared to the production of de-spiritualized and standardized types, not individuals.[52]

For Walsh, diplomatic recognition implied responsibility for the nation seeking it, specifically the obligation to respect, rather than undo, international law. "We hear much of the rights attaching to nationhood," he noted; "[but] we hear less of the obligations resulting from membership in the great family of nations." International peace was an impossibility if Soviet Russia was accorded recognition without acknowledging these obligations, because a "peace which reposes on purely utilitarian grounds, to the exclusion of natural and international law, is an edifice built on shifting ground, forever exposed to the unpredictable whirlwinds of human passion."[53]

In a June 1931 speech to the National Foreign Trade Council, Walsh stated: "Destroy confidence and good faith among nations and the whole structure of international relations crashes to the ground. That is the crime of Soviet Russia today." The Soviet Union's confiscation of foreign property in 1917 and its repudiation of international debts struck at the economic heart of international comity. "As foreign traders concerned with the fabric of world commerce," he stated, "we cannot overlook [this] patent fact." Such practices as Walsh described were "cornerstones of Soviet policy," and "a direct menace to the stability of the world."[54]

For Walsh, the United States had three choices on the recognition question. The first was what he called "honorable recognition," granted in return for Moscow's repudiating its goal of international revolution. The second choice was "dishonorable recognition," with no conditions imposed on Soviet Russia. The third choice was "continued non-recognition" until such time as the Soviet government disavowed the Third International. This last choice, Walsh asserted, was the right choice, "the logical response of America's traditional recognition policy."[55]

Walsh regarded the recognition issue in apocalyptic terms. The United States, with democracy as its modus operandi and Christianity as its bulwark, faced a political system seeking to eradicate both. Speaking to antirecognitionists in Washington, D.C., on April 18, 1933, he stated that, at the core of the issue, "two civilizations diametrically opposed in their principles, their practices, and their objectives, come face to face before the supreme tribunal of public opinion in a manner that has no precedent in international relations."[56]

AMERICAN CATHOLICS AND RECOGNITION: AN OVERVIEW

Franklin D. Roosevelt's 1932 election further increased recognitionist hopes. Unlike his predecessor, Roosevelt did not bear a strong anticommunist animus, and was amenable to opening diplomatic relations with the Soviet government. Robert Dallek notes that Roosevelt hoped both to open foreign markets and to discourage Japanese aggression in Asia by means of a Russian-American alliance.[57]

The antirecognitionists were not ready to concede the struggle, however. In March 1933, a petition signed by 673,586 Massachusetts voters opposing recognition was sent to the White House; in April, an antirecognition rally of six thousand, representing 160 organizations, was held in Washington. Although a State Department–sponsored survey of three hundred newspapers over a thirty-day period found little interest in the recognition issue, a survey of 1,139 periodicals by the internationalist American Foundation, found 63 percent in favor of recognition, 27 percent against, with the remaining 20 percent undecided.[58]

In his study of American Catholics during Roosevelt's first term, George Q. Flynn writes that, like the majority of Americans, Catholic support for the new administration's domestic endeavors was almost unanimous, given the desperation of the times. Their stand on recognition of Soviet Russia, however, was an area where Catholics were not in harmony with their fellow citizens. During the years 1930–33, Catholic leaders consistently voiced their opposition to the possibility of recognition.[59]

In the *Catholic World*, Paulist editor James Gillis declared that religious persecution, not economic gain or potential alliances, was the principal issue for Catholics. Gillis doubted that recognition would have any long-term economic effects, especially when dealing with such a "crafty, unprincipled, conscienceless, murderous group." In 1930, *Commonweal* editors opposed recognition of Soviet Russia because they felt "it was useless to attempt to deal with a government that placed no stock in international law or morality." Taking an economic tack, *America* argued that recognition would mean "fewer jobs for the American workingman, falling prices for domestic commodities, and a deepening of the [D]epression." In addition to its editorials, the Brooklyn *Tablet* organized antirecognition mass meetings, petitions, and demonstrations.[60]

The American bishops took a cautious approach to this issue. In early 1933, General Secretary Father John J. Burke sent a memorandum to the NCWC's Administrative Committee, asking their opinion on recognition. Comparing recognition to "inviting Al Capone and his gang into your home," Archbishop John G. Murray of Saint Paul, Minnesota, recommended no official response, but advised the bishops to continue working against recognition. Burke wrote Under-Secretary of State William Phillips that recognition "would be a grave mistake and would do unwarranted injuries to the institutions of our country." The NCWC never issued an official statement on recognition.[61]

Considering their long-standing anticommunism, Catholics were more divided over the issue of recognition than might be expected. Former New York governor and presidential candidate Alfred E. Smith, now a pro-business conservative, was among those supporting recognition of the Soviet Union on economic grounds. In April 1933, at an antirecognition rally in Washington, D.C., Walsh declared that Smith's "Russian views are not shared by so many American citizens of his own Faith who see eye to eye with him in most other respects." In May, Walsh came under attack in *Commonweal*, which stood with Walsh on spiritual grounds but felt that he dismissed the economic arguments too easily. In June, Walsh's friend and Georgetown colleague William Franklin Sands wrote *Commonweal*, supporting Walsh against the journal's May editorial. The division arising over this issue shows that American Catholics were never monolithically united on the anticommunist issue.[62]

"Leave It to Me, Father": Walsh, Roosevelt, and Recognition

By fall 1933, Roosevelt had taken decisive steps on this issue. In October, he instructed Henry T. Morgenthau and William C. Bullitt to approach Soviet officials about opening negotiations. Later that month, FDR announced that he invited Soviet Foreign Affairs Commissar Maxim Litvinov to Washington to discuss diplomatic recognition. At the same time, Robert Dallek writes, Roosevelt was aware that religious opposition posed "a serious problem." On the day he announced his invitation to the Soviets, he invited Walsh to the White House for a personal conference.[63]

According to Richard Gid Powers, FDR did so "as a gesture to quiet the predictable outrage of the Catholic community." He recognized Walsh as the leader of religious opposition to recognition. For the last three years, through his speeches, writings, and lobbying, Walsh had opposed recognition more consistently than any other American religious leader. In the course of their meeting, Roosevelt asked Walsh to prepare reports for him on Litvinov and on religious liberty in Russia. When Walsh warned him that the Soviets were difficult to deal with, Roosevelt replied: "Leave it to me, Father: I am a good horse trader."[64]

On October 21, 1933, Walsh issued a public statement regarding the upcoming negotiations. Roosevelt was not committed to a specific course of action, Walsh asserted; moreover, he had "complete confidence . . . that the pros and cons will be fully and justly considered." In what must have been a surprise to his fellow antirecognitionists, Walsh stated that

> continued public controversy and debate at this time appear to me to be superfluous and may prove dangerous. The President should not be hampered, or annoyed, or embarrassed, as he undertakes to fulfill his constitutional duty and exercise his constitutional prerogative in the conduct of our international relations. President Roosevelt has simply called for a conference to discuss the grave difficulties existing between two sovereign States.

The difficulties referred to included religious freedom in the Soviet Union, and the relationship between the Soviet government and the Third International. Should these be resolved, Walsh concluded, "I would be the first to support renewed diplomatic relations. This has been my public contention for ten years."[65]

Walsh sent a copy of his statement to the press, to the NCWC's press department, and to Roosevelt's secretary Marvin H. McIntyre. As Walsh wrote McIntyre, he had "received so many telephone calls . . . regarding my probable attitude in this important matter that I prepared and sent to the press the enclosed statement, which I trust will contribute something to the tranquility of mind needed for the forthcoming negotiations." To that end, he had changed the topic and title of an upcoming lecture from "Recognition of Soviet Russia" to "Capitalism at the Crossroads."[66]

In November, Roosevelt met personally with Litvinov. In order to appease religious groups, the ever-pragmatic FDR insisted on religious freedom for Americans in Soviet Russia. To this the Soviet government agreed and promised not to encourage revolutionary activity abroad. On November 17, 1933, Roosevelt formally accorded diplomatic recognition to the Union of Soviet Socialist Republics. Recognition was, writes Powers, "an enormous foreign policy triumph for the Soviets," one that "ended their isolation from the world community."[67]

Recognition of the USSR was generally well received by most Americans, especially business leaders. And even though most American Catholics did not endorse the move, they supported the President, who, *Commonweal* wrote, "sincerely did what he could and secured reasonable conditions for civilized human intercourse between Russia and the United States." George Q. Flynn cites Rooseveltian tact and Catholic gratitude as factors in their support. Rodger Van Allen suggests that Roosevelt's careful listening to Catholic opinion on recognition, and his insistence on including religion as a topic at the negotiations, were equally important factors. Van Allen calls FDR's meeting with Walsh "a diplomatic move which flattered American Catholics." James Martin Gillis did not comment on recognition, but this event marked the beginning of Patrick Scanlan's move toward the anti-Roosevelt camp.[68]

Walsh's actions during this period baffled many of his fellow Catholics. In particular, Patrick Scanlan was surprised by what he considered a sudden turnabout, writing Wilfrid Parsons, S.J., editor of *America*, on October 24: "I think Father Walsh in his statement bended [*sic*] over backward." He also insisted that Walsh's request "should not be seen as a gag on us [in the Catholic press]." Catholics, he continued, were "placed in a very difficult position because of the meeting with the Soviet at Washington. We want to be prudent but at the same time make the best fight for our rights that is possible."[69]

Many historians have also been baffled by Walsh's apparent retreat. Thus John B. Sheerin has commented: "Father Edmund Walsh was at first the most vocal Catholic critic of recognition (but later muted his criticism in a curious fashion)." Diplomatic historian Robert Paul Browder suggests that Roosevelt persuaded "Walsh to become more conciliatory," as does Robert Dallek, who also attributes Walsh's "remarkable turnabout" to FDR's persuasiveness. Edward M. Bennett writes that securing Walsh's cooperation was important for "insuring minimal opposition from the pressure groups." Denis Dunn writes that FDR simply charmed Walsh into giving "his blessing" to the Roosevelt-Litvinov Agreement.[70]

More recently, a different explanation of Walsh's seeming change of heart has emerged. Richard Gid Powers argues that Walsh never dropped his anti-Soviet outlook, but that he "was politician enough to see that the issue was settled and that there was no use arguing with the President." Indeed, Peter McDonough suggests, political instinct, caution, and adaptability were "Walsh's strong suit." Acutely aware of Washington's political climate, Walsh saw a Catholic triumphalist approach as potentially disastrous, and so did not push the issue; "if influence was to be extended, principles [had] to be expressed in line with a tact adapted to political realities."[71]

Another reason Walsh may have mitigated his opposition to Roosevelt's diplomatic move has been almost completely ignored. As a university administrator, Walsh realized that strongly opposing recognition of Soviet Russia might have negative repercussions for his students, many of whom would be seeking jobs in government after graduation. Walsh's correspondence indicates that he felt a deep responsibility to help his foreign service students find meaningful employment.[72]

Nevertheless, after November 17, Walsh continued to oppose recognition, arguing for its withdrawal on the grounds that Soviet Russia still encouraged revolution through the Third International. In November, Hamilton Fish's American Alliance inaugurated a four-part NBC radio series on Soviet propaganda in the United States, with Walsh as a featured speaker. "If the Soviet pleads inability to control the Third International," Walsh stated in December, "the Soviet Government does not exercise sovereignty and the United States should withdraw recognition." Writing to Patrick Scanlan in 1938, Walsh discussed "the grand mistake of recognition of Russia," which had "worked out exactly as those of us feared who know the Soviets. The pity of it is that pride and stubborn self-confidence triumphed over the cold facts, and thus led the government of the United States into the paths of humiliation and disillusionment."[73]

Edmund A. Walsh, the Great Depression, and the New Deal

In addressing the communist issue, Walsh inevitably addressed other issues as well. In a May 1934 speech at the University of Arizona, he elucidated the root causes of the Depression: "America, it has been charged, has been worshiping her golden calf and her material achievements." The country had achieved "the very definition of material success," he stated, but growth was "so over-developed on its physical side that the spiritual remained dwarfed and stunted through under-nourishment." Walsh attributed this to "pilots who had a better sense of motion than of direction." Industrialism's chief sin was that it "cultivated the spirit of things and discouraged things of the spirit."[74]

Walsh had long been aware of the dangers of what he regarded as unbridled materialism in American life. When Americans opted for mere wealth at the expense of their ideals and their moral obligations, they veered toward the injustice that bred communism:

> Greed begat reckless exploitation of human personalities. Exploitation begat class consciousness. Class consciousness begat crime at home and Communism abroad. Communism begat Bolshevism. Bolshevism sired the Soviet State and the Soviet State is the breeder of class hatred, world revolution and international atheism.

Communism's deadliest foe, Walsh concluded, was religion, which confronted "this evil progeny in every tongue and in every land," invoking "social justice, social charity and the saving lessons of her supernatural revelation" as its weapons.[75]

Walsh's main concern about the Great Depression was that it gave rise to communism. In a 1937 *Nation's Business* article, he characterized recent American industrial development as a mere "impulse, undisciplined and uncontrolled by planned reasoning." For Walsh, communism was "the lustiest offspring of the modern mind," the "illegitimate child of a reckless capitalism." He acknowledged "certain abuses" in industry, but he insisted that the Communist Party exploited these to its advantage as part of its plan to abolish democracy "the moment it is strong enough to do so." For Walsh, the main issue was not social injustice, but communist expansion: "I consider bolshevism with its inherent problems to be the most characteristic product of the industrial revolution, an industrial revolution which deified mere productivity alone."[76]

At its outset, Walsh supported the New Deal, but always with reservations. In a September 1933 radio address, he spoke about the "solemn obligation devolving on the people as a whole to see that the

Industrial Recovery Act does not fail," insisting that it was "wasted energy to debate what might, should or could have been done in its stead." Although he noted that many were "appalled . . . at the social, the economic, and the juridical audacity of many seemingly insignificant clauses hidden away in recent legislation," he suggested that "the constitutional aspects of the Act may be left for determination when we are sure that we are [still] going to have a Constitution!" Walsh concluded by urging a cooperative approach:

> Let the buying public buy until it hurts. . . . Let the selling public sell until it hurts. . . . To the producing public, which is labor, I would also say: Continue to cooperate until it hurts. That you have already done it generously all men know. That is why many sincere friends of labor hope that there will not be too much jockeying for the inside track, to the detriment of the common good, which would suffer grievously from artificial delays and unnecessary strikes.[77]

By 1934, however, Walsh was more openly opposed to the New Deal. Attacking the brain trusters, "the amateurs coming into Washington and laying down laws and procedures," he marveled that "the machine has not suffered more damage than it has."[78] In 1935, he commented: "We have no guarantee of perpetual immunity against fundamental change. . . . We have bought immunity thus far, and postponed the reckoning. . . . It is simply a race between the Treasury and disaster."[79]

Because of the urgency of the situation, David O'Brien writes, many American Catholics set aside their traditional distrust of any increase in government power and almost unanimously supported the New Deal from 1933 to 1935. By 1935, however, as economic pressures relaxed, divisions reappeared in the Catholic community; several Catholic leaders began to complain that, even though it had relieved some of the distress, the National Recovery Administration (NRA) was not achieving the actual work of reform as intended. By 1935, O'Brien writes: "American Catholicism again spoke with many voices on the issues of the day."[80]

Walsh believed that, because they were compulsory, the New Deal measures were bound to fail and simply could not "insure social justice." In his view, reform started with the individual, "upwards and outwards from the roots of character and moral persuasion. It cannot be imposed from the head downwards." By 1936, Walsh had concluded that "compulsion has failed, as ever it will and must, unless the free will of man cooperates." At the root of Walsh's outlook was his belief that "individualism" was the guiding force in creating "American civilization." This drive needed to be "reconciled with the broad civic responsibility which always attaches to power and influence."[81]

The Conservatism of Edmund A. Walsh

Before the 1930s, Walsh rarely addressed social issues, but the New Deal exposed his hitherto unseen conservatism. David Southern describes Walsh as a "a rock-ribbed conservative who had slight interest in social reform." David O'Brien identifies Walsh as a supporter of big business. Although most Catholic leaders supported the Democratic Party's endeavors during the New Deal era, others such as Alfred E. Smith and John J. Raskob were active in conservative organizations such as the Liberty League. The late Jesuit historian James Hennesey writes: "Smith, Raskob, and others represented a conservative element in the American Catholic mix never absent since the [republic's early] days when most Catholics were Federalists and then Whigs. . . ."[82]

Nowhere was Walsh's conservatism more apparent than in a 1935 letter to Commerce Secretary Daniel Roper. Referring to a recent speech brain truster Rexford G. Tugwell made to Midwest farmers as "open incitement to what is nothing less than class warfare," Walsh warned that efforts at dividing the American people might weaken cooperation between business and government, impeding the cause of social justice. "The Administration, I fear," he wrote, "has suffered in many of its higher and nobler endeavors from the exaggerated language of some of its subordinates." Walsh concluded with his own remedy for reform:

> The abuses of capitalism, which no one has condemned more openly than I have, will be cured only by the Christian principles of persuasion and an enlightened social consciousness. All attempts to do it by compulsion run counter to the experience of psychologists and those familiar with the stubborn instincts of human nature.[83]

Or, in the words of David O'Brien: "Walsh believed that only 'persuasion and enlightened social consciousness,' not 'compulsion,' could bring permanent recovery and reform."[84]

A prime example of Walsh's conservatism is seen in his work as a university administrator. During the Depression, employment opportunities in international business, trade, and government service, jobs for which the foreign service school's graduates competed, were severely limited when the State Department suspended all examinations for the diplomatic and consular services. School enrollment dropped from 300 in the 1932–33 academic year, to 275 in the following year; the curriculum focus shifted toward domestic business and economics so that graduates could more easily find work.

When the Federal Emergency Relief Agency offered seven million dollars in aid for students certified as needy by their colleges, Walsh opted not to apply. He argued that the recipient institution "must be prepared for an increasing amount of federal control and investigation," and that assistance of this sort tended to "pauperize the recipients." With the unanimous approval of the president and directors of the university, Walsh declared that "Georgetown would not participate in any shape or form in the federal relief."[85]

Generally speaking, Walsh moved in highly conservative circles. James A. Farrell, president of U.S. Steel (1911–32), was one of the foreign service school's main benefactors until his death in 1943. A staunch conservative, Farrell opposed trade unionism, refusing to negotiate with unions during the 1919 steel strike. In September 1931, U.S. Steel cut wages by ten percent, becoming the first major employer to break the 1929 agreement with President Hoover to maintain wage rates. For many years, Farrell was chairman of the highly conservative National Foreign Trade Council, whose annual convention Walsh used "as a medium of transmitting to various possible employers, records of students who are graduating this year and who would be in the field for positions."[86]

"A BULWARK OF STABILITY": WALSH AND THE ROLE OF EDUCATION IN 1930S AMERICA

For Walsh, higher education had an obligation to provide moral formation, a role he felt many American educators were neglecting. In 1930, he declared that American education "revealed symptoms of a disease not infrequent in individuals and nations that have risen rapidly to power and affluence." Walsh was particularly concerned about the modern elective system:

> Immature adventurers just released from high school have been encouraged to pick their way for four years through pedagogical cafeterias. Such a generation may achieve sophistication but not that humility which is the beginning of wisdom; it may acquire breadth but not depth, superficial information but little discrimination, and the fabric of its thought will be shoddy. The results are already apparent to every experienced educator who has not become fascinated by the lure of numbers.

Walsh affirmed the need for specialized training within the context of a liberal education, which he defined as "preparation for life in its entirety, not for any one specialized branch of human endeavor." The goal of Jesuit education was not merely to enrich individuals, but to prepare them for service in the interest of the public good. Such an education gave students "a fairer chance to qualify for the leadership which the university owes to the community."[87]

In a 1936 address to the National Catholic Educational Association, Walsh contrasted the Catholic theory of education with trends in the secular field. The difference, he argued, was not one of technique, but of underlying philosophy:

> If man is merely a highly organized social animal, but with no spiritual element or supernatural destiny, then obviously his material and biological well-being is the *summum bonum*. . . . If on the contrary man is conceived as a plant, not of earthly, but of heavenly growth, not only as an individual, but a person elevated to adoptive sonship of God, endowed with spiritual faculties and destined for immortality, obviously the pedagogy which derives from such first principles will be of a sharply different type.

By negating the moral factor, modern education gave wider opportunity for the communist "program of social discontent and world revolt against the principle of authority, against Christianity, against the democratic ideal" to take root and spread.[88]

In his 1938 speech to the National Education Association, Walsh addressed the question "Can satisfactory instruction in ethics and personal conduct be imparted in the public schools?" It "was a practical impossibility," he argued, "because of the traditional attitude of reserve always exercised in public institutions with respect to basic moral issues." Although the public schools could and did impart an "ethical culture" promoting civic virtues, ethics were ultimately based on religion. Ethics alone could not "bind the conscience with the moral obligation which religion alone demands. Remove religion, and morality will expire though manners and customs may survive, at least for a time. That is the plain record of history." Catholic schools, Walsh insisted, were not impelled by "hostility to the public schools." Their primary motive was a "sense of inescapable duty to conscience." Because their educational system included moral formation, Catholics believed that they could provide a well-rounded education, which in turn fulfilled a civic obligation, providing "a bulwark of stability in defense of those civil and religious liberties which have been so cruelly oppressed elsewhere and which one day may make their last stand in America."[89]

In championing the Catholic contribution to American life, Walsh articulated the growing confidence among Catholics that was behind the "Catholic Revival" movement. Between 1920 and 1960, writes Philip Gleason, the revival "proclaimed and attempted to actualize the ideal of a Catholic culture set over against and in opposition to modern culture"; Catholic institutions of higher education were an integral part of this movement. For Walsh, Catholicism was

> not only a religion but a culture, which has profoundly affected the form, the content, and the specific temperament of [W]estern civilization. It is not only a faith but a habit of thought, a way of living in society, and a normative psychology for reacting to external phenomena.[90]

In 1940, Georgetown's School of Foreign Service celebrated its twenty-first anniversary. Enrollment had reached 575, with students "from every State in the Union and virtually every country in the world." Alumni were serving in fifty-seven consulates and legations throughout the world. Walsh envisioned a special role for his own school, which "has ever tried to live up to the real meaning of its name—service—service at home, service abroad," with foreign service school graduates promoting American interests "through world friendship." At a time "when everyone has schemes to further the interest of international friendship," Georgetown promoted education as the primary means toward this end: "International peace through education! This is the aim and the purpose, and it will be the triumph of a college of the nations, the School of Foreign Service of Georgetown University, in the Capital of the United States of America."[91]

"JUSTICE IS THE FIRST OF THE MORAL VIRTUES": EDMUND A. WALSH AND THE FBI

Walsh was also interested in promoting peace at home, as his work with the Federal Bureau of Investigation indicates. Beginning in 1935, at J. Edgar Hoover's request, he lectured annually at the FBI's National Police Academy, a training school for police officers. Between 1935 and 1960, according to Steve Rosswurm, a "close and friendly relationship" existed between the American Jesuits and the FBI. The basis of this relationship, he argues, was a shared view of authority. Walsh and Hoover were both concerned over rising lawlessness in the 1930s. Walsh's lectures focused, not on communism, but on the moral decline that fostered a criminal mentality. Walsh felt well qualified to address this issue. "Religion," he asserted, "has had the longest clinical experience in the laboratory of human conduct." Legislation alone could not prevent crime, but religion could contribute to "human betterment" through moral formation of the individual.[92]

Walsh shared Hoover's belief in an authority that rested on a moral foundation. "I pointed out in class yesterday," he wrote Hoover in July 1937,

> that the Department of Justice in Government occupies an analogous position to the virtue of Justice among the other moral virtues. Justice is the first of the moral virtues and unless it prevails it is futile to speak of Wisdom, Temperance, Fortitude, or even Charity.

From 1935 to 1952, Walsh addressed academia, not primarily as an anticommunist, but as a moralist. His anticommunism was based upon his morals, and his morality was formed by religion.[93]

"THE ROMAN CATHOLIC CHURCH IS STILL THE GREATEST INTERNATIONAL OBSTACLE TO COMMUNISM TODAY"

Walsh argued that diplomatic recognition of the Soviet Union had strengthened the Communist Party's influence in the United States.

Since November 1933, CPUSA membership increased more than 300 percent. Estimating the total number of American communists at between 30,000 and 35,000, he warned that "each one of these is a trained agitator"; the communists were showing "very considerable activity" in exploiting industrial unrest. Walsh praised the American Federation of Labor, a trade union movement, as a "stabilizing element against revolution in this country."[94]

Having warned the public in 1935 that communists were trying to "foment domestic discontent," he declared in 1936 that

> subtle and hidden forces of alien origin inimical to both Christianity and democratic ideals will seek to confuse and embitter the popular mind, in their perennial hope of drawing profit from disunion and thereby creating an attitude of desperation. That is the appointed hour for extremists of the Communist School to make their bid for power. And dictators flourish when democracy declines.[95]

Speaking to high school student visitors at Georgetown, Walsh described the average Communist as an utterly ideological creature, one who

> does not go about his work of destroying Christianity and democracy in a casual or disorganized manner. He has a definite program divided into appropriate chapters and verses. He takes the long-range view and systematically prepares his disciples for their task of world revolution.[96]

In December 1934, Walsh testified before a Congressional hearing on communist and Nazi propaganda in the United States. Like communists everywhere, American communists did not operate alone, he explained; they were "skilled propagandists of an un-American conspiracy, each capable of leading thousands of less-informed and less-determined men," making them potential "social dynamite in the present unsettled times." Driving home his point, he asserted that

> the executive committee of the Communist International does not place its final hope in the 25,000 enrolled members of its American section, nor in the 200,000 to 300,000 sympathetic affiliates, but in the 12,000,000 unemployed in the United States, in the uncataloged millions of discontented, in the immaturity of propagandized youth, in "advanced" intellectuals, and in disloyal professors occupying strategic positions of trust in schools, colleges, and universities.[97]

In November 1936, Walsh alleged that Moscow directed American communists to support Roosevelt in the presidential campaign. In reality, however, the importance of communist support for Roosevelt in the 1936 election is doubtful at best. Indeed, as Walsh himself admitted, "the results of the November elections have given rise . . . to a belief that Communism is a negligible force in the United States and hence its doctrines and activities should not be taken too seriously." But the communist danger was not in the number of votes, however. Rather, it was in the communists themselves, "the leaven that hopes to embitter the masses," who rely on

2,000,000 friends in affiliated organizations, on the sympathetic idealist whose intelligence is not always equal to his emotional impulses, on the growing number of school teachers, professors, writers, and subtle propagandists who are trained to play ceaselessly on the social resentments of the masses until legitimate economic complaints are transformed into class hatred. Social justice is their slogan. But class warfare is their aim.[98]

In January 1936, at "The Catholic Answer to Communism" conference in New York, he declared: "The Roman Catholic Church is the greatest international obstacle to communism today." But, he was quick to note, anticommunism did not mean "unqualified approval of capitalism." Indeed, the best way to fight communism was "widespread application of social justice principles . . . that have been enunciated by Popes Leo XIII and Pius XI." Although Walsh did not give a specific plan, he concluded: "The best minds of Christendom should be set to this task."[99]

Confident that Christianity would emerge as the victor in this struggle, Walsh invoked historical precedents. "Every historic heresy," he wrote in 1935, "has been met by the contemporary intellects of Christian scholars across the ages." To reinforce his point, Walsh quoted the German theologian Karl Adam:

The Rock of Peter stills stands unshaken on the banks of the Tiber. . . . In the midst of our [W]estern civilization, there is still an authority, older than all the states, firmer than all the thrones, more powerful than all dictatorships, more sacred than the laws of nations. . . . But this authority in our midst lives by the eternal will of Christ, spirit of His spirit, power of His power. . . . And on this Rock rests the [W]estern Church.[100]

At the University of Detroit in 1938, Walsh responded to Earl Browder's call to American Catholics to join the CPUSA in the fight for social justice: Browder was merely extending "a gloved hand to his most feared enemy, the Catholic Church." Furthermore, it would "require more than sterile invocation of Thomas Jefferson and Abraham Lincoln to convince Americans of the underlying democracy of Moscow." Like all communists, Browder sought to hide his ideological motives until he achieved power. Walsh concluded that Browder was "biting on granite—which may sharpen his dialectics but will leave no trace on the rock."[101]

WALSH AND SPAIN

In 1931, following the overthrow of the monarchy, a republic was established in Spain, one that was essentially a parliamentary coalition of liberals, conservatives, anarchists, socialists, and communists. Over the next five years, its gradual drift to the Left became increasingly pronounced. Anticlerical legislation disestablished the Church, excluded religious orders from education, and dissolved the Society of Jesus in Spain.[102] In July 1936, a military rebellion led by General Francisco Franco, backed by ultraconservative Spanish groups, attempted to overthrow the republic. The ensuing Spanish Civil War consisted of a three-year struggle between Franco's Nationalists, supported by Italy and Germany, and the Republican Loyalists, supported by Soviet Russia. An outburst of anticlerical violence took place that horrified Catholics worldwide, one described by José Sánchez as "unparalleled in Catholic history." Within a few weeks, more than five thousand clergy and the faithful were killed, and churches were burned throughout Spain. The Republican regime was unable to control the violence.[103]

American public opinion, according to diplomatic historian F. Jay Taylor, "became inflamed in an almost unprecedented manner. The issue was hotly debated—from the pulpit, in the halls of Congress, on college campuses, in the editorial columns of the press, and through every agency designed to influence opinion."[104] Taylor notes that the Church's position in Spain "was an issue which for many people throughout the world transcended the implications of the Spanish Civil War."[105] Richard Gid Powers writes that, whereas non-

Catholics tended to understand the war as "part of the struggle between democracy and fascism," American Catholics insisted that the
real issue was "the persecution of the Spanish Church by a commu-
nist-controlled government."[106] In the words of Richard Traina, Spain
soon became "an international battleground."[107]

The dominance of the communists in Spain by 1936, the dissolu-
tion of the Jesuit order there, and the seizure of their property by the
Republican government drove *America* under the editorship of
Father Francis X. Talbot, S.J., to take the lead in the pro-Franco
Nationalist cause among American Catholics. Sánchez writes: "Much
of the idealization of the Spanish Church, its leaders, and General
Franco, stemmed from its pages."[108] A few days after the outbreak of
the war, Talbot called a meeting of New York's Catholic journalists to
determine a common editorial position on Spain, a meeting attended
by a member of Franco's junta. In February 1937, Talbot attacked the
"anti-Christian propaganda and practices of the Loyalist government,
composed as it [was] of Communists, anarchists, syndicalists, and
atheistic groups in Spain."[109] In October 1937, he warned that in the
event of a victory, the Republican regime "would not stop until the
whole of Spain [was] Sovietized."[110]

Both the *Commonweal* and the *Catholic Worker* attempted to take
a neutral stance, arguing that neither side could be endorsed in good
conscience. For George Shuster of the *Commonweal*, the Catholic
position failed to account for the presence of Mussolini and Hitler,
and wrongly accused all Loyalists of being Bolsheviks.[111] "One's
human affections for embattled priests and religious," wrote Shuster,
"leads one to side with Franco, but one's love for the timeless mission
of the Church leads one to believe that he may, after all, prove to be
the greater of two evils."[112] John LaFarge accused Shuster of betray-
ing the Church, standing by as neutral while Catholicism in Spain
was being destroyed. Indeed, Talbot argued, although "collaboration
with Fascism is possible for the Catholic Church [,] collaboration
with Communism is absolutely impossible. . . . Mr. Shuster can be a
Fascist and a fervent Catholic; he cannot be a Communist and a
Catholic." As a result of Shuster's stance, *Commonweal* lost a quarter
of its subscribers. Rather than sacrifice his intellectual honesty, Shuster resigned.[113]

In 1937, Catholics opposed Eleanor Roosevelt's proposal to bring
Basque refugee children to the United States as an attempt to elicit

Loyalist sympathy. Indeed, Walsh complained that the Roosevelt administration "was pressuring government employees to support the Spanish Republican cause."[114] In September 1938, he wrote to Talbot about a circular being passed out in the Department of Labor on behalf of the Loyalist position: "It is significant that the authorities seem to wink at this sort of thing, but apply drastically their prohibitions in other cases which do not appeal to them personally." Walsh concluded: "I believe this specific and documented incident should be given wide publicity, and in the language it deserves."[115]

This letter represents the only instance of Walsh's active participation in the pro-Franco cause. Though supportive of the Nationalists, he seems to have deferred to Talbot as the principal American Jesuit opponent of the Republican government. Even as most Catholics of the time concerned themselves with his issue, Edmund Walsh remained steadfastly focused on American communist activity.

"The Two Standards": Ignatian Spirituality as a Factor in Walsh's Anticommunism

Informationes et Notitiae was established in 1934, writes Peter McDonough, as "a periodic compendium of anticommunist news items and essays for circulation within the Society of Jesus."[116] In an article entitled "The Two Standards of 1935," Walsh stressed what he considered to be at the core of the struggle between communism and Christianity: "The world is face to face today with the necessity of making a momentous choice. There are two signs in the heavens, one clearly discernible from that hill outside Moscow, and the other from the Pincio." Communism demanded "the abolition of all religious belief and practice," and its goal was to "impose atheism by force on the individual, the family, the State, the world."[117]

Directly opposing it, Catholicism took confidence in the "Divine guarantee" that Christ would be with it "to the end of this world"; because of this, "the Catholic Church will not recoil nor retreat nor compromise. She must perish first, if that were possible." The Society of Jesus was to lead the opposition; Jesuits were called upon to fight "the common enemies of Christianity and civilization. The one is atheism, the other Communism."[118]

Although Walsh had been stressing the struggle between Catholicism and communism as a constant theme for several years, here he consciously situated the struggle within the context of Ignatian spirituality. Jesuit novices are required to make a thirty-day retreat known as the "Spiritual Exercises of Saint Ignatius." Each week of the retreat has a specific theme: the foundation of the Christian life, Christ's life, his Passion and death, and the new life of God's people. Called "the heart of Jesuit spirituality" by historian R. Emmett Curran, the spiritual exercises form the cornerstone of Jesuit identity, collectively and individually.[119]

During the thirty days, the exercises require extensive use of the imaginative powers. In the first week, Ignatius asks the retreatant to envision two "standards" (Ignatius uses *standard* to denote the banners of opposing armies): "The one of Christ, our supreme leader and Lord, and the other of Lucifer, the deadly enemy of our human nature." Christ is the "Commander-in-Chief of all the good," whereas Satan is "the chief of the enemy." In meditating on Satan's standard, Ignatius directs the retreatant to "consider how [Satan] summons innumerable demons, and scatters them, some to one city and some to another, so that no province, no state of life, no individual is overlooked . . . how he goads them on to lay snares for men and bind them with chains."[120]

The goal of the "two standards," writes Karl Rahner, is for the retreatant to reach a decision that will affect his entire life. Ignatius, he writes, "wants the exercitant to note that the power of the devil is everywhere operative." Commenting on this meditation, David Fleming writes: "Jesus adopts a strategy which is just the opposite of Satan: try to help people, not enslave or oppress them." The image of the two standards is undoubtedly black and white. Fleming notes, however, that Ignatius's "outlook on the world was a good deal more medieval than ours."[121]

Throughout his career, Walsh's anticommunism relied on imagery taken from the "Spiritual Exercises." For example, he wrote in 1930 that the Soviet Government was "an international menace which strikes at the very foundations of Christian civilization." In a 1933 speech, he described the recognition issue in terms of "two civilizations diametrically opposed in their principles, their practices, and their objectives come face to face." The Soviet mindset, he told the Fish Committee, divides "the world . . . into two entities, two groups.

It seems to draw a line right through humanity, and you fall on one side or the other."[122]

According to the first principle of the "Spiritual Exercises," and the guiding principle for the Christian life: "Man is created to praise, reverence, and serve God our Lord, and by this means to save his soul." The communist, Walsh argued, also had "certain *first principles* which he assumes to be true, not subject to discussion and certainly incapable of refutation"; indeed, the communist had "a complete philosophy of action" and was "in fact, far more dialectical and metaphysical than his enemies credit him with being.[123]

Outside the Society of Jesus, Walsh never referred to the "Spiritual Exercises," but they played an important factor in shaping his anticommunism. For Walsh, Soviet communism was not merely a political system, it was what Ronald Reagan would later term "an evil empire," struggling with Christianity for the soul of the human race. Domestic radicalism could not be taken lightly, because it was the enemy's vanguard, much like the enemy described in the meditation on the two standards. Although Steven Avella and Thomas Kselman have discussed Marian piety as a factor in American Catholic anticommunism, the influence of particular spiritual charisms on particular Catholic anticommunists has been almost completely ignored.

"An Institution by Himself": The Modus Operandi of an Anticommunist

In April 1934, Father General Ledochowski directed the American Jesuits to assume leadership in "in our Society's project of a worldwide systematic warfare against the common enemy of Christianity and civilization." Calling for greater coordination of anticommunist activities, he insisted that "the hour has come when these isolated efforts must become general." To lead this project, Ledochowski chose Walsh because, according to Peter McDonough, he believed Walsh could lend "visibility among American Jesuits to a social campaign that Ledochowski wanted to mount on a world scale."[124]

Although Walsh served as the chairman of the Inter-Province Committee on Communism and Atheism, McDonough notes that he soon lost interest in the operation, in coordinating national Jesuit activity, and in getting his fellow Jesuits involved in social analysis and action. Indeed, Walsh "was so busy traveling and managing the Georgetown operation that his contribution was confined to arranging the publication of *Informationes et Notitiae.*" In the School of Foreign Service, Walsh "had created a niche ingeniously suited to the world of Washington politics," and was "practically an institution by himself."[125]

McDonough's comments serve to point out two key aspects of Walsh's approach to anticommunism. First, even though he belonged to a religious community, Walsh was an individualist who worked best on his own. And second, whereas Ledochowski envisioned the Inter-Province Committee as a sort of think tank for Catholic social thought, and Walsh's role as leader of that effort, Walsh saw himself as, and was in fact, an activist and administrator rather than an academic theorist. Nonetheless, Walsh's activity with the committee served to elucidate some key aspects of his work as an anticommunist.[126]

In a 1936 letter to the American Provincials referring to Ledochowski's call for action, Walsh stressed that Jesuits were teachers, not policy makers. Their task was to exercise a *moral* influence on policy makers. "The Jesuit's vocation," he wrote, "lies in the spiritual domain, as a teacher, an expounder of principles and a moralist." This could be done in the classroom, teaching subjects such as economics, sociology, international law, or ethics. Walsh acknowledged that the danger lay in "determining where intellectual and moral guidance ends and where political leadership begins. The former is clearly within our vocation. The latter is definitely forbidden."[127]

During the 1936 presidential campaign, Walsh commented further on the need for Jesuits to avoid direct political involvement. In the November issue of *Informationes et Notitiae,* he insisted that the American Jesuits best served their cause "by scrupulously maintaining a non-partisan attitude in domestic politics." As Father Charles Coughlin and Monsignor John A. Ryan publicly argued over the merits of the New Deal and the Roosevelt administration, Walsh took the occasion to make a public statement berating priests who are "campaigning vigorously in a party sense." Although he never referred to Ryan or Coughlin directly, it was clear that he disapproved of their actions.[128]

CATHOLIC ANTICOMMUNISMS IN THE 1930s: AN OVERVIEW

As Walsh's comments show, Catholic anticommunism took a variety of forms during the 1930s. "The soil is rich for the seeds of Bolshevist agitation," a New York priest wrote *Commonweal* in 1930, "and they are being scattered lavishly. . . . I believe that if to-day or to-morrow there appeared a man of magnetic personality, an apostle of social revolt, fires would soon flame up in many places; possibly to meet in some great conflagration."[129] Patrick F. Scanlan of the Brooklyn *Tablet*, described by James T. Fisher as "perhaps the most influential diocesan paper in America," put the matter more calmly: "We have often had periods of unemployment in this country, but this is the first one we ever heard of them given as an excuse for communism."[130] This seeming calmness, however, belied Scanlan's obsessive hatred of communism, a hatred that was fueled by a strong minority consciousness, a hyperpatriotism, and by what Fisher calls "an absolute obsession with Catholic-Jewish conflict" in 1930s New York.[131]

Dorothy Day, who with Peter Maurin was the founder of the Catholic Worker movement, took a different view. Although Day competed with communists for the allegiance of the urban poor, her deeper motivation was to live in radical solidarity with the poor: she held "American society up against the basic Christian teachings of love and brotherhood and challenged Catholics to act honestly on the result." Day's biographer, William D. Miller, writes that her "attitude toward communism was anything but inflamed." Day considered communism a "heresy," but she regarded communists as misguided idealists capable of great generosity and self-sacrifice. Indeed, many Catholics regarded the Catholic Worker movement as "the intelligent Catholic's answer to communism."[132]

Jesuit scholar Donald Crosby describes Fulton J. Sheen as Catholic anticommunism's "philosopher and prophet." Communism was a major focus of Sheen's work as a philosophy professor at The Catholic University of America, in countless lectures, and on radio and television. A neo-Thomist, Sheen sought to "make St. Thomas functional, not for a school, but for the world . . . a remedy against the anarchy of ideas, riot of philosophical systems and breakdown of spiritual forces." Sheen viewed communism as a philosophical challenge and strove to construct a "Christian response to [this] challenge of the times."[133]

John LaFarge and James Martin Gillis both addressed communism in relation to larger concerns. According to Richard Gribble, Gillis viewed relativism as the major problem of the day, paving the way for communism. LaFarge addressed but did not limit his attention to communism. David Southern writes that LaFarge "just considered it the worst of all the isms that he lumped under modernism: secularism, materialism, liberalism, and atheism."[134]

The most famous, and notorious, Catholic anticommunist of the 1930s was Detroit priest Charles E. Coughlin, who entered radio during the 1920s to fight anti-Catholicism. During the Depression, Coughlin achieved national renown by calling for economic reform and making Catholic social thought accessible to a wide audience. In 1932 Coughlin supported Roosevelt with cries of "Roosevelt or Ruin"; in 1933, he called the New Deal "Christ's Deal." Much of Coughlin's appeal lay in simple answers to complex economic questions. By 1934, he believed his own rhetoric. When he realized that the Roosevelt administration did not, he ranted about plutocrats and communists in the government. By 1936, firmly anti-Roosevelt, Coughlin started a newspaper, *Social Justice*, and a political party, the Union Party. When the party candidate received less than 2 percent of the vote, Coughlin retired temporarily from the public eye, having lost much of his earlier support.

In January 1938, he returned to espouse a rabid anticommunism that soon degenerated into anti-Semitism. In July, he published the *Protocols of the Elders of Zion* in his newspaper. In November, he praised Kristallnacht as a defense against communism. By then, his support came from cities where Irish-Jewish tensions ran high. In January 1940, FBI agents arrested New York Coughlinites seeking to create an anti-Semitic terrorist campaign. In early 1942, when Coughlin praised Hitler and Mussolini, *Social Justice* was banned from the mails; under pressure from both his bishop and the government, he reluctantly withdrew from public life, his reputation reduced to a pitiful shadow of his former prestige.[135]

Richard Gid Powers sees Coughlin as an example of what he calls "irresponsible" anticommunism. "What America needed from anticommunism in the thirties," Powers writes, "was a principled defense of democracy against both communism and insurgent fascism." Several Catholic leaders decried irresponsible anticommunism. For examples, as biographer Francis L. Broderick notes, John A. Ryan, who authored the 1919 Bishops' Program of Social Reconstruction, regarded communism as less harmful than "certain professedly anti-Communist propaganda, which in reality [was] directed against social justice." And, according to Thomas T. Blantz, Father Francis J. Haas, director of the National Catholic School of Social Service, who served on various government committees during the 1930s, also belittled the communist threat, which he considered to be largely "a ploy on the part of industry."[136]

Although Scanlan and Coughlin shared a similar outlook on and approach to communism, they had little in common with Ryan's approach to the issue. They had even less in common with Dorothy Day's philosophy. Each of these prominent American Catholic anti-communists gave communism a different priority; their individual approaches often contrasted dramatically and sometimes radically. Very often the only thing that held them together was doctrine. In short, there were as many forms of Catholic anticommunism as there were Catholic anticommunists.

"THE CATHOLIC CHURCH MUST AND WILL RESIST EVERY TOTALITARIAN HERESY": EDMUND A. WALSH AND THE WINDS OF WAR

On April 5, 1939, Walsh testified before the Senate Foreign Affairs Committee on the Neutrality Laws. Because of the impact of public opinion, he argued, there was "no neutrality left in the world." He noted that American opinion was generally divided between two groups: the "extreme internationalists," who urged immediate intervention, and the "strict isolationists," who demanded complete avoidance of European affairs. Although he believed that both groups went too far, Walsh contended: "Self-interest dictates the necessity of cooperating in the prevention of another world catastrophe."[137]

American Catholics, writes George Flynn, did not take a unified stance on foreign policy in the late 1930s. Catholics were a diverse group, consisting of pacifists, nationalists, disillusioned First World War crusaders, Anglophobes, anticommunists, and League of Nations supporters. "I believe," said Walsh in September 1939, "that I can fairly interpret Catholic opinion as a whole when I say that every possible effort must be made to resist and counteract the contention that we must inevitably become involved in the European war." Walsh was "wholly in sympathy . . . with any movement designed to create an equally positive and stubborn resistance to the spread of that psychology." Moreover, he claimed there were "very few" Catholic leaders "who would be sympathetic to the war spirit."[138]

If war was inevitable, Walsh stated in his testimony before the Senate, it was because the last war ended "in tragedy, disillusionment, and an accumulation of injustices now fully realized." It was from an unjust peace, he contended, that Hitler's rise to power drew strength, setting the stage for future conflicts. Unless morality was accepted and implemented as the basis of international law, attempts at peace were bound to fail.[139]

Walsh traced the recent failure of the League of Nations to settle the Ethiopian crisis to what he regarded as the league's lack of moral authority. Although he respected Woodrow Wilson's endeavors to establish a lasting peace, he regarded Wilson's legacy as ultimately a "disservice." In failing to ensure that a just peace was achieved, Wilson's program failed to provide for the future. One Georgetown alumnus recalled Walsh's description of international law as

> only a control, . . . not a cure of evil human passions—that reformation of conduct must begin within the intellect, the will, the heart of mankind, proceeding from consciousness of human solidarity—that tranquility of order constitutes the definition of peace, whether individual or civic or international.

Or, as Walsh himself put it in a 1935 article: "The legislative and punitive powers of the State cannot hope unaided to extirpate crime any more than statutes enacted by Congress can insure social justice or the League of Nations create universal peace." Instead, it was best to rely on forming moral character, individual and national, as "the best contribution to human betterment."[140]

Walsh disliked the idea of coming to Russia's aid in the event of war. In 1939, he railed against the interventionists who supported powers that "for the moment, are called democracies," but were in fact the "most undemocratic, the most terroristic, and the most despotic government[s] in Europe." In 1941, when the Lend-Lease program was under way, he wrote:

> Is it unreasonable to demand of the Soviet beneficiary of American aid, and possibly of American blood, that they abandon their private

and special hatred of the first of the four freedoms in exchange for those common liberties which the other embattled democracies are so stoutly defending? They cannot have it both ways.

When he came to realize that a Soviet-American alliance was a foregone conclusion, however, Walsh praised Roosevelt for bringing up the question of religious liberty with Stalin, asserting that "the good wishes and the great expectations of all right-thinking Americans will be with him."[141]

Because both fascism and communism were anti-Christian, Walsh felt there was little to choose between them. At a December 1938 rally to protest anti-Semitic persecutions, he attacked the "subtle inflection of absolutism and arrogant autocracy now riding the air." Persecution of Christians and Jews, he suggested, was perhaps inevitable under dictatorships. Walsh had long been aware of the Nazi danger. In 1930, after visiting Europe, he had commented that a Nazi victory might lead to a repudiation of the Versailles Treaty, an end to reparation payments, and renewed military intervention. In 1935, Walsh warned an audience against the "offensive and false nationalism" arising in certain nations.[142]

Even as Walsh opposed Nazism, however, he also expressed views bordering on the anti-Semitic. In a February 1938 *Atlantic Monthly* article, Walsh discussed Jewish participation in the Russian Revolution, the roots of which he traced to a capitalism that departed from "Christian principles" during the Industrial Revolution. "The Jew was not the cause of the Russian Revolution," he wrote, "but the *entrepreneur*, who recognized his main chance and seized it shrewdly and successfully." But then he went on to note: "The accusation, which [Jews] resent, of being considered the Old Moneybags of Society, the proverbial pinchpenn[ies] of the ages, antedates the appearance of Christianity." Walsh's article concluded, somewhat unsatisfactorily: "Both Christendom and Jewry can fairly say, '*Peccavimus*.'"[143]

After Pearl Harbor, George Q. Flynn writes, American Catholics stopped debating foreign policy. Catholic isolationists and interventionists alike promoted patriotism, although they remained suspicious of America's Soviet ally. "The School of Foreign Service of Georgetown University," Walsh wrote Roosevelt on December 18, 1941, "is responding unreservedly to the call of the country as voiced by its Commander-in-Chief"; he was putting aside past differences in the interest of the war effort:

> Whatever legitimate diversity of opinion may have existed previously in the field of foreign policy has now vanished. I had certain misgivings respecting relations with Soviet Russia, as you may recall, and discussed them quite frankly with you in past years. But all that lies buried somewhere in the waters of Pearl Harbor. If my voice or pen can serve at this time, please consider them at your disposal.[144]

The month before, at a Mass sponsored by the Catholic War Veterans at Saint Patrick's Cathedral, Walsh had stated: "War is creeping nearer and nearer to these shores." Attacking what he called the "whispering campaign of innuendoes" that the Church was profascist, he had described fascism, communism, and democracy as the three "claimants for men's souls today." Walsh had urged the veterans to take stock in their American and Catholic heritage in the face of impending war:

> What has the Church to say to American democracy as it prepares to enter the blood-soaked arena where a world revolution is in progress? . . . It bids America remember how much of the democracy derives from the oldest church in Christendom. That, Catholic War Veterans, is your special and specific heritage. The teachings of your Church and your individual behavior give notice to the world that the Catholic Church must and will resist every totalitarian heresy, foreign or domestic, because of her trusteeship in the dignity of the human personality. Every modern Caesar, Fascist, Communist or Nazi, will first seek to annihilate the Christian Church if he will annihilate democracy. Religion forms the basic foundation of democracy.[145]

CONCLUSION

Walsh was an idealist who sought to promote the moral element in international affairs. He saw the growth of domestic radicalism, not simply as a response to injustice, but as part of a worldwide plan to destroy Christianity, the bulwark of Western civilization. His interpretation of Ignatian spirituality led him to view this conflict in terms of a struggle between two powers vying for world domination. Although Walsh only began to formally articulate this view in the 1930s, the underlying assumptions were operative long before that and continued to influence his outlook throughout his career.

Unlike the Benedictine liturgist Virgil Michel, who emphasized the corporate basis of social reform within the context of the Mystical Body of Christ, Walsh was a conservative individualist in the Hooverite sense. Because he relied heavily on persuasion in his work as an activist and educator, he opposed what he considered the compulsory interventions of the New Deal. Morality, he argued, could not be imposed from above. In this sense, Walsh differed greatly from Monsignor John A. Ryan or Father Francis J. Haas, who sought to implement concrete programs of social justice. Social reform, however, was an area that was clearly outside Walsh's range of expertise, and his suggestions amounted to little more than reiterations of the social encyclicals in vague and general terms.[146]

For Walsh, the Church was a bulwark against the secularizing influences that gave birth to communism. The lack of a moral influence at work in the international realm gave rise to war. Walsh may have opposed Roosevelt's domestic programs, but he was no isolationist. He opposed Nazism (fascism) and communism as twin totalitarian heresies that threatened world peace. Even though he was anti-Nazi, however, Walsh also harbored anti-Semitic feelings, which he seldom articulated publicly. During the coming war, he would not repress his anticommunism, but would reshape it in such a way as to enable him to be both anti-Nazi and anticommunist at the same time.

4

"An American Geopolitics"
Walsh and Wartime Catholic Anticommunism, 1941–45

Throughout the Second World War, American Catholic Church leaders expressed "a cautious patriotism" that contrasted with popular support for the war. In an attempt to balance their prophetic role with their patriotic obligations, the American bishops avoided the jingoistic support tendered in previous wars and did not seek to "enhance their status by ingratiating themselves to the patriotic public." Despite internal division over the approaching war, however, the American hierarchy issued a statement supporting President Roosevelt on December 23, 1941, although, for a while, as Gerald P. Fogarty observes, "there was some doubt as to the unanimity of the American episcopate."[1]

Historian George Sirgiovanni contends that the war years constituted a unique period in the history of American anticommunism, when anti-Sovietism was not a mainstream view. Because of the wartime alliance, the Roosevelt administration discouraged criticism of the Soviet Union. Arthur Krock of the *New York Times* recalled that indiscriminate praise became "so much the fashion" that to disparage Soviet Russia was to "bring down the charge of sympathy with Fascism." During the war, the American Communist Party espoused an ultrapatriotic line, consciously avoiding divisive issues. By 1945, Richard Gid Powers contends, "anticommunism had the appearance of disloyalty," whereas communism "seemed almost respectable."[2]

Beneath the seemingly placid surface, however, there ran what Sirgiovanni terms "an undercurrent of suspicion" regarding the Soviet Union's postwar aims. A wartime survey conducted by the American Institute of Public Opinion showed that 45 percent of respondents considered the Soviet government inherently immoral. In another wartime survey, between 30 and 40 percent of the respondents doubted that the Russians could be trusted to cooperate with the West once the war ended. Thus the wartime alliance did not completely reverse previous anticommunist views; it merely put them in abeyance.[3]

Along with conservative politicians such as Texas Congressman Martin Dies and conservative journalists such as George Sokolsky, conservative Catholic spokespersons formed the core of wartime anticommunism. Although they accepted the wartime alliance on pragmatic grounds, they maintained that the Soviet Union had not modified its revolutionary program. *Catholic World* editor James Gillis, for example, viewed the Soviets as temporary military partners, but could not repudiate his view of them as essentially sinister. "A fact," Father Gillis wrote, "is a fact. I do not believe in the elasticity of truth." In the Brooklyn *Tablet*, Patrick Scanlan warned readers "not to be gullible toward attempts to sell us the idea that Communism is only a political system peculiar to Soviet Russia and without international implication." Stalin, he argued, had "not suddenly sprouted wings nor suddenly found himself beneath a golden halo of democracy and freedom."[4]

In focusing on Edmund A. Walsh's anticommunism during the Second World War, this chapter more closely examines a period in the history of American Catholic anticommunism that has been largely overlooked, a period for its growth after the war, when it would reach its zenith. Although Walsh remained the foremost Catholic expert on Soviet political theory and practice, during the war he also emerged as the premier American Catholic interpreter of geopolitics, a school of political thought whose influence grew dramatically during and after the Second World War.[5]

Like Scanlan and Gillis, Walsh did not retract his anticommunist views during the war. Unlike them, however, he was actively involved in promoting the war effort, in his capacity as a university administrator, and as a lecturer and consultant for the War Department. Just as he tempered his antirecognition stance in 1933 during the Roosevelt-Litvinov negotiations, so during the war Walsh shifted his attention to Nazism, which he regarded as the greatest danger then threatening international stability. This shift on Walsh's part was not mere pragmatism, however. Geopolitics allowed Walsh to balance his anti-Nazi and anti-Soviet priorities in a way that did not compromise his fundamental beliefs regarding the Soviet Union. Walsh's wartime anticommunism cannot be fully understood apart from his growing interest in geopolitics, and his increased implementation of a geopolitical framework.

GEOPOLITICS, GERMANY, AND GEORGETOWN

The term "geopolitics" is best understood in a threefold sense. First, it refers broadly to politics on the world stage, in which nation-states are the primary players. Second, and more specifically, it refers to the way in which the world's geographical resources and the political drive of nation-states both influence and are affected by one another. Third, it refers to the academic discipline that developed in nineteenth-century Europe and gained increasing attention as the process of globalization intensified during the twentieth century.[6]

The underlying notions governing geopolitical thought had been recognized by policy makers and political philosophers long before its development as an academic discipline, notes British political scientist Brian Blouet. Citing Captain Alfred Thayer Mahan's *The Influence of Seapower upon History* (1890) and Frederick Jackson Turner's "The Significance of the Frontier in American History" (1893) as early and influential geopolitical treatises, Blouet sees in the still earlier Louisiana Purchase (1803) and Monroe Doctrine (1823), and in the later annexation of Hawaii (1896) and building of the Panama Canal (1903), clear examples of how the United States "employed geopolitical policies long before the term *geopolitics* came into use."[7]

Although the Swedish social scientist Rudolf Kjellen introduced the term *"Geopolitik"* in 1899, the two most significant theorists to develop geopolitical thought were renowned German geographer Friedrich Ratzel and British geographer and statesman Sir Halford Mackinder. An ardent advocate of German world power (*Weltmacht*), Ratzel first proposed the notion of *Lebensraum* or "living space," which viewed the state as a biological organism in search of additional living space. The Darwinian overtones of Ratzel's theory became evident as he proclaimed the right of stronger nations to acquire additional "living space" at the expense of weaker ones.[8]

Mackinder's long career included a professorship at the London School of Economics and a turn as high commissioner to South Russia from 1919 to 1920. In January 1904, he delivered a paper to the

Royal Geographical Society titled "The Geographical Pivot of History," proposing that the major international struggle of the new century would be for domination of the Eurasian continent, the world's largest land mass. In his 1919 book *Democratic Ideals and Reality*, Mackinder elaborated on his thesis with this famous statement: "Who rules East Europe commands the Heartland: Who rules the Heartland commands the World-Island: who rules the World-Island commands the world." Both Ratzel's notion of *Lebensraum* and Mackinder's "heartland" thesis attracted increased interest during the Second World War and the Cold War.[9]

The most influential German geopolitical thinker to emerge during the interwar period was the soldier-scholar Karl Haushofer (1869–1945). After retiring from the army in 1919 as a major general, Haushofer, who had earned a doctorate at the University of Munich, subsequently taught geography there. He soon established himself as the major German spokesman on geopolitics. Through his *Institut für Geopolitik* and its journal *Zeitschrift für Geopolitik*, in forty books and hundreds of articles, and through his radio programs, he both expounded and expanded on Ratzel and Mackinder. David Murphy, a historian of German *Geopolitik*, writes that Haushofer "was a ubiquitous presence in the German media . . . spreading the message of Germany's shortage of living space 'by a thousand channels.'"[10]

Like Ratzel, Haushofer viewed the state as a natural organism whose prosperity hinged on *Lebensraum*, forcing competition for earth space with other states. Geoffrey Parker writes that Haushofer's *Geopolitik* was "founded on an environmental determinism" that justified expansion at the expense of weaker states. Adapting Mackinder's thesis, Haushofer developed a theory by 1941 that the earth was divided into three main regions dominated by three major powers: the Americas, dominated by the United States; Europe and Africa, or "Eurafrica," dominated by Germany; and Asia, dominated by Japan.[11]

Historians have debated the extent of Haushofer's ties to the Nazi regime, particularly with regard to his influence in policy-making circles. At Munich, Haushofer had taught Rudolf Hess, an officer in Adolf Hitler's regiment during the First World War and an early member of the Nazi party, with whom he developed close personal and intellectual ties. Imprisoned with Hitler at Landsberg Castle after the aborted Munich putsch of November 1923, Hess later became Hitler's private secretary and most devoted follower, ranking after Hitler and Goering in the Nazi hierarchy.[12]

Brian Blouet contends that Haushofer, whom Hess introduced to Hitler, tutored the two in geopolitics and advised them both on geopolitical issues through the 1930s, and that that Hitler's autobiography *Mein Kampf* "exhibits the *Geopolitik* style." He further contends that Haushofer participated in negotiations between Germany and Japan, where he had once served as a military attaché. On the other hand, Blouet also notes that Haushofer fell out of favor with the Nazi regime around 1938 (by which time Hess's influence in party circles was slight) when he failed to advocate unbridled German expansionism in Central and Eastern Europe.[13]

Countering the view that Haushofer as the "diabolical mastermind behind Nazi conquest" and "evil genius" guiding Hitler's foreign policy, David Murphy denies that Haushofer, or geopolitics in general, was a significant influence upon Hitler, who used "whatever justifications he wished" as the need arose. Indeed, though he acknowledges Haushofer's role in popularizing geopolitical thought during the 1920s and 1930s, Murphy contends that geopolitics was less of an influence during the Nazi regime than it had been during the Weimar era. Thus Haushofer would appear to have been more successful as a publicist than as a policy maker.[14]

In an August 1952 address at the Army War College, Walsh recalled his first encounter with German geopolitics in 1924. After his return from Soviet Russia, Walsh recalled discovering a copy of *Zeitschrift für Geopolitik* in Georgetown's library:

> From that new, highly intellectualized magazine, from the geopolitical discussion in it and the type of maps drawn, I realized here was something more than a conventional place geographer. It showed a dynamic force at work. It showed a global perspective. It showed the slow building up of a philosophy of power for the German government.

He was intrigued by Haushofer's use of Mackinder, whose thesis he regarded as "one of the most brilliant hypotheses of modern political science." Based on this recollection, it would appear that Walsh was among Haushofer's first American readers.[15]

Although his lectures and writings during the 1930s make it clear that communism and not geopolitics was his main concern, Walsh's February 1940 Georgetown lecture on German geopolitics received generous attention from the *New York Times*. In it, he asserted that, as Hitler's chief adviser on foreign affairs, Haushofer oversaw "hundreds of very competent, if very fanatical, experts" who planned the details of Hitler's world conquest. Moreover, Nazi ideology was directly attributable to Haushofer's geopolitical teachings:

> The social and human composition of all sovereign nations now dominates the new concept of the diplomatic as well as the military objectives of the German state. The partition of Poland, then, and the assault on Finland are but so many incidental but predetermined moves on the vast checkerboard of international politics. . . . Austria was the bishop taken by Germany, Czecho-Slovakia was the castle taken by Germany, Poland was the queen taken by Germany, Latvia, Lithuania and Estonia were the pawns taken by Russia.

This lecture marks Walsh's public debut as an interpreter and promoter of geopolitical thought. He would expand this role throughout the decade—as a professor and administrator at Georgetown, where he much enlarged the place of geopolitics in the curriculum; as a government official, lecturing on geopolitics to military personnel throughout the nation; and as a popularizer, speaking to the larger American public to increase its awareness of this new discipline, which was exerting such an influence in the modern world.[16]

In 1942 a substantial amount of geopolitical literature began to appear in the United States. One political scientist commented: "Geopolitics has migrated from Germany to America." Among the preeminent American scholars in the fledgling field were Nicholas J. Spykman of Yale, who organized the Yale Institute of International Studies in 1935, and Isaiah Bowman, who had served as chief territorial specialist of the American Commission at Versailles and later as president of Johns Hopkins University. Indeed, "the greatest intellectual challenge to German *Geopolitik*," observes Geoffrey Parker, "arose in wartime America, in the form of a new geopolitics."[17]

GEORGETOWN AND THE SECOND WORLD WAR

After Pearl Harbor, Georgetown historian Joseph Durkin writes, the university "went 'all out'" in support of the war. In February 1942, Walsh issued a public statement, declaring that "the issues involved [in the war] transfer it bodily and totally into another moral category."

By 1943, more than 70 faculty members and 3,300 alumni were on active military duty, while more than 500 students belonged to the reserves. American higher education itself also prepared to meet the needs of "total war," a trend in which Georgetown wholeheartedly participated.[18]

In early 1942, under guidelines approved by the federal government and the Conference of American Colleges and Universities, the foreign service school revised its curriculum "to meet the needs of a nation committed to total war." The course "Political Economy of Total War," which became a requirement for upperclassmen, aimed to trace the "origin, development and influence of the *Institute of Geopolitics* founded by Haushofer in Germany." The 1942 course catalogue described geopolitics as "one of the most powerful weapons used by the Axis Powers," one that could "no longer be neglected." Campus Army and Navy ROTC programs trained future officers, while Walsh offered specialized courses on political and geographic warfare for military officers working in Washington.[19]

In the fall of 1943, the War Department designated Georgetown as a center for the recently established Army Specialized Training Program (ASTP), a pet project of Secretary of War Henry Stimson. The ASTP differed from the First World War's Student Army Training Corps (SATC) program in that the ASTP sent *soldiers* to school, whereas the SATC inducted *students* into military service while they remained on campus to finish their education. During the Second World War, the Army chose 190,000 draftees for specialized training at American colleges and universities. The School of Foreign Service was designated as a center for language and area studies, with Walsh as director. About 1,800 ASTP members lived at Georgetown while studying there. In 1944, the program was disbanded and the soldiers sent to European Theater of Operations (ETO) to fill the manpower gap.[20]

In *Contending with Modernity*, Philip Gleason notes that only 8 of the 116 colleges and universities participating in ASTP were Catholic, and that, of these, Georgetown had the largest program. Even though Walsh supported the war effort, however, he had reservations about its potential effects on higher education and wrote to that effect in October 1942 to Georgetown professor William S. Culbertson. In 1943, Walsh would put the war effort in a larger perspective:

> For the educators of America, total mobilization of the intellect and will as well as the body of democracy now becomes part of their teach-

ing function. To assist in grappling with the present emergency in such realistic fashion as to insure victory for the Allied Nations, is, for the duration, the controlling objective of higher education. But the permanent things of life—spiritual truth, moral ideals and cultural progress—will not be neglected or minimized at Georgetown.

American higher education, he concluded, "has not surrendered to the evil of total and permanent militarism," but merely strengthened "its physical side for the protection and preservation of its soul."[21]

From the start of the foreign service school, geography was a standard requirement. Although courses in "Applied Geography" indirectly addressed geopolitical issues, specific courses on geopolitics were not offered at the school before the war. That was to change in 1944: "Hereafter," announced the school catalogue of that year, "a course on the true influence of geography in determining an equitable, sound and practical foreign policy for the United States will form part of the regular curriculum."[22]

Although Walsh had followed the growth of German geopolitics during the 1930s, when he taught courses on the Constitution, Soviet history and politics, English, and research methodology, he did not teach a geopolitics course until 1942.[23] In 1941, he was a guest lecturer on *Geopolitik* in Professor William S. Culbertson's "Political Economy of Total War." Walsh's relationship with Culbertson, a prominent Washington attorney and lieutenant colonel in the Army Reserves who had taught at the School of Foreign Service since 1921, was to be a significant factor in his development as a geopolitical expert.[24]

In 1942, Walsh offered his own course on geopolitics, a class he would teach for the rest of his academic career. In the course syllabus, Walsh elaborated on the war's true significance:

> The conflict is between the rights of individual men, endowed with the dignity of human personality and elevated to the adoptive sonship of God, on the one side, and the dehumanized, totalitarian state of Fichte, Hegel, Treitschke, Nietzsche, Hitler and the Tanaka Memorial of Japan on the other. That means not a world campaign of conventional belligerents [but] a World Revolution seeking to capture the soul of humanity.

In response to Haushofer's *Geopolitik*, Walsh proposed the creation of an "American geopolitics," based on "international justice, international honor and mutuality of international respect." An American geopolitics did not aim to create "a new imperialism," but to fulfill the "heavy obligations . . . attaching to great power and economic influence."[25]

WAR DEPARTMENT LECTURER AND GEOPOLITICAL CONSULTANT

Every winter since 1924, Walsh had presented a public series of ten lectures, which became known as the "Winter Ten." One Washington newspaper estimated that the series attracted approximately 1,800 people annually. The last set of these lectures, "America Faces Total War," presented in early 1942, focused on "the various phases of military, economic, and industrial mobilization for war," as well as on war's "political and moral aspects." Walsh discontinued the series because he had been assigned to address a much larger audience: the United States Army.[26]

Over the next three years, he would lecture on international relations for the War Department at military posts and officer training schools nationwide, offering lecture courses for junior officers at the War College, the Command and General Staff General School, and the Judge Advocate General School. John F. Parr, a foreign service alumnus who later served as dean, recalled: "Father Walsh's sense of military and naval affairs was very deep seated in his personality and intertwined in his sense of patriotism." In the postwar era, Walsh continued to lecture for the military at the Air University, Maxwell Field, Alabama, and at the War College.[27]

In addition to his lectures, Walsh was closely involved with the U.S. Army's Geopolitical Section, Military Intelligence Division, General Staff, established on June 8, 1942, under General George V. Strong, with Lieutenant Colonel William S. Culbertson as its first chief and a full-time staff of eight. The section's objectives were to

> study physical, economic, political and ethnological geography in order to advise on measures of national security and assurance of continued peace in the post-war world, as well as to conduct such studies as may be demanded for the immediate prosecution of the war.

More specifically, it was tasked with "the gathering and analysis of data upon which the formulation of military policy may be based."[28]

"Geopolitics has captured the imagination of the academic world," Culbertson wrote General Strong in June 1942. He suggested, therefore, that the new unit engage the services of American scholars as consultants; during its short life span, the Geopolitical Section relied on the expertise of several university professors. Among those educators "called upon from time to time" were Walsh, Nicholas Spykman of Yale, Harold Sprout, Edward Mead Earle, and Dana Munro of Princeton, and Derwent Whittlesey of Harvard. On December 2, 1942, Walsh was officially appointed an "Expert Consultant."[29]

But Walsh was far more than a consultant. In his unpublished autobiography, Culbertson described him as "a pioneer in the constructive study of German geopolitics," as one "directly associated with the founding of the geopolitical section," and as chief among those educators lobbying the War Department to establish a geopolitical unit in the spring of 1942. In "a strong letter" to Secretary of War Henry L. Stimson in May 1942, Walsh stressed the need for such a unit. Indeed, Culbertson concluded, his role in creating "an American geopolitics" left "a lasting impression on the military planning and strategy of the American nation."[30]

In a September 1942 presentation to the Geopolitical Section, Walsh insisted that geopolitical planning was "one of the most important elements" in the Nazi program. The United States was "late, but not too late, in developing the methods and techniques of Geopolitics." The misuse of geopolitical analysis was "no reason for avoiding it or even for apologizing for its use in our strategy and in our planning for security." A global approach to the problems of strategy and security, he suggested, could be best done in the War Department, free from any special interest which might operate elsewhere.[31]

The Geopolitical Division was discontinued in June 1943, when its personnel were absorbed into the newly created Office of Strategic Services. Although, as Culbertson noted, Walsh was "much concerned over the discontinuance of the work which we were doing," the change did not affect his work for the War Department, which continued throughout the war. His consulting and lecturing served to enhance his image as a popular interpreter of geopolitics, inaugurated a closer relationship with the military that lasted for the rest of his career, and marked an increasingly collaborative relationship with other scholars also active in the new academic discipline.[32]

Together with Professor Joseph P. Chamberlain of Columbia University, Walsh founded the Institute of World Polity in 1945, an organization committed to "the discussion and systematic research of questions affecting international relations and the foreign policy of the United States." Located at the School of Foreign Service, the institute remained in existence until 1972. "A permanent philosophy of international relations," its founding statement declared, "must be established and maintained if the errors and tragedies of the past are to be avoided in the future." Among the founding participants were William S. Culbertson, Constantine E. McGuire, Samuel Flagg Bemis of Yale, Karl Brandt of Stanford, Edward Mead Earle of Princeton, Quincy Wright of the University of Chicago, and former *America* editor Wilfrid Parsons, S.J.[33]

WALSH AND THE NAZI THREAT

For Walsh, *Geopolitik* was a discipline with "no conscience." What began as a "Darwinian process" under Ratzel reached its apogee in Haushofer's research, freed "from moral obligation and spiritual control." For Walsh, Haushofer was representative of intellectuals who "cynically insisted that science had nothing to do with values or moral considerations." What distinguished Haushofer from other scholars, however, was that as Hitler rose to power, "the prestige and function of geopolitics ascended with him." As a result, geopolitics became "a dynamic driving rod in the mechanics of statecraft."[34]

German geopolitics was the climax of a secularization process Walsh traced back to the sixteenth century. Although many Catholic leaders identified the Reformation as the source of modern problems, Walsh blamed the Renaissance. In exalting "material beauty and artistic brilliancy," he argued, the Renaissance produced "a paganism of taste, charm and refinement" that "corrupted the soul of Europe and squandered the supernatural heritage of Christendom." Combined with the Industrial Revolution and its ethos of individualism, which he regarded as Protestant-inspired, the effect of the Renaissance was to shift "men's gaze earthward":

The Renaissance of Catholic Italy worshiped the contours of man's body, his raiment, his art, his rediscovered classics, ornaments, and food; the Industrial Revolution of Protestant England shifted the idolatry to his mass production of anything capable of being priced and marketed. Both missed the value of man per se. . . . Both prepared the soil for the emergence of Prussia, whose historic tendency has been to minimize law and exalt force.[35]

As a result, the modern world faced a choice between "the value of power and the power of values." To meet the crisis, Walsh proposed an American geopolitics rooted in "international justice, international honor, the sanctity of the given word, and mutuality of international respect," a geopolitics that, unlike its German counterpart, was to be guided by a moral compass rooted in religion. "So long as religion survives," he declared, "so long will the American way of life survive."[36]

A DOUBLE REVOLUTION: GERMAN AND SOVIET GEOPOLITICS

For Walsh, the Soviet Union posed a long-range threat after Germany's defeat. Both communism and Nazism, he insisted, had an "identical objective—World Revolution." In an address to Culbertson's Geopolitical Section, Walsh maintained that, although his views about the Soviets were well known, he welcomed military cooperation against a dangerous enemy: Nazi Germany "is now our mortal enemy and so long as Russia cooperates in the task of defeating that menace, we are rightly and justly supporting her military effort." Nevertheless, Walsh called for Stalin's pledge to defend "those freedoms which inspire our present total mobilization":

> What the Christian world and the democracies would welcome would be the thrilling news that complete religious freedom has been restored, that the Third International has been retired to the archives, not temporarily but permanently, and that Soviet Russia [is adhering] to the principles of the Atlantic Charter.[37]

In a 1944 address to the League of Catholic Women in Boston, Walsh voiced his opposition to both "the Germanic program of world revolution" and "Russia's special geopolitics." Moscow abandoned the Third International in 1943, Walsh believed, because it no longer required "the subterfuge of a so-called private organization"; by 1944, it was "increasingly evident" that the Soviet Union aimed to "re-establish her own frontiers and intervene elsewhere in Europe according to predetermined and self-created norms, without waiting for consultation or collective action." The Allies needed to face "realistically the political effects of Russia's triumphant march into Western Europe."[38]

In an October 1944 address to the Te Deum Forum in Illinois, Walsh declared that Poland's future was "the acid test of the sincerity and international integrity of the great powers." Soviet Russia was "obviously . . . staking out her claims in the post-war world," whereas the Allies were "holding honorably to the agreement not to cheat the starter's gun." Though he acknowledged Russia's military contributions, he condemned what he perceived as its "concomitant attempt to profit by the present world tragedy and under cover of the confusion incident to global warfare seek to expand a way of life hostile to Christianity and Democracy." Not to acknowledge Soviet Russia's revolutionary aims even in the middle of the war, he insisted, was to "commit intellectual suicide."[39]

Poland, George Sirgiovanni observes, was a major concern for the wartime anticommunists, who saw the Polish issue as a test of American willingness to enforce the self-determination principles of the 1941 Atlantic Charter, and who saw Poland's fate as a sign of Europe's immediate future. American Catholics, in particular, feared a Catholic nation coming under communist control. Indeed, as Richard Gid Powers points out, "the great issue of the war for Catholic anticommunists was the future of Poland"; Catholics "made it clear that they would judge the success of the war by the fate of Catholic Poland and Lithuania."[40]

At a December 1944 conference on the future of Soviet-American relations, Walsh declared that the United States and the Soviet Union "will probably emerge from this holocaust as the two most powerful units in the family of nations," although "our relations with Soviet Russia will certainly not be easier or more promising." The war did not modify the Soviet revolutionary impulse, Walsh asserted, but only restrained it through "pragmatic diplomacy." Soviet Russia entered the war "on purely geopolitical grounds which were progressively revealed as the war developed." Soviet geopolitics differed from Nazi geopolitics in that the Nazis "loudly advertised their *Lebensraum* motivation—and failed. The Russians said nothing and succeeded." The Russian Revolution had not ended, Walsh asserted, but was "only now entering on its most important external phase."[41]

As victory approached, Walsh continued to stress the importance of geopolitics, but increasingly emphasized the Soviet geopolitical threat. Indeed, Walsh's wartime anticommunist discourse was expressed in an increasingly geopolitical vocabulary. Paraphrasing Mackinder in 1944, he advised Americans: "Do not forget that Moscow lies much nearer to the pulse of Eurasia, India, and China than do London and Washington." Shortly before the end of the war, at Washington's British Mission, he stated: "With the annihilation of the German *Geopolitik*, a new form [of] geopolitics is asserting itself in Eastern and Central Europe," with the Soviets "succeeding brilliantly in acquiring domination of Mackinder's heartland." It was an error, he warned his audience, "to consider the Russian Revolution as over."[42]

Walsh saw a new empire, "a Pan-Slavic Confederation, under Communist auspices," in the making. The "manner and ruthlessness" of Soviet annexations, he declared, would "amaze and shock" Americans. In a 1945 speech at the University of Pittsburgh, Walsh defined what he considered the "guiding principles of Soviet Geopolitics":

> the outright absorption of territory; the creation of "spheres of influence," the promotion of sympathetic relations with independent states through "advantageous pacts and the big brother technique"; "reciprocal guarantees and shared economic privilege" with more remote areas; the coordination of worldwide communist activity through "instructed national groups, by cultural interchange, by cautious propaganda and still more cautious channeling of essential directives through diplomatic and commercial agents."[43]

WALSH AND NUREMBERG

The Allies had developed plans for the occupation of Germany well in advance of victory. The U.S. Group Control Council for Germany, for example, was activated in London in the autumn of 1944. An American planning agency before the actual occupation, the Group Control Council assumed leadership of the military government in Germany under General C. W. Wickersham. In the fall of 1945, the council was replaced by the Office of Military Government of the United States for Germany (OMGUS) under General Lucius D. Clay. In September 1949, control over German domestic affairs passed to the Federal Republic of Germany, and John J. McCloy assumed the office of U.S. High Commissioner for Germany.[44]

As early as 1943, the Allies began discussions on how to deal with war crimes and criminals. At the Teheran Conference, Stalin proposed executing some fifty thousand German officers, while Churchill suggested punishing a few key members of the Nazi elite. The Americans took a more moderate approach, calling for a trial. Part of the reason for this, Frank Ninkovich suggests, was that "American hatred of Germans was not deeply rooted." While he notes that there "was reason enough for enmity," Americans did not view all Germans as Nazis. The enmity that did exist, though never as extreme as among the other Allies, was a "consequence of the war, not its cause."[45]

In 1945, the Allies signed an agreement creating the International Military Tribunal. Operating on the principle that "individuals have international duties which transcend the national obligations of obedience imposed by the individual state," the tribunal specified three categories of crimes: crimes against peace, war crimes, and crimes against humanity. Nuremberg, previously the scene of stupendous Nazi rallies, was chosen for its historic significance. The defendants included Herman Goering, Rudolf Hess, and Joachim von Ribbentrop, Hitler's foreign minister. President Truman appointed Supreme Court Justice Robert H. Jackson as the American chief of counsel. In operation from November 1945 through August 1946, the tribunal delivered 10 death sentences, 3 life imprisonment sentences, and 3 acquittals. Although debates arose regarding their objectivity and their legality, the trials represented a major step toward defining standards of civic and international morality.[46]

Walsh was a direct participant in these events. In the summer of 1945, he was assigned to Justice Jackson's staff as an "Expert Consultant" on religious matters and geopolitics to investigate and document the Nazi persecution of the Christian churches and to prepare a statement on the role of Haushofer's geopolitics in German foreign policy. Between August 1945 and September 1946, Walsh collected affidavits from witnesses documenting Nazi religious persecution. In October, in his capacities as representative of the U.S. government and as geopolitical expert, Walsh interviewed Haushofer on his connection to the Nazi regime.[47]

In April 1945, Walsh was contacted by a member of General Clay's staff about his willingness to participate in the upcoming trials. Joseph Keenan of the AFL, then serving as General Clay's labor adviser in Germany, offered the position to Walsh, who accepted it. In his diary, Walsh noted that he was asked "to prepare a case, from geopolitics, showing how the German *Geopolitikers* had corrupted the German mind and prepared people for cooperating in the criminal attack on Europe." Colonel Howard A. Brundage of the Judge Advocate General Corps queried Walsh whether the Holy See would prepare a list of war criminals. Walsh replied that this was unlikely because, if it were to do so, its "universal religious mission . . . would be compromised."[48]

Walsh was enthusiastic about his new assignment, which, he wrote, would be "very valuable for [the] good" of Georgetown and the Jesuit order, and which would be "perhaps supreme in importance" among his "assignments from both [the] U.S.A. and Vatican."[49] Zaccheus J. Maher, the American assistant in the Jesuit Curia, shared his enthusiasm:

> This latest call which has come to you from our government is in my humble opinion the most momentous you have ever received, far more so than the one on which you served so well in Russia some years ago. . . . If . . . while working at the reconstruction of Germany you can guide the leaders of our nation in the contact they have eastward, then indeed you will have deserved doubly well of Church and country.

"What a consolation it is to us," Maher concluded, "and how proud we feel of the Society, as we see how the Holy See almost instinctively turns to her, as St. Ignatius wished that it might, for missions of unique difficulty."[50]

On July 15, Walsh received news of his official appointment as an "Expert Consultant," with an "assimilated rank" equivalent to a field-grade officer. Walsh's Provincial approved "provided I was not used in any capacity not befitting a priest." On July 18, Walsh accepted the appointment with the understanding that he "would not . . . appear as a prosecutor of individual war criminals [nor] as a witness in public trials [and that his] status [would] be confined to consultant on religious matters and on the role of geopolitics as a violator of International Law." Walsh's orders specified that he was to prepare a statement for the International Military Tribunal on geopolitics and to investigate religious persecutions "insofar as specific acts violated International Law." In his diary, Walsh wrote enthusiastically: "We are at a point of history to create a *new* conception of international law."[51]

In August, Walsh left for Europe, where he conferred with Justice Jackson, who had just met with Pius XII and Monsignor Domenico Tardini of the Secretariat of State in an attempt to secure Vatican assistance in supplying evidence for the trial. Although, according to Jackson, Pius feared that the trials "might degenerate into an indiscriminate revenge program," the Holy See nevertheless supplied Jackson's office copies of correspondence between the Vatican and Germany, including copies of Pius's diplomatic protests, which Walsh, an accomplished linguist, helped translate. "With charity but with firmness and justice," Walsh explained in a newspaper interview, "the Holy See will point out specific measures adopted by the Nazi government to destroy the Catholic Church in Germany and occupied countries."[52]

Although the present controversy regarding the Holy See and Nazi Germany centers on Pius XII's alleged "silence," Walsh's diary suggests that the Vatican was far from silent in connection to the Nuremberg trials. Indeed, as Jackson would later write, the process of documenting religious persecution, which otherwise would have been a laborious task, was "greatly expedited and aided by documents provided for us by the Vatican." It was clear to everyone, Jackson explained, that "we had no purpose to serve except to lay the truth before the Tribunal," and that the Vatican's aid was not intended to signify an "attitude toward the guilt or innocence of any particular defendant." Walsh sifted through the papal documents, conducted interrogations, and gathered material that was "of great value to us."[53]

PERSECUTIONS: CHRISTIAN AND JEWISH

In August 1945, Jackson advised Walsh to "get signed and authentic personal testimony from Church leaders as to specific offenses," allowing him to create his own itinerary. In ten months, Walsh traveled more than 35,000 miles. During his travels throughout the former Nazi territories, he interviewed 185 people, among them members of the German and Austrian hierarchy, laity, and Protestant ministers. "My job," he told an American reporter in November, "is to prove [religious persecution] juridically, . . . not passionately or revengefully, . . . so that it will meet the severest legal standards and stand the test of history."[54]

Walsh's interviewees ranged from a French Jesuit imprisoned in a concentration camp, to Cardinal Theodor Innitzer of Vienna, whose praise for Hitler's *Anschluss* is still controversial. In October 1945, Walsh visited the Vatican, where Monsignor Tardini told him it was "a shame and disgrace that Poland, the first country to be invaded and which resisted the Nazis, should have been sold down the river and handed over to the Communist dictatorship." Walsh's final report, Tardini insisted, proved that

> religion . . . was one of the things that stood in the way of a totalitarian regime. And, of course, Hitler considered the Catholic Church to be the No. 1 obstacle among religious sects because of its large size, closely-knit organization, and the powerful Vatican.

Walsh argued that National Socialism did not propose to openly abolish religion, "but merely to distort it to the Nazi cause." His study showed that the Nazi "first principle" was "the utter domination of religious organizations."[55]

Curiously, however, Walsh's public and private writings make little reference to the Nazi death camps (the term "Holocaust" was not coined until the 1950s). In October, he visited Dachau, where he "saw all the horror spots." Germany's "offenses are not only against International Law, the Hague Regulations and the Geneva Convention," he wrote in his diary,

> but against the very basic instincts and natural law itself of humanity. No code exists, no rules of evidence ever visualized the colossal conspiracy and atrocities committed at Dachau, Buchenwald and elsewhere, nor [is any] adequate to measure the program of complete extermination of [a] whole people.[56]

It is significant that Walsh's discussion of the Holocaust gave minimal attention to anti-Jewish persecutions. Although he did not attempt to deny them, it is clear that both personally and professionally, Walsh exhibited greater concern for the priests and Catholic Poles imprisoned in concentration camps.

In one sense, this may not be surprising, given the fact that his main task was to document the Nazi persecution of Christians rather than of Jews. At times, however, Walsh minimized anti-Jewish persecutions with a surprising insensitivity that even employed anti-Semitic imagery. Thus, in his 1948 book *Total Power*, he wrote:

> The Jews were hated as persons and on allegedly politico-economic grounds, and it was a comparatively easy police process to deal with the 6,000,000 individuals who formed the Jewish population of Germany. But Christianity was feared as a formidable spiritual obstacle to the conquest of total power because of the basic antagonism between its doctrines and the totalitarian metaphysics of National Socialism. What Nazism chiefly coveted from Jewry was its money, its property, and its material position in the economic organization of society.[57]

Although he adhered to stereotypes of Jewish affluence, Walsh no longer stressed Jewish radicalism in his post-Nuremberg writings, perhaps an indication of the effect his encounter with the death camps had upon him.[58]

WALSH'S INTERROGATION OF HAUSHOFER

Under house arrest in his south Bavarian home since the Allied occupation, Karl Haushofer had been questioned by American officers about his role in fomenting Nazi aggression. Jackson asked Walsh to take over the interrogation of Haushofer in late September, instructing him to have Haushofer prepare a final statement

> which shall point out the evil consequences of German geopolitics and why it developed the way it did. This admission from the acknowledged leader of the movement can then be published in Europe and America, particularly in university and scientific circles, with results which should be far more profitable from an educational point of view than would result from putting Haushofer in the dock as merely one more among the twenty-two already indicted.

Although Walsh had not previously conducted an interrogation before visiting Haushofer, he had witnessed Thomas J. Dodd's interrogation of Franz von Papen and DeWitt Clinton Poole's of Joachim von Ribbentrop.[59]

When Walsh first visited him at his home on September 25, 1945, Haushofer was a frightened old man in poor health, who immediately declared that he had never belonged to the Nazi Party. In early October, Walsh escorted Haushofer to Nuremberg for two interview sessions, during which Haushofer protested that "the Nazis had corrupted and distorted" his meaning. After Walsh persuaded Haushofer to compose a statement repudiating the Nazi applications of his teachings, he was returned to his home on October 10th with a certificate that he was not to be put on trial. On November 2nd, Walsh visited Haushofer and accepted his "Defense of German Geopolitics."[60]

In his November report to Jackson, Walsh concluded "that the evidence warranted the allegation that Haushofer was morally and legally guilty of participation in a premeditated crime of wanton aggressiveness." In a September memorandum, he had argued that, in providing the "scientific" arguments for Nazi aggression, German geopoliticians were "legally and morally guilty of participation in a premeditated crime of wanton aggression that resulted in the loss of many millions of lives, a staggering material destruction and widespread moral depravity." Citing the "role of geopolitics in corrupting education into a preparation for war," Walsh considered Haushofer and his associates "basically as guilty as the better-known criminals."[61] In March 1946, Karl Haushofer and his wife committed suicide. After visiting their graves, Walsh wrote in his diary:

> I could not but think of the deep tragedy of this death by night, alone, in a lonely gulley, of the last of the geopoliticans! What an inscrutable destiny, that after 19 [years of] teaching and warning [the] U.S.A. about the teachings of Haushofer, I should today be kneeling over his suicide's body in one of the loneliest spots in Bavaria!

Walsh's brief interrogation of Haushofer significantly enhanced his reputation as a geopolitical expert. Indeed, a reporter for *Extension* magazine would claim in December 1946 that the War Department looked upon Walsh as "its own authority on geopolitics."[62]

WALSH'S ASSESSMENT OF NUREMBERG

As a "a diabolic evil loose in the world," Walsh wrote in his diary, Nazism should be judged "by the standards which it sought to destroy." The prosecutors tried to *prove the facts* and . . . to set such an example for posterity that no government or nation will ever dare to try it again." For Walsh, Nuremberg affirmed "the basic moral law which antedates and underlies both municipal and international law." The Soviet presence at Nuremberg clearly irked him because he considered them "guilty of the identical totalitarian persecution of religion." Indeed,

> while the Soviet judge at Nuernberg was cooperating with England, with France and the United States in condemning the breaches of international law committed by the Nazi conspirators, his own government was engaged in one of the most flagrant violations of all times.

Nonetheless, Walsh asserted: "What Russia is doing politically does not cancel out the guilt of Germany," nor could the Nazis "be absolved because of the Russians' present inequity in Poland and elsewhere."[63]

Walsh regarded the war crime trials as a success, praising Jackson's rulings as one of "the great state papers of American history." The trials marked "a distinct and important phase in the evolution of international law." For the first time in history, human rights violations were now treated on the same level as international crimes. For Walsh, two important lessons came out of the Nuremberg trials: "that nations cannot, because they are nations, escape punishment for gross offenses, and that civilization must respect the basic right of religious freedom."[64]

Not all Jesuits shared Walsh's enthusiasm for the trials, however. Writing for *America* in November 1946, Gustav Gundlach, a German Jesuit sociologist at the Gregorian University, expressed concern about their objectivity. Walsh responded that, although Nuremberg did not "exclude or minimize the fundamental moral issues," simply denouncing the Nazi crimes was inadequate. To authenticate "the legal and personal responsibility of each individual defendant," the prosecutors had "ransacked a continent for evidence." National self-interest, he declared, was "no longer a defense for international criminality." The prosecutors drew "the sleeping sword of indignation, too long encumbered by the cords of disputatiousness—and dare[d] to use it." The trials were not an act of vengeance, he concluded, but "an expression in legal terms of the conscience of humanity."[65]

The dangers addressed at Nuremberg, Walsh was careful to point out, "did not perish with Goering and his associates." The "next question on the order of the day for civilized thinking" was how to

deal with Soviet Russia, which was "now widely charged with com-
mitting the identical crimes which brought heavy retribution on the
Nazi conspirators," and whose aggressive expansionism, violation of
human rights, and persecution of religion were the new challenges
facing the postwar world. If "moral cowardice or shameful appease-
ment or political expediency" prevailed, Walsh warned, then the nations of the world must prepare for "new holocausts" and "a still
more ghastly conflict."[66]

TOTAL POWER: THE BOOK

It was to address the Soviet issue that Walsh published his third
book in 1948, *Total Power: A Footnote to History*, which drew on his
experience at Nuremberg, his diaries, his correspondence, and other
collected documentation. In 1947, shortly after Walsh had completed
his manuscript, Thomas Dodd had urged him to find a publisher
because several books on the Nuremberg trials were soon likely to
appear. The published work was not simply an account of Walsh's
work in Germany, however; it was an extended meditation on both
the Nazi German and Soviet Russian abuses of power, the roots of
totalitarianism, and America's role in the postwar world. Whereas
Germany and Russia embodied "power without law," Walsh wrote,
"power controlled by justice obedient to eternal law is the destined
mission of America."[67]

"The tragedy of Karl Haushofer," *Total Power* begins, was his participation in the "nationalizing" of scholarship. Under Haushofer,
geopolitics became a weapon supplying "an allegedly scientific basis
and justification for international brigandage." For Walsh, Nazism
raised a deeper issue: "What one really beheld in the prisoner's dock
at Nuremberg was a logical devolution in the despiritualizing of modern culture and the ultimate expression of an unbalanced and per-
verted humanism."[68]

For Walsh, totalitarianism in all its forms represented the "despiritualizing" of Western culture, a movement that was centuries in the
making. Whereas the medieval world had been "conscious of man's
spiritual and moral attributes," Machiavelli's "corrupted statecraft"
and Descartes' "philosophic doubt" had combined to create a
"schizophrenia of the intellect":

For four centuries the modern mind has been seeking order but inviting chaos. Renaissance, Reformation, Nationalism, Democracy, Industrial Revolution . . . and finally Totalitarianism—red, black, and brown
. . . were the stages through which Europe passed in search of its soul
and in quest of political stability.[69]

For Walsh, this struggle did not end in 1945. The Second World
War was an "interlude, a ghastly and inhuman *entr'acte*" in which
Germany "snatched the scepter of world revolution" from the Soviets. Hitler, he contended, was "a parenthesis in the text. The scepter
has now returned to Moscow." Soviet expansion, he warned, "prom-
ises to turn out to be the most important geopolitical demonstration
of modern times." True to Mackinder's "celebrated theory of power,"
Walsh stated, Soviet Russia had gained control of the "heartland"
through recent annexations in eastern Europe.[70]

Ideology continued to be the driving force behind Soviet expansionism, which Walsh depicted in religious terms. As the "evangelist
of world communism," Soviet Russia could not stand still. The "target
of her messianic psychology," he argued, was "the human soul," and
the free world the "most coveted goal of her apostolate." At the start
of the Cold War, Walsh saw a fundamental conflict emerging: "The
lines are drawn for a deeper conflict between absolutism and freedom of the spirit, between two antagonistic philosophies of life that
can no longer be disguised under political pretexts or disputed as
technicalities." Walsh called on the United States, as heir to the "cultural values" inherited from its European "parent," to assume leadership in the struggle against "the autocracy of the steppes."[71]

Like Walsh's previous books, *Total Power* received mixed reviews.
Whereas the reviewer for *The Library Journal* praised Walsh's "pro-
vocative thinking," and Hans Kohn commended his "critical understanding and moving eloquence" in the *New York Times*, Walsh's
confrere Robert Graham found the book a "somewhat disjointed
work" in *America*, and Valentine De Balla, even as he saw it as a
"powerful and comprehensive searchlight into the jungle of our postwar problems" in the *Catholic World*, allowed that the book might
have been "better organized."[72]

Professor Waldemar Gurian, a German émigré and editor of Notre
Dame's *Review of Politics*, offered the most extensive and telling criticism. However sound his ideas, Gurian wrote, Walsh's style was

"loose and disorganized," and his book was weak on ideological analysis. To give a convincing history of ideas, it was not enough "to accumulate quotations and list many names." Moreover, Walsh's treatment of the Middle Ages seemed to ascribe "all evil exclusively to modern times." Though "embarrassed to be so critical about a book by such a distinguished writer," Gurian nonetheless deemed his criticism to be "in the interest of the reputation of Catholics among students of modern totalitarianism." Indeed, he regretted that "the imperfections of Father Walsh's chapters may be misused to discredit the ethical principles and basic views on men and history which he presents, but which he does not support with a precise and differentiating study of the concrete socio-historical material." Thus, even though Walsh may have been the most renowned Catholic spokesperson on geopolitics, his views did not go unchallenged by his fellow Catholic scholars.[73]

THE UNITED NATIONS AND AMERICA'S ROLE
IN THE POSTWAR WORLD

Beginning in 1943, the establishment of an international organization became the subject of serious discussion among the Allies. In April 1945, the representatives of more than three hundred nations met in San Francisco to form the United Nations. The charter was signed in June and the U.S. Senate ratified it the following month. As Joseph Rossi, S.J., notes, however, many American Catholics, largely because of Soviet membership, were skeptical about the new organization's potential effectiveness. Walsh himself was not entirely enthusiastic, observing that "economists and competent specialists . . . will be pouring water into a sieve unless the superstructure of the world's external organization be informed and vitalized and spiritualized by something more universal than international economic policy." Furthermore, he argued, unless Poland received "just and adequate treatment," the U.N. would "enter on its career with a blot on its escutcheon.[74]

The war, Walsh stated in May 1945, proved that the United States would "never again be taken lightly by any power on the face of the earth." He called on the nation, having achieved an unprecedented degree of physical and industrial strength, to provide "evidence to the world of greatness of mind, refinement of spirit and nobility of conduct." The failure to meet this challenge, he warned, would mean "another chapter in the oft-repeated annals of cultural decadence." The United States had entered on its "hour for greatness":

> Under our very eyes a new pattern of civilization is being woven on the thundering loom of time. Into that fabric must go the image of a city mounted on [a] foundation of moral values, adorned with dignity of human personality and rendered cohesive by acceptance of universal law.

Walsh saw it as postwar America's "proffered destiny" to "cast her great weight on the side of spiritualized leadership, true world democracy and against totalitarianism whether openly practiced or cynically disguised."[75]

The month before, he had called on the nation to provide "leadership of mind, soul and heart" to the postwar world. For Walsh, this was clearly the task of the United States, and not the United Nations:

> Let her dare to proclaim, first to her own people and then to all her allies . . . that external devices, leagues to enforce peace and proportionate representation will all prove ropes of sand against recurrent violence unless the spirit of man be purged of the gross materialism and worship of speed, motion and external form which have characterized the modern mind since the Renaissance and the Industrial Revolution. The Four Freedoms, Atlantic Charters, Bills of Rights, Freedom of the Seas and International Law have never yet nor will be secured by economists, statesmen or financial wizards. These externalities are legalized reaction to something that lies deep and invisible within the human soul.

America was to provide a spiritual model for the world, a notion directly traceable to John Winthrop's image of the "City on a Hill." For Walsh, the true determinant of American greatness was not its military power, nor its high standard of living, nor yet its economic influence abroad. Rather, it was the extent to which Americans lived up to their democratic principles, and recognized the religion of their civilization. The United Nations was bound to be ineffective because it did not ground itself on a spiritual footing.[76]

CONCLUSION: CATHOLIC ANTICOMMUNISM
AT THE END OF THE SECOND WORLD WAR

Throughout the war, anticommunism among Catholics operated at all levels, from bishops to clergy to laity. In 1942, Father John F. Cronin, S.S., who taught philosophy and economics at Saint Mary's Seminary in Baltimore, noted "a notable and alarming resurgence of Communist activity throughout the United States in recent months," particularly in the labor movement. According to Cronin, the communists exploited "the favorable attitude towards Russia induced by her heroic defense and consequent contribution to the cause of the United Nations." Cronin called for an increase in labor schools "to educate leaders . . . in Catholic social principles," and "expert training" for priests directing diocesan social programs.[77]

In early 1944, Archbishop Amleto Cicognani, the apostolic delegate, wrote to Archbishop Edward Mooney, chairman of the NCWC's administrative board, expressing the hope that "the Bishops, Clergy and Faithful of the United States will take cognizance of the increasingly serious danger of Communism, which the Holy See has condemned in fulfillment of its divine mission for the salvation of souls." At their November 1944 meeting, the bishops of the NCWC asked Father Cronin to produce a detailed "confidential report" on domestic communism, which was distributed at their 1945 meeting.[78] In addition, the NCWC sent a questionnaire on communism to each diocese. "The average person seems to view Russia as unquestionably our greatest friend, militarily," the respondent from Florida's Saint Augustine diocese stated,

> but along with this great admiration there goes a sort of "suspended judgement" about a lot of questions involving Russia which formerly were uppermost in the mind of the average American. Among these questions is Communism. For the present the public has conveniently put this question aside without answering it.[79]

Although it may have been reined in, Catholic anticommunism did not simply return to the stable during the war years. James Gillis and Patrick Scanlan may have been the more outspoken wartime anticommunists, but they were never lone voices crying out in an American Catholic wilderness. In 1945, American Catholics entered the Cold War with a well-developed set of assumptions about the

Soviet Union. In the case of Edmund A. Walsh, the war experience actually sharpened his anticommunism through his increased use of geopolitics. However much Walsh regarded communism as a greater threat than fascism, his geopolitical framework allowed him to shift emphasis from one to the other as the international political scene changed, while providing an intellectual consistency to his arguments.

During the war, Geoffrey Parker writes, a division arose among American geopolitical scholars between realists and idealists. In a 1941 address to the American Political Science Association, Nicholas J. Spykman of Yale advocated a realist postwar world of power balances and spheres of influences. Although Spykman died in 1943, Brian Blouet contends that his worldview "was to become dominant in American foreign policy in the Cold War era." On the other hand, according to Parker, the "idealist viewpoint was most radically voiced by Edmund Walsh." The geopolitical debate during the Second World War presaged the realist-idealist debate among American foreign policy makers during the Cold War, where Walsh also championed the idealist perspective.[80]

In his 2000 essay on Walsh's geopolitics, the geographer Gearóid Ó Tuathail / Gerard Toal describes Walsh as "one of the leading figures" in promoting geopolitics as an academic discipline in the United States." Walsh's participation in the geopolitical discourse of the 1940s represented a significant if underappreciated effort to address the relation between religion and culture. His work embodied the Jesuit "permeationist" approach; seeing geopolitics not just as an academic debate, but also as "an omnipresent spiritual struggle," he used the prevailing intellectual terminology to evangelize the culture from within. For Walsh, the United States and Soviet Russia were, indeed, the "two standards" facing the world in 1945.[81]

5

"The Spiritual and Material Menace Threatening the Present Generation"

Walsh and Catholic Anticommunism in the Cold War, 1946–56

Throughout most of 1952, at the peak of the Cold War, Edmund A. Walsh was busy lecturing to audiences nationwide on the Soviet threat to international freedom. In June, he summarized the progress of the conflict between the Soviet bloc and the West for basic training graduates at Lackland Air Force Base, Texas: "Seven years of steady planned conquest since 1945 have resulted in a new Communist Empire, the greatest in recorded history." Walsh assured the graduates that their service was needed as the world situation worsened:

> World War III has already begun . . . by open combat in Korea and in Indo-China, by guerilla [*sic*] warfare in Burma and Malaysia, . . . by political infiltration in Germany, France, and Italy, and by increasing mobilization of manpower war potential in the satellite lands behind the Iron Curtain, as well as within the confines of the Soviet Union.

By fulfilling Lenin's revolutionary ambitions, the Soviets were making open warfare between Soviet Russia and the West "inevitable."[1]

In September, lecturing on Soviet geopolitics at the Army War College, Walsh remarked that his own anticommunism, formerly deemed "intransigent and extreme," was now understood to be based on "cold reality." Citing statistics, he declared that "approximately one-third of the human race" was "subjected directly or indirectly to the Kremlin." The Far East was already under communist control, and western Europe stood in danger of conquest. The transatlantic region was free for the moment, but Soviet Russia's attempts to expand beyond "her heartland" made even that area unsafe from Soviet inroads.[2]

On November 15, however, at a dinner honoring his fiftieth anniversary as a Jesuit, Walsh suffered the first of a series of strokes that would end his public career and leave him an invalid until his death in October 1956. The period from 1946 to 1952, Louis Gallagher notes, was the busiest of Walsh's life; during these Cold War years, his "public strictures against the evils of communism and the Soviet expansion gained renewed credibility and respect . . . in the diplomatic community and in the higher reaches of government."[3] Indeed, according to journalist Louis Farrar,

> religious and political leaders—from the President's executive office to the halls of the people on Capitol Hill—go to him for authoritative guidance as to the devious plans and purposes of the Communist leaders. They have found him ready, wanting to speak clearly and lucidly on Communism—its causes and possible cures.

Walsh had gone "unheeded for years," Farrar concluded. "But he is *not* unheeded today."[4]

This chapter focuses on Walsh's anticommunism during the years 1946–52, when his long-held views intersected with the larger political currents of the day. His last book, *Total Empire*, which dealt with Soviet expansion, was a 1951 bestseller. By then, anticommunism was obviously a popular topic. In his public addresses, as a member of the presidential commission that advocated universal military training in 1947, and as an advocate of atomic might, Walsh justified one colleague's description of him as the "best known American Jesuit of his era." During the realist-idealist debate in foreign policy, when American policy makers sought to determine whether ideology or realistic political objectives motivated Soviet expansionism, Walsh injected a religious element into the debate. In 1952, he emerged as the Catholic champion of idealism, challenging George Kennan to publicly debate the issue.[5]

In their 1992 study of Father John Cronin and Baltimore labor, Joshua B. Freeman and Steve Rosswurm note that, although scholars agree that the Catholic Church played a leading role in Cold War anticommunism, "detailed studies of Catholic anti-communism are rare."[6] In 1978, Donald Crosby's *God, Church, and Flag* focused on the relationship between Joseph McCarthy and American Catholics; in 1984, Kathleen Gefell Centola examined the anticommunist rhetoric of American bishops and Catholic journalists. David O'Connor's

2000 study of grassroots Catholic organization illustrates how the anticommunist impulse permeated all levels of American Catholic life.[7] This chapter offers the first extended treatment of a leading Catholic anticommunist whose chief contribution to the movement was as an interpreter of Soviet Russian objectives during the Cold War.

THE ORIGINS OF THE COLD WAR AND THE
RISE OF THE ANTICOMMUNIST CONSENSUS

The historiographical debate over who "started" the Cold War has outlived the conflict itself. The traditionalist school of interpretation blamed Stalin's ideologically motivated expansionism. In contrast, the revisionist school emphasized realism, arguing that the new postwar power balance, not Soviet fanaticism, caused the conflict. Revisionists such as Thomas Paterson stress America's own expansionist impulses. In recent years, however, scholars have come to agree that the Cold War was not caused by one side or the other. James T. Patterson, for example, writes that, in 1945, the United States and the Soviet Union emerged as the world's two most powerful nations, creating "a new and highly unsettled world that bred insecurity on all sides." According to Patterson, it was the "different geopolitical concerns" of the two nations that made discord unavoidable, producing a five-decade struggle whose foundations were ideological, economic, and political.[8]

By the time of the Cold War, Ronald Steel writes, foreign affairs became the "nation's highest priority." At the same time, according to Richard Gid Powers, anticommunism "moved from the margins to the center of American politics." The emerging postwar anticommunist consensus was motivated by twin concerns: international communism and its domestic counterpart. These twin concerns intersected in the years 1950–54, when the Korean conflict and the attempts by Wisconsin Senator Joseph McCarthy to expose sedition on the part of American communists and their fellow travelers brought anticommunism to a fever pitch. During the postwar years, anticommunist sentiment and activity permeated American political and cultural life, from the Executive Office to the local school district, in the labor movement, and in the arts and media.[9]

WALSH AND SOVIET GEOPOLITICS

Throughout the Cold War, Walsh warned policy makers about "the new geopolitics that is now standing knocking with an imperial summons at the gates of the west." The Soviets were merely the "successors of the Nazi totalitarians," and Soviet Russia was a "new claimant for the hegemony of Europe." Soviet expansion in eastern Europe, he insisted, was nothing more than a "continuation of the Russian Revolution," setting the stage for "a deeper conflict between . . . two antagonistic philosophies of life which can no longer be disguised under political pretexts or disputed as technicalities." In a May 1948 address to the National Industrial Conference Board, Walsh described the situation in geopolitical terms:

> The more firmly the absolutism of Marxian Communism intrenches itself on the continent of Europe, the nearer its domination approaches an Atlantic world made contiguous by the technology of aviation and the inevitability of widespread atomic knowledge. To that extent we are involved and irreparably involved.[10]

Walsh argued that the Soviets explicitly employed Haushofer's theories. Their expansion was "not typically Marxian," he argued, but "Germanic." In a speech to the Army War College in 1952, Walsh suggested that "there are members of the old Haushofer school in Russia today." He was certain that "nothing will satisfy the Politburo in Moscow except the ultimate control of the continent of Europe and the imposition of Communism on its populations." Citing the Italian elections of 1948, in which the Christian Democrats defeated the communists, Walsh argued:

> If Italy had fallen into the lap of Moscow, and if the Iron Curtain had progressed that far westward, not one but three or four victims of the creeping imperialism of Marxian Communism would surely have been involved, and communism would have advanced that much nearer to the English Channel and the Atlantic World.

For Walsh, the Kremlin was composed of "trained revolutionaries," and any "statesman or negotiator who fails to recognize that objective is a victim of either moral or intellectual myopia."[11]

After the Second World War, the world was divided into two blocs competing for global influence, precipitating crisis after crisis, from the spring crisis of 1948 in Czechoslovakia and the subsequent Berlin airlift, through the 1980s arms race. According to Brian Blouet, the Cold War saw the triumph of geopolitics, and in particular of Sir Halford Mackinder's view, as a primary interpretive tool for policy makers. Thus, while the Soviets tried to eject the West from the western and eastern fringes of Eurasia, the West sought to check Soviet expansion. Milan Hauner agrees with Blouet, writing that Mackinder "substantially influenced the postwar U.S. policy of containing Moscow's expansionist appetite along the Eurasian rimland."[12]

Melvyn Leffler argues that a geopolitical sensibility permeated American policy making throughout the Cold War. He notes, for example, that a 1945 Joint Chiefs of Staff study expressed concern over Soviet domination of Eurasia. In 1948, a paper drafted by National Security Council staff concluded that Russian expansion "would be strategically and politically unacceptable to the United States." The paper, known as "NSC 20/4," was the first comprehensive review of American policy toward the Soviet Union, and showed Mackinder's influence:

> Between the United States and the USSR there are in Europe and Asia areas of great potential power which if added to the existing strength of the Soviets would enable the latter to become so superior in manpower, resources and territory that the prospect for the survival of the United States as a free nation would be slight.

The growth of geopolitics as a policy-making tool enhanced Walsh's status with the Truman administration, and explains why he was frequently asked to lecture on the topic to the military.[13]

HARRY S. TRUMAN AND THE RISE OF
THE NATIONAL SECURITY STATE

Between 1945 and 1950, American-Soviet relations moved from alliance to mutual apprehensiveness, and then to unequivocal antagonism. Roosevelt, who did not believe that a totalitarian government necessarily generated a totalitarian foreign policy, presumed that recovery rather than expansion would be Stalin's postwar priority. When he succeeded Roosevelt, Harry S. Truman had virtually no experience in foreign affairs; unlike Roosevelt, he "liked things in black and white." Truman considered Stalin a "world bully," who took advantage of American generosity at Yalta, but who might still be "brought around" if handled firmly. The 1946 Iranian crisis, which ended when Soviet troops withdrew from Iran in April, marked the beginning of Truman's "get tough" policy toward the Soviet Union.[14]

The Truman administration sought to determine an explanation for the sources of Soviet conduct. In the "Long Telegram" of February 22, 1946, George F. Kennan, a career foreign service officer stationed in Moscow, responded to the State Department's request for an interpretation of Stalin's motives. As Daniel Yergin explains, Kennan argued that Stalin was not ideologically motivated, but had to portray the West negatively to justify his rule. He also believed that the Soviets did not have the necessary strength for conquest, were in no hurry, and could be *contained by the adroit and vigilant application of counterforce at a series of constantly shifting geographical and political points.*" Although Kennan considered the Soviets impervious to reason, he regarded them as "highly sensitive to the logic of force," ready to "withdraw . . . when strong resistance is encountered at any point." Elaborated in a 1947 *Foreign Affairs* article under the pseudonym "X," Kennan's containment theory became, in Yergin's words, a "bible for American policymakers."[15]

As a result, Kennan became the foremost advocate of realism in American foreign policy. According to historian Richard Crockatt, the realist regards self-interest as the driving force in international relations. The nation-state pursues rationally conceived objectives, and conflicts of interests propel world affairs. No militarist, Kennan insisted that American efforts to ensure its own stability at home weakened the Soviets far more than preoccupation with an illusory military threat. In his memoirs, he berated the tendency "to divide the world neatly into Communist and 'free world' components . . . and to search for general formulas to govern our relations with one or the other." (Walsh, as will be shown later in this chapter, rebuked Kennan for failing to do just that.) If Roosevelt was too naive for Kennan, Truman was too fundamentalist.[16]

When Greece and Turkey faced the threat of communist takeover in 1947, and Great Britain could no longer provide them financial and military support, Truman gave his "All-out speech" to Congress on March 12, 1947, calling for 400 million dollars in aid to the two nations. In what became known as the "Truman Doctrine," the president declared that the world faced a choice between two "alternative ways of life." The first was

> based upon the will of the majority, and is distinguished by free institutions, representative government, free elections, guarantees of personal liberty, freedom of speech and religion, and freedom from political oppression. The second way of life is based upon the will of a minority forcibly imposed upon the majority. It relies upon terror and oppression, a controlled press and radio, fixed elections, and the suppression of personal freedoms.

Truman's successful appeal was a "declaration of Cold War" and announced America's new role as defender of the free world. Dean Acheson conceived its underlying premise, known as the "rotten apple" theory. Unless the United States used its power to curtail Soviet influence in one area, communism might spread from nation to nation.[17]

In a June 1947 Harvard commencement address, Secretary of State George C. Marshall proposed that America invest in the economic reconstruction of Europe. Fearing that economic breakdown might strengthen the Soviet communist appeal, the United States poured 17 billion dollars into Europe between 1948 and 1952. The bulk of the support went to key industrial nations, as opposed to those with large communist parties. The Marshall Plan both created an economic environment favorable to capitalism and integrated western Europe into an American-dominated alliance against Stalin.[18]

The Truman Doctrine, the Marshall Plan, Kennan's containment theory, and Acheson's "rotten apple" theory all contributed to accelerating the Cold War. In 1947, Congress passed the National Security Act, which incorporated all service branches into the Department of Defense, established the Air Force as its own branch, and created the Central Intelligence Agency and the National Security Council. To create a "preponderance of power" over the Soviets, the United States increased the level of production from 50 atomic bombs in 1948 to 300 in 1950. Although Truman and Acheson agreed with Kennan on the need to curtail Soviet expansion, they emphasized what Acheson termed "situations of strength." John Lewis Gaddis contends that Acheson, who succeeded Marshall as secretary of state in 1949, viewed strength "as almost an end in itself, not as means to a larger end."[19]

Walsh viewed the Truman Doctrine as "a collateral application of the principles established at Nuremberg," and praised Truman for recognizing communism as "the fountainhead of the spiritual and material menace threatening the present generation." This event marked a diplomatic turning point, as opposition to Soviet expansion became "a cardinal principle of American foreign policy." The rapid response of the United States to Britain's withdrawal from Greece and Turkey was "an index of awakened responsibility in high places." Walsh praised the Marshall Plan for its commitment to alleviate the economic distress that fomented the rise of communism.[20]

Taken together, Walsh saw the Truman Doctrine and the Marshall Plan as together disclosing "the slowly-forming will-power of the United States." Americans were beginning to grasp "the significance of the challenge to Western Civilization which Marxian Communism involves and they are fortifying their soul and mobilizing the physical resources to meet it."[21] The best response to this challenge, Walsh argued in a 1948 newspaper interview, was "demonstrable power controlled by conscience and respect for other people." Appeals to "moral instincts" were as useless in dealing with the Soviets as they had been with the Nazis. The only remaining alternative, he believed, was "the argument of strength justly and righteously employed."[22] Walsh's reasoned positions on this issue no doubt contributed to his appointment to the presidential advisory commission assigned to investigate the feasibility of a peacetime draft.

UNIVERSAL MILITARY TRAINING: A HISTORICAL OVERVIEW

In October 1945, addressing a joint session of Congress, Truman proposed a project for Universal Military Training (UMT), a program that would require one year of military training for all physically fit eighteen-year-olds. Comparing the enterprise to the pre-First World War Plattsburg movement, George Q. Flynn writes that UMT's goal was to produce a "reservoir of trained manpower" for future wars. Its implications for what many regarded as the "Prussianization" of American youth, however, soon raised strong opposition among a variety of groups as an unnecessary expansion of state power. In December 1946, Truman appointed a nine-person advisory commission to investigate the program's feasibility. The commission endorsed

UMT in a June 1947 report entitled "A Program for National Security." In March 1948, Truman appealed to Congress to implement his program; Congress declined, but allowed the Selective Service System to remain in place.[23]

Although John Lewis Gaddis contends that Truman promoted UMT "largely as a show of 'resolve' for the Russians," Michael Hogan considers it an integral part of Truman's national security program. According to Hogan, Truman saw national security as demanding constant readiness on the part of both civilians and the military. To meet the objections of those who considered the program undemocratic, Truman invoked the "citizen soldier" tradition of Revolutionary days. In citing a tradition that extended back to the roots of American democracy, he suggested that UMT could serve as a "program of moral renovation" for American youth.[24]

Opposition to UMT was strongest among religious organizations, pacifist groups, educators, labor, and agriculture, whose combined influence, according to Gaddis, kept UMT "from ever receiving serious consideration." American labor viewed the draft as a strikebreaking tool; legislators such as Senator Robert Taft saw it as an impractical alternative to increased air power. That America had never before had a peacetime draft helps explains the strong opposition it aroused. Nonetheless, Hogan concludes that the struggle over UMT was an "important chapter in the history of American state making, another attempt to forge the instruments of national security without creating a garrison state on the ruins of American democracy."[25]

In November 1944, the American bishops opposed passage of a compulsory military training bill "until after the end of the war and we know what the international situation will be." They argued instead for an extension of Selective Service to meet wartime needs. In November 1945, although recognizing "the need for preparedness," the NCWC advocated an investigation into ways of abolishing the draft worldwide, but indicated that it would accept a peacetime draft if "found necessary." The bishops advocated that military manpower needs be met, as much as possible, with voluntary enlistments. In the event of a peacetime draft, they asked that the military "work with recognized moral leadership to correct certain policies and attitudes which have wrought grave moral damage to great numbers of young people in the armed services during the past five years." The bishops' response to peacetime draft proposals reflected what Gerald Sittser has called "cautious patriotism." This caution also made their stance open to a variety of interpretations during the UMT debate.[26]

THE UMT COMMISSION: APPOINTMENTS AND OBJECTIONS

Realizing the extent of the popular opposition to UMT, the Truman administration sought means to answer the criticisms. In October 1946, Secretary of War Robert P. Patterson suggested that Truman appoint a commission composed of nine "civilians of outstanding caliber who are recognized authorities in the several fields of national interest involved." Secretary Patterson proposed that the commission include experts in the fields of international affairs, education, and law, and that it also be representative of women, religion, and labor. Such a commission's findings would be "an unimpeachable source," and would answer "the basic questions raised with regard to international relations, atomic warfare, interference with education and impact on the civil economy."[27]

Secretary Patterson suggested Walsh as a possible Catholic representative. In November, Truman asked Walsh, who willingly agreed. On December 20th, Truman announced the formation of an advisory commission, made up of "recognized authorities in their several fields who have the confidence of the American people," to examine both the need and feasibility for universal military training and to submit a report of their findings. In addition to Walsh, commission members included former presidential counsel Samuel I. Rosenman; public and industrial relations consultant Anna Rosenberg; Chicago attorney Truman K. Gibson Jr.; Harold W. Dodds, president of Princeton University; Karl T. Compton, president of the Massachusetts Institute of Technology; Charles E. Wilson, president of General Electric; Joseph E. Davies, former ambassador to the Soviet Union; and Daniel Polling, editor of the *Christian Herald*.[28]

Although the commission was intended to represent a wide variety of viewpoints, objections were immediately raised over its alleged pro-UMT bias. In January 1947, Professor Huston Smith of the University of Denver wrote Truman that, because five of its nine members had already declared their support for UMT, "it does not appear that this is a balanced committee." On the front page of its January 9, 1947 issue, under the headline "President Appoints Rubber Stamp Commission," the *Conscription News* described Walsh as a "former army instructor . . . sympathetic to conscription," and suggested that Truman had "carefully selected" him over the many Catholics who opposed conscription.[29]

Walsh's presence on the commission gave rise to strong objections among Catholics and non-Catholics alike. In January 1947, David Ludlow, a New Jersey architect, asked Truman why Walsh was selected when "the Catholic Church is strongly against conscription." Cassie Jane Winfrey of San Diego asked that Walsh, whose presence on the commission she held to be "a violation of Church and State," "be excluded from all contact, official or unofficial, with the War Department." "His policy-making activities." Winfrey declared, "[could] result in nothing but disaster for the United States and for civilization." Fred Geier asked Walsh to correct "the impression that [he was] speaking for all Catholics." James Mangan, an alumnus of Chicago's Loyola University, was amazed to see a Jesuit "endorsing Peacetime Conscription," and asked Walsh to "issue a release stating that [his] views are not necessarily the views of the Society of Jesus."[30]

American Catholics and UMT

Richard Gribble writes that American Catholics "on all sides rejected [the UMT] proposal." *America* called it a "dangerous experiment"; James M. Gillis called it "madness and a preliminary to national suicide." Patrick Scanlan, as anticommunist as ever, was unable to overcome his fears of "Prussianization" to endorse Truman's program; indeed, Father William J. Miller, S.J., president of the University of Detroit, denounced the program as "fascist." Yet, even though the American Catholic press generally opposed peacetime conscription, strong divisions appeared among the hierarchy, as mentioned earlier, and the NCWC wavered over issuing a public statement on the subject.[31]

In July 1947, William P. Montavon, director of the NCWC's Legislative Bureau, wrote Monsignor Walter Carroll, the conference's executive secretary, that the UMT commission had requested "an authoritative statement" from the conference. In September 1947, the Administrative Board approved a statement by the bishops "in the event that our views were asked for by the Congress." The bishops insisted that any conscription legislation be "temporary in character and designed to meet international emergency conditions"; that it include exemptions for clergy and theological students; and that it provide for the "moral, physical and religious welfare of the trainees." The bishops concluded with a plea for "eventual disarmament among nations and the cessation of military training."[32]

During the public debate over UMT, two American cardinals, Dennis P. Dougherty of Philadelphia and Francis J. Spellman, archbishop of New York and military vicar for the Armed Forces, expressed conflicting views on the subject. In what Margaret Reher calls "one of his rare public interventions," Dougherty opposed UMT, serving as honorary president of the National Council against Conscription. Although he did not object to "temporary wartime conscription," Dougherty considered "permanent peacetime conscription" to be "a radical departure from the American tradition" and "foreign to the ideals of democracy"; indeed, he saw UMT as a potential "occasion of moral ruin for untold thousands of our American youth." Furthermore, he insisted, peacetime conscription provoked rather than prevented war. "Why is peacetime military training bad for Germany," he asked, "and good for America?"[33]

For his part, Spellman, whom Gerald Fogarty describes as "the most influential American Catholic prelate of his age," publicly endorsed Truman's program. On March 17, 1948, Truman included UMT in a list of measures he submitted to Congress. That evening in New York, at a dinner for the Friendly Sons of Saint Patrick, Truman renewed his appeal. Spellman, who was also at the dinner, commented:

> I hate war. And it is because I hate war that I must put my trust in men who know better than I the dangers that beset America, and if these men, chosen by the vote and the confidence of the American people, believe that preparedness will prevent war, then I, who love my country better than I love my life, cast my vote, as a private American citizen, for universal military training.[34]

Although Donald Crosby has called him "the political leader of Catholic anticommunism," Spellman might more precisely be called "the most visible anticommunist in the American episcopate during the Cold War."[35]

The advisory commission was, in fact, biased in favor of Truman's program, and Walsh saw it as his role to persuade the public of its merits. He therefore attempted to interpret the hierarchy's statements in such a way as to justify UMT. During the commission's meetings, Walsh argued that the hierarchy's statements "substantially coincide" with the commission's recommendations, insisting that if "the international situation demands it, then [it] would not be opposed." Although the bishops had opposed the language of the previous UMT bills, he insisted that they had "very little opposition to the substance. . . . I don't think we could say that they were against the idea or the principles." Furthermore, he asserted, their previous statements on the subject left "the door wide open" for a pro-UMT interpretation. Walsh said that one bishop told him: "If the need be demonstrated, all right. [But] you have to demonstrate the need."[36]

"SOMETHING MORE THAN MERE WORDS"

Demonstrating the need was the commission's raison d'être. Between December 20, 1946 and April 12, 1947, the commission held twelve meetings at the White House. At the first meeting, Karl Compton was elected chairman; in his absence, Walsh served as acting chairman. Admitting he was "particularly sensitive to seeing people call us the New Nazis and the New Fascists," he noted that the American people had "never had conditions such as the British and the Germans had." "How would New York act," he asked, "how would Philadelphia act under that complete demoralization and disruption of all control that took place there? As I see it, it is precisely to forestall such a development that this program is chiefly designed."[37]

Western Europe, he would later say, stood at the crossroads between democracy and totalitarianism. Unless America showed a willingness to help, Europe might "be forced into a camp that it wouldn't want to go into." To those who argued that the Soviets were simply "bluffing," he retorted that their

bluff has succeeded to the extent of acquiring 270,000 square miles. That was done by military power, done by setting up governments and then holding them by power. So you don't persuade me about it being a bluff. . . . Unless you can back up your ideals and your hopes by something more than mere words, then the steam-roller goes on and on and on.[38]

Walsh viewed military training as a moral growth opportunity for directionless American youth who "breathe the air as if it were commonplace." The UMT program would make them appreciate what they had been given. He opposed any recompense for military service, however, calling the G.I. Bill "a huge national bonus." In a national emergency, military service was the obligation of every citizen, and he insisted that the government should not attempt to "buy the services of men to perform a civic duty." Walsh hoped that a nationwide program of military training for high school graduates might lead to a revival of the principles that pervaded the Federalist era. For Walsh, that period constituted "the golden days of American political thought," when freedom was "something that [Americans] were creating and not something handed to them on a platter, as we have received it."[39]

Walsh helped compile the sections of the advisory commission's report that dealt with the nation's spiritual and moral strength and with the international situation. The commissioners submitted their 445-page report to President Truman in May 1947. In sum, they recommended universal military training "as a wise and prudent investment in American security, liberty, and prosperity." "The only convincing reason for our affirmative decision," Walsh wrote a colleague in June 1947, "was national security in the present worsening situation." Walsh's participation highlighted his unique contribution to Catholic anticommunism during the early Cold War. Although Spellman also favored UMT, neither he nor any other Catholic anticommunist brought the kind of political expertise to the debate that Walsh possessed.[40]

On June 18, 1947, Walsh testified on behalf of UMT before the Senate Armed Services Committee. If "a reasonable psychology" prevailed in the world, he stated, the program would be unnecessary, but might was "the only argument" that worked with the Soviets. Modern warfare enlarged the "scope and extent of one's civil duties." As a result, national defense measures reached deeper into every community. "The belief that you can win over a totalitarian government with sweetness and light," he declared, "is a delusion that time is gradually uprooting." Walsh concluded that America "ran the same danger now as we did in 1939," but that Stalin was a far greater threat to world peace than Hitler had been. Michael Hogan places Walsh among those who argued that "America's democratic political identity and traditional values had to be adapted to its new responsibilities in an age of total war."[41]

The debate over universal military training has significant implications for the historian of American Catholic anticommunism. It is unfortunate that a debate that involved the two leading American prelates and prompted the wrath of many Catholics has been so neglected by scholars. Though Dougherty, Scanlan, and Gillis were every bit as anticommunist as Spellman, and though all agreed that Soviet communism posed a danger, they could not agree on an appropriate response. The issue of expanded federal power, in this case a peacetime draft, had implications that many of them were unwilling to confront. Even at the height of the Cold War, then, Catholic anticommunism was never a monolithic movement.[42]

Walter I. Giles, Walsh's secretary from 1944 to 1950, notes that whereas the Jesuit's anticommunism alienated him from the Roosevelt administration, it earned him Truman's great esteem. For Truman, Walsh served in two roles on the UMT advisory commission: Catholic spokesperson and expert on Soviet political theory and practice. In 1948, the president appointed Walsh to another panel, the Commission on Religion and Welfare in the Armed Forces; Walsh served as one of several consultants on American policy toward Germany for the State Department's Policy Planning Staff in September 1948, during George Kennan's tenure. He also served on the U.S. Merchant Marine Academy's Academic Advisory Board that same year. In 1950, he participated in a New York State Regents committee to recommend materials for studying communism. By then, Walsh was not only a prominent advocate of Truman's Soviet policy; he was also an active participant in the making of Cold War policy.[43]

GEORGETOWN AND THE COLD WAR

In October 1949, Walsh established the Institute of Languages and Linguistics as a department of the School of Foreign Service. Envisioned as an interdisciplinary project, the institute was to integrate language studies with cultural and geographical studies; its goal was "to train individuals to use languages as links and not as barriers between peoples." As such, it was a "natural evolution" of the school. At Nuremberg he recruited Colonel Leon Dostert, a 1928 School of Foreign Service graduate serving on Eisenhower's staff, to be the first director. Dostert had developed a foolproof system of simultaneous language translation involving a multichannel headphone system, which he first employed at Nuremberg and later at the United Nations. Under Dostert, Maggie Reichard Wolf writes, the institute "gained almost instant fame as the first of its kind in the Western world." Its establishment was a pivotal event as Georgetown "developed more and more as an international university."[44]

Under Walsh, the School of Foreign Service actively participated in the Cold War. In conjunction with the State Department, he wrote Justice Robert Jackson in November 1950, the school was offering intensive courses in American history, international law, and foreign relations to future German diplomats.[45] During that same year, Dostert made arrangements with the Air Force to send officers for specialized courses at the school. In October 1952, William S. Culbertson reported that, for the past two years, he had taught his "Psychological Warfare" course to between thirty and ninety Air Force officers every semester.[46] In January 1952, Walter Bedell Smith, director of the Central Intelligence Agency, thanked Walsh for assigning Dostert as a part-time consultant to the agency, and for Walsh's own "considerable and direct services in behalf of national defense."[47] In September 1952, at an Army War College lecture, Walsh expressed a "sense of privilege in having been permitted over many years to share in the defense of this country in the field that is permitted to me."[48]

Georgetown was not the only Jesuit university to have a close relationship with government authorities during the Cold War. In 1950, Father Thurston Davis, S.J., dean of Fordham College, established the Institute of Contemporary Russian Studies as an academic center. The Army Map Service and the CIA helped fund the institute's research activities, and its Russian-language program received federal aid through the National Defense Act. Although the institute closed in 1969, its existence demonstrates the extent to which Catholic higher education was an active participant in the Cold War. Ellen Schrecker, Lionel Lewis, and, indeed, most historians of the academy during the Cold War have focused on how McCarthyism affected the secular universities; Sigmund Diamond has explored the cooperation between Ivy League schools and government agencies in those years. With few exceptions, however, scholars have continued to neglect Catholic colleges and universities.[49]

THE ROAD TO NSC-68

By the summer of 1949, Daniel Yergin notes, Truman seemed to be emerging as the victor in the Cold War. Two events quickly and drastically altered this perception, however. In August, the Soviet Union successfully detonated its first atomic bomb. In October, Chinese communists under Mao Zedong overthrew Chiang Kai-shek's Nationalist regime. Cold War historian Lisle Rose writes that the combination of these events "produced soul-wrenching terror." Raymond Garthoff recalls that the breaking of the American nuclear monopoly "had a powerful psychological impact." American policy makers began to conclude that diplomatic accommodation with the Soviets was impossible. Frank Ninkovich writes that by the end of 1949, "Washington was beginning to shift its view on Soviet ideology away from Kennan's reassuring assertions that the Soviet leaders were realists."[50]

As a result, American foreign policy took a sharply militaristic turn that reached its climax in the Korean conflict. George Kennan resigned as director of the Policy Planning Staff in protest. Ninkovich contends that although an American nuclear monopoly had postponed the debate over how deeply Soviet leaders were committed to communism, an underlying belief always existed among policy makers that acquiring the bomb would immediately heighten Soviet aggression. Leffler argues that Truman wanted to maintain a "configuration of power in the international system that was preponderantly to America's advantage." In January 1950, Truman called for the development of the hydrogen bomb. Soon afterward, he asked his advisers to reexamine the national objectives in the Cold War.[51]

Kennan's successor, Paul Nitze, supervised the project, which resulted in the creation of National Security Council Document 68 (NSC-68), presented to Truman in April. NSC-68 provided the guidelines for the next generation of diplomats and foreign policy experts. Unlike Kennan, Nitze saw a fanatical ideology impelling Soviet expansionism, making conflict with the United States inevitable. He therefore recommended a rapid military buildup that included hydrogen bombs. In NSC-68, Richard Gid Powers writes, "the underlying issue of the cold war was the moral clash between the values of freedom and communism." Section 4 of NSC-68, for example, is entitled "The Underlying Conflict in the Realm of Ideas and Values between the U.S. Purpose and the Kremlin Design." Unlike Kennan's strategy, "NSC-68 thus aimed not at containing the Soviet system, but destroying it," writes Walter LaFeber.[52]

Walsh and the Militarization of American Foreign Policy

Although he did not have access to NSC-68, Walsh was familiar with the underlying principles that marked this shift in American foreign policy. He lauded "the new diplomacy of power, getting up our courage and talking in monosyllables to Russia." Addressing Washington's Cosmopolitan Club in 1951, he declared:

> It is no longer the style to shrug off Communist manifestoes and propaganda as intended for domestic consumption and not to be taken too seriously. I no longer hear the smooth palliations I once heard from a distinguished now deceased President of the United States in 1933 in his study in the White House: "Leave them to me, Father; I am a good horse trader."

For Walsh, the Roosevelt years were "days of great error," but he hoped that the "costly errors" of Yalta and Potsdam might serve as "lamps to our feet in the future."[53]

Since his return from Russia in 1924, Walsh had insisted there had been no basic change in Soviet aims. "All I have to do," he told a military audience in 1952, "is to change the date on my 1924 manuscript and give it to you in terms of 1952. There is no basic change whatsoever."[54] Walsh praised the American commitment to the Korean Conflict as "a turning point . . . in the growth to full stature of American leadership." The communists assumed "the United States had gone soft," but they soon learned that "America had not lost its soul." For Walsh, Korea was an opportunity for the United States to "dare to take the leadership for which the world is yearning." The time had arrived, he insisted, for the nation to exercise its "destined mission" of might "controlled by justice obedient to the eternal law." This mission included the use of atomic weapons.[55]

<h2 style="text-align:center">WALSH AND THE BOMB</h2>

Walsh believed that the Soviets would have atomic production capacity by 1950, after which point they would attack the United States. This belief led him to advocate what is known as the "first strike" principle in atomic warfare. In a May 1948 interview, Walsh stated that if the nation had evidence of a pending attack from Russia, it had the right to attack first as a self-defense measure. He argued, however, that American leaders needed strong "evidence and proof" of a direct threat. In June 1948, lecturing at the Industrial College of the Armed Forces, Walsh said: "Catholic theology, and I think any form of Protestant theology that I know of—Christian theology in general—in fact, the Natural Law gives any man the right of self-defense."[56]

Walsh's views on atomic warfare attracted greater notice as the Korean conflict escalated. On December 6, 1950, in response to a question during a lecture at Brown University, he stated: "I know of no moral conviction to force me to wait for an atomic bomb attack first. How a dead man can release an atomic bomb I do not know."[57] On December 24, 1950, Walsh elaborated his views in the *Washington Star*. The Soviets, he insisted, had been stockpiling atomic weaponry in preparation for an attack on the United States.

> Neither reason nor theology, nor morals, require men or nations to commit suicide by requiring that we must await the first blow from a power with no moral inhibitions and when, as in the case now under consideration, the attack would surely include bombardment by atomic missiles.

Walsh cited natural law in arguing that the state had the right "to repel an unjust aggressor by means reasonably adapted and proportionate to the nature of the attack." If the President had "moral certitude" of a pending attack, he would be morally justified in taking "defensive measures proportionate to the danger." Because he viewed the Soviet Union as inherently immoral, Walsh did not see certitude as a problem. The death of Russian civilians, he wrote, would be a "regrettable effect, not intended as such." The president's main intention was to prevent the Soviet Union from destroying the United States, as it had sworn to do. At the same time, Walsh stressed the "appalling responsibility" laid on the intelligence community to make sure that such an event was in the works. He concluded that Soviet protests of peaceful intentions were "only the actors' lines of a prepared script designed to distract the audience from an approaching Pearl Harbor."[58]

Walsh's article elicited strong responses. One Washingtonian wrote disgustedly: "If this is the true teaching of Christianity, I would prefer to be a heathen." The *Christian Century* called Walsh's article "shocking." Moral certitude was impossible, the editor argued, "and the pretense that it is possible opens the door to our own demoralization." If governments employed Walsh's approach, "the collapse of civilization" was ensured. The editorial concluded that Walsh's line of argument showed "how far the casuistry for which his order is noted can be carried."[59]

Walsh appears to have relied heavily on Saint Thomas Aquinas's theory of "double effect." According to Aquinas, if a person's action is directed toward a virtuous result, then the evil effects incurred are not morally imputable to that person. The evil effect of the action must not be willed in itself. In the September 1944 issue of *Theological Studies*, the Jesuit moral theologian John C. Ford had described how this line of reasoning (which he did not endorse) applied to obliteration bombing:

> The bombing has a good effect, the destruction of war industries, communications, and military installations leading to the defeat of the enemy; it also has an evil effect, the injuring and death of innocent civilians (and the destruction of their property). The damage to civilian life (and property) is not intentional; it is not a means to the production of a good effect, but is merely its incidental accompaniment.[60]

Walsh's stress on the end goal ignored the morality of the means employed, revealing his blindness toward the larger implications of atomic warfare—and the limits of Catholic idealism.

Throughout the 1940s, American Jesuits had debated the morality of atomic warfare. Although John Ford had accepted the "just war" theory, he had distinguished between the bombing of "well-defined military objectives" and obliteration bombing, which involved large residential areas. Ford had argued against double effect because "the alleged proportionate cause is speculative, future, and problematical, while the evil effect is definite, widespread, certain, and immediate." Wilfrid Parsons, former editor of *America*, had taken the opposite view. In 1947, as chairman of the Ethics Committee for the Catholic Association for International Peace (CAIP), Parsons had justified a retaliatory nuclear strike, but had not addressed its implications for the opposing civilian population, in an attempt, suggests William Au, to reconcile Catholic moral teaching with America's need to provide adequate military power in its own defense.[61]

Walsh's 1950 position, however, seems to have been unique among the American Jesuits at this time. Whereas Parsons had accepted a responsive attack, Walsh actually sanctioned preemptive nuclear measures against the Soviet Union. None of the intricate subtleties present in John Ford's argument appears to have troubled Walsh. Indeed, it might be said that his position on this issue was more akin to that of fundamentalist Protestant ministers than to that of his fellow Jesuits.

By 1950, Paul Boyer writes, "Cold War obsessions overrode earlier atomic fears." As a result, moral discourse on the bomb was muted, and the American peace movement went into a virtual coma. Catholic opinion on war and peace was highly divided. Boyer places Walsh among those religious leaders who during the early Cold War manifested "an increasing inclination to defend the moral legitimacy, under certain circumstances, of using atomic bombs." The CAIP, founded in 1928, supported the just war theory. In contrast, the *Catholic Worker* refused to accept military preparation as the "only way to defend human freedoms." The Redemptorist moral theologian Francis J. Connell declared that the atomic bomb did not ethically differ from cannons or rifles, whereas the Catholic pacifist Gordon C. Zahn argued the reverse.[62]

TOTAL EMPIRE: THE BOOK

Walsh's last book, *Total Empire*, was published in the summer of 1951. The first half of the book offers a critique of Soviet revolutionary theory. Even in 1950, he contended, the average American was "still slow" to grasp "the most formidable challenge since the barbarian hordes from the North overran the capital of embattled Rome during the twilight of the Empire." While the events of 1949–50 brought "a sudden awakening to the reality of the danger," he wrote, the Soviets had never displayed any "confusion or divided counsel." Soviet aims were consistent since 1917:

> The Revolution never relaxes though it has sometimes stumbled. It changes tactics and personnel but never renounces its program of planned chaos. It shifts gears and reduces speed but never loses direction or sight of its objectives. It gains or loses momentum but never changes its inner nature or renounces responsibility to itself. It substitutes new forms and places of attack but never relents in its conspiracy for world domination.[63]

As Walsh went on to explain, in forming his dialectical materialism, communism's underlying philosophy, Marx applied the nineteenth-century German philosopher Georg Wilhelm Friedrich Hegel's dialectics to the study of history to create a theory of class conflict as the driving force in human affairs. For Marx, revolution arose in response to the exploitation of the proletariat, and the ensuing clash produced a classless society. Lenin concretized Marxian theory in his revolutionary writings by combining a "certitude of intellect and fortitude of will" to make Hegelian dialectics a political reality.[64]

The second part of *Total Empire*, entitled "The Wasted Years," traced the evolution of a more aggressive foreign policy. Because moral appeals left the "Hegelians of Moscow cold and unresponsive," American military might had to reach a level where an aggressor "will think more than twice before provoking another devastating conflict." The main issue in the arms buildup was not the cost, but "the alternative possibilities," primarily a nuclear attack. Walsh again endorsed "first strike," arguing that total war extended the target zone to include "whole peoples as peoples." The United States government had "an obligation" to safeguard the lives of its citizens, especially when facing a "power with no moral inhibitions." He stressed the need for a high "measure of certitude" on the part of policy makers, concluding: "We are embarked on a kind of cosmic poker game for the highest stakes in history."[65]

Total Empire appeared at a time when the American public was increasingly apprehensive about the Soviet threat. In July, the book was listed as number 6 on the *Washington Star*'s nonfiction list, and as number 15 on the *New York Times* list for "general sales." Reviewer Mikhail Koriakov in the *New York Times*, though noting its inaccuracies, unsubstantiated generalizations, and "unconvincing" historical parallels, nonetheless considered *Total Empire* a "timely book." In January 1952, the Catholic Writers Guild presented Walsh its award for the best nonfiction book. Although, in its reliance on polemical over scholarly argumentation, *Total Empire* has not held up over the years, either as history or as political science, it must be again remembered that Walsh wrote as an activist attempting to persuade the public of the Soviet threat.[66]

1950: THE RISE OF JOSEPH McCARTHY

The popular reception of Walsh's last book provides an indication of how anticommunism had taken on new strength in American life after 1945. Domestic anticommunism experienced a rebirth in 1945 when Mississippi Congressman John Rankin resurrected the House Un-American Activities Committee (HUAC), whose purpose was to investigate "the extent, character and objects of un-American propaganda activities in the United States." In 1947, Truman's Executive Order 9835 initiated an anticommunist purge of the executive branch that was duplicated at other levels of government. The 1947 Taft-Hartley Act required union officials to sign an anticommunist affidavit; individual unions conducted their own purges. In October 1949, eleven members of the CPUSA national board were found guilty under the 1940 Smith Act of advocating the violent overthrow of the U.S. government. Between 1946 and 1956 in New York City, 379 teachers and professors lost their positions as a result of alleged Communist affiliations.[67]

In July 1948, the HUAC launched an investigation of Alger Hiss, president of the Carnegie Endowment for International Peace. A prominent New Dealer and former State Department official who had been with Roosevelt at Yalta, Hiss was charged with spying for the Soviets. Whittaker Chambers, a former member of the CPUSA and a self-confessed spy, declared that Hiss had passed secret government documents to him during the 1930s. On January 21, 1950, Hiss was convicted of perjury and sentenced to five years' imprisonment. The Hiss case highlighted the spreading fear of domestic subversion.[68]

Domestic and international anticommunism intersected in 1950 as Joseph R. McCarthy raised antiradical fears to a fever pitch. Elected to the Senate from Wisconsin in 1946, McCarthy attracted little notice until he opted to focus on the communist issue. On February 9, 1950, he inaugurated the era of "McCarthyism" with an address before the Republican Women's Club of Wheeling, West Virginia: "I have here in my hand a list of 205—a list of names that were known to the Secretary of State as being members of the Communist Party and who nevertheless are still working and shaping policy in the State Department." McCarthyism did not arise out of a vacuum. The Hiss and Smith Act cases, the loss of China to the communists, and the various exposés by HUAC were all significant factors that contributed to its growth. Richard Gid Powers writes that McCarthy's lists made him "the most feared man in America."[69]

McCarthy initiated a four-year reign of fear unprecedented in American history. In late 1953, as chairman of the Senate Committee on Government Investigations and the Permanent Subcommittee on Investigations, he launched an inquiry into subversive activity within the U.S. Army. By then, many Americans came to view his charges as containing more form than substance. During the Army-McCarthy hearings, his political credibility was weakened when the Army charged McCarthy and his chief counsel, Roy Cohn, with seeking privileges for G. David Schine, a member of McCarthy's committee recently drafted into the Army. In December 1954, the Senate officially censured McCarthy for contemptuous and denunciatory behavior, a move that proved the coup de grâce to his political career—and the sunset of American anticommunism.[70]

WALSH, McCARTHY, AND THE COLONY DINNER OF 1950

On January 7, 1950, Walsh had attended a dinner at Washington's prestigious Colony Restaurant arranged by Georgetown professor Charles Kraus, who invited attorney William A. Roberts and Senator McCarthy. On March 14, journalist Drew Pearson, writing in the *Washington Post*, had accused Walsh of planting the seeds of McCarthyism during the dinner. As Pearson related the story, McCarthy had wanted a catching theme for his reelection campaign. Among the topics that McCarthy's dinner companions suggested were seaway projects and pension plans, neither of which had interested him. Finally, Walsh had told McCarthy that "any Senator who consistently attacked Communism would have a great appeal for the voters." Acting on Walsh's advice, McCarthy had then delivered his notorious speech at Wheeling. Pearson's source for the story was most likely Roberts, who occasionally represented Pearson and who, Tyler Abell writes, also served as a "source of news leaks."[71]

In May 1950, without naming Walsh, Pearson had written that several Georgetown Jesuits, "acting unofficially and as individuals," were advising McCarthy. In November 1951, he had repeated his charges: "Originally, McCarthy got his Communist purge idea from a Catholic professor at Georgetown University, Father Edmund A. Walsh." The story had spread rapidly. *The Churchman* had written in 1951 that McCarthy "only fires the guns that are made for him by Father Edmund Walsh, S.J." The *Christian Century* had offhandedly referred to Walsh as McCarthy's adviser. In June 1953, journalist I. F. Stone had written that McCarthy "has had the guidance of Father Walsh." Donald Crosby notes that Pearson's tale "soon became an accepted part of McCarthy lore."[72]

"The debate over whether the 'Colony dinner' actually ever occurred—or whether it occurred as Drew Pearson reported it—has spawned an interesting literature in its own right," writes Mark Massa in *Catholics and American Culture*. Thomas C. Reeves, McCarthy's most sympathetic biographer, though acknowledging that the Pearson story "has been accepted by virtually every historian since," concludes that the "significance of the event . . . has been magnified greatly." Even a scholar as sympathetic to Walsh as Richard Gid Powers assumes that McCarthy "often consulted the Georgetown Jesuits like Edmund Walsh who were bulwarks of Catholic anticommunism."[73]

In the first published work on the senator, *McCarthy: The Man, the Senator, the "Ism,"* which appeared in 1952, authors Jack Anderson and Ronald W. May wholeheartedly endorsed Drew Pearson's account. This is not surprising, considering that Anderson worked on Pearson's staff from 1947 to 1969. Because the book was the first to address McCarthyism, scholars have tended to treat it as a primary source. Many scholars, including Robert Griffith and James Chace, have accepted the story wholeheartedly. Others, such as Richard Fried, accept the Pearson account, but argue that McCarthy was already an active anticommunist before the dinner. Still others, such as Robert Ingalls in his 1981 biography of McCarthy, trace McCarthyism to the Colony dinner but do not mention Walsh. In one form or another, then, the Colony dinner story has entered the canon of Cold War historiography.[74]

Although Louis Gallagher does not mention McCarthy in his biography of Walsh, another Jesuit scholar, Donald Crosby, provides the most complete and responsible assessment of the Walsh-McCarthy connection in his 1978 study of McCarthy and American Catholicism, Noting that Walsh never wrote or spoke about McCarthy in public, Crosby asserts that Walsh privately bet Pearson one thousand dollars he could not prove the Colony dinner story. Pearson ignored the challenge. In Crosby's account, Walsh most likely thought a public response would only "glorify Pearson's story." His refusal to answer Pearson's charges, however, lent credence to the growing conviction that Walsh had instigated McCarthy's anticommunism and attendant rise to national prominence.[75]

That the two met is beyond doubt, Crosby insists, and that they discussed communism is more than likely. He points out, however, that Walsh did not make it a practice to coach politicians, and it is doubtful he would have made an exception in the case of a little-known junior senator from the Midwest; indeed, notes Crosby, this would have been "completely out of character for him." At the same time, it is easy to understand why Pearson's account could have gained such widespread credence. The idea of a priest—especially one the late Monsignor George Higgins described as "almost the symbol of clerical anticommunism in Washington"—inspiring an Irish Catholic senator to mount an anticommunist crusade made sense to many. Nonetheless, Crosby concludes, "future historians would do well to consign it to the oblivion it has long deserved."[76]

Recent scholarship tends to support Crosby's analysis. Thomas Reeves argues that McCarthy was on the anticommunist bandwagon long before he met Walsh. Foreign service school historian Seth Tillman points out that "all that can be stated with reasonable certitude is that the dinner took place, that the participants discussed the politics of anti-communism, and that a month later, on February 9, Senator McCarthy made his notorious accusation." More tellingly,

Tillman finds no evidence of further contact between the two after the dinner; he also notes that Walsh's main interest was international communism, not domestic subversion. Arthur Herman, McCarthy's most recent biographer, concurs with Tillman on this point. Like Crosby, Herman concludes that Pearson's story "has no . . . basis in hard fact."[77]

There are other reasons why Walsh would have had little to do with McCarthy. Walsh never engaged in McCarthy's populist brand of political activity. Whereas McCarthy painted himself as the champion of the common man, Walsh never made any pretenses in this direction. Furthermore, by January 1950, Walsh was a Washington celebrity; he had no need to cultivate the favor of an unknown politician with whom he shared few interests. Indeed, of the four attendees at the Colony dinner, the person most familiar to the public eye in January 1950 was Edmund A. Walsh.[78]

Only once did Walsh venture into the field of domestic anticommunism, and then only when asked. In November 1950, at the request of the FBI, Walsh reviewed Max Lowenthal's *The Federal Bureau of Investigation* for the *Washington Post*. Hoover wanted a reviewer to publicly refute Lowenthal's account, which had been touted as a "scathing historical study of the bureau." Walsh attacked the Lowenthal book as an "an indictment" that smeared the bureau as a menace to civil liberties. "It will take some tall persuading," Walsh commented, "to get such a verdict from the American people." The book's sole merit, he wrote, was as "a quick reference manual for all hostile elements, foreign and domestic, who seek ammunition for destroying confidence in one of our most trusted security agencies." Hoover thanked Walsh for helping to "unmask the real and sinister motive behind the book."[79]

WALSH AND KENNAN: THE DEBATE THAT NEVER WAS

The international scene was still Walsh's main concern. On July 27, 1952, he spoke at Colgate University's Conference on American Foreign Policy, an event attended by over one hundred government officials and foreign dignitaries. In "The Spiritual Aspect of Foreign Policy," his most complete treatment of the subject, and one that affirmed his position as the leading Catholic idealist, Walsh reminded

American policy makers that they faced a conflict "between spirit and ideals on the one hand, and armed materialism on the other." The "real challenge" they faced was to make "confidence in our American heritage" and reliance on the "spiritual faith entrusted to Christendom . . . the anchor of stability for the West." The Cold War was not limited to Korea, he asserted. Because it involved "two interpretations of man's nature and ultimate destiny," conflict would occur "wherever men exist and the Communist agitator appears."[80]

In the Soviet philosophy, human beings had "no spiritual character or immortal destiny." That such a philosophy should exist in any nation was bad enough, but the Soviets wanted to extend their system worldwide. At the same time, Walsh declared that a rising secularism in the West contributed to the growth of communism.

> The wanton flirting with irreligion during the exuberant naturalism of the 19th century; the excesses of the Industrial Revolution, with its neglect of social justice; the arrogance of cold rationalism; the scepticism of shallow thinkers in a position to influence public opinion; the joyful sniping at moral values from academic chairs

encouraged men and women to have "faith in nothing—except in the impossibility of faith in anything." In stark contrast, however, the communists "never lost confidence in their own brand of certitude."[81]

Walsh then directed his attack toward realism in American foreign policy, particularly as it was manifested in George F. Kennan's 1951 book, *American Diplomacy, 1900–1950.* Walsh charged Kennan with minimizing the moral element in international relations. Kennan seemed to deny that "state behavior is a fit subject for moral judgement." Although he acknowledged that self-interest played some part at every level of statecraft, Walsh accused Kennan of overemphasizing this factor and of implying that "there is no place for the concept of right and wrong in judging the actions of a sovereign state." Such a view, he asserted, was "in flat contradiction to the public policy expressed by a long line of American presidents, statesmen and secretaries of state." Citing the Nuremberg proceedings, he argued that "observance of the moral law . . . has been a constant theme in American state papers." Walsh concluded by "publicly asking Mr. Kennan what he means by now arguing that Stalin is not subject to the moral laws of the whole human race?"[82]

In the summer of 1952, Kennan was in Moscow, serving as ambassador to the Soviet Union. On August 2, Charles E. Bohlen, counselor for the State Department, enclosing a copy of Walsh's address, wrote Kennan that "Father Walsh at Colgate's conference on American foreign policy took issue with some of the statements in your book concerning the use of moral judgements, etc. in international affairs," and that Walsh had told him "with great regret he felt compelled to take issue with you on this moral question." Bohlen acknowledged that Kennan's stance on morality "has caused considerable comment and may be subject to the interpretation Walsh puts on it." Fortunately, he noted, the press did not pursue this topic and there was "no public controversy over the matter."

After reading Walsh's address, Kennan prepared a letter to the *New York Times* refuting Walsh's charges. Bohlen, however, advised him against sending it. To tackle a subject "involving so much theology and metaphysics as that of moral law would raise considerable controversy in church and other circles here." Kennan chose to follow Bohlen's advice, thereby avoiding a debate. Walsh, notes Kennan's biographer David Mayers, emerged as one of Kennan's earliest critics:

> Since the early 1950's, when Father Edmund Walsh took Kennan to task for his statement at Chicago that the United States ought not make itself into a slave of international law and morality, various critics have charged him with believing that there is no concept of right and wrong in judging the actions of independent states—except in making Machiavellian determinations about expediency.[83]

"THE UNITED NATIONS, IN ITS TRUE SENSE"

In addressing the spiritual aspect of foreign policy to a military audience in 1948, Walsh declared:

> I think I may say I am a member of one of the oldest peace organizations in the world; a member of the United Nations, in its true sense. Therefore, anything that can affect the peace of the world is of very great interest—and should be—to the spiritual powers as well as to the material and the political.

In August 1952, Walsh reserved the right "to criticize severely when in my opinion public policy seems to me to be counter to the best wishes of the United States." Although he was clearly a conservative,

Walsh never publicly identified with a political party. When asked whether he was a Democrat or a Republican, he replied that the question was irrelevant because, as a resident of the District of Columbia, he was ineligible to vote.[84]

Clarifying the Church's role in the Cold War in a sermon at New York's Saint Francis Xavier Church in October 1951, Walsh explained that, because the Church, "with the wisdom of age-long experience," realized that material power alone was insufficient in the present struggle, it concentrated on "the spiritual strengthening of man's intellect, man's will and man's faith." Over the centuries, it had seen many "many a totalitarian Caesar" come and go. In a rare triumphalist statement, Walsh asserted:

> Caesar has often put his booted heel on what he fondly hoped was the corpse of Christianity only to have the immortal one arise and chant a requiem for the tyrant's soul when his little hour has run out. That is why Moscow hates the Catholic Church and fears it too.

In strengthening America's spiritual resolve, the Church helped bolster democracy worldwide.[85]

Walsh's anticommunism was ecumenical. In May 1951, Walsh and Daniel A. Polling, who served together on the UMT advisory commission, delivered a joint radio address over the Mutual Broadcasting System. The topic of their address was "Faith to Meet the Present Danger." Citing the work of military chaplains, Walsh noted that this was not the first time "a Baptist minister and a Catholic priest have stood shoulder to shoulder in common defense of our American heritage." For both Walsh and Polling, communism struck "deep at the heart of our common Christian heritage." The Cold War was not just a military threat, but a "deeply human menace that affects all men." They therefore called for a mobilization of the nation's spiritual and moral resources, no less than its military resources.[86]

Walsh and Catholic-Protestant Relations

In April 1952, the Georgetown University community formally celebrated Walsh's golden jubilee in the Society of Jesus. In May, commenting on media coverage of the event, the *Christian Century* asked whether any other Roman Catholic—legislator, cabinet member, Supreme Court justice, cardinal, layman—has had an influence on the policy of the United States government since World War I to compare with the head of the Georgetown University School of Foreign Service.

In January of the year before, the *Century* had written: "Father Walsh is believed by many observers of the Washington scene to have more influence than any other Roman Catholic in the national capital." Recognizing the school's success in training and placing future diplomats, the *Century* had asked then why "American Protestantism has been content to leave in Jesuit hands this educational opportunity at the national capital." Continued indifference in this area, it had warned, "could become virtual default on Protestantism's part."[87]

The postwar years saw a heightening of Protestant-Catholic tensions, the result of growing pains as the United States moved from being a Protestant-oriented society to a nation of recognized religious pluralism and, more particularly, the result of Catholic lobbying for federal aid to parochial schools, Catholic prominence in the anticommunist movement, and the debate over an American embassy to the Vatican. The creation of Protestants and Other Americans United for the Separation of Church and State (POAU) in 1948 was clear evidence that Catholics were gaining a nationwide influence equal to that of Protestantism. And where anti-Catholicism of the 1920s had been dominated by reactionary Protestants with little or no ecclesiastical training, postwar anti-Catholicism emanated from Protestants of all backgrounds, liberal and conservative, led by well-trained clergy and educated laypersons.[88]

The preeminent postwar anti-Catholic was an ordained minister and distinguished civil servant, Paul Blanshard, whose 1949 book *American Freedom and Catholic Power* almost immediately sold out its first printing and was a best seller for six months. Mark Massa writes that, although Blanshard's "classically liberal fears" envisioned a Catholic laity that was overly acquiescent to "Rome's hegemonic designs," many American Catholics entered the middle-class mainstream with great ease during the postwar years, a development Blanshard failed to recognize. Characterizing Blanshard's dichotomy between laity and hierarchy as "unduly simplistic," Massa argues that the bishops manifested a similar receptivity to the surrounding culture. Blanshard never referred to Walsh directly, but Walsh's public prominence undoubtedly fueled his anxiety, and may have contributed more significantly to Protestant-Catholic tensions than has been previously assumed.[89]

ILLNESS AND DEATH

On November 15, 1952, a testimonial dinner sponsored by Georgetown's alumni association at the Mayflower Hotel celebrated Walsh's golden jubilee. Among the 462 guests were diplomats, business leaders, clergy, military personnel, educators and members of the press. Seated on the dais were three bishops, four generals, three university presidents, six ambassadors and eight judges. E. D. Merrill, president of the Washington Board of Trade, thanked Walsh in the name of the business community for "spreading the American way of life." General J. Lawton Collins, U.S. Army Chief of Staff, presented Walsh a Certificate of Appreciation from the Army. Archbishop Amleto G. Cicognani, the Apostolic Delegate, congratulated Walsh on behalf of Pope Pius XII, praising "the great deeds of his life," particularly his establishing the School of Foreign Service. This occasion clearly marked the apogee of Edmund A. Walsh's career.[90]

The same occasion, however, would also mark the end of Walsh's career. "During my speech at the dinner," he wrote John Parr in December 1953, "I realized that I was not well. I was perspiring constantly and my heart thumping like a bass drum." Walsh had, in fact, suffered a slight stroke, one that was "inevitable," the doctors at the Georgetown University Hospital had told him, "because of the heavy schedule [he had] always carried." Over the next year, Walsh, diagnosed with severe arteriosclerosis, would endure subsequent strokes, although, in December 1954, while living at Georgetown's Faculty Infirmary, he still hoped to return to work, and even contemplated writing a biography of Lenin.[91]

Walsh was what would today be called a "workaholic," who often went to his office late in the evening. Indeed, as his secretary, Walter Giles, recounts, Walsh "did much of his work from 11 or 12 at night to about 5 A.M., and would sleep a few hours in the morning." According to Gallagher, Walsh had a "habit of extending his workday into the early hours of the approaching dawn"; it was therefore no surprise to him that Walsh "finally succumbed to exhaustion under a burden of overwork." Walsh once told Georgetown alumnus William McKevitt that "he didn't become passably intelligent until midnight."[92]

In June 1955, Walsh was appointed "Regent Emeritus of the School of Foreign Service," but he continued to be listed as "Vice President of the University." Father Frank Fadner, a graduate of the London School of Economics, succeeded Walsh as regent. Father William F. Maloney, Walsh's Provincial, thanked him for bringing "national and international prestige to the University," praising him as "a magnificent son of Saint Ignatius." The *Washington Post* commented that Walsh's official retirement "marks the end of an era for this important institution." The *Washington Star* wrote that Walsh's name was so closely connected with Georgetown that "it is hard to think of him as being separated from it."[93]

Walsh died on October 31, 1956, three weeks after his seventy-first birthday. The *New York Times* called him "a long-time leader in the fight against world communism"; the *Washington Post* credited him with having "a powerful influence on American diplomatic thinking" and mourned the loss of "a beloved educator and friend": the Washington *Times-Herald* recalled Walsh as one of the District's "most familiar and certainly . . . one of its most influential figures." The Washington *Catholic Standard* ascribed Walsh's success to his "application of the Faith to the problems of national and international scope." *America* provided what was perhaps the most fitting eulogy to Walsh's career:

> Priest, author, lecturer, administrator, diplomat, director in 1922 of the Papal Relief Mission to Russia, consultant at the Nuremberg trials, organizer of Georgetown's Institute of Languages and Linguistics—his life was a litany of achievements.[94]

CONCLUSION

Walsh's career provides a useful perspective for examining the larger history of American anticommunism. During the years examined in this chapter, anticommunism reached its high-water mark, moving into the mainstream of American political life. For nearly thirty years, Walsh had lectured and written extensively on Soviet communism, its philosophy and its goals. By 1952, it is no exaggeration to say that he was probably the best-known Catholic anticommunist in the United States. In publicly challenging Kennan's realism, Walsh cemented his status as the foremost American Catholic idealist. As Walter Giles had observed: "Seldom has the cliché—'a legend in his own time'—been truer than it was of Edmund Walsh."[95]

Walsh lauded America's newfound role as leader of the free world, stressing the nation's obligation to provide a model of virtuous government for the international community. In doing so, the nation had to struggle against secularizing trends and reaffirm the moral element in civic and international life. This new role, he argued, would inevitably lead to a showdown with Soviet Russia, whose goal was to eradicate the Christian and democratic principles underpinning American life. Although many Catholic leaders advocated an aggressive Soviet policy, only Walsh did so from the perspective of an accomplished geopolitical scholar and expert on Soviet political theory, as his work with the UMT advisory commission shows.

Drew Pearson's account of the Colony dinner has overshadowed all other aspects of Walsh's career, leading scholars to overlook the significant role he played in Catholic anticommunism during the early Cold War. Even at the height of the anticommunist consensus, Catholic anticommunism was never a united movement, as evidenced in the debates over peacetime conscription and atomic warfare. Furthermore, Walsh's activity was only one aspect of a complex and multilayered movement. Where John Cronin emphasized communism's domestic manifestations, Fulton Sheen addressed its philosophical implications, and Walsh focused on its international aspect. And however much Dorothy Day and Patrick Scanlan agreed that communism was a threat, they had little else in common. These differences should compel historians of Catholic anticommunism to reexamine long-held assumptions.[96]

In 1964, identifying insecurity as the driving force in American anticommunism, Richard Hofstadter, professor of history at Columbia University, contended that American anticommunists sought to prove their Americanism and achieve insider status. Hofstadter's contention is amply supported by how historians have treated Catholic anticommunism. David Caute, for example, suggests that the Cold War brand of "high-proof superpatriotism" offered Catholics the chance to be good Americans. In his study of Cold War Brooklyn, Francis Henry Touchet contends that Cold War anticommunism gave

Catholics "a golden opportunity to join the great consensus and achieve Americanization," although Kathleen Centola berates those same Catholics for their "irrational preoccupation with Communism."[97]

As his career eloquently attests, however, Walsh's anticommunism was anything but an expression of insecurity. A longtime political insider in Washington, Walsh had no need to prove his Americanism, and status anxiety played no role in his career. Rather, his anticommunism was an expression of confidence that grew out of his attempt to bring Catholic principles to bear in the field of international relations. Although minority consciousness certainly played a significant role for many Catholic anticommunists, to argue that they were all so motivated is to ignore the complexity of the anticommunist impulse in mid-twentieth-century American Catholicism.

Epilogue

Walsh's strokes removed him from the public arena just as Catholic anticommunism was reaching its high-water mark. By 1954, Mark Massa writes, "a deep fissure" had emerged among Catholics over Joseph McCarthy, his aims, and his tactics.[1] Although many Catholics supported the senator, Catholic endorsement was never unanimous.[2] Division appeared in the Catholic press: *Our Sunday Visitor* and the Brooklyn *Tablet* supported McCarthy, whereas *Commonweal* and *America* condemned him as irresponsible and reckless. In the Senate, Dennis Chavez of New Mexico, a Catholic, led the opposition to his Wisconsin colleague. In April 1954, within days of one another, Cardinal Francis Spellman publicly endorsed McCarthy, and Chicago Auxiliary Bishop Bernard J. Sheil denounced him.[3]

In the wake of his censure by the Senate in December 1954, McCarthy descended into obscurity as rapidly as he had ascended to fame. His excesses, and those of his followers, had thoroughly discredited any legitimate contentions anticommunists may have had. As a result of the Army-McCarthy hearings, Richard Gid Powers notes, liberal anticommunists began to move away from the anticommunist consensus that had characterized the early Cold War. By the time Barry Goldwater ran for president in 1964, anticommunism had come to be associated with right-wing extremism, a stereotype that Goldwater himself found hard to shake. Furthermore, the extreme hysteria of right-wing organizations such as the John Birch Society helped contribute to anticommunism's increasingly disreputable public image.[4]

The 1960s marked the beginning of what Powers calls American Catholicism's "long goodbye to anticommunism." John F. Kennedy's election to the presidency, which overturned many long-held assumptions regarding what it meant to be an American Catholic, was an important factor in this decline. Even more influential was the pontificate of John XXIII, which redefined the Church's relationship with the modern world. In his 1961 encyclical *Mater et Magistra*,

John wrote that colonialism was a bigger problem than communism, prompting the rising conservative Catholic spokesman William F. Buckley to remark: "Mater si, Magistra no!" By then, anticommunism had ceased to be a unifying element for the American Catholic community.[5]

With the Second Vatican Council and the social upheaval of the 1960s, anticommunism became less of a priority for American Catholics. Other issues came to the forefront, chief among them poverty, race, war, and renewal of the Church. Although fewer Catholics embraced anticommunism with the fervent enthusiasm of earlier years, Catholics continued to compose a high percentage of anticommunists.[6] Patrick Allitt notes that Catholic laypersons such as William F. Buckley and Michael Novak played a fundamental role in shaping the conservative intellectual movement from the 1950s through the 1980s, although theirs was but one of many Catholic voices. "In 1950," writes Allitt, "the U.S. Catholic Church spoke with one voice and regarded itself as a homogeneous body. By 1970 even the appearance of unanimity had vanished."[7]

By the late 1960s, the American hierarchy assumed an increasingly prophetic voice on issues of war and peace. In "Human Life in Our Day" (1968), the bishops began to question the morality of American military involvement in Southeast Asia. In 1971, their "Resolution on Southeast Asia" denounced the Vietnam War.[8] The 1983 letter of the American Bishops, "The Challenge of Peace," argued that anticommunism was not a fit reason for the use of nuclear weapons: "In simple terms, we are saying that good ends (defending one's country, protecting freedom, etc.) cannot justify immoral means (the use of weapons that kill indiscriminately and threaten whole societies)." By then American Catholic anticommunism had ceased to have any kind of institutional basis.[9]

Although it is impossible to predict how Walsh would have reacted to these changes, it is fair to say that his brand of anticommunism would have made little sense to a subsequent generation. This may help explain why he was forgotten so quickly. Thus to argue that American democracy and Catholicism were mutually reinforcing would not have elicited the same response in 1970 that it did in 1950. Indeed, in 1983, the American bishops directly refuted the arguments that underscored Walsh's endorsement of nuclear warfare, saying that anticommunism was no longer a sufficient rationale. His depiction of the Christian-communist conflict in black and white terms would not have held the same urgency at a time when John XXIII was calling for dialogue between Marxists and Christians. His stress on Christendom would have made little sense in the breakdown of the neo-Scholastic consensus that characterized 1960s Catholicism.[10]

There would never be another Catholic anticommunist like Edmund A. Walsh. No other American Catholic leader in the twentieth century would achieve his status as an expert on Soviet communism and geopolitics, or as an advocate of idealism in American foreign policy. His true significance was not as a scholar, where his legacy is scant, but as an anticommunist activist, an organizer of international relief work, and an educational pioneer. In the words of Georgetown professor Carroll Quigley, writing in 1959:

> Father Walsh was a man of action rather than a scholar. I do not mean that he was not a scholar, for he was constantly thinking, planning, and organizing with a remarkably quick and able mind. But I do mean he was never satisfied merely with thought or merely with words. . . . Thus he was a man of action and as such a leader. In any group, he became, almost at once, the center of attention and of decision.[11]

Walsh's successor as regent of the School of Foreign Service, Father Frank Fadner, S.J., called him a "storybook Jesuit."[12] His story is an important chapter in the history of Catholic anticommunism in the United States, one that has been overlooked for far too long.

NOTES

For the sake of conciseness in second and subsequent instances, the following abbreviations have been used to cite works in the notes:

ARAC   American Relief Administration Collection, Bakhmeteff Archive, Rare Book and Manuscript Collection, Columbia University, New York

ARAP   American Relief Administration Papers, Herbert Hoover Presidential Library, Long Branch, Iowa

CFP   Charles Fahy Papers, Library of Congress, Manuscript Division, Washington, D.C.

Diary   Diary of Edmund A. Walsh, S.J., kept during his earlier years in Europe (1912–14), Edmund A. Walsh, S.J., Papers (see EAWP)

EAWP   Edmund A. Walsh, S.J., Papers, Lauinger Library, Special Collections Division, Georgetown University, Washington, D.C.

FBI File   U.S. Federal Bureau of Investigation, "Subject: Edmund A. Walsh," file 62–32073, sec. 1 (in possession of Patrick J. McNamara)

Fish Committee U.S. House of Representatives, Special Committee to Investigate Communist Activities in the United States, 71st Cong., 2nd sess., part 1

GUA   Georgetown University Archives, Lauinger Library, Special Collections Division, Georgetown University, Washington, D.C.

GUSFS   Georgetown University School of Foreign Service

JEDP   Joseph E. Davies Papers, Library of Congress, Manuscript Division, Washington, D.C.

JHOP   John H. Ohly Papers, Harry S. Truman Presidential Library, Independence, Mo.

LJGP   Louis J. Gallagher, S.J. Papers, Archives of the New England Province of the Society of Jesus, College of the Holy Cross, Worcester, Mass.

NCWCF   National Catholic Welfare Conference Files, Archives of The Catholic University of America, Washington, D.C.

Neutrality Hearings   U.S. Senate Committee on Foreign Relations, *Neutrality, Peace Legislation, and Our Foreign Policy: Hearings,* 76th Cong., 1st sess., part 1

Nuremberg Diary   Private writings and correspondence of Edmund A. Walsh, S.J., during his stay at Nuremberg (1945–46; no. 1 = May 1945; no. 2 = August–November 1945; no. 3 = November 1945–October 1946), Edmund A. Walsh, S.J., Papers (see EAWP)

OF-FDR   Official Files, Franklin Delano Roosevelt Presidential Library, Hyde Park, N.Y.

OF-HST   Official Files, Harry S. Truman Presidential Library, Independence, Mo.

OGSSF-NCWCF   Office of the General Secretary Subject Files, National Catholic Welfare Conference Files (see NCWCF)

P-SA   Parr-Smith Archive, Lauinger Library, Special Collections Division, Georgetown University, Washington, D.C.

PACUT   Presidential Advisory Commission on Universal Training (December 1946–May 1947)

PC   Provincial's Correspondence, Archives of the Maryland Province of the Society of Jesus, Roland Park, Md.

PPF   President's Personal File

PRCQ   Permission Required to Cite or Quote

RG 59   Record Group 59 (Records of the Department of State Relating to the Internal Affairs of Russia and the Soviet Union), National Archives, General Records of the Department of state, College Park, Md.

RHJP   Robert H. Jackson Papers, Library of Congress, Manuscript Division, Washington, D.C.

Russian Diary   Diary of Edmund A. Walsh, S.J., kept during his stay in Soviet Russia (1922–23), Edmund A. Walsh, S.J., Papers (see EAWP)

SFS   School of Foreign Service, Georgetown University

SFSP-GUA   School of Foreign Service Papers, Georgetown University Archives (see GUA)

WNHM-ARAC   W. N. Haskell Manuscripts, American Relief Administration Collection (see ARAC)

WSCP   William S. Culbertson Papers, Library of Congress, Manuscript Division, Washington, D.C.

Yearbook   Georgetown University School of Foreign Service, *Yearbook, February 1919–February 1920, Including Report of the Foundation Exercises*

INTRODUCTION

1. See Powers, *Not without Honor: The History of American Anticommunism*.

2. See McNamara, "A Study of the Editorial Policy of the Brooklyn *Tablet* under Patrick F. Scanlan, 1917–1968."

3. "Curriculum Vitae of Edmund A. Walsh, S.J.," and "Rev. Edmund Aloysius Walsh, S.J.," in file 702, box 11, Edmund A. Walsh Papers, Lauinger Library, Special Collections Division, Georgetown University, Washington, D.C. (hereafter EAWP).

4. "Rev. Edmund A. Walsh, S.J., Biographical Notes," in file 702, box 11, EAWP.

5. See L. J. Gallagher, "Father Edmund A. Walsh." Random House rejected Gallagher's manuscript in 1959, on the grounds that there was "not a market large enough" for such a book; see Paul LaPolla to Louis J. Gallagher, S.J., September 3, 1959, in file 654, "Gallagher, Louis (Faculty)," Georgetown University Archives, Lauinger Library, Special Collections Division, Georgetown University, Washington, D.C (hereafter GUA). Gallagher's correspondence seems to indicate that he was working on a biography as early as 1954; see Edward B. Bunn to Father Provincial, July 29, 1954, in folder 113, box 2, EAWP. The Louis J. Gallagher, S.J., Papers at the Archives of the New England Province of the Society of Jesus, College of the Holy Cross, Worcester, Mass. (hereafter LJGP), provide no further insight into the writing of his book.

6. L. J. Gallagher, *Edmund A. Walsh, S.J.: A Biography*. For reviews see J. F. Gallagher, "Biography"; Sullivan, "Review of *Edmund A. Walsh, S.J.*"; Dollen, "Ambassador of Mercy."

7. See Hull, "The Holy See and Soviet Russia, 1918–1930: A Study in Full-Circle Diplomacy."

8. See McDonough, *Men Astutely Trained: A History of the Jesuits in the American Century*, 72, 74; Powers, *Not without Honor*, 52; Ó Tuathail / Toal, "Spiritual Geopolitics: Father Edmund Walsh and Jesuit Anticommunism."

9. It may be worth noting that I often found more on Walsh in non-Catholic than in Catholic archival sources. The presidential papers of every chief executive from Warren G. Harding to Dwight D. Eisenhower except Calvin Coolidge contained a generous amount of material on Walsh. This was especially true of the collections in the Harry S. Truman Presidential Library, Independence, Mo. The only Catholic archives I consulted as frequently were the Lauinger Library, Special Collections Division at Georgetown and the National Catholic Welfare Conference Files at The Catholic University of America.

10. Bell, *The Radical Right*; Caute, *The Great Fear: The Anti-Communist Purge under Truman and Eisenhower*, 21.

11. Powers, *Not without Honor*, 426.

12. Ibid., 66, 132, 427, 15.

13. Halsey, *The Survival of American Innocence: Catholicism in an Era of Disillusionment, 1920–1940*, 2–6.

CHAPTER 1: EDMUND A. WALSH: BOSTONIAN, JESUIT, ACTIVIST, AND EDUCATOR

1. On the evolution of international relations as an academic discipline, see McCaughey, *International Studies and Academic Enterprise: A Chapter in the Enclosure of American Learning*; Kirk, *The Study of International Relations in American Colleges*, 2–5; Schulzinger, *The Making of the Diplomatic Mind: The Training, Outlook and Style of United States Foreign Service Officers, 1908–1931*, 3–15.

2. Heinrichs, "Bureaucracy and Professionalism in the Development of American Career Diplomacy"; Barnes and Morgan, *The Foreign Service of the United States: Origins, Development and Functions*, 196–97; Ilchman, *Professional Diplomacy in the United States: A Study in Administrative History*, 132.

3. The only full-length history of the foreign service school is Tillman, *Georgetown University's School of Foreign Service: The First 75 Years*. Also useful are Nevils, *Miniatures of Georgetown, 1634–1934: Tercentennial Causeries*, 239–57; and Durkin, *Georgetown University: First in the Nation's Capital*, 97–106.

4. Nevils, *Miniatures*, 240; Tillman, *School of Foreign Service*, 4.

5. Georgetown University School of Foreign Service, *Yearbook, February 1919–February 1920, Including Report of the Foundation Exercises* (hereafter *Yearbook*), 10–11. This booklet contains course and faculty listings for the school's first year.

6. Ibid., 12.

7. See Kohn, *American Nationalism: An Interpretive Essay*; Dohen, *Nationalism and American Catholicism*, 15; on John Winthrop's image, see Ahlstrom, *A Religious History of the American People*, 147.

8. O'Brien, *Isaac Hecker: An American Catholic*, 109.

9. Ireland, *The Church and Modern Society: Lectures and Addresses*, 10–11, 178. See also Cross, *The Emergence of Liberal Catholicism in America*, 109–10; Wangler, "Myth, Worldviews and Late Nineteenth Century American Catholic Expansionism."

10. *Yearbook*, 39, 43; unidentified clipping, February 16, 1919, and clipping from *Philadelphia Catholic Standard-Times*, May 17, 1919, in "SFS 1918–1919" file, School of Foreign Service Papers, Georgetown University Archives, Lauinger Library, Special Collections Division, Georgetown University, Washington, D.C. (hereafter SFSP-GUA).

11. *Yearbook*, 12.

12. Ibid., 12–13.

13. Tillman, *School of Foreign Service*, 11. On the program at George Washington University, see Kayser, *Bricks without Straw: The Evolution of George Washington University*, 259.

14. Gleason, *Contending with Modernity: Catholic Higher Education in the Twentieth Century*, 22. In his 1958 study, Edward Power wrote: "Most of the substantial innovations in Catholic higher education were initiated by Georgetown." Power, *A History of Catholic Higher Education in the United States*, 216.

15. Walsh is first listed as a Ph.D. in the 1919 Georgetown catalogue. At a 1914 meeting of the American Provincials, in order to meet the growing standardization of requirements in American higher education, it was agreed that doctorates should be conferred on Jesuit college and university presidents, as well as on deans. Presumably, this line of reasoning led to the conferring of Walsh's honorary degree at the birth of the School of Foreign Service (hereafter SFS). For background on the 1914 meeting, see Leahy, *Adapting to America: Catholics, Jesuits and Higher Education in the Twentieth Century*, 40.

16. Information on Walsh's early years is from the biography by his childhood friend and fellow Jesuit, L. J. Gallagher, *Walsh*, 1–3. See also L. J. Gallagher's extended obituary in "Walsh." On Walsh's father, see clipping from *Boston Pilot*, September 19, 1914, 8; on the family, see "Brave Catholic Priest, Dramatic Figure in Russia, Is Boston Man," *Boston Post*, April 15, 1923, both in folder 746, box 12, EAWP.

17. James Martin Gillis, as quoted in Gribble, *Guardian of America: The Life of James Martin Gillis, C.S.P.*, 249. For the larger context, see Higham, *Strangers in the Land: Patterns of American Nativism, 1860–1925*, chap. 4; McConnell, "Reading the Flag: A Reconsideration of the Patriotic Cults of the 1890's," 103; O'Leary, *To Die For: The Paradox of American Patriotism*.

18. T. H. O'Connor, *Boston Catholics: A History of the Church and its People*, 114–15. Not until the episcopate of William Henry O'Connell (1907–44) did institutionalism gain momentum; for a contrast with the earlier period, see O'Toole, *Militant and Triumphant: William Henry O'Connell and the Catholic Church in Boston, 1859–1944*, 79–80. See also Kane, *Separatism and Subculture: Boston Catholicism, 1900–1920*.

19. "Speeches and Remarks Made at the Jubilee Dinner Honoring Edmund A. Walsh, S.J., on His Fiftieth Anniversary as a Member of the Society

of Jesus, Mayflower Hotel, Washington, D.C., November 15, 1952," 26–27, in "Walsh, Edmund A.: Golden Jubilee Celebration" file, box 86, Charles Fahy Papers, Library of Congress, Manuscript Division, Washington, D.C. (hereafter CFP). For patriotic demonstrations in South Boston, see T. H. O'Connor, *South Boston, My Home Town: The Story of an Ethnic Neighborhood,* 104–6, 121. Before joining the Jesuits, Walsh had applied to Annapolis, where he claimed to have received an appointment; see John Parr, "Mes Trois Mousquetaires—My Three Musketeers—Rev. Edmundus Aloysius Walsh, S.J., and the World Wars," unpublished manuscript, 1981, in folder 8, box 1, Parr-Smith Archive, Lauinger Library, Special Collections, Georgetown University, Washington, D.C. (hereafter P-SA).

20. At the 1919 inauguration of the SFS, historian and future Georgetown president W. Coleman Nevils stated: "We Americans love to watch the growth of our country . . . and with her growth we love to trace the increase of usefulness on the part of Georgetown University. It was in 1815 that we received our charter. A few years after the war with Mexico we opened our School of Medicine in 1850; and our graduate school in 1855. The wounds of the Civil War were scarcely healed when our School of Law grew forth and was welcomed. At the close of the victorious Spanish War we reared our noble hospital, quickly followed by the opening of our School of Dentistry." Nevils, *Miniatures,* 242. See also Curran, "Georgetown's Self-Image at the Turn of the Century."

21. "Speeches and Remarks, November 15, 1952," 27, in CFP.

22. Chief Justice Edward D. White, as quoted in Durkin, *Georgetown,* 86.

23. On McCormick, see McDonough, *Men Astutely Trained,* 219–20, 394–97. See also Hennesey, "American Jesuit in Wartime Rome: The Diary of Vincent A. McCormick, S.J." Hennesey notes that the McCormick papers in the Archives of the New York Province of the Society of Jesus in New York City are extremely sparse.

24. For insights into Walsh's personality and outlook, see the diary he kept during this period, in folder 125, box 2, EAWP (hereafter Diary). For instance, Walsh berates the Irish for not being American enough, for seeming "to be ashamed of their own nation—content to crawl along if allowed—no ambition to rise above conditions of past. They cling to old live-from-day-to-day spirit and with a sort of cynical determination to act as if they have been downtrodden for centuries and that it is useless to attempt modern ways and improvements. There is no confidence but apathy." Ibid., November 28, 1912.

25. Ibid., November 10, 1912.

26. Ibid., April 1 and 28, 1913, May 9, 1913.

27. Ibid., August 3, 1914. It is interesting to note that Walsh's grades at this time were either very high or very low, with little variation in between;

see "Meldungsbuch des Studier Edmund A. Walsh," in folder 714, box 11, EAWP. Clearly, his interests lay in topics other than the moral theology, canon law, and the New Testament courses for which he was registered. Unfortunately, no letters to or from Walsh have survived from this period of his life.

28. L. J. Gallagher, *Walsh*, 96. On Walsh's appointment as prefect, see the Georgetown University House Diary, May 30, 1918, GUA. I am grateful to Professor R. Emmett Curran for sharing his research from his forthcoming second volume of the university's history.

29. Consultors' Minutes, June 9, 1918, GUA (courtesy of Emmett Curran).

30. Donlon to Wernz, April 1913, in Maryland Province Correspondence, Archivum Romanum Societatis Jesu, MD 16 XII 4, Jesuit Curia, Rome (courtesy of Emmett Curran). It is not clear whether Creeden was familiar with the earlier plan, but it is almost certain that a young scholastic such as Edmund Walsh would not have been privy to such an undertaking.

31. Jay P. Dolan, *The American Catholic Experience: A History from Colonial Times to the Present* (Garden City: Doubleday, 1985), 353–54. For the origins of the NCWC, see McKeown, *War and Welfare: American Catholics and World War I*, 84, 154; Sheerin, *Never Look Back: The Career and Concerns of John J. Burke*, 36–55; Slawson, *The Foundation and First Decade of the National Catholic Welfare Council*, chap. 1. As will be shown in the second chapter of this study, Walsh had great respect for John Burke and his work at the NCWC.

32. McShane, *"Sufficiently Radical": Catholicism, Progressivism, and the Bishops' Program of 1919*, 197.

33. Creeden to Rockwell, December 1918 and July 28, 1919; in Provincial's Correspondence, Archives of the Maryland Province of the Society of Jesus, Roland Park, Md. (hereafter PC; courtesy of Emmett Curran).

34. O'Malley, *First Jesuits*, 90; Buckley, *The Catholic University as Promise and Project: Reflections in a Jesuit Idiom*, 62.

35. It should be noted, however, that not all Jesuits approved of the school. William O'Brien recalls that there was always a rift between the SFS and the College of Arts and Letters. Interview with Dr. William V. O'Brien, professor emeritus of government, Georgetown University, January 31, 1999. Walter Giles, Walsh's longtime assistant, recalled that several Georgetown Jesuits believed the SFS had no place in Jesuit education, labeling it the "foreign school"; see Watkins, *Footnotes to History: Selected Writings and Speeches of Edmund A. Walsh, S.J.*, 19. In the school's early years, Coleman Nevils wrote, some of the Jesuits in the older departments felt "a certain amount of undue publicity was being given to so young a child." Nevils, *Miniatures*, 257. SFS historian Seth Tillman maintains that the de-

spite the diversity of views among faculty and students, "the Jesuit tradition has remained strong. Its effect has been to hold before the curriculum and the academic environment an appreciation of and sensitivity to *values*— Christian values in the inclusive, ecumenical sense in which Christian values include the universal principles of all faiths." Tillman, *School of Foreign Service*, 18. I consider Tillman's to be the best explanation of Jesuit permeationism and its influence on the SFS.

36. Henri J. Wiesel, S.J., to William V. Repetti, S.J., November 25, 1958, in "Founding of SFS" file, "SFS 1918–1931" box, SFSP-GUA.

37. Quigley, "Constantine McGuire: Man of Mystery." McGuire was a financial consultant who reputedly included the Vatican among his clients. The whereabouts of his papers are unknown. See also "Constantine McGuire, Hemisphere Economist," *Washington Post*, October 25, 1965, in "SFS 1918–1919" file, SFSP-GUA.

38. Quigley, "Constantine McGuire," 13. Quigley writes that McGuire held a lifelong grudge against Harvard for denying him a professorship, which he attributed to anti-Catholic bias at the university. This may have been an additional reason why he approached a Catholic university such as Georgetown with his school proposal.

39. Ibid., 14; Tillman, *School of Foreign Service*, 4; see also Consultors' Minutes, June 9, 1918, in GUA 531–1 (courtesy of Emmett Curran).

40. J. DeSiqueira Coutinho, "In the Halls of Georgetown University (Some Events in the School of Foreign Service, 1919–1960)," unpublished manuscript, n.d., in "SFS 1918–1919" file, SFSP-GUA. McGuire later said that only Coutinho and Walsh knew about his meeting with Creeden; Quigley, "McGuire," 14.

41. "Memorandum on a School for the Diplomatic and Consular Service," May 1918, in "SFS 1918 (?) Memo on Origin of SFS" folder, SFSP-GUA. The memorandum is written with the casual expertise of one familiar with government circles, which neither Walsh nor Creeden would have had at this time.

42. Creeden to Rockwell, December 1918, in PC.

43. Tillman, *School of Foreign Service*, 25; Beaulac, "Edmund A. Walsh, S.J.," in Georgetown University, *On the Hilltop: Reminiscences and Reflections on Their Campus Years by Georgetown Alumni*, 9; McKevitt, *The Hilltop Remembered*, 38; interview with Dr. William V. O'Brien, January 31, 1999; Hearne, "Father Walsh in the United States," 22. As a scholastic, Walsh revived the college Dramatic Association; see *Georgetown College Journal* (February 1910): 180.

44. Interview with Rev. Joseph T. Durkin, S.J., Georgetown University, September 27, 1999. Louis Gallagher seems to support this assertion as he describes Walsh's time as a seminarian: "As a student of Philosophy at

Woodstock College [Walsh] realized and took advantage of the fact that he was living, studying and recreating with a community of future scholars from whom he could glean more knowledge in a few hours of conversation than he could accumulate in weeks from library shelves." L. J. Gallagher, *Walsh*, 4.

45. The reasons for Walsh's appointment to the SATC remain shrouded in mystery; archival sources give no indication as to why he was appointed. Only one other Catholic educator was appointed, Father Peter Guilday, professor of Church History at The Catholic University of America. On Catholic colleges and the SATC, see Gleason, *Contending with Modernity*, 72–78. Walsh had previously indicated a desire to serve as military chaplain; see Walsh to "Dear Fr. Rector," June 25, 1918, in folder 50, box 1, EAWP. There is a possibility that Creeden, Walsh, or both volunteered for the position, but no manuscript exists to support such a contention.

46. Schlesinger, *The Age of Roosevelt*, vol. 1: *The Crisis of the Old Order, 1919–1933*, 37–38. See also Schaffer, *America in the Great War: The Rise of the War Welfare State*, 31–63.

47. On the SATC, see Kennedy, *Over Here: The First World War and American Society*, 55–57; Gruber, *Mars and Minerva: World War I and the Uses of Higher Learning in America*, 213–18; Levine, *The American College and the Culture of Aspiration, 1915–1940*, 27–32.

48. L. J. Gallagher, *Walsh*, 11. Philip Gleason suggests that Walsh's SATC experience may have been the seed of the SFS; Gleason, *Contending with Modernity*, 75. In later years, Walsh claimed the idea of a foreign service school first came to him in Europe in 1914; see Healey, "Diplomat Priest." If so, Walsh's diary gives no indication of it; this later claim may have been a case of historical revisionism. Unfortunately, other than statistics, he left no observations on the schools he visited.

49. Walsh to Creeden, November 23, 1918, in "SFS 1918–1919" file, SFSP-GUA. On Joseph Farrell, see "Fr. Jos. A. Farrell," in folder 275, box 15, Faculty Files, GUA; Creeden to Rockwell, June 1919, in PC; Consultors' Minutes, April 30, 1919, in GUA 531–1. On James A. Farrell, see Forbes, *Men Who Are Making America*, 37–66.

50. Walsh to Creeden, November 23, 1918, in "SFS 1918–1919" file, SFSP-GUA.

51. William Franklin Sands to Edmund A. Walsh, May 17, 1936, in William Franklin Sands Papers, Philadelphia Archdiocesan Historical Research Center, Overbrook, Pa.

52. School of Foreign Service, *Peace Bulletin*, no. 2 (January 7, 1919), in "SFS 1919" file, SFSP-GUA. Among others, McGuire contacted William S. Culbertson of the Tariff Commission; see C. E. McGuire to W. S. Culbertson, September 6, 1919, in "Diaries" file, box 4, William S. Culbertson Pa-

pers, Library of Congress, Manuscript Division, Washington, D.C. (hereafter WSCP).

53. Louis J. Gallagher, S.J., as quoted in Tillman, *School of Foreign Service*, 2; Quigley, "McGuire," 15.

54. Beaulac, "Walsh," in Georgetown University, *On Hilltop*, 7; Tillman, *School of Foreign Service*, 11.

55. Paul H. Coughlin, "The Things That Are More Excellent," in Georgetown University, *On Hilltop*, 62.

56. Walsh, *The History and Nature of International Relations*.

57. Interview with Dr. William V. O'Brien, January 31, 1999.

58. Edmund A. Walsh, S.J., "Adequate School Training in Commercial History, An Address Delivered at the Seventh National Foreign Trade Convention, San Francisco, May 12, 1920," in file "1920 SFS," SFS box 1918–1931, GUA; "Draft of Remarks by the Regent, Friday, January 14, 8:15 P.M., Auditorium of the National Museum," in "Academic Exercises Commemorating the Founding of SFS, 2/17/19" folder, SFSP-GUA. Even though the Washington speech is placed in a folder dated 1919, events mentioned in the speech could not have taken place before 1921.

59. Edmund A. Walsh, S.J., "Address Delivered at Exercises in Commemoration of Fifth Anniversary of the Founding of the School of Foreign Service, November 21, 1924," in "SFS 1924" folder, SFSP-GUA (hereafter Walsh, "Fifth Anniversary," in SFSP-GUA).

60. Walsh, *History and Nature*, preface (pages are unnumbered in this book).

61. Walsh, "Fifth Anniversary," in SFSP-GUA.

62. May, *The End of American Innocence: A Study of the First Years of Our Own Time, 1912–1917*, 6–8; Halsey, *The Survival of American Innocence: Catholicism in an Era of Disillusionment, 1920–1940*, 2, 5.

63. Gen. W. Ledochowski to Rockwell, Rome, December 22, 1919, in Maryland Province Correspondence, Archivum Romanum Societatis Jesu, MD 16 XII 4, Jesuit Curia, Rome; Hanselman to Creeden, Rome, February 3, 1920, in GUA 413–6 (both courtesy of Emmett Curran).

64. Constantine E. McGuire to Edmund A. Walsh, November 5, 1920, in "1920 SFS" folder, SFSP-GUA.

CHAPTER 2: "WHAT THINK YE OF RUSSIA?": WALSH AND
CATHOLIC ANTICOMMUNISM IN THE 1920S

1. For historical background on Jesuit tertianship, see Ruhan, "The Origin of the Jesuit Tertianship: Meaning, Interpretation, Development"; O'Malley, *First Jesuits*, 298–301. Not all fully formed Jesuits take the fourth

vow; those who do (Walsh included) become "professed" fathers; those who do not are "spiritual coadjutors."

2. Excerpt of letter from Ledochowski to Walsh, Rome, July 8, 1922, in folder 94, box 2, EAWP (the note to Creeden from Walsh is at the bottom of this letter, and is dated October 8, 1922). Walsh's letters to Creeden from Paray-le-Monial written prior to February 1922 indicate he had no idea what the Vatican had in mind for him, and that he planned on returning to Georgetown for the 1922–23 academic year; for example, see Walsh to Creeden, Paray-le-Monial, January 12, 1922; Walsh to Creeden, Paray-le-Monial, January 19, 1922; W. Coleman Nevils to Walsh, Georgetown, February 5, 1922; all in folder 94, box 2, EAWP.

3. Powers, *Not without Honor,* 52. The only extended account of Walsh's anticommunist activity in the 1920s is in ibid., 111–13. Hull writes that Walsh did not speak Russian when he began relief work in the Soviet Union. Hull, "Holy See," 72–73.

4. L. J. Gallagher, "Walsh," 25.

5. For the revisions in the curriculum see Georgetown University School of Foreign Service (hereafter GUSFS), *Catalogue, 1925 (Winter 1924),* 50, *Catalogue, 1926,* 41, 50, and *Catalogue, 1927,* 21, resp.

6. Pipes, *A Concise History of the Russian Revolution,* 360. See also Nove, *An Economic History of the USSR,* 81; Figes, *A People's Tragedy: The Russian Revolution, 1891–1924,* 739–45.

7. Pipes, *Concise History,* 199, 344–46, 356–60. For a firsthand account of the famine see Bechhofer, *Through Starving Russia: Being the Record of a Journey to Moscow and the Volga Provinces in August and September 1921.*

8. Weissman, *Herbert Hoover and Famine Relief to Soviet Russia, 1921–1923,* xiv; Burner, *Herbert Hoover: A Public Life,* 136; Smith, *An Uncommon Man: The Triumph of Herbert Hoover,* 92, 196; Patenaud, "Herbert Hoover's Brush with Bolshevism." Along with the NCWC, the other groups at the August 24, 1921, Washington meeting were the American Friends Service Committee, the Red Cross, the Federal Council of Churches, the Jewish Joint Distribution Committee, the YMCA, the YWCA and the Knights of Columbus. See Hull, "Holy See," 55–57; Weissman, *Hoover,* 175; Fisher, *The Famine in Soviet Russia, 1919–1923: The Operations of the American Relief Administration,* 161. In the fall of 1921, the Knights of Columbus had expressed interest in sending a representative to Russia, but later decided not to, and left relief work to the NCWC. Ironically, Walsh was their choice for representative; see D. J. Callaghan to C. A. Herter, October 12, 1921; Christian A. Herter to Perrin C. Gilpin, October 14, 1921; Perrin Gilpin to C. A. Herter, October 15, 1921; all in "ARA Personnel File: Walsh, Edmund J. [*sic*], 1921–1952," box 75, American Relief Administration Papers, Herbert Hoover Presidential Library, Long Branch, Iowa (hereafter ARAP).

9. The Vatican Archives are presently available only through 1922, making it unlikely that the definitive history of Vatican-Soviet relations will emerge anytime in the near future. Useful sources are Hull, "Holy See," which is the definitive account of the Papal Relief Mission's operations. Also useful are Zatko, *Descent into Darkness: The Destruction of the Roman Catholic Church in Russia, 1917–1923*; Stehle, *Eastern Politics, 1917–1979,* chaps. 1–2; Graham, *Vatican Diplomacy: A Study of Church and State on the International Plane*; "Catholic Relief Mission to Russia," in Wieczynski, *The Modern Encyclopedia of Russian and Soviet History*, 6:138–40; Floridi, *Moscow and the Vatican*, chap. 1; Jedin, *History of the Church*, vol. 10: *The Church in the Modern Age*, 24, 60–62, 509–10.

10. Hansjakob Stehle contends that the Kerensky government hoped to establish diplomatic relations with the Vatican; Stehle, *Eastern Politics*, 15. Father Edward Juniewicz, who was a seminarian in Petrograd at the time of the October Revolution, summarized the attitude that prevailed among Catholics in Russia at the time: "When the October Revolution burst upon Russia, I in common with other Catholics welcomed the change because we had been persecuted under the old regime. Firing in the streets was for me, then a student in the Petrograd Theological Seminary, the dawning of a new era. . . . But how soon did we find our hopes vain. Our new masters have turned themselves upon us and are intent on the destruction of all religion, and with a sad heart we find they are no better than the previous." Father Edward Juniewicz, as quoted in Hull, "Holy See," 189.

11. Graham, *Vatican Diplomacy*, 352.

12. John J. Burke to Herbert Hoover, March 4, 1922, in "Communism: Russia; Famine: 1922" file, Office of the General Secretary Subject Files, National Catholic Welfare Conference Files, Archives of The Catholic University of America, Washington, D.C. (hereafter OGSSF-NCWCF). For background on the NCWC's affiliation with the ARA, see "Minutes of the General National Committee, August 25, 1921"; Memorandum from McMahon to Burke, August 26, 1921; Memorandum from Burke to McMahon, August 26, 1921; Phone message from Colonel Haskell to Mr. McMahon, August 26, 1921; all in "Communism: Russia; Famine: 1921" file, OGSSF-NCWCF. For background on the NCWC's struggle against suppression, see Sheerin, *Never Look Back*, chap. 4; Slawson, *Foundation*, 137–78. For Cardinal O'Connell's point of view, see O'Toole, *Militant*, 199–200; Slawson, *Foundation*, 137. See also Shelley, "The Oregon School Case and the National Catholic Welfare Conference."

13. Slawson, *Foundation*, 142–43; Hull, "Holy See," 73. Hull mentions the citizenship requirement. Hansjakob Stehle suggests that the Holy See chose an American director in order to attract the support of the "rich Americans"; Stehle, *Eastern Politics*, 32. He does not seem to take into ac-

count the terms of the Riga Agreement. Cardinal O'Connell had gotten the consistorial congregation at the Vatican to issue the condemnation of the NCWC on February 25, 1922.

14. I discovered the Georgetown connection in Father Joseph Farrell's faculty file at Georgetown; see folder 275, "Farrell, Joseph A. S.J. 239–6," box, in the Varia Collection, GUA. This folder contains an obituary of Farrell and a letter to him from Walsh on the occasion of Haskell's death. This was the second time that Walsh's connection with Farrell helped him. The first was Walsh's introduction to James A. Farrell, whose endowment helped establish the School of Foreign Service. On Haskell, see "Haskell, William Nafew." In 1931, Haskell wrote a memoir of his work in Russia entitled "A Russian Panorama." The typewritten manuscript was never published, but is kept in four folders in the W. N. Haskell Manuscripts, American Relief Administration Collection, Bakhmeteff Archive, Rare Book and Manuscript Collection, Columbia University, New York (hereafter WNHM-ARAC). It provides an overall view of the relief work; without going into great detail on his appointment, it makes clear that Walsh had ultimate control over personnel. See also W. N. Haskell, "Affiliated Organizations," 2, in folder 4, WNHM-ARAC. On Haskell's choice of Walsh see Cablegram S.248, March 15, 1922, in "ARA Personnel File: Walsh, Edmund J. [sic], 1921–1952," box 75, ARAP. In an interview during the late 1940s, Walsh stated that Haskell had written to him at Paray-le-Monial about the relief work in 1921, and had aroused his interest in the work. Although there is no correspondence in the EAWP to substantiate this, nonetheless it becomes clear that Walsh's appointment was clearly not an overnight decision; see "Reverend Edmund A. Walsh, S.J., 1885–."

15. Cablegram from Walsh to Burke, Paray-le-Monial, February 13, 1922; Burke to Walsh, February 17, 1922; Walsh to Burke, Rome, February 28, 1922, all in "Communism: Russia: Famine: 1922" file, OGSSF-NCWCF. In a 1923 newspaper interview, Walsh stated that Haskell had asked the Vatican for permission to appoint him as relief director; see "Brave Catholic Priest, Dramatic Figure in Russia, Is Boston Man," *Boston Post*, April 15, 1923, in folder 746, box 12, EAWP. Cablegram from Walsh to Burke, Paray-le-Monial, February 13, 1922; John J. Burke to Herbert Hoover, March 4, 1922, both in "Communism: Russia: Famine: 1922" file, OGSSF-NCWCF. Walsh to Creeden, Rome, March 3, 1922, in folder 94, box 2, EAWP. In Walsh's Russian diary, he refers to "all that W. N. H. [Haskell] and Mr. H. [Hoover] had already done" for the Papal Relief Mission; Edmund A. Walsh, S.J., diary, March 1, 1922, in folder 125, box 2, EAWP (hereafter Russian Diary). See also Louis J. Gallagher, S.J., "A Twentieth Century Jesuit," unpublished memoir, n.d., 20, in LJGP; Hoover, *An American Epic*, vol. 3: *Famine in Forty-Five Nations, The Battle on the Front Line, 1914–1923,*

500–501. All of these sources attest to the close relationship that existed between Walsh and Haskell. The EAWP collection at Georgetown does not contain any correspondence between Walsh and Haskell, nor does the Haskell collection at Columbia.

16. Russian Diary, February 28–March 7, 1922. Walsh gives all the details of his two weeks in Rome under the one entry listed above. Strangely enough, Hull does not cite this document, or even acknowledge its existence, in his study, nor has any scholar before or after him made use of this highly valuable source.

17. Pipes, *Concise History*, 336–38.

18. For more on the thinking behind the Soviet antireligious campaign, see Mayer, *The Furies: Violence and Terror in the French and Russian Revolutions*, 476; Peris, *Storming the Heavens: The Soviet League of the Militant Godless*, 26–27.

19. Mayer, *Furies*, 476.

20. Pipes, *Concise History*, 333–42; Mayer, *Furies*, 449–78; Peris, *Storming*, 2.

21. Peris, *Storming*, 21; Husband, *"Godless Communists": Atheism and Society in Soviet Russia, 1917–1932*, 48.

22. Husband, *"Godless Communists,"* xiii.

23. Ibid., xii.

24. Ibid. In 1924, Leon Trotsky described his ideal of the "new Soviet man" that would emerge from the revolution: "Man will, at last, begin to harmonize himself in earnest. . . . He will want to master first the semiconscious and then also the unconscious processes of his own organism [and] subordinate them to the control of reason and will. . . . Man will make it his goal to master his own emotions, to elevate his instincts to the heights of consciousness . . . to create a higher sociobiological type, a superman. . . . The average human type will rise to the heights of an Aristotle, Goethe, Marx. And beyond this ridge, other peaks will emerge." Leon Trotsky, as quoted in Pipes, *Concise History*, 25.

25. Russian Diary, May 21, 1922.

26. Although its official title was the "Pontifical Relief Mission," what I have chosen to call the "Papal Relief Mission" is also referred to as the "Vatican Mission" and the "Papal Mission."

27. This account of the beginnings of the Papal Relief Mission has been summarized from Russian Diary, May 3–31, 1922. For the letter that Walsh presented to Harding, see Pope Pius XI to President Warren G. Harding, May 15, 1922, in microfilm reel 220, file 1661, "Pope Pius XI," Warren G. Harding Papers, Library of Congress, Microfilm Collection, Washington, D.C. In his diary, Walsh claims that Gasparri had him write a draft of the letter he presented to Harding; see Russian Diary, May 7–13, 1922. This

may well be the case, but in the absence of other sources, it is impossible to verify. For the affiliation with the ARA, see Richard S. Emmett to Frank C. Page, June 16, 1922, in "ARA Personnel File: Walsh, Edmund J. [*sic*], 1921–1952," box 75, ARAP.

28. Official papal declaration, as quoted in Hull. "Holy See," 78.

29. Hull, "Holy See," 90. See also Gallagher, "Twentieth Century Jesuit," 19, in LJGP.

30. For a list of Papal Relief Mission membership, see Ryan, *The Papal Relief Mission in Russia,* 5; see also Hull, "Holy See," 101. Although the Society of Jesus played a major role in the organization and operation of the mission, the work was not exclusively a Jesuit enterprise. In his diary, Walsh suggests that this was to lessen the jealousy that might arise among other religious communities; see Russian Diary, March 1, 1922. According to the March 1922 agreement between Cardinal Pietro Gasparri and Vaclav Vorofsky, as quoted in Hull, "Holy See," 59–60, any envoys that the Holy See might choose to send could not belong to "nationalities or political formations hostile to Soviet Russia."

31. Monsignor Giuseppe Pizzardo, as quoted in Stehle, *Eastern Politics,* 43.

32. Pizzardo as quoted in Russian Diary, May 13, 1922.

33. Haskell, "Russian Panorama," 2, in folder 2, WNHM-ARAC.

34. Stehle, *Eastern Politics,* 29. See also Zatko, *Descent,* 111. U.S. State Department officials frequently commented on the intense scrutiny to which the Soviets subjected the Vatican relief workers; see F. W. B. Coleman to "The Honorable Secretary of State," Riga, Latvia, February 14, 1923, file 861.404/86, microfilm reel 316, Record Group 59 (Records of the Department of State Relating to the Internal Affairs of Russia and the Soviet Union, 1910–29), National Archives, General Records of the Department of State, College Park, Md. (hereafter RG 59). Coleman's letter also expresses the suspicion of Vatican "efforts to disintegrate the Russian Orthodox Church."

35. Hull, "Holy See," 101. Hull's 1970 dissertation is an extremely detailed work, the most complete of its kind. He does not, however, use sources that I have employed, such as the correspondence between Walsh and John J. Burke in the NCWCF collection at the Archives of The Catholic University of America. The Walsh-Burke papers are important for tracing the diplomatic role that is crucial to the formation of his anticommunism. Until now the only scholar to make reference to them has been John Sheerin; see Sheerin, *Never Look Back,* 86–88. I agree with Hull's assessment that the Holy See did have a strong philanthropic motivation in helping the millions of starving Russians. At the same time, however, Vatican officials very much wanted to take steps that would lead to the reestablish-

ment of the Church in a country where it had operated for centuries under discrimination from the Orthodox establishment.

36. For the text of the apostolic epistle, see Pius XII, "Annus fere iam est." See also Carlen, *Papal Pronouncements, A Guide: 1740–1978*, vol. 1: *Benedict XV to Paul VI*, 88, no. 13:10. Hull, "Holy See," 79–80; Walsh to Burke, October 9, 1922; Burke to Walsh, November 29, 1922, both in "Communism: Russia: Famine: 1922" file, OGSSF-NCWCF; on estimates of Catholic financial contributions worldwide, see Zugger, *The Forgotten: Catholics of the Soviet Empire from Lenin through Stalin*, 152. Although no exact numbers are available, $2,000,000 is probably a fair estimate. See Walsh to Burke, September 13, 1922; in "Communism: Russia: Famine: 1922" file, OGSSF-NCWCF. See also Walsh to Burke, January 18, 1923; Burke to Walsh, February 14, 1923; Walsh to Burke, March 16, 1923; Walsh to Burke, June 14, 1923; all in "Communism: Russia: Famine: 1923–1928" file, OGSSF-NCWCF.

37. Walsh to Burke, Theodosia, Crimea, August 13, 1922, in "Communism: Russia: Famine: 1922" file, OGSSF-NCWCF. In November, Burke wrote Walsh: "I know something of the magnitude of the task that rests upon your shoulders"; Burke to Walsh, November 19, 1922, in "Communism: Russia: Famine: 1922" file, OGSSF-NCWCF. I believe there is a parallel between Walsh and Burke's careers, which they were both aware of, and which historians have neglected. Whereas Burke sought to bring a Catholic influence to bear at the national level through the creation and subsequent work of the NCWC, Walsh sought to do the same at the international level through his School of Foreign Service and his anticommunist activism.

38. For the opening of the Papal Relief Mission, see Gallagher, "Twentieth Century Jesuit," 50, in LPGP; Walsh, "Papal Relief in Russia"; L. J. Gallagher, "With the Papal Relief Mission in Russia"; Walsh to Gasparri, September 3, 1922, in folder 381, box 6, EAWP. In October 1922, Walsh told Creeden that he was learning foreign trade "from another angle now, in the school of experience"; Walsh to Creeden, Moscow, October 8, 1922, in folder 94, box 2, EAWP. See also Ray Meyer, "University Professor is at Work in Russia," unidentified news clipping, August 13, 1922, in folder 746, box 12, EAWP.

39. Walsh, "Papal Relief," 35.

40. Walsh to Creeden, Moscow, March 27, 1922, in folder 94, box 2, EAWP. See also Hull, "Holy See," 2, 134, 151, 215; L. J. Gallagher, *Walsh*, 53.

41. Gallagher, "Twentieth Century Jesuit," 61, in LJGP; Walsh to Burke, August 13, 1922, in "Communism: Russia: Famine: 1922" file, OGSSF-NCWCF. See also Walsh to Burke, January 18, 1923, in "Communism: Rus-

sia: Famine: 1923–1928" file, OGSSF-NCWCF. This is not to undermine Walsh's significant administrative ability, but rather to delineate the many tasks he found himself dealing with upon arrival in Russia.

42. Gallagher, "Twentieth Century Jesuit," 62, 72, in LJGP. On Farrell's appointment, see Walsh to Burke, Moscow, October 30, 1922; Walsh to Burke, Moscow, November 15, 1922; Letters of introduction by John J. Burke [for Farrell], November 17, 1922; Burke to Haskell, November 17, 1922; Walsh to Burke, November 22, 1922, all in "Communism: Russia: Famine: 1922" file, OGSSF-NCWCF.

43. L. J. Gallagher, *Walsh*, 31. See also Cieplak to Walsh, December 6, 1922, in Szczesniak, *The Russian Revolution: A Collection of Documents Concerning the Suppression of Religion by the Communists, 1917–1925*, 103–4. On Archbishop von der Ropp's imprisonment, see Zugger, *Forgotten*, 125–26. Although Zugger's book is useful in parts, it suffers greatly from narrative incoherence; it adds little to the existing literature on the events of 1922–23, uncritically relying on outdated sources such as Zatko and unreliable accounts such as Stehle. Furthermore, it makes no use of Hull, and incorrectly lists the mission director as "Edward A. Walsh."

44. Walsh to Gasparri, as quoted in L. J. Gallagher, *Walsh*, 28–29. See also Zugger, *Forgotten*, 176–77; Hull, "Holy See," 151; Cieplak to Walsh, December 19, 1922, in Szczesniak, *Russian Revolution*, 104–5. On the Soviets' failure to respond to his letters, see Walsh to Gasparri, January 22, 1923; Pizzardo to Walsh, December 14, 1922, both in folder 383, box 6, EAWP.

45. Walsh to Burke, January 18, 1923, in "Communism: Russia: Famine: 1923–1928" file, OGSSF-NCWCF; Walsh to Gasparri, January 22, 1923, in folder 383, box 6, EAWP.

46. Walsh to Gasparri, March 20, 1923, in folder 384, box 6, EAWP. Zugger, *Forgotten*, 178; Hull, "Holy See," 176–78; Stehle, *Eastern Politics*, 46; The most balanced account of the clergy trial is in Hull, "Holy See," 178–205. *New York Herald* journalist and former British officer Captain Francis McCullagh, an eyewitness to the trial and a strong anticommunist, devoted an entire book to the trial; see McCullagh, *The Bolshevik Persecution of Christianity*. Although useful as an eyewitness account, McCullagh's book suffers from polemic incoherence. *New York Times* reporter Walter Duranty was less sympathetic toward the clergy than McCullagh, but his account is more readable; see Duranty, *I Write As I Please*, 202–7.

47. Pipes, *Concise History*, 338. See also "Prelates Receive Death Sentence," NCWC News Service, April 5, 1923, in "Communism: Russia: Cieplak" file, OGSSF-NCWCF; "Catholic Priests, Bold during Trial, Score Bolshevism," *New York Herald*, April 5, 1923, in folder 746, box 12, EAWP.

48. Zugger, *Forgotten*, 180. See also Hull, "Holy See," 267–93.

49. L, J. Gallagher, *Walsh*, 43; Hull, "Holy See," 191. On the American protest and the harsh sentences, see Telegram from Secretary of State

(Hughes) to President Harding, March 28, 1923; Telegram from Harding to Hughes, March 28, 1923; Hughes to Houghton, March 28, 1923, all in U.S. Department of State, *Foreign Relations of the United States, 1922*, vol. 2, pp. 815–17.

50. Stehle, *Eastern Politics*, 46. Walsh viewed anti-Polish sentiment as a big factor in Soviet hostility against the Catholic Church. Before the trials, Walsh wrote Cardinal Gasparri: "It has been one of my most delicate duties to convince the Soviet officials that *Catholic* does not necessarily mean *Polish* and consequently something political." Walsh to Gasparri, January 1, 1923, in folder 383, box 6, EAWP.

51. Christian Herter to DeWitt Clinton Poole, April 12, 1923, in file 861.404/124, microfilm reel 316, RG 59.

52. Walsh to Burke, April 5, 1923, in "Communism: Russia: Famine: 1923–1928" file, OGSSF-NCWCF.

53. Walsh to Gasparri, May 13, 1923, in folder 385, box 6, EAWP. See also "Visits Cieplak in Prison," *New York Times*, May 15, 1923, 3; "Dr. Walsh Visits Msgr. Cieplak in His Prison," NCWC News Service, n.d., both in "Communism: Russia: Cieplak" file, OGSSF-CWCF. Cieplak's conduct made a deep impression on Walsh, who participated in the preliminary stages of Cieplak's canonization. By that time, however, Walsh's own health was declining, and he was unable to make any significant contribution to the cause; see Msgr. Valerian Meysytowicz to "Dear Father," May 10, 1954; Louis J. Gallagher, S.J., to Rev. Francis Domanski, S.J., both in folder 411, box 6, EAWP.

54. Walsh to Gasparri, May 24, 1923; Walsh to Pizzardo, May 2, 1923, both in folder 385, box 6, EAWP. Walsh to Gasparri, January 22, 1923, in folder 383, box 6, EAWP.

55. Holmes, "Religion in Revolutionary Russia." See "Dr. Grant Discusses Soviet Executions," *New York Times*, n.d., in folder 746, box 12, EAWP. The Grant clipping was found in Walsh's papers, an indication of the importance he attached to it. Walsh collected articles from all sources, and these are available in the Walsh Papers at Georgetown. On his copy of a *New York Times* article claiming that the pope ordered the Russian clergy to resist, Walsh wrote "LIES!"; see "Says Pope Ordered Resistance to Soviet," *New York Times*, May 24, 1923, in folder 746, box 12, EAWP.

56. See [Gillis], "Editorial Comment." On James Gillis's early years as editor of *Catholic World*, see Gribble, *Guardian*, 83–93.

57. [Tierney], "Russia and Oregon." On the Oregon School Bill, see Tyack, "The Perils of Pluralism: The Background of the Pierce Case"; Holsinger, "The Oregon School Bill Controversy, 1922–1925."

58. [Scanlan], "Bolshevism in Operation." See also McNamara, "Brooklyn *Tablet*, 27–30.

59. In his study of English Catholic press reaction to the clergy trials, James Flint writes: "No longer were [English Catholics] willing to suppose that the new regime in Moscow consisted of sincere if perhaps misguided idealists, or of harmless though bungling dreamers, or even of wild orators full of oratory and violence. Instead, it appeared that the Bolsheviks had proven themselves to be cruel and determined ideologues whose nefarious designs included the destruction of Christ's Church. Hostility to whatever might pass by the name of Bolshevism or Communism was the natural result." Flint, "English Catholics and the Bolshevik Revolution: The Origins of Catholic Anti-Communism," 5.

60. Walsh to Burke, March 16, 1923, in "Communism: Russia: Famine: 1923–1928" file, OGSSF-NCWCF.

61. Walsh to Burke, May 24, 1923, in "Communism: Russia: Famine: 1923–1928" file, OGSSF-NCWCF. In June 1922, Walsh wrote Burke: "The Mission upon which I was dispatched to the United States by the Holy See would be notably advanced if I could use the publicity machinery of the National Catholic Welfare Council in the dissemination of literature regarding the present appalling conditions in Russia." Walsh to Burke, June 8, 1922, in "Communism: Russia: Famine: 1922" file, OGSSF-NCWCF. Walsh had also asked Father Edward Garesche, editor of the Jesuit journal *Queen's Work*, to publicize the events in Russia; E. F. Garesche, S.J., to John J. Burke, December 13, 1922, in "Communism: Russia: Famine: 1922" file, OGSSF-NCWCF.

62. Walsh to Burke, June 18, 1923, in "Communism: Russia: Famine: 1922" file, OGSSF-NCWCF. For Walsh's anonymous articles, see [Walsh], "The Martyrdom of the Russian Church," "Russia," and "Jottings from Innsbruck about Russia." On Walsh's camera work, see "Reds Dose Relief with Propaganda," *New York Herald,* April 10, 1923, in folder 746, box 12, EAWP. The text of the articles is repeated almost verbatim in other articles that do bear Walsh's name, using the same anecdotes and incidents. In addition, the rhetoric and the themes expounded in the anonymous articles are identical.

63. Walsh to Burke, January 18, 1923; Walsh to Burke, June 18, 1923, both in "Communism: Russia: Famine: 1923–1928" file, OGSSF-NCWCF.

64. Walsh to Burke, April 23, 1923, in "Communism: Russia: Famine: 1923–1928" file, OGSSF-NCWCF.

65. Edmund A. Walsh, S.J., "Memorandum on Council of 'Living Church' (Bolsheviks Church) Held in Moscow during Week Apr. 29–May 5, 1923," in folder 385, box 6, EAWP. For further background on the Second Church Council of the Living Church, see also Pipes, *Concise History,* 340–41.

66. See Filene, *Americans and the Soviet Experiment, 1917–1933*, 84, 86.

67. Halsey, *American Innocence*, 1–8; see also Massa, *Catholics and American Culture: Fulton Sheen, Dorothy Day, and the Notre Dame Football Team*, 7–8. On the division within American Protestantism, see Handy, *A Christian America: Protestant Hopes and Historical Realities*, 159–84; Hudson, *Religion in America: An Historical Account of the Development of American Religious Life*, 159–81; Ahlstrom, *Religious History*, 915.

68. Russian Diary, May 21, 1922.

69. Walsh to Gasparri, October 12, 1923, in folder 387, box 6, EAWP. For similar expressions, see Walsh to John J. Burke, April 23, 1923, in "Communism: Russia: Famine: 1923–1928" file, OGSSF-NCWCF. What were Walsh's influences? It is true that Irish Catholic feelings toward their Jewish neighbors were never hospitable, but Walsh's writings betray no such influence from his early years. Although he studied at Innsbruck, noted for its anti-Semitic slant, he was only there for a short while, and the diary he kept during this time does not express any anti-Semitic sentiment. On Innsbruck, see Tentler, *Seasons of Grace: A History of the Catholic Archdiocese of Detroit*, 301; for further context, see O'Brien, *American Catholics and Social Reform: The New Deal Years,* 10–13.

70. Carroll, *Constantine's Sword: The Church and the Jews, A History,* 435.

71. Unnamed French Jesuit, as quoted in Schultenover, *A View from Rome: On the Eve of the Modernist Crisis*, 77.

72. Jesuit General Luis Martín, as quoted in ibid., 82–83.

73. Jesuit journal *Month*, August 1919 editorial, as quoted in Flint, "English Catholics," 12–13. For a later treatment of the same theme in a Jesuit periodical, see "Hungary—The Red Terror and the Jewish Problem."

74. Higham, *Strangers*, 277–86. The *Protocols*, published by Henry Ford in his 1920s *Dearborn Independent* and by Father Charles Coughlin in the 1930s, chronicled the alleged plans of a cabal of Jewish bankers to achieve world domination. During the 1930s, Nazi Germany used the "document" to justify much of its anti-Semitic persecutions. Anti-Semitism was also present in American higher education during this era. In 1918, in a lecture at the University of Minnesota, one professor, as quoted in Gruber, *Mars and Minerva*, 241, asserted that "a surprising number of revolutionaries" were Jews, and were "particularly dangerous, because centuries of suffering at the hands of the government had made [them] bitter [men]." A useful overview is available in Bayor, "Klans, Coughlinites and Aryans Nations: Patterns of American Anti-Semitism in the Twentieth Century."

75. Powers, *Not without Honor*, 78.

76. For Walsh's private expressions of anti-Semitism, see Walsh to Burke, March 27, 1922, in "Communism: Russia: Famine: 1922" file; Walsh to

Burke, April 23, 1923, in "Communism: Russia: Famine: 1923–1928" file, both in OGSSF-NCWCF. See also Walsh to Pius XI, October 3, 1923, in folder 387, box 6, EAWP. Interestingly, these expressions are always directed in private letters to his fellow priests, never to lay people, although this is by no means to imply that the addressees necessarily shared the same outlook. Such could certainly not be said of Pius XI, who attacked anti-Semitism in the later years of his reign; see McDonough, *Men Astutely Trained*, 134–35; Southern, *John LaFarge and the Limits of Catholic Interracialism*, 230–38.

77. Haskell, "Russian Panorama," 58, in folder 3, WNHM-ARAC. See also Hull, "Holy See," 210.

78. For further background on the ARA's famine relief, see Weissman, *Hoover*, 165, 172, 174; Pipes, *Concise History*, 360; Edmondson, "An Enquiry into the Termination of Soviet Famine Relief Programmes and the Renewal of Grain Export, 1919–1923," 382; Rhodes, "An Ohio Kitchen Inspector and the Soviet Famine of 1921–1922: The Russian Odyssey of Henry C. Wolfe," 199.

79. Walsh to Burke, July 20, 1923, in "Communism: Russia: Famine: 1923–1928" file, OGSSF-NCWCF; Walsh to Creeden, July 20, 1923, in folder 18, box 1, EAWP. In later years, the rumor developed that Walsh himself had been secretly consecrated at this time. Gallagher writes that Walsh enjoyed encouraging the rumor; L. J. Gallagher, *Walsh*, 89. Andrew Greeley recalls: "I never met Father Edmund Walsh, though among the Jesuits at the seminary I attended (St. Mary of the Lake at Mundelein), he was thought to be something of a living legend. It was told that he always had episcopal robes in his closets because he had been ordained a bishop ('consecrated' we would have said in those days) when he was sent to Russia, and ordained priest[s] secretly in Russia. Whether or not that's true, I don't know, but it certainly is a good story." Andrew M. Greeley to Patrick J. McNamara, April 21, 1998.

80. Cardinal Pietro Gasparri, as quoted in Hull, "Holy See," 218.

81. Walsh to Creeden, September 27, 1923, in folder 94, box 2, EAWP. For further background on Walsh's last months in Soviet Russia, see L. J. Gallagher, *Walsh*, 67; Hull, "Holy See," 218. By this time, contributions had dropped considerably in the wake of the clergy trials; see Walsh to Burke, June 14, 1923, in "Communism: Russia: Famine: 1923–1928" file, OGSSF-NCWCF.

82. Walsh to Burke, July 20, 1923, in "Communism: Russia: Famine: 1923–1928" file, OGSSF-NCWCF. Walsh to Gasparri, August 2, 1923; Walsh to Gasparri, August 31, 1923, Walsh to Gasparri, September 3, 1923; all in folder 386, box 6, EAWP. Walsh to Creeden, September 27, 1923, in folder 94, box 2, EAWP; Walsh to Pope Pius XI, October 3, 1923, in folder

387, box 6, EAWP. See also Zugger, *Forgotten,* 188–89. On April 9, 1924, however, they finally freed Cieplak, who made his way to Rome and then to the United States, where he died in New Jersey in December 1925. Hansjakob Stehle contends that the Soviets had an extraordinary dislike for Walsh, whence it might be deduced that they did not want Walsh to get credit for freeing the archbishop; see Stehle, *Eastern Politics,* 49.

83. Walsh to Gasparri, August 24, 1923; Walsh to Gasparri, September 21, 1923; Walsh to Gasparri, September 28, 1923; all in folder 386, box 6, EAWP. Walsh to Gasparri, October 12, 1923; Walsh to Gasparri, November 26, 1923; all in folder 387, box 6, EAWP. See also Gallagher, *Edmund A. Walsh,* 63.

84. Walsh to Gasparri, August 1923, as quoted in Hull, "Holy See," 212.

85. Walsh to Gasparri, August 1, 1923, in folder 386, box 6, EAWP. See also Walsh to Gasparri, November 26, 1923, in folder 387, box 6, EAWP.

86. Walsh to Creeden, September 27, 1923, in folder 94, box 2, EAWP. Hull, "Holy See," 227–32; L. J. Gallagher, *Walsh,* 81; Stehle, *Eastern Politics,* 51–52. Two German priests on the Papal Relief Mission staff remained for a few weeks after Walsh, until they were forced out by the Soviets; Hull, "Holy See," 231–32.

87. Walsh to Burke, January 7, 1924, in "Communism: Russia: Famine: 1923–1928" file, OGSSF-NCWCF; Walsh to Creeden, December 11, 1923, in folder 94, box 2, EAWP; "Report on Russian Relief Presented at Vatican by Rev. Father Walsh, S.J.," *Northwest Record,* January 20, 1924, in folder 746, box 12, EAWP; Hull, "Holy See," 234; Jedin, *History of Church,* 10:511. I have also followed Walsh's itinerary as listed in his diary; see Russian Diary, December 3, 1923–January 9, 1924.

88. Hull, "Holy See," 1, 242–46; Zugger, *Forgotten,* 228–40. On April 8, 1929, the All-Russian Central Executive Committee of the Soviet States issued the Law on Religious Associations, which nationalized all church property and denied juridical rights to religious bodies, the final blow to organized religion in Russia.

89. Hull, "Holy See," 247.

90. On the Papal Relief Mission's success, see L. J. Gallagher, *Walsh,* 76; Hull, "Holy See," 2–3. On Walsh and the CNEWA, see McGuiness, "The Call of the East: The Early Years of the Catholic Near East Welfare Association"; Stern, "Catholic Near East Welfare Association"; Gaffey, *Francis Clement Kelley and the American Catholic Dream,* 1:358–59; L. J. Gallagher, "Walsh," 42; Cohalan, *A Popular History of the Archdiocese of New York,* 257; "Catholics Launch Near East Drive"; "Pope Congratulated on Fifth Anniversary." See also Edmund A. Walsh to Archbishop Michael J. Curley, December 14, 1928, in Michael J. Curley Papers, Archdiocese of Baltimore Archives, Baltimore; Edmund A. Walsh to Cardinal George W. Mundelein,

November 11, 1926, in Madaj Collection, Archdiocese of Chicago's Joseph Cardinal Bernardin Archives and Records Center, Chicago.

91. McGuiness, "Call of East," 37; L. J. Gallagher, "Walsh," 48; Fogarty, *The Vatican and the American Hierarchy from 1789 to 1965*, 234; Walsh, "Pius the Eleventh, Champion of Truth." According to John Parr, who taught at the School of Foreign Service under him, Walsh was "never on intimate terms with H.H. Pope Pius XII, as he had been with his predecessor." Parr, "Mousquetaires," 15, in P-SA.

92. For an overview of the Church-state conflict in Mexico during this period, see Vinca, "The American Catholic Reaction to the Persecution of the Church in Mexico, 1926–1936"; Slawson, *Foundation*, 242, 245, 282, 285; Quirk, *The Mexican Revolution and the Catholic Church, 1910–1929*. On Burke's role, see Whitley, "Father John J. Burke, C.S.P., and Mexican Church-State Relations, 1927–1929."

93. On Walsh's role in the Church-state negotiations in Mexico, see Sheerin, *Never Look Back*, 139–56; Fogarty, *Vatican and American Hierarchy*, 234; Kauffman, *Faith and Fraternalism: The History of the Knights of Columbus*, 312; Gaffey, *Kelley*, 2:82–83. For newspaper accounts of Walsh's role, see "Walsh Calls Accord Harbinger of Peace"; "Way Seen as Laid for Lasting Peace"; "Father Walsh Lauds Portes Gil Accord."

94. Walsh, *The Fall of the Russian Empire: The Story of the Last of the Romanovs and the Coming of the Bolsheviki*, 7. Richard Gid Powers writes: "Walsh's academic training was in Russian history, which brought him to the attention of the Pope in 1922 when he needed a director for the Papal relief mission to Russia." Powers, *Not without Honor*, 52. I strongly disagree with Powers. Before 1922, Walsh never took, or taught, a class of any kind on Russia. It was only in 1921, as pointed out in chapter 1, that Constantine McGuire stressed to him the importance of Russian studies. For further elaboration of this point, see Georgetown University School of Foreign Service, *Announcement 1921–1922*, ser. 2, bull. 2, rev., 7–8, 23, 35. Upon returning from Russia, he never took a course or pursued any degree in this field. If he later became known as an expert on Soviet Russia, he was a *self-taught* expert.

95. Walsh to Burke, December 12, 1923; see also McCullagh to Walsh, December 1, 1923; McCullagh to Burke, October 25, 1924; all in "Communism: Russia: Cieplak" file, OGSSF-NCWCF.

96. McCullagh, *Bolshevik Persecution*; for a review of McCullagh's book, see Will, "Destroying Religion in Russia."

97. Walsh to Creeden, September 27, 1923, in folder 94, box 2, EAWP. Throughout Walsh's time at Georgetown, and long after, intellectuals fleeing from Soviet rule found a welcome home, and occasionally tenure, "on the hilltop."

98. Filene, *Americans and Soviet Experiment*, 65–66, 287.

99. Ibid., 65, 96; On American responses to the October Revolution, see Gardner, *Safe for Democracy: The Anglo-American Response to Revolution, 1913–1923*, 130–37; Strakhovsky, *American Opinion about Russia, 1917–1920*, xii, 3–9, 30, 45. On the Soviets' view of relations with the United States in 1920s, see Sivachev and Yakovlev, *Russia and the United States: U.S.-Soviet Relations from the Soviet Point of View*, 82–83, 94–95; on Secretary of State Hughes's "steadfast refusal to acknowledge the reality of the Soviet state," see Bennett, *Recognition of Russia: An American Foreign Policy Dilemma*, 57; Wilson, *Ideology and Economics: U.S. Relations with the Soviet Union, 1918–1933*, 14.

100. Powers, *Not without Honor*, 20.

101. Murray, *Red Scare: A Study in National Hysteria, 1919–1920*, 276; Glazer, *The Social Basis of American Communism*, 70–71; Schlesinger, *Age of Roosevelt*, 1:66.

102. Powers, *Not without Honor*, 43–67, 426. On Ralph Easley's anticommunist activity, see Zerzan, "Understanding the Anticommunism of the National Civic Federation." The papers of the National Civic Federation, essential to any scholar of American anticommunism in the 1920s, are housed at the New York Public Library.

103. Allitt, "Anti-Communism and American Catholics," 105.

104. Crosby, *God, Church, and Flag: Senator Joseph R. McCarthy and the Catholic Church, 1950–1957*, 5. Socialist-related issues were also present in the conflict between Corrigan and New York priest Edward McGlynn, whose support of single-tax theorist Henry George after Corrigan forbade him to campaign in George's favor led to his excommunication; see Donnelly, "Catholic New Yorkers and New York Socialists, 1870–1920." Despite its ambitious title, Donnelly's dissertation is essentially a treatment of the McGlynn case. For brief overviews of Catholic anticommunism, see Allitt, "Catholic Anti-Communism"; Crosby, "The Politics of Religion: American Catholics and the Anti-Communist Impulse."

105. Higham, *Strangers*, 175–82; Kauffman, *Patriotism and Fraternalism in the Knights of Columbus: A History of the Fourth Degree*, 39.

106. Higham, *Strangers*, 179; Kauffman, *Patriotism*, 43–44. A useful study of prewar anti-Catholicism at the local level is Margulies, "Anti-Catholicism in Wisconsin Politics, 1914–1920."

107. Kauffman, *Patriotism*, 44–48. For publications of this period, both pro and con, dealing with socialism and the Catholic Church, see Husslein, *The Pastor and Socialism: A Paper Read Before the Ecclesiastical Round Table of the Priests of the Ohio Valley*; Kress, *The Red Peril*; Ryan, *Social Reform on Catholic Lines*; Bohn, *The Catholic Church and Socialism*; Lockwood, *The Priest and the Billy Goat*; Clancy, *Catholicism and Socialism*;

Ameringer, *Communism, Socialism, and the Church*; De Leon, *Abolition of Poverty: Socialist versus Ultramontane Economics and Politics (Originally Published in Response to Public Address of Rev. Thomas I. Gasson, S.J., in Boston, 1911)*. Although the above listing is by no means exhaustive, it does testify to the issue's urgency in the prewar years. For a historical overview, see Doherty, "The American Socialist Party and the Roman Catholic Church, 1901–1917." On John Noll, see Hutton, "Catholicity and Civility: John Francis Noll and the Origins of *Our Sunday Visitor*"; Ginder, *With Ink and Crosier: The Story of Bishop Noll and His Work*.

108. Unnamed Mississippi constituent, as quoted in Cuddy, "'Are the Bolsheviks Any Worse Than the Irish?': Ethno-religious conflict in America During the 1920's," 32. See also Higham, *Strangers*, chap. 10; Curry, *Protestant-Catholic Relations in America, World War I Through Vatican II*, chap. 1; Perrett, *America in the Twenties: A History*, 76–83; Parrish, *Anxious Decades: America in Prosperity and Depression, 1920–1941*, 121–22; for general reference, see Williams, *The Shadow of the Pope*. On Catholic response to anti-Catholicism, see Dumenil, "The Tribal Twenties: 'Assimiliated' Catholics' Response to Anti-Catholicism in the 1920's."

109. *Tablet*, February 9, 1918, 5. See also McNamara, "Brooklyn *Tablet*," 27–29, 34–35. On the rise of the Ku Klux Klan, see Jackson, *The Ku Klux Klan in the City, 1915–1930*.

110. Walsh to Pizzardo, March 12, 1924, in folder 96, box 2, EAWP.

111. L. J. Gallagher, *Walsh*, 81–82.

112. Georgetown University School of Foreign Service, *Catalogue, 1925*, Winter ed., 46.

113. Georgetown University School of Foreign Service, *Catalogue, 1926*, 41, 60–62. See also "Lecture Course Opened to Public," undated news clipping, in folder 747, box 12, EAWP. The lectures began at the Smithsonian in 1924, moved back to Georgetown, and then to Constitution Hall; L. J. Gallagher, *Walsh*, 83. Drew Pearson, who during the 1950s accused Walsh of being the driving force behind McCarthyism, claimed that Walsh made Georgetown a center of opposition to Soviet Russia in the 1920s and 1930s. According to Pearson: "Father Walsh had a profound effect upon State Department personnel through his Foreign Service School. By training young diplomats at his Foreign Service School, Father Walsh also gave an anti-Russian slant to American foreign policy for many years." Pearson, "Johnson Girls and Catholicism," *Washington Post*, July 9, 1965, in folder 770, box 12, EAWP. Pearson overestimates the pace at which the school's graduates made their presence felt in policy-making circles; see Tillman, *School of Foreign Service*, 15.

114. Walsh to Pizzardo, March 12, 1924, in folder 96, box 2, EAWP; "Lecture Course Opened to Public," *Washington Star*, n.d., in folder 747, Box,

EAWP. L. J. Gallagher, *Walsh,* 84; "Papal Relief Will Be on World Basis, Father Walsh Predicts," *Catholic Watchman,* February 16, 1924, in folder 746, box 12, EAWP. See also "Papal Mission Sets Mark," *New York Times,* May 19, 1924, 7; unidentified clipping, May 22, 1925, "Father E. A. Walsh's Talk on Russia Leaves Audience Spellbound," unidentified clipping, all in folder 748, box 12, EAWP.

115. *Washington Post,* November 3, 1956, in folder 703, box 11, EAWP. In a 1952 interview, DeWitt Clinton, a career diplomat who served in Russia in 1921, attested to Walsh's credibility: "The situation in '21 in Russia was far worse than anything I ever saw [but] I never saw Russia at its worst. The man who can tell you about that is Father Edmund Walsh down at Georgetown University, who went in representing the Vatican to relieve them in 1921 and 1922. He can show photographs that will turn your stomach." DeWitt Clinton Poole Memoir (1952; 3 vols.), PRCQ, no. 95, vol. 1, 134, Oral History Research Office, Columbia University, New York. See also L. J. Gallagher, "Walsh," 38.

116. Dwight D. Eisenhower, "Remarks by the President at Georgetown University, Washington, D.C., at the ceremonies dedicating the Edmund A. Walsh School of Foreign Service, October 13, 1958," in "PPF 22-C Georgetown University" file, box 678, White House Central Files, Dwight D. Eisenhower Library, Abilene, Kansas.

117. McEvitt, *The Hilltop Remembered,* 38; L. J. Gallagher, *Walsh,* 86; Roberts, "Alsop's Faded Georgetown"; Quigley, "Father Walsh as I Knew Him," 232. Roberts refers to the founding of Georgetown as a village in 1703, not to the university's founding in 1789.

118. Filene, *Americans and Soviet Experiment,* 270; Mark, "October or Thermidor? Interpretations of Stalinism and the Perception of Soviet Foreign Policy in the United States, 1927–1947." Filene writes: "The Soviets preached un-American atheism, collectivism, and class dictatorship, but they also preached efficiency, progress, and democracy of a sort—and did so with the messianic fervor and invocation of historical destiny which had become characteristic of American ideals. This overlapping relationship was largely responsible for American dissension and consternation about the Soviet regime during the 1920s. When regarded in one perspective, the Communists were demoniacal enemies; in another they were harsher but more effective Progressives or even capitalists." Filene, *Americans and Soviet Experiment,* 283.

119. "Soviet Russia's Conditions"; Walsh, "Soviet Russia's Foreign Policy Does Not Justify U.S. Recognition Yet"; "Soviet Assailed at D.A.R. Congress."

120. "Priest Attacks Rule of the Soviet."

121. "Address of Rev. Edmund A. Walsh, S.J.," 45–46, in "American Relief Administration Related Materials" file, WNHM-ARAC.

122. Ibid., 49.

123. Ibid.

124. "Barriers Raised by Evil Soviet Theories Prevent Recognition of Russia by U.S.," *Washington Star*, May 24, 1925, in folder 746, box 12, EAWP; unidentified clipping, "Walsh Warns D.A.R. of Soviet Peril," in folder 750, box 12, EAWP; Walsh, "Some Observations of the Soviet Problem," 13.

125. Walsh, *Fall of Russian Empire*, xii–xiii. Previews appeared in the *Atlantic Monthly* in monthly installments just before publication; see Walsh, "The Fall of the Russian Empire: 1. The Plot Played by a Woman," "The Fall of the Russian Empire: 2. The End of the Monarchy," and "The Last Days of the Romanovs."

126. Walsh, *Fall of Russian Empire*, vii.

127. "Review of *The Fall of the Russian Empire*"; Johnston, "Russia's Revolution as an Episode in the Human Tragedy"; Dulles, "Back-Wash of the War."

128. Kellock, "The Innocence of Father Walsh"; Clarkson, "What Think Ye of Russia?"

129. Hull, "Holy See," 10; interview with Rev. Joseph T. Durkin, S.J., Georgetown University, September 29, 1999.

130. Walsh, *Fall of Russian Empire*, 5–6. Walsh also took a verbal swing at recognition supporters in his definition of *liberal:* "Etymologically, the term 'liberal' has obvious relation to freedom of some sort. Up to the close of the eighteenth century it had no political significance, being applied to cultural freedom, 'a liberal education,' 'the liberal arts,' and so forth. . . . In the twentieth century it denotes a curious variety of claimants who range from sincere crusaders and unprejudiced thinkers to illiberal bigots, cranks, and intellectual dilettantes. For the latter category it frequently serves as a convenient cloak to mask a mental or moral incapacity to face and take a positive stand on serious issues. These are the straddlers, the dabblers, and the *poseurs*, who applaud the most contradictory theories, however ridiculous, rather than strain their nerves by a too close application of logic or endanger their reputation for broadness and tolerance by a public exhibition of their thought processes." Ibid., 55.

131. Ninkovich, *The Wilsonian Century: U.S. Foreign Policy since 1900*, 2, 11.

132. "Urges New Peace Tribunal."

CHAPTER 3: "THE TWO STANDARDS": WALSH AND AMERICAN
CATHOLIC ANTICOMMUNISMS, 1929–41

1. For a useful survey of events surrounding the rise of American radicalism in the Depression, see Parrish, *Anxious Decades*.

2. Frank, "Prelude to Cold War: American Catholics and Communism," 39, 42, 50. Frank provides a brief but useful survey unavailable elsewhere; he notes that, by 1937, there were more than three hundred periodicals addressed to Catholic readers in the United States.

3. O'Brien, *American Catholics*, 82.

4. See Powers, *Not without Honor*, 426; Frank, "Prelude to Cold War," 50. The intra-Catholic debate surrounding the communist issue in the first half of the twentieth century may well be likened to the current debate surrounding abortion.

5. "Three Faiths Join in Assailing Soviet," 1; Rosswurm, "Manhood, Communism, and Americanism: The Federal Bureau of Investigation and the American Jesuits, 1935–1960," 13.

6. Jedin, *History of Church*, 10:511; Moody, *Church and Society: Catholic Social and Political Movements, 1789–1950*, 48. Useful documentary sources include Ehler and Morrall, *Church and State through the Centuries: A Collection of Historic Documents with Commentaries*, 378–617; Barry, *Readings in Church History*, vol. 3: *The Modern Era, 1789 to the Present*, 330–37, 370–80, 407–18. On LaFarge and the unissued encyclical *Humani Generis Unitas*, see Southern, *LaFarge*, 230–37.

7. Duffy, *Saints and Sinners: A History of the Popes*, 260–61; Holmes, *The Papacy in the Modern World, 1914–1978*, 57, 93, 111–13, 116; Aubert, *The Church in a Secularized Society*, 555. Despite his harsh assessment, Duffy does acknowledge that Pius XI took a stronger stand toward fascism before his death. In an obituary of Pius he wrote for *America* in 1939, Walsh depicted him as preeminently an anticommunist: "Pius XI, obviously, will take his place in history as the Pope of the Conciliation. He will likewise be distinguished as the Pope of Catholic Action and the Great Encyclicals such as *Quadragesimo Anno*. But in the opinion of the present writer, his early recognition of the danger to the world inherent in Communism and Bolshevism will merit a high place among the greatest of Popes." Walsh, "Pius the Eleventh," 463.

8. McDonough, *Men Astutely Trained*, 65; Southern, *LaFarge*, 216. For a more favorable view of Ledochowski, see Slattery, "In Memoriam: Very Rev. Fr. Vladimir Ledochowski."

9. Father General Wlodimir Ledochowski, as quoted in McDonough, *Men Astutely Trained*, 68. David Southern notes that Ledochowski and Pius XI shared a strident anticommunism, and he goes so far as to suggest that the general's influence "was probably one of the major reasons the Holy See had been more lenient toward Hitler's brand of tyranny than Stalin's"; Southern, *LaFarge*, 232. Southern makes no mention, indeed, seems altogether unaware, of Pius XI's experience as nuncio to Poland during the war with Russia in 1920, in which he showed the strength of his anticommunist convictions.

10. Zugger, *Forgotten*, 210, 242–44; Hull, "Holy See," 243.

11. Hull, "Holy See," 246.

12. Ibid.; Powers, *Not without Honor*, 111. On devotion to Our Lady of Fatima during the Cold War, see Kselman and Avella, "Marian Piety and Cold War in the United States." Anticommunism in American Catholic spirituality *before* the Cold War is a highly neglected topic, and one that certainly deserves further exploration by scholars.

13. Spalding, *The Premier See: A History of the Archdiocese of Baltimore*, 360; Archbishop Michael J. Curley, as quoted in Powers, *Not without Honor*, 110–11. No indications as to whether Walsh actually wrote the text of Curley's letter is provided either in the EAWP at Georgetown or in the Michael; J. Curley Papers at the Archdiocese of Baltimore Archives, Baltimore.

14. Walsh to "Right Reverend and Reverend Clergy," n.d., in folder 97, box 2, EAWP; "Martyrs in Russia Estimated at 6,000."

15. Walsh, *Why Pope Pius XI Asked Prayers for Russia on March 19, 1930: A Review of the Facts in the Case Together With Proofs of the International Program of the Soviet Government*, 19, 76. Soviet scholar Daniel Peris describes the League of the Militant Godless as the Soviet government's "organizational centerpiece to bring atheism to the masses." By 1932 the League had 5.5 million members, and its own newspaper, *Bezbozhnik* (The Godless); see Peris, *Storming*, 2. See also Walsh, "A Roman Catholic Indictment," in which he details the league's work in Russia, as well as Russian persecution statistics; "Moscow's Reply to the Pope in Line with Expectations"; "Three Faiths Join"; "Martyrs in Russia."

16. Walsh, "Misleading the Public."

17. Ibid., 16; "Misleading the Public Again"; "'Time' Limps in Again"; Heyden, "A Record of the Controversy between Fr. Edmund A. Walsh and *Time*."

18. L. J. Gallagher, *Walsh*, 89.

19. Schlesinger, *Age of Roosevelt*, 1:66; Leuchtenberg, *The Perils of Prosperity, 1914–1932*, 241; Kennedy, *Freedom from Fear: The American People in Depression and War, 1929–1945*, 11.

20. Kennedy, *Freedom from Fear*, 10–11. See also Wattenberg, *Historical Statistics of the United States: From Colonial Times to the Present*, 135; Schlesinger, *Age of Roosevelt*, 1:167; Leuchtenberg, *Franklin D. Roosevelt and the New Deal, 1932–1940*, 1.

21. Raymond Mosley, as quoted in Kennedy, *Freedom from Fear*, 11. See also Leuchtenberg, *Roosevelt*, 25. For a view sympathetic to Hoover, see Schwarz, "Hoover and Congress: Politics, Personality and Perspective in the Presidency"; Kennedy, *Freedom from Fear*, 91, 94; Fausold, *The Presidency of Herbert C. Hoover*, 124; Burner, *Hoover*, 249; Hoover, *Memoirs*, vol. 2: *The Cabinet and the Presidency, 1920–1933*, 301–19.

22. Klehr, *The Heyday of American Communism: The Depression Decade*, ix. Freeman, *In Transit: The Transport Workers in New York City, 1933–1966*, 71. Freeman quotes one TWU member who testified before the newly established House Un-American Activities Committee (the Dies Committee) in 1938 on the communist appeal: "[They] were willing to spend money—to pay for lawyers and give us as much protection as could be given. So I felt that those people were really interested in the working class." Ibid. In the 1932 presidential election, the CPUSA received 103,000 votes, as opposed to 21,000 in 1928; see Heale, *American Anticomunism: Combating the Enemy Within, 1830–1970*, 101.

23. Glazer, *Social Basis*, 92–93; A. Fried, *Communism in America: A History in Documents*, 98; Klehr, *Heyday*, xi; see also Powers, *Not without Honor*, 93.

24. For a useful overview of the historiographical debate, see Isserman, "Three Generations: Historians View American Communism"; Draper, *The Roots of American Communism*, 395, and *American Communism and Soviet Russia: The Formative Period*, 441. For the revisionist school, see Schrecker, *No Ivory Tower: McCarthyism and the Universities*; Naison, *Communists in Harlem during the Depression*; Ottanelli, *The Communist Party of the United States: From the Depression to World War II*; Klehr, *Heyday*, xi, 10, 416; Klehr, Haynes, and Fuisov, *The Secret World of American Communism*, 17–18; Klehr and Haynes, *The American Communist Movement: Storming Heaven Itself*, 177. For an account sympathetic to Klehr and Haynes, see A. Fried, *Communism in America*, chap. 3.

25. Sivachev and Yakovlev, *Russia*, 99; see also Powers, *Not without Honor*, 88. There were limits to the success of Fish's committee. The British historian M. J. Heale suggests that the absence of a Red Scare in the early 1930s "owed a great deal to the deflation of confidence in American institutions." Heale, *American Anticommunism*, 103.

26. U.S. House of Representatives, Special Committee to Investigate Communist Activities in the United States, *Hearings* (hereafter Fish Committee, *Hearings*), 1:1. See also Ogden, *The Dies Committee: A Study of the Special House Committee for the Investigation of Un-American Activities, 1938–1944*, 24–25.

27. Fish Committee, *Hearings*, 1:6.

28. Ibid., 1:15, 16, 18, 19. Walsh repeated this charge throughout the decade. In a 1932 address, he stated: "No informed man accepts the platitude that the Soviet Government and the Third International are different organizations. . . . Conspiracy against the peace of the world cannot be palliated by the stale subterfuge that it is only the left hand of the Communist Party—the Communist International—which is striking blows at this moment at world stabilization, and not the right hand—the Soviet Govern-

ment—which, on the contrary, is being held out in gestures of international friendship or in cunning appeals for loans and recognition." Edmund A. Walsh, S.J.,"International Peace through International Justice," An Address at the Sixth General Assembly, American Conference of Institutions for the Establishment of International Justice, U.S. Chamber of Commerce, May 4, 1932, 5–6, in folder 236, box 3, EAWP.

29. Ibid., 25–26; Fish Committee, *Hearings*, 4:15. Walsh later claimed that Stalin was encouraging American communists to draw "revolutionary profit from the prevailing economic crisis in their homeland." Walsh, "The Basic Issue in the Recognition of Soviet Russia," 195.

30. Fish Committee, *Hearings*, 1:28.

31. Ibid., 1:25; 4:8, 15. The original manuscript of Walsh's testimony before the Fish Committee is in folder 200, box 3, EAWP.

32. Powers, *Not without Honor*, 114; Troncone, "Hamilton Fish, Sr., and the Politics of American Nationalism, 1912–1945," a sympathetic account of Fish's activity. The *American Mercury* placed Walsh among "the amateur detectives who have entertained the Fish Committee." Ogden, *Dies Committee*, 24.

33. Hamilton Fish, Jr., to Walsh, May 28, 1931, in folder 14, box 1, EAWP; Walsh to Hamilton Fish, Jr., October 18, 1932, in folder 55, box 1, EAWP. It is worth noting that Walsh's testimony at the Fish Committee brought him to the attention of the Federal Bureau of Investigation. The oldest document in Walsh's FBI file is a copy of his remarks to the committee; see "Subject: Edmund A. Walsh," file 62–32073, sec. 1, Federal Bureau of Investigation (hereafter FBI File). (When I contacted the bureau to request the file for Edmund A. Walsh, I was informed that no such file existed. I am grateful to Steve Rosswurm, therefore, for providing me with a copy of this file.)

34. Pipes, *Communism: A History*, 58, 103.

35. Walsh, *The Last Stand: An Interpretation of the Five-Year Plan*, 71, 73; Edmund A. Walsh, S.J., as quoted in L. J. Gallagher, *Walsh*, 185.

36. Walsh, *Last Stand*, 123, 268, 35, 306.

37. L. J. Gallagher, *Walsh*, 185; Drury, "Review of *The Last Stand*," 658–59; Rorty, "More Truth About Russia"; "Four New Books on Russia"; "Books in Brief." One reader wrote *Commonweal* in 1932: "I am convinced Father Walsh's book hurts the principles he champions because of his lack of objectivity in stating the facts." "Two Views of Russia," 290. In his assessment of *The Last Stand*, Eduard Mark correctly places Walsh among those 1930s American scholars stressing the primacy of ideology in Soviet political thought and practice, although he incorrectly assumes that Walsh was a spokesman for the American Catholic Church on this issue; Mark, "October or Thermidor? Interpretations of Stalinism and the Perception of Soviet Foreign Policy in the United States, 1927–1947," 941.

38. Filene, *Americans and Soviet Experiment*, 92, 98; Wilson, *Ideology and Economics: U.S. Relations with the Soviet Union, 1918–1933*, 67. See also Davis and Trani, *The First Cold War: The Legacy of Woodrow Wilson in U.S.-Soviet Relations*. For a prorecognition view, see Robins, "United States Recognition of Russia Essential to World Peace and Stabilization," 272, 275. On William E. Borah, see Maddox, *William E. Borah and American Foreign Policy*; Borah, "The Argument for Diplomatic Relations."

39. Bennett, *Recognition of Russia*, 94; L. J. Gallagher, *Walsh*, 89, and "Walsh," 38. Walsh used his annual lecture series at Georgetown to address the recognition issue; see "Schedule of Lectures, 1930, The School of Foreign Service, Georgetown University; Announcing the Annual Course of Lectures on Soviet Russia at Georgetown University under the Auspices of the School of Foreign Service, 1932," in "Communism: Russia" file, OGSSF-NCWCF.

40. See "Says Soviet Envoys Plot Revolutions."

41. Walsh, "Basic Issue," 195, 196, 197; see also "Demands Roosevelt Give Soviet Stand." For further attacks on Senator Borah, see "Soviet Is Assailed at D.A.R. Meeting."

42. For the text of Walsh's NBC radio address, see Walsh, "America, Russia and George Bernard Shaw," 490, 491. See also Powers, *Not without Honor*, 113.

43. Walsh, "America," 489, 493, 494; L. J. Gallagher, *Walsh*, 87; see also Powers, *Not without Honor*, 113. Walsh sent copies of his address to the State Department, the War College, members of Washington's diplomatic community, and members of the press; see Memo to Salb and Trainor, November 13, 1931, in folder 93, box 2, EAWP.

44. Walsh, quoted in "Will Join in Protest against Rule of Stalin," *New York Times*, February 21, 1933, 22; and "The Catholic Church in Present-Day Russia," originally published in *Catholic Historical Review*, 18, no. 2 (July 1932): 177–204.

45. Edmund A. Walsh, S.J., "Capitalism at the Crossroads, The Nation's Task for 1933," unpublished manuscript, in folder 183, box 2, EAWP.

46. Edmund A. Walsh, S.J., as quoted in *Congressional Digest*, October 1933, 243, 245; Walsh, "Basic Issue," 195.

47. Walsh, "Rights and Obligations of Citizenship under the Constitution."

48. Edmund A. Walsh, S.J., "William Gaston of North Carolina," speech delivered at the University of North Carolina, Chapel Hill, November 28, 1938, in Watkins, *Footnotes*, 163.

49. "Excerpts from a speech of Reverend Edmund A. Walsh, S.J., Ph.D., Vice-President of Georgetown University at the fiftieth anniversary of the founding of the Elks in the City of Washington, February 11th, 1932," in folder 217, box 3, EAWP.

50. Edmund A. Walsh, S.J., "Capitalism at the Crossroads," unpublished manuscript, in folder 184, box 3, EAWP.

51. Ibid.

52. "Extracts from an Address Delivered by Edmund A. Walsh, S.J., at the 35th Annual Convention of the Eastern Commercial Teachers' Association, April 15, 1933," in folder 197, box 3, EAWP.

53. Ibid.

54. Edmund A. Walsh, S.J., "Foreign Trade and International Stability (Speech given to the Twelfth Annual Convention of the National Foreign Trade Council, June 26, 1931)," in folder 225, box 3, EAWP.

55. Walsh, "Basic Issue," 199–200.

56. Ibid., 193.

57. Dallek, *Franklin D. Roosevelt and American Foreign Policy, 1932–1945*, 78–79.

58. Bishop, *The Roosevelt-Litvinov Agreements: The American View*, 10; Dallek, *Roosevelt*, 79.

59. Flynn, *American Catholics and the Roosevelt Presidency, 1932–1936*, 95, 141.

60. Gribble, *Guardian*, 146–47; "Father Walsh on Russia," *America*, 74; "Father Walsh on Russia," *Commonweal*, 187; O'Brien, *American Catholics*, 80.

61. Sheerin, *Never Look Back*, 212–13.

62. O'Brien, *American Catholics*, 80; Walsh, "Basic Issue," 193; "Father Walsh on Russia," *Commonweal*, 4.

63. Dallek, *Roosevelt*, 80; Filene, *Americans and Soviet Experiment*, 207. A complete account of Roosevelt's reasons for espousing recognition of the Soviet Union will probably never be available because "FDR's ability to shroud motivation and conceal the inner spring of executive action has given rise to one misconception after another." Marks, *Wind over Sand: The Diplomacy of Franklin D. Roosevelt*, ix.

64. Powers, *Not without Honor*, 113–14. For the details of Walsh's meeting with Roosevelt as recounted by Walsh, see L. J. Gallagher, "Walsh," 69–70.

65. "President's Hands Free, Says Walsh"; see also Memorandum to Miss McNulty from Press Department [NCWC], October 23, 1933, in "Communism: Russia: 1933" file, OGSSF-NCWCF.

66. Walsh to Marvin H. McIntyre, October 21, 1933, in file 220a, "Russia," Official Files, Franklin D. Roosevelt Presidential Library, Hyde Park, N.Y. (hereafter OF-FDR). This letter and its accompanying notations suggest that Walsh may have discussed this matter already with the president. FDR wrote at the bottom of this letter: "Mac: Thank him and tell him I appreciate it. FDR."

67. Powers, *Not without Honor*, 113. See also Dallek, *Roosevelt*, 80; Filene, *Americans and Soviet Experiment*, 207.

68. See Burns, *Roosevelt: The Lion and the Fox*, 190; Flynn, *American Catholics*, 239; Van Allen, *The Commonweal and American Catholicism: The Magazine, the Movement, the Meaning*, 46; Gribble, *Guardian of America*, 147. On Scanlan and recognition of the Soviet Union, see McNamara, "Brooklyn *Tablet*," 51–53.

69. Patrick F. Scanlan to Wilfrid Parsons, October 24, 1933; Wilfrid Parsons to Patrick F. Scanlan, October 25, 1933, both in folder 25.0, box 5.0, Wilfrid Parsons Papers, Lauinger Library, Special Collections Division, Georgetown University, Washington, D.C.

70. Sheerin, *Never Look Back*, 212; Browder, *The Origins of Soviet-American Diplomacy*, 122; Dallek, *Roosevelt*, 79; Bennett, *Recognition of Russia*, 94–96. Of President Roosevelt's persuasive ability, Dennis J. Dunn writes: "Changing minds was FDR's specialty. He was a gifted orator and took justifiable pride in his ability to move the people. He was also a charming person and he used his charm to win over political opponents or to gain influential endorsements for a new initiative. . . . After visiting one-on-one with Roosevelt, most political leaders were putty." Dunn, *Caught between Roosevelt and Stalin: America's Ambassadors to Moscow*, 22. David Kennedy, in *Freedom from Fear*, 98, describes Roosevelt as a "master reconciler."

71. Powers, *Not without Honor*, 114; McDonough, *Men Astutely Trained*, 71–73.

72. See Memorandum to Father Walsh from "H.," February 20, 1930, in folder 57, box 1, EAWP; Walsh to Coleman Nevils, October 22, 1937, in folder 99, box 2, EAWP.

73. "The American Alliance of the United States, Inc., Radio Broadcast Series on Recognition of Soviet Russia," in "Communism: Russia: 1933" file, OGSSF-NCWCF; see also "Asks End of International"; Walsh, "What Recognition of Russia Means." Walsh to Patrick F. Scanlan, January 24, 1938, in folder 65, box 1, EAWP.

74. Edmund A. Walsh, S.J., "What Is Progress? An Address to the Graduating Class of 1934, University of Arizona, Tucson, Arizona, at the Baccalaureate Exercises, May 27, 1934," 12, 2, 5, 6–7, in FBI File.

75. Ibid. See also "Draft of remarks by the Regent, Friday, January 14, 8:15 P.M., Auditorium of the National Museum," in "Academic Exercises Commemorating the Founding of SFS, 2/17/19" folder, SFSP-GUA.

76. Walsh, "The Third American Crisis," "Communism for World War, Says Fr. Walsh," and "Extracts from Address Delivered April 15, 1933," in EAWP.

77. "Recovery or Disaster." During the 1930s, Walsh often made statements that could be construed as decidedly antilabor or, at the least, as

insensitive to the plight of American workers. In 1935, Walsh praised Americans suffering through the Depression: "For six years this Nation has been in the throes of a nation-wide catastrophe that would have shattered the very foundations of any government whose people are not so broadly tolerant, so casual, and so resilient as our own." Walsh, "Challenge to Religion," 189.

78. "Fight against NRA Is Laid to Moscow."

79. "M.S.C. Class Told Civil War Is Here," *New York Times*, June 15, 1937, 9. Walsh offered a scathing description of brain trusters to a gathering of Catholic educators: "a certain type of professor who prostitutes academic freedom to an unacademic conspiracy against the very foundations of Christian morality . . . ; who advances class hatred by a sneering and superior attitude toward those inferior breeds outside his caste who dare to dissent from his self-decreed infallibility. We who live in Washington have observed the intolerance and illiberality of such mandarins when transplanted to positions in the government and clothed with brief authority. There is still a remnant of them rushing from department to department, each with a dictator's baton in his briefcase, hoping and planning and scheming for enlarged but centralized power." Walsh, "Education and Freedom Under Democracy," 95.

80. O'Brien, *American Catholics*, 51.

81. Walsh, "Democracy's Answer to Communism," 31; "M.S.C. Class Told Civil War Is Here"; Walsh, "Religion and the Modern Mind."

82. Southern, *LaFarge*, 217; O'Brien, *American Catholics*, 57; Hennesey, *American Catholics: A History of the Roman Catholic Community in the United States*, 254, 269.

83. Walsh to Daniel C. Roper, December 13, 1935, in file 36, "Press 1935," OF-FDR. Roper told Roosevelt: "I am a great admirer of Dr. Walsh and have found him in repeated conferences on various lines sympathetic with the general objectives of the administration"; see Memorandum to FDR from Daniel C. Roper, December 14, 1935, in file 36, "Press 1935," OF-FDR.

84. O'Brien, *American Catholics*, 57. O'Brien writes: "There were only a few business-oriented attacks on the New Deal in Catholic periodicals, but several prominent Catholics who claimed to be supporters of the New Deal were disturbed by attacks on business leadership by prominent administration spokesmen." Ibid., 57. In a 1935 article that sounds suspiciously pro–big business, Walsh wrote that religion "must resist the rule of *irresponsible* wealth; it must steadfastly oppose the concentration of political and economic power in the hands of the few who possess financial power. By that it is not insinuated that men of wealth and fortune should be excluded from good repute nor looked upon with suspicion or hostility. Such men often

prove excellent public officials, and have contributed notably to government and the public good by their talents, their administrative experience, and their philanthropies." Walsh, "Challenge to Religion," 190.

85. Edmund A. Walsh, S.J., as quoted in Tillman, *School of Foreign Service*, 22–23. In an April 1932 speech at Georgetown, Walsh stated: "I think you will agree with me that no institution stands more fearlessly for the natural right of property, for order in the state and respect for constituted authority, whether human or divine, than the Catholic Church." Walsh, "Capitalism at Crossroads," in folder 184, box 3, EAWP. It should be noted that in 1935, Georgetown did finally accept federal aid for the SFS students, so long as the money went directly to the students and not to the school itself.

86. Kennedy, *Freedom from Fear*, 23, 87. On the National Foreign Trade Council's annual convention, see Memo to Father Walsh from "H.," February 20, 1930, in EAWP; Walsh to Coleman Nevils, October 22, 1937, in folder 99, box 2, EAWP. In early 1922, Walsh secured for Farrell permission to erect a private chapel in his residence, writing John Creeden: "How much do you think it would be worth? $50,000?" Walsh to "Dear Fr. Rector," February 7, 1922, in file 94, box 2, EAWP. Walsh moved among the more conservative elements of Washington society, which the WSCP at the Library of Congress confirm. Culbertson, a Washington attorney and Georgetown faculty member, kept copies of dinner invitation lists, which read like a *Who's Who* of 1930s Washington conservatives. Frequently present at the same Sunday dinner parties were conservative senators, judges, and renowned conservatives such as former President Hoover, with whom Walsh maintained close ties from his ARA days. See "Sunday—May 17th," in "1936" file, box 15, WSCP.

87. "Academic Diet in Colleges Is Too Soft and Lower Schools Are Faulty."

88. Walsh, "Education and Freedom," 89, 95.

89. Walsh, "Ethical Standards in High School Instruction"; see also "Studebaker Denies Facing Pressure."

90. Walsh, "An Epistle to the Romans: *Modern Style*," 241; Gleason, *Contending with Modernity*, 146.

91. "University Unit is 21 Years Old." Walsh had good reason to celebrate. In 1936, Georgetown faculty member William Franklin wrote him: "You have become an acknowledged center of influence." William Franklin Sands to Walsh, May 17, 1936, in William Franklin Sands Papers, Philadelphia Archdiocesan Historical Research Center, Overbrook, Pa.

92. Walsh, "Challenge to Religion," 185, and "Religion," 385–86.

93. Walsh to J. Edgar Hoover, July 23, 1937, in FBI File; see also J. Edgar Hoover to Walsh, August 12, 1937, in same file; Rosswurm, "Manhood," 14.

94. "Fight against NRA." On the growth of Communist Party membership during the Depression, see Glazer, *Social Basis*, 92–93, 133. Glazer estimates that CPUSA membership grew from 7,500 in 1930 to an all-time high of 55,000 in 1938. New York formed nearly one-quarter of the national membership in 1934, and one-half by 1938.

95. "Communism for World War"; "Announcing the Annual Course of Lectures by Edmund A. Walsh, S.J., at Georgetown University (1936)," in "Communism: General" file, OGSSF-NCWCF.

96. "Union Sodality Convenes at Georgetown University; Delegates Discuss Communism."

97. U.S. House of Representatives, Special Committee on Un-American Activities, *Investigations of Nazi Propaganda Activities and Investigation of Certain Other Propaganda Activities: Public Hearings*, 139.

98. "Reds Seen Backing Roosevelt"; Walsh, "The Great Fallacy." On FDR's relationship with the CPUSA, see Burns, *Roosevelt*, 243; Klehr and Haynes, *American Communist Movement*, 80–81; Ottanelli, *Communist Party*, 103–5.

99. *New York Times*, April 15, 1936, 23.

100. Walsh, "Education and Freedom," 98; Karl Adam, as quoted in ibid., 100.

101. "Father Walsh Answers Browder."

102. For an overview of the Spanish civil war, see Bolloten, *The Spanish Civil War: Revolution and Counter-Revolution*. For a general survey of American responses, see Guttmann, *The Wound in the Heart: American Response to and Interpretation of the Spanish Civil War*. For an overview of the American Catholic response, see Valaik, "American Catholic Dissenters and the Spanish Civil War, 1936–1939"; Hennesey, *American Catholics*, 272.

103. Sánchez, "The Spanish Civil War and American Catholics."

104. F. J. Taylor, *The United States and the Spanish Civil War*, 7.

105. Ibid., 143.

106. Powers, *Not without Honor*, 134.

107. Traina, *American Diplomacy and the Spanish Civil War*, 4.

108. Sánchez, "Spanish Civil War," 1346.

109. F. J. Taylor, *Spanish Civil War*, 148.

110. Van Allen, *Commonweal*, 61; Valaik, "American Catholic Dissenters," 539.

111. O'Brien, *Public Catholicism*, 181; see also O'Brien, *American Catholics*, 88.

112. George N. Shuster, *Commonweal*, April 23, 1937, 716, as quoted in Blantz, *George N. Shuster: On the Side of Truth*, 86.

113. O'Brien, *American Catholics*, 89. Years later, George Shuster recalled that, as he was leaving *Commonweal*, "it occurred to me that for Catholic

New York the outside world was either Communist or Fascist, and that therefore they had opted for Fascism." George N. Shuster, as quoted in Hennesey, *American Catholics*, 272. For the Talbot quote, see O'Brien, *Public Catholicism*, 181.

114. Powers, *Not without Honor*, 135.

115. Walsh to Talbot, September 2, 1938, in folder 66, box 1, EAWP.

116. McDonough, *Men Astutely Trained*, 74. From the start, it was clear that *Informationes et Notitiae* was restricted to Jesuit use: "By direction of Father General these communications for the present are to be considered *ad usum nostrorum tantrum.*" *Informationes et Notitiae*, no. 4 (June 1935), i.

117. Walsh, "The Two Standards in 1935." From the Pincian Hill, or Pincio, the cupola of Saint Peter's Basilica on the western horizon is clearly visible.

118. Ibid.

119. Curran, *American Jesuit Spirituality: The Maryland Tradition, 1634–1900*, 5. See also O'Malley, *The Fifth Week*, xiii.

120. Puhl, *The Spiritual Exercises of St. Ignatius: Based on Studies in the Language of the Autograph*, 60. In arguing for the importance of Ignatian imagery as an influence on Walsh's anticommunism, I do not imply that other anticommunist Jesuits would have reached the same conclusions in their own experience of the spiritual exercises. John LaFarge, for example, did not employ this imagery to any significant extent in his own writings. See Southern, *LaFarge*, 216.

121. Rahner, *Spiritual Exercises*, 169, 172; Fleming, *A Contemporary Reading of the Spiritual Exercises: A Companion to St. Ignatius' Text*, 34, xiii.

122. "Martyrs in Russia"; Walsh, "Basic Issue,"193; Fish Committee, *Hearings*, 1:15.

123. Puhl, *Spiritual Exercises*, 12; Walsh, *The Last Stand*, 170.

124. Ledochowski, "Letter of Very Rev. Fr. General to the Provincials of the American Assistancy and Canada"; McDonough, *Men Astutely Trained*, 74. See also Southern, *LaFarge*, 217; Walsh to "Reverend and Dear Father," May 15, 1935, in folder 99, box 2, EAWP; "Minutes of the Inter-Province Meeting on Communism and Atheism."

125. McDonough, *Men Astutely Trained*, 74.

126. Although Walsh endorsed a living wage, unemployment insurance, and social security, his specific reform suggestions were generally vague. In a 1936 commencement address at Georgetown, he suggested creating an economic council composed of representatives from capital and industry, labor, agriculture, the professions, religious and other groups, which would "legislate for the good of all the people, not for any section or specific industry" to do what "Congress cannot or will not do." Walsh's suggestions show

the influence of the 1931 encyclical *Quadragesimo Anno*. The economic council would not be an official body, he stated, but "in such a house of national welfare . . . no one group could hope to secure advantages for any special interest. Such an organized economic body would preserve the organic unity of society, be a powerful auxiliary to government and disarm the visionary and the bolshevik." "Social Council Urged for Nation by Walsh," 13. See also Walsh, "Democracy's Answer." In 1931, he urged "a chastened sense of fellowship between employer and employed, such as existed in the medieval guilds, based on the consciousness of a common origin and a supernatural destiny." Walsh, "America," 499.

127. McDonough, *Men Astutely Trained*, 72.

128. Walsh, "Editorial"; "Walsh Denies Political Stand by Catholic Church," *Washington Herald*, October 15, 1936, in folder 757, box 12, EAWP.

129. New York priest's letter to *Commonweal*, as quoted in Broderick, *Right Reverend New Dealer: John A. Ryan*, 192.

130. Fisher, *The Catholic Counterculture in America, 1933–1962*, 74; "From the Managing Editor's Desk," *Tablet*, June 26, 1930, 9.

131. Fisher, *Catholic Counterculture*, 85–86. Ronald Bayor writes that, although the *Tablet* was "ostensibly a Catholic newspaper, it actually represented a mainly Irish viewpoint." Bayor, *Neighbors In Conflict: The Irish, Germans, Jews, and Italians of New York City, 1929–1941*, 175–76. On Patrick F. Scanlan in the 1930s, see McNamara, "Brooklyn *Tablet*," chap. 2.

132. O'Brien, *American Catholics*, 209; Miller, *Dorothy Day: A Biography*, 262. See also Fisher, *Catholic Counterculture*, 90; Miller, *A Harsh and Dreadful Love: Dorothy Day and the Catholic Worker Movement*.

133. Crosby, *God, Church, and Flag*, 15. On Bishop Fulton J. Sheen, see Reeves, *America's Bishop: The Life and Times of Fulton J. Sheen*; Massa, *Catholics*, 86.

134. Gribble, *Guardian*, 146; Southern, *LaFarge*, 216.

135. The first reliable study of Father Charles E. Coughlin was Tull, *Father Coughlin and the New Deal*, still a fine account. An insightful study of Coughlin as a person, containing interviews previously unavailable, is Marcus, *Father Coughlin: The Tumultuous Life of the Priest of the Little Flower*. The best study of Coughlin's ideology and its place within the larger historical framework is Brinkley, *Voices of Protest: Huey Long, Father Coughlin and the Great Depression*. Also useful are Tentler, *Seasons of Grace*, 332–42; Athans, *The Coughlin-Fahey Connection: Father Charles E. Coughlin, Father Denis Fahey, C.S.Sp., and Religious Anti-Semitism in the United States*. A recent and irresponsible work that adds nothing to the historiographical debate surrounding Coughlin's ideology is Warren, *Radio Priest: Charles Coughlin, The Father of Hate Radio*.

136. Powers, *Not without Honor*, 117–18, 129, 132; Broderick, *Right Reverend*, 234; Blantz, *A Priest in Public Service: Francis J. Haas and the New Deal*, 113. See also Ryan, *The Church and Socialism, and Other Essays*.

137. "Moves to End Jam on Neutrality Act"; Key Pittman to Walsh, April 26, 1939, in folder 63, box 1, EAWP. U.S. Senate, Committee on Foreign Relations, *Neutrality, Peace Legislation and Our Foreign Policy: Hearings*, 481 (hereafter *Neutrality Hearings*).

138. Flynn, *Roosevelt and Romanism: Catholics and American Diplomacy, 1937–1945*, 7, 22; Walsh to Herbert Hoover, September 20, 1939, in "Walsh, Rev. Ed. A." file, box 247, Post-Presidential Individual Papers, Herbert Hoover Presidential Library, Long Branch, Iowa.

139. *Neutrality Hearings*, 480.

140. Dan O'Connell, "Father Walsh and Japan," *Foreign Service Courier* 5, no. 12 (1957): 12–25, in folder 703, box 11, EAWP; "Walsh Calls Wilson Ideal a 'Disservice,'" *Washington Post*, March 21, 1936, in folder 757, box 12, EAWP; Walsh, "Religion,"385–86. In 1931, Walsh wrote: "In world relations it is the heart of humanity that must be won. Commendable indeed are naval conferences, agreements of limitation of armaments, pacts for the outlawry of war, economic conventions, and similar laudable attempts to eliminate the dangers of international warfare by limiting both the occasions and the physical instrumentalities of war. But they furnish inadequate guarantees of peace unless simultaneously we disarm the spirit of hatred and distrust among nations as well as among individuals, tranquilize men's hearts, and educate them to mutual respect and confidence." Walsh, *Last Stand*, 253–54.

141. *Neutrality Hearings*, 481; "Moscow Statement on Religion Disappoints White House Circles"; "Mgr. Walsh Backs Moves"; Walter Lippmann, "Russia, America, and Mr. Roosevelt," undated clipping in "ARA Personnel File—Walsh, Edmund J. [sic], 1929–1932," box 75, ARAP. On opposition to Lend-Lease, see Cole, *Roosevelt and the Isolationists, 1932–1945*, 374–79, 409–22, 436–44; Freidel, *Franklin D. Roosevelt: A Rendezvous with Destiny*, 347–48, 361–63. In 1936, Walsh told the National Catholic Educational Association that international communism was waiting for the nations to "embark again on reciprocal homicide" and "that will be its opportunity to strike a telling blow against democracy. *New York Times*, April 15, 1936, 23. See also Walsh, *Last Stand*, 50–51.

142. "Faiths at Capital Hit Persecutions"; "Fears War Menace in German Election"; "Federal Officials Accused As 'Reds'"; see also "Castle Backs Hull on Neutrality Aim."

143. Walsh, "Epistle." Other Jesuits expressed similar views during this period. At a 1934 meeting of the Jesuit Philosophical Association of the Eastern States, Rev. J. F. X. Murphy, S.J., professor of History at Boston

College, delivered a paper entitled "The Problem of International Judaism." As reported in the *New York Times,* after praising "the Jew's tremendous capacity for spiritual insight and growth," he berated "the intense clannishness of the Jew . . . the root element in his character that makes the Jew a problem today as he was to the Romans of old." He concluded that the "Jewish problem . . . arises because of the different intellectual and moral ideals of the Hebrew as opposed to the Christian ideal, which, of course, not all Christians live up to." Murphy said that Jews "who lost connection with their religion do harm by their lack of morals in their influence on the stage, the motion pictures and above all the daily press." Rev. J. F. X. Murphy, as quoted in "Fight against NRA." *America*'s editor Wilfrid Parsons defended Murphy's speech, stating that the Jesuit "had no intention of joining himself to any anti-Semitic movement." In 1931, Walsh referred to foreign bankers financing the Five-Year Plan as "Shylocks"; Walsh, *Last Stand,* 131.

144. Flynn, *Roosevelt,* 185, 179; Walsh to Franklin D. Roosevelt, December 18, 1941, in PPF 7883, OF-FDR.

145. "Catholic Veterans at Special Mass."

146. On Virgil Michel, see Paul Marx, *Virgil Michel and the Liturgical Movement.*

CHAPTER 4: "AN AMERICAN GEOPOLITICS": WALSH AND WARTIME CATHOLIC ANTICOMMUNISM, 1941–45

1. Sittser, *A Cautious Patriotism: The American Churches and the Second World War,* 2; Hennesey, *American Catholics,* 276; Fogarty, *Vatican and American Hierarchy,* 276.

2. Sirgiovanni, *An Undercurrent of Suspicion: Anti-Communism in America during World War II,* 3–7, 189; Heale, *American Anticommunism,* 96–102; Powers, *Not without Honor,* 156, 169.

3. Sirgiovanni, *Undercurrent,* 1–2, 188.

4. Ibid., 147; James Gillis and Patrick F. Scanlan, as quoted in McNamara, "Brooklyn *Tablet,*" 90. On James Gillis's wartime stance, see Gribble, *Guardian,* 164–73.

5. A 1947 biographical sketch for *Catholic Authors* stated: "One of the great authorities in the United States on the Russian question is Dr. Edmund A. Walsh. For the past eighteen years he has made a close study of Russian affairs, and has written several books, articles, and pamphlets on the subject. He has lectured on Russia over 2,000 times, having appeared in practically all the leading cities of the United States. His library contains

over 3,000 books on foreign affairs, and his office is full of maps, pictures, and posters that betray his interest in the Soviet State." "Reverend Walsh."

6. For the growth of geopolitics as an academic discipline, I have found Blouet, *Geopolitics and Globalization in the Twentieth Century*, and Parker, *Western Geopolitical Thought in the Twentieth Century*, to be particularly helpful.

7. Blouet, *Geopolitics*, 7; see also, Musicant, *Empire by Default: The Spanish-American War and the Dawn of the American Century*, 3–10; Hunt, *Ideology and U.S. Foreign Policy*, 153. For a more recent discussion of the rise of American geopolitical consciousness, see Zimmermann, *First Great Triumph: How Five Americans Made Their Country a World Power*. One scholar of German geopolitics writes that "Mahan, in his day, earned renown as a modern, maritime Clausewitz." Murphy, *The Heroic Earth: Geopolitical Thought in Weimar Germany*, 3.

8. On Friedrich Ratzel, see Blouet, *Geopolitics*, 28–30; Parker, *Western Geopolitical Thought*, 11; Murphy, *Heroic Earth*, 10.

9. On Sir Halford Mackinder, see Blouet, *Halford Mackinder: A Biography*, and *Geopolitics*, 11, 27–28, 51. On Mackinder and Russia, see Hauner, *What Is Asia to Us? Russia's Asian Heartland Yesterday and Today*, chap. 7.

10. This summary of the main tenets of Haushofer's *Geopolitik* is taken from Blouet, *Geopolitics*, 56–62. Blouet, ibid., 61, estimates that *Zeitschrift für Geopolitik* reached a circulation of 700,000 during the 1930s. On the journal's influence, see also Parker, *Western Geopolitical Thought*, 57, 61; Murphy, *Heroic Earth*, 106.

11. Blouet, *Geopolitics*, 57, 60; Parker, *Western Geopolitical Thought*, 61. Blouet, *Mackinder*, 178, writes that Mackinder was "the prestigious outsider quoted to buttress established orthodoxy" in Germany.

12. Overy, *Interrogators: The Nazi Elite in Allied Hands, 1945*, 119.

13. Blouet, *Geopolitics*, 60–61.

14. Murphy, *Heroic Earth*, vii–viii. According to Blouet, *Mackinder*, 190, "Haushofer was not an original thinker, and he combed the work of writers like Curzon, Mackinder, Holdich, Fairgreave, Mahan, Bowman, and Kjellen (author of the term *geopolitics*) for ideas to buttress his arguments."

15. Edmund A. Walsh, S.J., "Geopolitical Position of the United States (Lecture to the Army War College, August 26, 1952)," 17–18, in folder 234, box 3, EAWP. Walsh's friend and longtime Georgetown faculty member Carroll Quigley asserted that Walsh only became interested in geopolitics by the late 1930s; see Quigley, "McGuire," 20.

16. "Pan-Europe Called Aim of Nazi Drive." For evidence of his strong interest in German affairs during the 1930s, see Walsh to Hamilton Fish Armstrong, July 16, 1934, in Hamilton Fish Armstrong Papers, Seely-Mudd Collection, Princeton University, Princeton, N.J.

17. Blouet, *Geopolitics*, 54, 120–21, 123; Parker, *Western Geopolitical Thought*, 5, 102; for the development of geopolitical thought in North America, see esp. chap. 7. The diplomatic historian Michael Hunt suggests that a major reason for the popularity of geopolitics among American scholars during the Second World War and thereafter was that "first-generation Wilsonians" were seeking out a less moralistic-sounding vocabulary than had been used in the previous conflict. The new technology "narrowed the gap between nations so developments half a world away could affect foreign policy as never before." Hunt, *Ideology*, 152.

18. Durkin, *Georgetown*, 113–14; GUSFS, *War Bulletin 3*, 8; "Press Release for February 28, 1942," in folder 325, box 5, EAWP.

19. Tillman, *School of Foreign Service*, 23–24; GUSFS, *Undergraduate Courses in Foreign Service, Business and Public Administration (War Bulletin 1)*, 14. See also "Course in Geopolitics," *Times Herald*, September 17, 1942, in folder 763, box 12, EAWP. A useful explanation of the difference between the ASTP and the SATC is available in Durkin, *Georgetown*, 95–96. Durkin notes that Georgetown had an Army ROTC program dating back to the First World War.

20. Gleason, *Contending with Modernity*, 211–15; "Walsh, Biographical Notes," in folder 702, box 11, EAWP; Tillman, *School of Foreign Service*, 24; GUSFS, *War Bulletin 4*, 7.

21. Gleason, *Contending with Modernity*, 213; Walsh to Culbertson, October 31, 1942, in "July–December 1942" file, box 22, WSCP; Edmund A. Walsh, S.J., "The Function of Education in Total War," in GUSFS, *War Bulletin 3*, 15.

22. GUSFS, *War Bulletin 4*, 25–26. Tillman, *School of Foreign Service*, 14.

23. For a list of Walsh's course offerings in the prewar years, I have consulted the following course catalogues from the period, all of which are available in Georgetown's Lauinger Library: GUSFS, *Catalogue, 1931–1932*, 15, *Catalogue, 1933–1934*, 10; *Catalogue, 1937*, 14; *Catalogue, 1938–1939*, 10, *Catalogue, 1939–1940*, 10, *Catalogue, 1940–1941*, 10, and *Undergraduate Course in Foreign Service Catalogue, 1941–1942*, 10, resp.

24. GUSFS, *Undergraduate Curriculum, 1945*, 10; "Political Economy of Total War, Second Semester [January 9, 1942]," in "Jan.–June 1942" file, box 22, WSCP; see also "Lecturers in the Course 'Political Economy of Total War,' from October 1941 to May 1942," in same file. Culbertson wanted to teach a course later on called "Political Economy of Total Peace"; see Culbertson to Walsh, January 15, 1947, in "Jan.–June 1947" file, box 29, WSCP.

25. "Course on Geopolitics, Lecturer: Edmund A. Walsh, S.J., [1942]," 8–9, in folder 331, box 5, EAWP. In 1945, Walsh taught a course entitled "Distorted Geopolitics—Germany, Japan"; GUSFS, *Fall Quarter (October 1–December 21, 1945)*, 10.

26. "Dr. Walsh to Give Series of Lectures on U.S. and Total War," *Washington Star*, January 28, 1942, in folder 762, box 12, EAWP; "Dr. Edmund Walsh to Give Lecture Series," *Catholic Review*, February 6, 1942, in folder 762, box 12, EAWP.

27. "Curriculum Vitae," 2, in EAWP; "Walsh, Biographical Notes," 2–3, in EAWP; Parr, "Mousquetaires," 15, in P-SA. For a firsthand description of Walsh's lecture tours, see Walsh to Hoover, June 20, 1942, in "Walsh, Rev. Ed. A." file, box 247, Post-Presidential Individual Papers, Hoover Presidential Library, Long Branch, Iowa. See also Walsh to Evelyn Walsh McLean, January 10, 1945, in "Walker-Wilson" file, box 8, Evelyn Walsh McLean Papers, Library of Congress, Manuscript Division, Washington, D.C. On Walsh's positive reception by the military see William S. Culbertson, "Memorandum for General Crowell, July 7, 1943," in "Chapter XXVI" file, box 95, WSCP (Culbertson chapter files contain material from his unpublished autobiography "Ventures in Time and Space").

28. "Personnel of Analysis Section, June 18, 1943," in "Analysis Section, War Department, General Staff, Miscellaneous, 1943, n.d." file, box 180; "Memorandum No. 61: Subject: Geopolitical Section, Military Intelligence Service, June 18, 1942"; see also "Concerning the Organization of the Geopolitical Section, August 3, 1942," in "July–Dec. 1942" file, box 22; Edmund Meade Earl to Henry L. Stimson, June 2, 1943, in "Chapter XXVI" file, box 95, all in WSCP. On the arguments advanced on behalf of a geopolitical division, see Lt. Colonel William S. Culbertson, "Memorandum for the Secretary of War, Subject: The Analysis Section, June 3, 1943," in "Jan.–June 1943" file, box 22, WSCP. During the war, Culbertson served as a member of the Planning Group, Office of Strategic Services (1943–44), as chairman of the Special Economic Mission to North Africa, the Middle East and Italy (1944), and worked in technological intelligence in Germany (1945); see Culbertson, "Chapter XXVI" file, in box 95; "Colonel Culbertson's Army Assignments during World War II," in "1945" file, box 26, all in WSCP.

29. "Memorandum for General Strong: Subject: Geopolitics, June 6, 1942," in "Chapter XXVI" file, box 95; "Personnel of Analysis Section, June 18, 1943," in "Analysis Section, War Department, General Staff, Miscellaneous, 1943, n.d." file, box 180, both in WSCP; Walsh to Lt.-Col. W. S. Culbertson, December 7, 1942, in folder 100, box 2, EAWP.

30. Culbertson, "Chapter XXVI" file, box 95, in WSCP. For Stimson's response to Walsh's letter of May 30, 1942, see Henry L. Stimson to Walsh, June 6, 1942, in "Chapter XXVI" file, box 95, WSCP: "I fully agree with you that, of all the Government agencies, the War Department is best suited to take the lead in this important work, and to this end a Geopolitical Section has been set up in the Military Intelligence Division of the General Staff.... I am greatly appreciative of the splendid work which you have been doing

for the War Department on your lecture tours." See also "A Tribute to the Reverend Edmund A. Walsh, S.J., by Dr. William S. Culbertson, Honorary Chairman, Symposium on Training for the Foreign Service," 2–3, in "Chapter XXV" file, box 94, WSCP. Walsh's letter of May 30, 1942, is available in neither the EAWP nor the WSCP.

31. Edmund A. Walsh, S.J., as quoted in William S. Culbertson, "Memorandum for General Kroner, September 21, 1942," in "July–Dec. 1942" file, box 22, WSCP.

32. Culbertson to Henry L. Stimson, February 15, 1945, in "Jan.–June 1945" file, box 26; William S. Culbertson to Brig. Gen. Benedict Crowell, August 26, 1943, in "Chapter XXVI" file, box 95, both in WSCP.

33. "*Institute of World Polity*, Statement of Purpose, Organization and Methods, Washington, January 20, 1945," in "Jan.–June 1945" file, box 26, WSCP; "Walsh, Biographical Notes," 3, in EAWP. Tillman, *School of Foreign Service*, 31; GUSFS, *War Bulletin 4*, 24.

34. Walsh, "Geopolitics and International Morals,"12–13, 15, 27, 22. See also E. A. Walsh, "Review of *Geopolitics, The New German Science*, by Andrew Gyorgy," *American Journal of International Law*, October 1944," 1, in folder 229, box 3, EAWP. Walsh did see some good coming out of the Haushofer school: "Among the beneficial consequences of the exaggerated German '*Geopolitik*' must be counted, first, the sharpening and focussing of our knowledge respecting the power-potential of all the major areas of the world." Edmund A. Walsh, S.J., "Russia and Her Future Potential— Military and Industrial—Seminar, Discussion, Army Industrial College, Wednesday, April 18, 1945," 1, in folder 279, box 4, EAWP.

35. Walsh, "Geopolitics," 26–27.

36. Ibid., 35, 36; "Religion Mainstay of U.S., Dr. Walsh Tells D.A.R. Parley," *Times Herald*, May 4, 1942, in file 762, box 12, EAWP.

37. Walsh, "Geopolitics," 36. "Press Release for April 11, 1942," in folder 325, box 5, EAWP. See also "Dr. Walsh Proposes that Stalin Pledge Freedom's Defense," *Washington Star*, 11 April 1942, in folder 762, box 12, EAWP. Culbertson, "Memorandum for General Kroner, September 21, 1942," in "July–Dec. 1942" file, box 22, WSCP.

38. "Soviet Russia and the Peace of Europe, Address to the League of Catholic Women, Boston, March 19, 1944," 4, 7, 9–11, 15, in folder 297, box 4, EAWP.

39. "Press Release, Springfield, Ill., October 11, 1944," in folder 294, box 4, EAWP. See also Frank A. Hall to Monsignor [Michael J.] Ready, October 12, 1944, in "Communism: Russia: 1944–1945" file, OGSSF-NCWCF; "Declares Russia is Self-Seeking," *New York Sun*, October 12, 1944, in "ARA Personnel File, Walsh, Edmund J., 1921–1952," box 75, ARAP; "Russia's Aid Seen Lagging."

40. Sirgiovanni, *Undercurrent*, 86, 158; Powers, *Not without Honor*, 175. See also LaFeber, *America, Russia and the Cold War, 1945–1992*,15; L. E. Davis, *The Cold War Begins: Soviet-American Conflict over Eastern Europe*, 38–61.

41. Edmund A. Walsh, S.J., "Future Relationship of the United States and Russia," National Institute of Social Sciences, Panel Discussion, December 13, 1944, New York City, 1, 6–8, in folder 228, box 3, EAWP.

42. Edmund A. Walsh, S.J., "Present and Future of Russia, Auditorium, University of Pittsburgh, Jan. 15, 1945," 9, in folder 262, box 4, EAWP; Edmund A. Walsh, S.J., "Speech before the British Mission, Wash., D.C., March 28, 1945," 2–4, in folder 230, box 3, EAWP.

43. Walsh, "Geopolitics," 39. On Walsh's wartime lectures on Soviet geopolitics to the military, see Brigadier General D. Armstrong to Walsh, April 11, 1945, in folder 51, box 1, EAWP.

44. Zink, *The United States in Germany, 1944–1955*, 26–29, 282; Zienike, "The Formulation and Initial Implementation of U.S. Occupation Policy in Germany." For an overview on the U.S. occupation of Germany, see Gimbel, *The American Occupation of Germany: Politics and the Military, 1945–1949*. See also Wiggers, "Creating International Humanitarian Law (IHL): World War II, the Allied Occupations, and the Treaties That Followed." Also useful is Blantz, *Shuster*, chap. 8.

45. Ninkovich, *Germany and the United States: The Transformation of the German Question since 1945*, 30–31.

46. Ibid., 31–32.

47. "Walsh, Biographical Notes," 3, in EAWP; "Curriculum Vitae," in EAWP; L. J. Gallagher, *Walsh*, 146, 148, 149–150, 151, 156; Parr, "Mousquetaires," 15, in P-SA.

48. "E. A. Walsh, *Private*, Germany 1945, no. 1 (a) Control—(b) Judge Advocate General's Office, USA (appointment and date up to leaving Washington)" (hereafter Nuremberg Diary no. 1), May 29, 1945, in folder 126, box 2, EAWP.

49. Ibid., May 8, 1945.

50. Zaccheus J. Maher, S.J., to Walsh, May 30, 1945, in ibid., May 30, 1945; Maher went on to say: "It is extremely important that your association in this mission be made known to the Holy Father and to Fr. Vicar. You yourself will know best when and how to best advise them, whether through the Apostolic Delegate or other confidential channels." On Maher, see McDonough, *Men Astutely Trained*, 161–69.

51. *Nuremberg Diary*, no. 1 (July 15, 1945; July 18, 1945; July 23, 1945). Walsh's War Department identification card and information sheet are in folder 438, box 7, EAWP. His information sheet lists him as "field-grade officer—assimilated rank." Official title is "Expert Consultant." Walsh's

traveling orders are in folder 439, box 7, EAWP. For a list of contacts, see "To Be Seen in Germany" [1945], in folder 441, box 7, EAWP.

52. Justice Robert H. Jackson, as quoted in "Edmund A. Walsh. Private. Europe 1945. From August 21, 1945 to Nov. 3, 1945. (incl.)" (hereafter Nuremberg Diary no. 2), August 31, 1945, in folder 126, box 2, EAWP. "Dr. Walsh Translates Letters from Vatican to Nazi Leaders," unidentified clipping, November 26, 1945, in file 763, box 12, EAWP; "Vatican's Document on Nazis Ready for Court, Walsh Says," *Washington Star*, January 6, 1946, in file 764, box 12, EAWP. On Monsignor Domenico Tardini, see Blet, *Pius XII and the Second World War: According to the Archives of the Vatican*, 7–8.

53. "Re Documents Furnished by the Vatican on Persecution of the Churches, Used at Nuremberg," n.d., in "Nuremberg War Crime Trial Offices—U.S. Chief of Counsel—The Vatican" file, box 111, Robert H. Jackson Papers, Manuscript Division, Library of Congress; see also Healey, "Diplomat Priest," 20; "Re Documents Furnished by the Vatican on Persecution of the Churches, Used at Nuernberg," n.d.; Kenneth Leslie to Robert H. Jackson, August 28, 1946; Robert H. Jackson to Kenneth Leslie, September 4, 1946, all in "Nuremberg War Crimes Trial Offices—U.S. Chief of Counsel—The Vatican" file, box 111, Robert H. Jackson Papers, Library of Congress, Manuscript Division, Washington, D.C. (hereafter RHJP). John Parr recalls that Walsh's presence on Jackson's staff "gave rise to the informal belief that he was an informal Vatican observer. However this may be, he never was on intimate terms with His Holiness Pope Pius XII, as he had been with his predecessor." Parr, "Mousquetaires," 15, in P-SA. George P. Morse, who served as General William Donovan's aide in the Office of Strategic Services, helped Walsh prepare the brief on the persecution of the Christian Churches. He recalls that Walsh was highly regarded by Jackson; interview with George P. Morse Jr., at Georgetown University, August 21, 2002.

54. "Jackson Lauded for Nuremberg"; Healey, "Diplomat Priest," 19; "Dr. Walsh Says Nazi Victory Meant End of Church in Reich," unidentified clipping, November 16, 1945, in file 764, box 12, EAWP.

55. Nuremberg Diary no. 2, August 31, 1945, September 14, 26, 28, and 29, 1945, October 1 and 30, 1945, November 4, 1945; see also Healey, "Diplomat Priest," 20. Monsignor Tardini's comments are in the October 30, 1945, diary entry.

56. Nuremberg Diary no. 2, September 2 and October 11, 1945.

57. Walsh, *Total Power: A Footnote to History*, 101. Gerald Sittser writes that American Churches in general "were so concerned about the suffering of Christians in Europe that they neglected to intervene on behalf of the Jews." Sittser, *Cautious Patriotism*, 215.

58. In his study of Irish-Jewish conflict in Depression-era New York City, Ronald Bayor writes that, after the Second World War, "anti-Communism,

though still strong, no longer had an anti-Semitic emphasis. Perhaps the revelation of the Nazi atrocities at this time muted this and other anti-Jewish feelings." Bayor, *Neighbors in Conflict,* 165. I suspect that this may have been a significant factor in Walsh's case as well.

59. See folder 636, box 10, in EAWP; Nuremberg Diary no. 2, September 18–20, 1945. For a summary of the interrogations done with Haushofer before Walsh took over, see "Secret Enclosure, Evaluation Report 55, 5 June 1945, Combined Intelligence Objectives Sub-Committee, Interrogation of Dr. Karl Haushofer, Professor of Geo-Politics at the University of Munich," in "Chapter XXVI" file, box 95, WSCP. On the interrogation, see "Testimony of Karl Haushofer, Taken at Nürnberg, Germany, 5 October 1945, 1445–1600, by Colonel Howard A. Brundage, JAGD, OUSCC," in folder 635, box 10, EAWP. See also Walsh, *Total Power,* 12.

60. Walsh, *Total Power,* 3, 11, 12, 17. See also Ernst H. Feilchenfeld to William S. Culbertson, February 5, 1946, in "Jan.–June 1946" file, box 27, WSCP. It seems that Walsh went into the interrogations with a predetermined agenda: "The conspiracy of Haushofer in his application of geopolitics was an entirely unprecedented device which transcends previous categories of conspiracy and should not be judged by the rules drawn up for the more conventional statutory crimes. The moral law is more comprehensive, less systematized than penal laws and hence cannot be confined to rules drawn for crimes on a lesser scale. The crimes of this war must be judged not only by a court of Int[ernational] Equity courageous enough to supply the defects and inadequacies of enacted, positive law. Too much adherence to the latter conventions may result in some of the major conspirators, e.g., Haushofer, escaping justice." Nuremberg Diary no. 2, September 2, 1945. For the text of Haushofer's "Defense of German Geopolitics," see Walsh, *Total Power,* 344–53.

61. "Report on Professor Karl Haushofer of the University of Munich and the influence of his *Geopolitics,* Prepared for Justice Jackson, by Dr. Edmund A. Walsh, Consultant, 2 November 1945," 1–2, 3, 4, 10, 15, 18, in folder 644, box 10, EAWP; Walsh had suggested "*not* rounding up every guilty geopolitician," but "indict[ing] a chosen example, i.e., General Karl Haushofer and concentrat[ing] on him as the symbol and chief instigator of the entire geopolitical movement." See also "Memorandum on the Role of Haushofer and Geopolitics, 10 September 1945," in folder 633, box 10, EAWP.

62. "Edmund A. Walsh. *Private.* Europe 1945 III From Nov. 4, 1945 to July 1, 1946 to Oct. 2, 1946" (hereafter Nuremberg Diary no. 3), March 15, 1946, in folder 126, box 2, EAWP; Healey, "Diplomat Priest," 19. At least one scholar has speculated that Walsh may have overemphasized his role in the Haushofer case, in order to enhance his own reputation. In his study of

Walsh's geopolitics, Gearóid Ó Tuathail / Gerard Toal writes: "Even in 1948 after he had interviewed Haushofer and the U.S. Army had determined that he was not particularly important to the Nazi state or close to Hitler, Walsh was wont to exaggerate Haushofer's influence and his own prescience about him." Ó Tuathail / Toal, "Spiritual Geopolitics," 202.

63. Nuremberg Diary no. 3, October 30, 1945, November 4, 1945; "Russians Hit for Hypocrisy in Diplomacy," unidentified clipping, March 4, 1947, in folder 764, box 12, EAWP.

64. "Jackson Lauded." See also "Dr. Walsh Attributes to Jackson Start of World Jurisprudence," *Washington Star*, March 4, 1947; Jackson to Walsh, March 5, 1947, both in "Walsh" file, box 21, RHJP. "Nuremberg Staff Doubts Trials' Legality," *Times-Herald*, July 10, 1946, in file 764, box 12, EAWP; "American Staff at Nürnberg Dubious over Trials' Legality," *Times-Herald*, July 10, 1946, in file 764, box 12, EAWP; Healey, "Diplomat Priest," 19–20, 56, 63.

65. Gundlach, "Moral Estimate of the Nuremberg Trial"; Walsh, "Comments and Corollaries."

66. Walsh, "Comments," 154. See also Walsh to Jackson, December 22, 1948, in "Nuremberg War Crimes Trial, Post-Trial Material Correspondence, W–Z" file, box 114, RHJP.

67. Thomas J. Dodd to Walsh, March 15, 1947, in folder 9, box 1, EAWP; Walsh, *Total Power*, vi, 330. "Power and might," Walsh wrote in 1945, "are not necessarily evil and unjust. Great power can be used and might be thrown into a policy, without thereby destroying justice. Size of itself is no sin—but the *use* of it can be a sin. The challenge is to the purity of our conscience, and not to be dodged by the bare fact of being a victor possessed of might. The justice of God is emphasized by all theological writers—tempered by charity and mercy, but by no means ever frustrated by lack of precedent or dubious jurisdiction. Government is a participation in the divine economy and should not be afraid of recognizing the responsibility." Nuremberg Diary no. 3, November 4, 1945.

68. Walsh, *Total Power*, 16, 241, 7, 17, 78, 178.

69. Ibid., 172, 176, 181. The "seeking order but inviting chaos" quotation is potentially subject to much distortion. Gearóid Ó Tuathail / Gerard Toal points out correctly that, although Walsh was an *antimodernist* who espoused an "idealized medievalism," he was by no means *antimodern*; Ó Tuathail / Toal, "Spiritual Geopolitics," 194–95.

70. Walsh, *Total Power*, 247, 259, 260–61.

71. Ibid., 37, 218, 262, 328.

72. "Walsh, Edmund A., S.J., *Total Power: A Footnote to History*"; Kohn, "Story of Haushofer"; Graham, "A 'Footnote' on Nuremberg"; De Balla, "Review of *Total Power*." Walsh's manuscript was rejected by at least one

publisher, Simon and Schuster. See Don Congdon to Walsh, April 16, 1947, in folder 53, box 1, EAWP.

73. Gurian, "Review of *Total Power: A Footnote to History*." A European refugee and specialist on communism who came to the University of Notre Dame during the 1930s, Gurian founded the *Review of Politics* in 1939 to serve as "a national forum for Catholic political philosophy celebrating the Catholic interpretation of contemporary and social events." Gurian and his associates, although "avowedly anti-positivist, anti-behaviorist, and anti-secular," avoided polemics and party politics. Gleason, *Contending with Modernity*, 267. Walsh's writing style in *Total Power* smacks of Victorian melodramatics, peppered with classical allusions and Shakespearean quotations. Thus, for example: "History is loud with explosions as the outraged conscience of the people finally asserts itself against domestic tyrants." And the "sadism" of the concentration camps "far surpassed the cruelties of Nero, Caligula, or Heliogabalus"; Rudolf Hess is referred to "this Caligula." Walsh, *Total Power*, 92, 93, 125, 128.

74. For background on American Catholic attitudes toward the United Nations, see Rossi, *American Catholics and the Formation of the United Nations*, 109; Gribble, *Guardian*, 197, 199; "The Problems of Peace, An Address by Edmund A. Walsh, S.J., The Mayflower Hotel, May 10, 1945, before the Business and Professional Women's Club of Washington," in folder 264, box 4, EAWP; see also "Walsh Says Security Hinges on Just Treatment of Poles," *Times-Herald*, May 11, 1945, in file 763, box 12, EAWP.

75. "Problems of Peace, May 10, 1945," in EAWP.

76. "The Role of the United States in the Post War World, An Address by Edmund A. Walsh, S.J., April 3, 1945, before the Export Managers Club, New York City," in folder 272, box 4, EAWP.

77. "Communist Activities: Report by Rev. John F. Cronin, S.S., St. Mary's Seminary, Baltimore, Md. [Nov. 5, 1942]," 1, 2, 5, in "Communism: General: 1939–1942" file, OGSSF-NCWCF. On Cronin, see Freeman and Rosswurm, "The Education of an Anti-Communist: Father John F. Cronin and the Baltimore Labor Movement"; Powers, *Not without Honor*, 212–13; Spalding, *Premier See*, 361, 377–78.

78. Archbishop Amleto G. Cicognani to Archbishop Edward Mooney, February 18, 1944, in "Communism: General: 1944" file, OGSSF-NCWCF; Spalding, *Premier See*, 361.

79. "Diocesan Confidential Questionnaire on Communism, Commissioned by the National Catholic Welfare Conference with Responses from the Diocese of St. Augustine, Florida, 1945."

80. Parker, *Western Geopolitical Thought*, 103, 111, 115; Blouet, *Geopolitics*, 121.

81. Ó Tuathail / Toal, "Spiritual Geopolitics," 188, 203.

CHAPTER 5: "THE SPIRITUAL AND MATERIAL MENACE
THREATENING THE PRESENT GENERATION": WALSH AND
CATHOLIC ANTICOMMUNISM IN THE COLD WAR, 1946–56

1. Edmund A. Walsh, S.J., "An Address to the Graduates of 1952, Lackland Air Force Base, San Antonio, Texas, Friday, June 20, 1952," in folder 241, box 4, EAWP.

2. "Address by Reverend E. A. Walsh, S.J., before the Army War College, Carlisle Barracks, PA, 2 Sep 52: 'The United States in the World Today,'" in folder 178, box 3, EAWP.

3. Louis J. Gallagher, S.J., as quoted in Tillman, *School of Foreign Service,* 31.

4. Louis D. Farrar, "The Man behind a Mighty Mission," unpublished manuscript for *Washington Religious Review,* in folder 713, box 11, EAWP. See also "Curriculum Vitae," 2, in EAWP; L. J. Gallagher, *Walsh,* 227, and "Walsh," 65.

5. For the "best known quote," see "Curriculum Vitae of Edmund A. Walsh, S.J.," 2, in folder 702, box 11, EAWP. In 1960, Sister Dorothy Jane Van Hoogstrate offered the following comparison, which will serve as a useful point of reference for this study: "The Realist generally maintains that he faces life as it is, not as it should be. With this approach he justifies his skepticism about the ability of nations to transcend self-interest, or to curb the inevitable international conflict by appeals to principle or by resort to institutional devices. The Idealist pursues such goals as justice among nations, enduring peace, the spiritual and material advancement of mankind, respect for international law, and cooperation in a juridical organization." Van Hoogstrate, *American Foreign Policy, Realists and Idealists: A Catholic Interpretation,* viii.

6. Freeman and Rosswurm, "Education of Anti-Communist," 218.

7. Crosby, *God, Church, and Flag*; Centola, "The American Catholic Church and Anti-Communism, 1945–1960: An Interpretive Framework and Case Studies"; D. L. O'Connor, "Defenders of the Faith: American Catholic Lay Organizations and Anticommunism, 1917–1975." O'Connor focuses on the Catholic War Veterans, the Catholic Daughters of the Americas, the Cardinal Mindszenty Circles, and the Blue Army.

8. Paterson, *Meeting the Communist Threat: Truman to Reagan,* 45, 53; LaFeber, *The American Age: United States Foreign Policy at Home and Abroad since 1750,* 434–37; Gaddis, *Russia, The Soviet Union, and the United States: An Interpretative Essay,* 156; Yergin, *Shattered Peace: The Origins of the Cold War and the National Security State,* 5, 239; Patterson, *Grand Expectations: The United States, 1945–1974,* 82, 90. For a useful his-

toriographical essay, see Leffler, "The Interpretive War over the Cold War, 1945–1960."

9. Steel, "The Domestic Core of Foreign Policy," 23; Powers, *Not without Honor*, 191.

10. "Address by Rev. Edmund Walsh Before the General Session of the Thirty-Second Annual Meeting of the National Industrial Conference Board, May 26, 1948," 10, in folder 249, box 4, EAWP. See also "Father E. A. Walsh, 'Soviet Geopolitics,' The Industrial College of the Armed Forces, Washington, D.C., 25 April 1947," in folder 292, box 4, EAWP; "Retreat Is Alternative to 'Decent Peace,' Dr. Walsh Declares," *Washington Post*, April 21, 1947, in file 764, box 12, EAWP.

11. Edmund A. Walsh, S.J., *New Geopolitics in Europe and Asia*, 10 June 1948 (Restricted), Publication no. 161, the Industrial College of the Armed Forces, Washington, D.C., 23, 37, in folder 252, box 4, EAWP. See also Walsh, "Geopolitical Position, August 26, 1952," 29–30, in EAWP. "Address before National Industrial Conference Board, May 26, 1948," 13, in EAWP. See also "Walsh Delays Return Home until after Italians Vote," *Washington Star*, April 18, 1948, in folder 765, box 12, EAWP.

12. Blouet, *Geopolitics*, 12, 133–34; see esp. chap. 7, "The Cold War and the Triumph of Geopolitics"; Hauner, *What Is Asia?* 237; Leffler, "Interpretive War," 120.

13. Leffler, "The American Conception of National Security and the Beginnings of the Cold War, 1945–1948," 147; Gaddis, *Strategies of Containment: A Critical Appraisal of Postwar American National Security Policy*, 57.

14. On Truman's propensity for "black and white," see Paterson, *Communist Threat*, 53; Dallek, *The American Style of Foreign Policy: Cultural Politics and Foreign Affairs*, 185. On Truman's inexperience in foreign affairs, see LaFeber, *American Age*, 434; Gaddis, *Russia, Soviet Union*, 168, and *The United States and the Origins of the Cold War, 1941–1947*, 351; Yergin, *Shattered Peace*, 73.

15. Yergin, *Shattered Peace*, 169, 170, 389, 402–3; see also LaFeber, *American Age*, 449–51. Kennan entitled his July 1947 *Foreign Affairs* "X" article "The Sources of Soviet Conflict."

16. Crockatt, *The Fifty Years War: The United States and the Soviet Union in World Politics, 1941–1991*, 7; Yergin, *Shattered Peace*, 282, 389; see also Mayers, *George Kennan and the Dilemmas of U.S. Foreign Policy*, 321; Kennan, *Memoirs, 1925–1950*, 323–24. For Kennan, the idealist approach "confuses public understanding of international issues more than it clarifies it. It shackles and distorts the process of decision-making. It causes questions to be decided on the basis of criteria only partially relevant or not relevant at all. It tends to exclude at many points the discrimination of judgement and the prudence of language requisite to the successful conduct of the affairs of a great power." Ibid., 324.

17. For the text of Truman's March 12, 1947, speech, see Girard, *America and the World*, 185. See also LaFeber, *America, Russia*, 49, and *American Age*, 453–55; Yergin, *Shattered Peace*, 284; Powers, *Not without Honor*, 189.

18. See LaFeber, *American Age*, 455–57; Yergin, *Shattered Peace*, 306–7, 309, 314–17.

19. Yergin, *Shattered Peace*, 469; LaFeber, *American Age*, 457–59; Leffler, *A Preponderance of Power: National Security, The Truman Administration, and the Cold War*, 323–24; Hogan, *A Cross of Iron: Harry S. Truman and the Origins of the National Security State, 1945–1954*, 330. Gaddis, *Strategies of Containment*, 82, 83.

20. Walsh, *Total Power*, 319–21; "Address before National Industrial Conference Board, May 26, 1948," 17, in EAWP; "Walsh, *New Geopolitics*," in EAWP.

21. "Address before National Industrial Conference Board, May 26, 1948," 2, in EAWP.

22. "Geopolitics and the Trouble with Russia," *PM*, May 26, 1948, in folder 765, box 12, EAWP. See also "Passage from an Address by the Reverend Edmund A. Walsh, S.J., at the Mayflower Hotel, Monday Evening, November 22, 1948," 1, 2, in folder 244, box 4, EAWP; Edmund A. Walsh, S.J., as quoted in *Congressional Digest*, October 1947, 254, 256.

23. O'Sullivan and Meckler, *The Draft and its Enemies: A Documentary History*, 162–63, 196; Flynn, *The Draft, 1940–1973*, 8, 90, 94; Donovan, *Conflict and Crisis: The Presidency of Harry S. Truman, 1945–1948*, 136–37. Until recently, Truman's Universal Military Training program has been a largely neglected topic. For the two most thorough treatments, see Hogan, *Cross of Iron*, chap. 4, and Flynn, *Draft*, chap. 4.

24. Gaddis, *United States and Origins*, 63; Hogan, *Cross of Iron*, 120, 124.

25. Gaddis, *United States and Origins*, 341; Flynn, *Draft*, 98; Hogan, *Cross of Iron*, 121–22, 136.

26. Huber, *Our Bishops Speak, 1919–1951*, 234, 237–38; Sittser, *Cautious Patriotism*, 39.

27. "Memorandum for the President of the United States, 7 October 1946," in Official Files, Harry S. Truman Presidential Library, Independence, Mo. (hereafter OF-HST).

28. Harry S. Truman to Walsh, November 20, 1946; Walsh to Truman, November 25, 1946; "Immediate Release, December 19, 1946," in "President's Advisory Commission on Universal Training" file, all in OF-HST. See also "Truman Picks Nine to Study Training, Offer Youth Plan." In choosing the commission, Truman's advisers noted that "previous attempts to pass this program failed at the opposition of clergy and educators"; see "Roster of Personnel of Commission," February 24, 1947, in John H. Ohly Papers, Harry S. Truman Presidential Library, Independence, Mo. (hereafter JHOP).

29. Huston Smith to Truman, January 15, 1947, in OF-HST; "President Appoints Rubber Stamp Commission," *Conscription News*, no. 88 (January 9, 1947): 1, 3, in JHOP.

30. David Ludlow to Truman, January 15, 1947; Cassie Jane Winfrey to Truman, November 17, 1947, both in OF-HST; Fred A. Geier to Walsh, October 15, 1947, in "Military Affairs File, UMT, June 1947," OGSSF-NCWCF; James T. Mangan to Walsh, June 2, 1947; Mangan to Walsh, October 24, 1947, both in folder 61, box 1, EAWP.

31. Gribble, *Guardian*, 181. For an overview of Scanlan's Cold War editorials, see McNamara, "Brooklyn *Tablet*," chap. 3. On Father William J. Miller, S.J., see Hogan, *Cross of Iron*, 129.

32. Mr. Montavon to Monsignor Carroll, July 17, 1947, in "UMT Materials" file; "Universal Military Training" [September 18, 1947], in "Military Affairs File, UMT, June 1947," both in OGSSF-NCWCF.

33. Reher, "Dougherty, Dennis Cardinal"; "Gist of Statement Made by Bishop Lamb Friday Afternoon to Senate Armed Services Committee on Behalf of Card. Dougherty [March 25, 1948]"; see also John M. Swomley, Jr., to "Dear Friend," April 25, 1947, both in "UMT Materials" file, OGSSF-NCWCF.

34. Fogarty, "Francis J. Spellman: American and Roman," 216; Cardinal Francis J. Spellman, as quoted in O'Brien, *Public Catholicism*, 221.

35. Crosby, *God, Church, and Flag*, 13. See also "Two Cardinals Have Varying Views on UMT," unidentified clipping, March 25, 1948, in "UMT Materials" file; "Congress Committee Hears Two U.S. Cardinals' Views on Military Training Issue," April 5, 1948, in "Military Affairs File, UMT, 1948–1950," both in OGSSF-NCWCF. Unfortunately, neither the Walsh Papers at Georgetown (EAWP) nor the Spellman Papers at Saint Joseph's Seminary, Dunwoodie, N.Y., contain any correspondence between the two leading Catholic advocates of UMT.

36. "Memorandum no. 3, Hearings on Universal Military Training, June 19, 1947," in "Military Affairs File, UMT, June 1947," OGSSF-NCWCF. See also "Report of First Meeting of the President's Advisory Commission on Universal Training [hereafter PACUT] at the White House, December 20, 1946, 10 A.M.," 11; "Report of Second Meeting of the [PACUT], Conference Room, White House, December 28, 1946, 10 A.M.," 131, 135; "Report of Fourth Meeting of the [PACUT], Conference Room, [White House,] January 10 and 11, 1947," 270, all in box 87, Joseph E. Davies Papers, Library of Congress, Manuscript Division, Washington, D.C. (hereafter JEDP).

37. "Report of First Meeting of the [PACUT] at the White House, December 20, 1946, 10 A.M.," 20, 21; "Report of Second Meeting of the [PACUT], Conference Room, White House, December 28, 1946, 10 A.M.," 56, 116, both in box 87, JEDP.

38. "Report of Tenth Meeting of the [PACUT], Conference Room, [White House,] February 21 and 22, 1947," 1380, in box 88, JEDP; "Report of Eighth Meeting of the [PACUT], Conference Room, [White House,] February 7 and 8, 1947," 1108; "Report of Seventh Meeting of the [PACUT], Conference Room, [White House,] January 31 and February 1, 1947," 861–63, both in box 87, JEDP.

39. "Report of Second Meeting of the [PACUT], Conference Room, White House, December 28, 1946, 10 A.M.," 116, in box 87, JEDP; "Report of Tenth Meeting of the [PACUT], Conference Room, [White House,] February 21 and 22, 1947," 1382; "Report of Twelfth Meeting of the [PACUT], Conference Room, [White House,] April 11 and 12, 1947," 1792–93, both in box 88, JEDP.

40. Edmund A. Walsh to "Mr. Walsh," June 2, 1947, in "UMT Materials" file, OGSSF-NCWCF. See also Anna M. Rosenberg to John H. Ohly, February 27, 1947; "Tentative Outline of Report," both in JHOP; "The President Receives Universal Training Report," *New York Times*, June 2, 1947, 5; "Nation Warned to Train Youth for Atomic War," unidentified clipping, June 2, 1947, both in file 764, box 12, EAWP.

41. For Walsh's testimony on UMT before the Senate Armed Services Committee, see "Memorandum no. 3, Hearings on Universal Military Training, June 19, 1947," in "Military Affairs File, UMT, June 1947," OGSSF-NCWCF; see also "Soviet Seen Having Atomic Bomb Soon," *New York Times*, June 19, 1947, 9; "Soviet Has Atom Secret, Says Walsh," *Washington Post*, June 19, 1947, both in folder 764, box 12, EAWP. On Stalin as a greater threat than Hitler, see "Commies Plan World Rule, Walsh Warns," unidentified clipping, 1946, in file 764, box 12, EAWP. Hogan, *Cross of Iron*, 138–39, 158.

42. Walsh continued to champion UMT after its rejection, expressing his support for UMT in March 1952 in a full-page newspaper advertisement with George C. Marshall and Albert Hayes of the American Federation of Labor. Walsh's statement read: "Nothing has transpired in the meantime to change my considered judgement. On the contrary, the Communist world revolution now dominates, directly or indirectly, nearly one third of the human race. And the end of the menace to political and religious freedom is not yet in sight." "Father Walsh Says: UMT Forces the Facts," unidentified clipping, March 3, 1952, in folder 767, box 12, EAWP. Although Walsh did not consider himself a "militarist by any means," neither was he a "pacifist in the current application of that term"; see "Geopolitics and Trouble with Russia," in EAWP; "Soldier Graves in Europe and Asia, July 1, 1948," 3–4, in folder 289, box 4, EAWP.

43. For Walter I. Giles's comments on role of Walsh's anticommunism in Roosevelt's and Truman's attitude toward him, see Watkins, *Footnotes*, 4.

For Walsh and the State Department's Policy Planning Staff, see "Minutes of Meeting[s,] 1947–1948," in box 32, "Minutes of Meetings," Records of the Policy Planning Staff, 1947–1953, RG 59; Miscamble, *George F. Kennan and the Making of American Foreign Policy, 1947–1950*, 148.

44. For an overview of the growth and development of the SFS Institute of Languages and Linguistics, see Wolf, "A Landmark at 50"; Fritschel, "The School That Father Walsh Built," 6; Durkin, *Georgetown*, 126–27.

45. Walsh to Jackson, November 3, 1950, in "Walsh" file, box 21, RHJP.

46. Culbertson to Walsh, October 2, 1952; see also Walsh to Culbertson, September 26, 1952, both in "July–Dec. 1952" file, box 35, WSCP; William S. Culbertson, "Personal Note for the Assistant to the President, February 16, 1953," in "Jan.–June 1953" file, box 36, WSCP. On Georgetown and the Air Force, see Culbertson to Harold Sprout, February 5, 1951, in "Jan.–June 1951" file, box 33, WSCP. See also L. E. Dostert, "To the Members of the Faculty Participating in the Psychological Warfare Training Program," in "Jan.–June 1951" file, box 33, WSCP. Walsh, "Address to Graduates of Lackland Air Force Base, June 20, 1952," in EAWP.

47. Walter B. Smith to Walsh, January 7, 1952, in folder 43, box 1, EAWP.

48. "Address before Army War College, 2 Sep. 52,"in EAWP.

49. For more on Fordham's Institute of Contemporary Russian Studies, see Jaskiewicz, "The Institute of Contemporary Russian Studies"; Schroth, *Fordham: A History and Memoir*, 221. On McCarthyism and the universities, see Schrecker, *No Ivory Tower*; Chomsky et al., *The Cold War and the University: Toward an Intellectual History of the Postwar Years*; Lewis, *Cold War on Campus: A Study of the Politics of Organizational Control*, chap. 1. For academic cooperation with the government in the first decade after the Second World War, see Diamond, *Compromised Campus: The Collaboration of Universities with the Intelligence Community, 1945–1955*.

50. On the psychological effects of Soviet Russia's acquiring the atomic bomb, see Rose, *The Cold War Comes to Main Street: America in 1950*, 313; Garthoff, *A Journey through the Cold War: A Memoir of Containment and Coexistence*, 7. For more on the diplomatic effects of the Soviet bomb, see Yergin, *Shattered Peace*, 470, 477, 479; Gaddis, *Russia, Soviet Union*, 193, 400. Walsh seems to have paid little attention to China. In 1948, he warned that, without American aid, China would soon "drop entirely into the hands of the expanding Communist Empire." Like Acheson, Walsh's main focus was on Soviet Russian communism, and he seems to have regarded the Chinese version merely as a less significant branch of the Soviet tree; see "Address before National Industrial Conference Board, May 26, 1948," 1, in EAWP. See also "Walsh Fears Far East Reds," *Times Herald*, April 21, 1948, in folder 765, box 12, EAWP.

51. Ninkovich, *Wilsonian Century*, 173; Leffler, *Preponderance of Power*, 330.

52. Powers, *Not without Honor*, 212–13; see also LaFeber, *American Age*, 481; Yergin, *Shattered Peace*, 401; Leffler, *Preponderance of Power*, 360. For a useful overview of the making of NSC-68, see Gaddis, *Strategies of Containment*, chap. 4. For the text of NSC-68, see Etzold and Gaddis, *Containment: Documents on American Policy and Strategy, 1945–1950*, 385–442.

53. Walsh, "Geopolitical Position, August 26, 1952," in EAWP; "Address to the Cosmopolitan Club, Washington, D.C., October 25, 1951," 3, in folder 246, box 4, EAWP; see also "Address before Army War College, 2 Sep. 52," in EAWP. Walsh restrained his criticisms of Roosevelt while the president was alive. See "On the Death of Franklin Delano Roosevelt, April 15, 1945," in folder 274, box 4, EAWP.

54. Walsh, "Geopolitical Position, August 26, 1952"; see also "Address before Army War College, 2 Sep. 52," 6, 19, both in EAWP.

55. "Faith to Meet the Present Danger: A Radio Discussion between Dr. Daniel A. Polling and the Very Reverend Edmund A. Walsh, S.J., for the Committee on the Present Danger, May 20, 1951," in folder 337, box 5, EAWP; see also "Synopsis of Lecture on Tuesday, November 13, 1951, at the Mayflower Hotel under the Auspices of the Saint Matthew's Book Forum by Edmund A. Walsh, S.J., Doc. Litt.," in folder 283, box 4, EAWP; "Address before National Industrial Conference Board, May 26, 1948," in EAWP.

56. "Geopolitics and Trouble with Russia," in EAWP; "Walsh, *New Geopolitics*," 46, in EAWP. For additional statements by Walsh on "first strike," see "Father E. A. Walsh, 'Soviet Geopolitics,' The Industrial College of the Armed Forces, Washington, D.C., 25 April 1947," 44–45, in folder 292, box 4, EAWP; "Russians Hit for Hypocrisy in Diplomacy," unidentified clipping, March 4, 1947; "Dr. Walsh Lauds Truman Plan to Halt Communism," unidentified clipping, March 26, 1947; "Russia to Challenge U.S. When Ready, Walsh Declares," unidentified clipping, 1947, all in folder 764, box 12, EAWP. See also "Historical Answer," *Time*, April 7, 1947, 24–25; "Memorandum no. 3, Hearings on Universal Military Training, June 19, 1947," 4, both in "Military Affairs File, UMT, June 1947," OGSSF-NCWCF; "Soviet Seen Having Atomic Bomb Soon." "Stalin Following Hitler's Tactics, Truman Aide Says," unidentified clipping, June 19, 1947, in folder 764, box 12, EAWP. "Sees Bomb Secret Lost: Father Walsh Tells FBI Group Russia Has Blueprints."

57. "Walsh Sees U.S. Justified in A-Bomb Attack on Soviets," *Washington Star*, December 6, 1950, in folder 766, box 12, EAWP. See also "Church Group Backs Use of Atomic Bomb."

58. "Father Walsh and the Bomb," *Washington Star*, December 24, 1950, in folder 766, box 12, EAWP. For Walsh's draft of the December 24, 1950,

Washington Star article, see Edmund A. Walsh, S.J., "Atom Bombs and the Christian Conscience," December 20, 1950, in folder 179, box 3, EAWP. See also "War for Ruin or Strike before Struck?" *Washington Star*, June 15, 1951; "Fr. Walsh States Use of Atom Bomb Justified if Soviet 'Pearl Harbor' Is Imminent," *Washington Post*, June 15, 1951, both in folder 766, box 12, EAWP; "Priest Justifies Use of Bomb for Defense."

59. "Father Walsh's Article," *Washington Star*, January 8, 1951, in folder 766, box 12, EAWP; "Jesuit Tries to Justify Use of A-Bomb."

60. Ford, "The Morality of Obliteration Bombing," 289. See also McNeal, *The American Catholic Peace Movement, 1928–1972*, 13, 183.

61. Ford, "Morality," 261, 284, 302, 309. John Ford had not changed his mind in 1960, when he wrote: "It is the fashion to say: 'But today war is different. War is total. Everybody, or almost everybody, in the enemy country contributes to the war effort. Everybody is more or less a combatant.' This is fallacious." Ford, "The Hydrogen Bombing of Cities," 99. On Wilfrid Parsons, see Au, *The Cross, the Flag, and the Bomb: An American Catholic Interpretation*, 14–17.

62. Boyer, *By the Bomb's Early Light: American Thought and Culture at the Dawn of the Atomic Age*, 340, 344, 345, 346; Piehl, "The Catholic Worker and Peace in the Early Cold War Era," 80, 89; McNeal, *American Catholic Peace Movement*, 2–3.

63. Walsh, *Total Empire: The Roots and Progress of World Communism*, 167–68, 39, 90.

64. Ibid., 115. For an argument similar to Walsh's, see Sheen, *Communism and the Conscience of the West*, 58–77.

65. Walsh, *Total Empire*, 209, 247, 253, 258–59.

66. "Sunday *Star* Weekly Book Survey," *Washington Star*, July 4, 1951; "The Best Sellers," *New York Times*, July 22, 1951, both in folder 765, box 12, EAWP. Koriakov, "'Who Rules the Heartland . . .'"; "Book Awards to Be Made." By comparison, Paul Blanshard's *Communism, Democracy and Catholic Power* was ranked number 14 on the *New York Times* list.

67. For a useful overview of the anticommunist purge under Truman and Eisenhower, see Caute, *Great Fear*. On the 1949 trial of CPUSA national board members, see Belknap, *Cold War Politics: The Smith Act, the Communist Party, and American Civil Liberties*; Steinberg, *The Great "Red Menace": United States Prosecutions of American Communists, 1947–1952*, 157–77. On teachers, see Zitron, *The New York City Teachers Union, 1916–1964: A Story of Educational and Social Commitment*, 212. On labor, see Levenstein, *Communism, Anti-Communism, and the C.I.O.*, 299–308.

68. Caute, *Great Fear*, 59–62; Weinstein, *Perjury: The Hiss-Chambers Case*, 505–23; Cooke, *A Generation on Trial: USA versus Alger Hiss*, 314–41.

69. Senator Joseph R. McCarthy, as quoted in Oshinsky, *A Conspiracy So Immense: The World of Joe McCarthy*, 109. See also Powers, *Not without*

Honor, 229, 240. Lisle Rose writes that the first Soviet atomic explosion and the Korean conflict were "dramatic bookends to the emergence of McCarthyism"; Rose, *Cold War*, 6.

70. T. Taylor, *Grand Inquest: The Story of Congressional Investigations*, 112–35; R. M. Fried, *Men against McCarthy*, 287; Caute, *Great Fear*, 107–8; Griffith, *The Politics of Fear: Joseph R. McCarthy and the Senate*, 254–69; Reeves, *The Life and Times of Joe McCarthy: A Biography*, 639, 665.

71. For details of the dinner and Pearson's comments, see Crosby, *God, Church, and Flag*, 48; Drew Pearson, "USSR and Back by Air Foreseen," unidentified clipping, 1951, in folder 766, box 12, EAWP; Abell, *Drew Pearson, Diaries, 1949–1959*, 79; interview with William V. O'Brien, professor emeritus of Government at Georgetown University, January 31, 1999. O'Brien contends that Professor Charles Kraus brought the group together not for ideological reasons (William Roberts was an active Democrat), but because he enjoyed bringing disparate characters together in a social setting. Roy Cohn confirms Kraus's role; see Cohn, *McCarthy*, 11. On Pearson and Roberts, see Abell, *Pearson*. On Pearson, see Anderson, *A "Washington Merry-Go-Round" of Libel Actions*.

72. Crosby, *God, Church, and Flag*, 48; Drew Pearson, "McCarthy Profited from the Lustron Deal," unidentified clipping, May 19, 1950, in folder 766, box 12, EAWP; Drew Pearson, "State Department Scores a Ten Strike," *Washington Post*, November 29, 1951, in folder 766, box 12, EAWP; for the *Churchman* quote, see "Who's Backing McCarthy?", *Winston-Salem Journal & Sentinel*, July 12, 1953, in folder 768, box 12, EAWP; "Jesuit Tries to Justify"; I. F. Stone, as quoted in Crosby, *God, Church, and Flag*, 49; Crosby, ibid. See also Abell, *Drew Pearson, Diaries, 1949–1959*, 118. Pearson was still repeating the story a decade after Walsh's death; see Drew Pearson, "Johnson Girls and Catholicism," *Washington Post*, July 9, 1965, in folder 770, box 12, EAWP. See also "Who's Backing McCarthy?" *Winston-Salem [N.C.] Journal and Sentinel*, July 12, 1953, in folder 768, box 12, EAWP.

73. Massa, *Catholics*, 68; Reeves, *McCarthy*, 202, 203; Powers, *Not without Honor*, 238.

74. The literature on McCarthy is immense. For accounts of the Colony dinner that accept Pearson's version, see Anderson and May, *McCarthy: The Man, the Senator, the "Ism,"* 172; Griffith, *Politics of Fear*, 29; Landis, *Joseph McCarthy: The Politics of Chaos*, 48; Anderson with Boyd, *Confessions of a Muckraker: The Inside Story of Life in Washington during the Truman, Eisenhower and Johnson Years*, 221; Chace, *Acheson: The Secretary of State Who Created the American World*, 236. David Oshinsky notes that Walsh denied the story; Oshinsky, *Conspiracy*, 107. See also R. M. Fried, *Men*

against McCarthy, 40–41; Ingalls, *Point of Order: A Profile of Senator Joe McCarthy*, 39–40. Lately Thomas contends that Walsh was a friend of McCarthy, but later repudiated him; Thomas, *When Even Angels Wept: Senator Joseph McCarthy—A Story without a Hero*, 85, 179.

75. Crosby, *God, Church, and Flag*, 50. Father William V. Repetti, S.J., the Georgetown University archivist who arranged the Walsh Papers (EAWP), jotted his notes on news clippings in the collection. According to Repetti, Walsh said he "would not consider answering a man like Drew Pearson and that he (Fr. W.) did not suggest that McC. take up Communism." See the notes Repetti wrote on the following clippings: Hugh Trevor-Roper, "Vicious Yet Hollow," London *Times*, February 7, 1960, in folder 770, box 12, EAWP; "Roberts Tells of 1950 Talk with McCarthy," unidentified clipping, February 16, 1954, in folder 768, box 12, EAWP; Drew Pearson, "State Department Scores a Ten Strike," *Washington Post*, November 29, 1951, in folder 766, box 12, EAWP.

76. Crosby, *God, Church, and Flag*, 51–52.

77. Reeves, *McCarthy*, 203; Tillman, *School of Foreign Service*, 32; Herman, *Joseph McCarthy: Reexamining the Life and Legacy of America's Most Hated Senator*, 97, 177.

78. A 1941 account of Washington social life, as quoted in Hart, *Washington at War, 1941–1945*, 37, described "Georgetown—the paradox where only the richest and poorest can afford to live [and where at] original parties . . . people as different as a Father Walsh, Liz Whitney, John L. Lewis, Wendell Wilkie and Gene Autry can be found conversing. . . ." See also "Did You Happen to See—Rev. Edmund A. Walsh, S.J.," *Times-Herald*, June 22, 1943, in FBI File.

79. Theoharis, *From the Secret Files of J. Edgar Hoover*, 312. Memorandum from Mr. Clegg to Mr. Tolson, November 10, 1950, in FBI File; Rosswurm, "Manhood," 14. Rosswurm suggests that it may have been Louis Nichols, head of the FBI's Crime Records Section, who contacted Walsh about reviewing Max Lowenthal's *The Federal Bureau of Investigation*. For Walsh's review, see Rev. Edmund A. Walsh, S.J., "'A Lawyer's Indictment in Mood of Persecutor,'" *Washington Post*, November 26, 1950, in folder 766, box 12, EAWP. See also J. Edgar Hoover to Walsh, November 27, 1950, in FBI File. Attorney Joseph Rauh, founder of Americans for Democratic Action (ADA), recalls the controversy surrounding the Lowenthal book: "The *Washington Post* decided it was too hot to handle with just one review, so they had two. Father Walsh of Georgetown was . . . pro-Hoover, and I was nominated to write the anti-Hoover review." Joseph Rauh, as quoted in Fariello, *Red Scare: Memories of the American Inquisition, An Oral History*, 139. See also O'Reilly, *Hoover and the Un-Americans: The FBI, HUAC, and the Red Menace*, 140–44.

80. Walsh, "The Spiritual Aspect of Foreign Policy," 641–42, 646.

81. Ibid., 641, 642, 643, 644.

82. Ibid., 644–45. See also Kennan, *American Diplomacy, 1900–1950;* "Father Walsh Hits Kennan for 'Anti-Moral' Approach," *Catholic Standard,* August 8, 1952, in folder 767, box 12, EAWP; " 'Dangerous' Views Charged to Envoy."

83. The Counselor of the Department of State (Charles E. Bohlen) to the Ambassador in the Soviet Union (George F. Kennan), *Personal and Secret* [Washington,] September 19, 1952, in U.S. Department of State, *Foreign Relations of the United States, 1952–1954,* vol. 8: *Eastern Europe; Soviet Union; Eastern Mediterranean,* 1045–47; Mayers, *Kennan and Dilemmas,* 321.

84. "Walsh, *New Geopolitics,*" 4, and "Geopolitical Position, August 26, 1952," 16–17, both in EAWP.

85. "Sermon Delivered by Reverend Edmund A. Walsh, S.J., Church of St. Francis Xavier, New York, October 14, 1951," in folder 351, box 5, EAWP.

86. "Faith to Meet the Present Danger: A Radio Discussion Between Dr. Daniel A. Polling and the Very Reverend Edmund A. Walsh, S.J., for the Committee on the Present Danger, May 20, 1951," 3, 6–7, in folder 337, box 5, EAWP.

87. "Fifty Years in Jesuit Order"; "Georgetown Aide Hailed"; "Where Protestantism Is Defaulting"; "Jesuit Tries to Justify." In 1947, the pastor of Timber Ridge Christian Church, High View, W. Va., referring to Walsh, complained to Truman about "the influence of the Vatican on our State Department"; Roy D. Coulter to Truman, September 3, 1947, in OF-HST.

88. Curry, *Protestant-Catholic Relations,* 40–41, 44, 50, 57, 59, 61; Allitt, *Catholic Intellectuals and Conservative Politics in America, 1950–1985,* 18–20.

89. Massa, *Catholics,* 1, 2; Patterson, *Grand Expectations,* 18; Kessner, *Fiorello H. LaGuardia and the Making of Modern New York,* 476. In later years, Paul Blanshard expressed optimism over the convening of the Second Vatican Council, and he modified his view of Catholicism as a result; see Blanshard, *Paul Blanshard on Vatican II.* To date, there is no biography of Blanshard. See also McGreevey, "Thinking on One's Own: Catholicism in the American Intellectual Imagination, 1928–1960."

90. "Rev. E. A. Walsh Honored," *New York Times,* November 16, 1952, 71; "Speeches and Remarks, November 15, 1952," 3, 5, 6, 19–20, both in folder 713, box 11, EAWP, and in "The Speaker's Table," in "Walsh, Edmund A.: Golden Jubilee Celebration" file, box 86, CFP. On General J. Lawton Collins, see Fisher, *Dr. America: The Lives of Thomas A. Dooley, 1927–1961,* 49–52.

91. Walsh to John Parr, December 17, 1953, in folder 7, box 1, P-SA. On Walsh's first stroke and apparent recovery, see "Father Walsh Suffers Slight Stroke," *Washington Post*, December 4, 1952; "Father Walsh Reported Recovering from Stroke," *Washington Star*, December 4, 1952; "Father Walsh Improved," *Catholic Standard*, December 12, 1952, all in folder 767, box 12, EAWP. See also "Rev. Edmund Walsh in Hospital," *New York Times*, January 4, 1953, 44; unidentified person to Rev. Vincent A. McCormick, S.J., January 17, 1953, both in folder 113, box 2, EAWP; Louis J. Gallagher, S.J., to Edward B. Bunn, S.J., March 18, 1953, in file 654, "Gallagher, Louis (Faculty)," GUA; "Father Walsh Incapacitated by Stroke," *Washington Post*, December 20, 1953, in folder 768, box 12, EAWP. Walsh to Parr, December 8, 1954, in folder 7, box 1, P-SA; J. Raymond Trainor to Parr, December 28, 1954, in folder 6, box 1, P-SA.

92. Walter I. Giles, as quoted in Fritschel, "School," 6–7; L. J. Gallagher, *Walsh*, 228, and "Walsh," 65; McEvitt, *Hilltop*, 38, 77; Farrar, "Man behind Mighty Mission," in EAWP; interview with George P. Morse Jr. at Georgetown University, August 21, 2002.

93. "Father Walsh Made Regent Emeritus," *Washington Post*, June 18, 1955, in folder 768, box 12, EAWP; William F. Maloney, S.J., to Walsh, June 10, 1955, in folder 61, box 1, EAWP. "Father Walsh Retires," *Washington Post*, June 19, 1955; "Father Walsh Retiring," *Washington Star*, June 21, 1955, both in folder 768, box 12, EAWP.

94. *New York Times*, November 1, 1956, 39; *Washington Post*, November 1, 1956, B2; "Edmund A. Walsh," *Washington Post*, November 3, 1956; *Times Herald*, November 2, 1956; "Father Edmund A. Walsh, S.J.," *Catholic Standard*, November 9, 1956, 8–9; *America*, November 17, 1956, all in folder 703, box 11, EAWP. "Father Edmund A. Walsh," *Evening Star*, November 2, 1956, in folder 769, box 12, EAWP.

95. Walter I. Giles, as quoted in Watkins, *Footnotes*, ix.

96. When asked where the *Tablet* and the *Catholic Worker* came together, Dorothy Day, as quoted in "The Catholic Press," replied: "Only at the Lord's table."

97. On Richard Hofstadter, see Powers, *Not without Honor*, 256–57. Caute, *Great Fear*, 21, 42; Touchet, "The Social Gospel and Cold War: The Melish Case," 402; Centola, "American Catholic Church," 1, 199, 594. See also Schatz, "American Labor and the Catholic Church, 1919–1950," 183. In 1955, Will Herberg wrote that "American Catholics still labor under the weight of the bitter memory of non-acceptance in a society overwhelmingly and self-consciously Protestant." Herberg, *Protestant-Catholic-Jew: An Essay in Religious Sociology*, 232.

EPILOGUE

1. Massa, *Catholics*, 80.

2. According to a Gallup poll taken of Catholics in January 1954, 58 percent supported McCarthy, 23 percent opposed him, while the rest declared themselves neutral. See DeSantis, "American Catholics and McCarthyism," 24; Oshinsky, *Conspiracy*, 305–7; Rogin, *The Intellectuals and McCarthy: The Radical Specter*, 91–92.

3. Crosby, *God, Church, and Flag*, 158–73.

4. Powers, *Not without Honor*, 304, 317, 318.

5. Ibid., 305; William F. Buckley, as quoted in ibid., 355. David O'Brien comments: "Pope John XXIII and President John F. Kennedy, those two idols of my generation, unwittingly shifted the fulcrum of Catholic life and permanently altered the Catholic conception of allegiance to God and country. 'What does it now mean to be an American Catholic?' is now an open question, in poker player's parlance, at both ends. The reforms of Pope John made it difficult to know what it meant to be a Catholic; the election of John F. Kennedy added the problem of defining the American Catholic." O'Brien, *The Renewal of American Catholicism*, xiii.

6. Powers, *Not without Honor*, 306.

7. Allitt, *Catholic Intellectuals*, x.

8. Powers, *Not without Honor*, 326. See also Nolan, *Pastoral Letters of the National Hierarchy, 1792–1970*, 604–7; 679–705.

9. See Avella and McKeown, *Public Voices: Catholics in the American Context*, 278. See also O'Brien, *Public Catholicism*, 245. On conservative Catholic response to the American bishops' 1983 letter, see Allitt, *Catholic Intellectuals*, 290–96.

10. See Gleason, *Keeping the Faith: American Catholicism Past and Present*, 33.

11. Quigley, "Father Walsh," 234.

12. Father Frank Fadner, S.J., as quoted in Fritschel, "School," 6.

BIBLIOGRAPHY

MANUSCRIPT COLLECTIONS

Archdiocese of Baltimore Archives, Baltimore
    Michael J. Curley Papers
Archdiocese of Chicago's Joseph Cardinal Bernardin Archives and
Records Center, Chicago
    Madaj Collection
Archives of the Catholic University of America, Washington, D.C.
    National Catholic Welfare Conference Files
Archives of the Maryland Province of the Society of Jesus, Roland
Park, Md.
    Provincial's Correspondence
Archives of the New England Province of the Society of Jesus, College of the Holy Cross, Worcester, Mass.
    Louis J. Gallagher, S.J., Papers
Archivium Romanum Societatis Jesu, Jesuit Curia, Rome
    Maryland Province Correspondence
Bakhmeteff Archive, Rare Book and Manuscript Collection, Columbia University, New York
    American Relief Administration Collection
Dwight D. Eisenhower Library, Abilene, Kans.
    President's Personal File, White House Central Files
Franklin Delano Roosevelt Presidential Library, Hyde Park, N.Y.
    Official Files
Harry S. Truman Presidential Library, Independence, Mo.
    Harry S. Truman Papers
    John H. Ohly Papers
    Official Files
Herbert Hoover Presidential Library, Long Branch, Iowa
    American Relief Administration Papers
    Post-Presidential Individual Papers
Lauinger Library, Special Collections Division, Georgetown University, Washington, D.C.

Georgetown University Archives
Edmund A. Walsh, S.J., Papers
Parr-Smith Archive
Wilfrid Parsons, S.J., Papers
Library of Congress, Manuscript Division, Washington, D.C.
Charles Fahy Papers
Evelyn Walsh McLean Papers
Joseph E. Davies Papers
Robert H. Jackson Papers
William S. Culbertson Papers
Library of Congress, Microfilm Collection, Washington, D.C.
    Warren G. Harding Papers
National Archives, College Park, Md.
    Record Group 59, General Records of the Department of State
Oral History Research Office, Columbia University, New York
    DeWitt Clinton Poole Memoir
Philadelphia Archdiocesan Historical Research Center, Overbrook,
Pa.
    William Franklin Sands Papers
Seely-Mudd Collection, Princeton University, Princeton, N.J.
    Hamilton Fish Armstrong Papers

PRINT AND UNPUBLISHED SOURCES

Abell, Tyler, ed. *Drew Pearson, Diaries, 1949–1959.* New York: Holt,
    Rinehart and Winston, 1974.
"Academic Diet in Colleges Is Too Soft and Lower Schools Are
    Faulty." *New York Times,* September 13, 1931, III, 2.
Ahlstrom, Sydney E. *A Religious History of the American People.*
    New Haven: Yale University Press, 1972.
Allitt, Patrick. "Anti-Communism and American Catholics." In *Ency-
    clopedia of American Catholic History,* edited by Michael Glazier
    and Thomas J. Shelley, 105–06. Collegeville, Minn.: Liturgical
    Press, 1997
————. "Catholic Anti-Communism." *Crisis,* March 1996, 22–26.
————. *Catholic Intellectuals and Conservative Politics in America,
    1950–1985.* Ithaca, N.Y.: Cornell University Press, 1993.

Ameringer, Oscar. *Communism, Socialism, and the Church*. Milwaukee: Milwaukee Social Democratic Publishing, 1913.

Anderson, Douglas A. *A "Washington Merry-Go-Round" of Libel Actions*. Chicago: Nelson-Hall, 1980.

Anderson, Jack, with James Boyd. *Confessions of a Muckraker: The Inside Story of Life in Washington during the Truman, Eisenhower and Johnson Years*. New York: Random House, 1979.

Anderson, Jack, and Ronald W. May. *McCarthy: The Man, the Senator, the "Ism."* Boston: Beacon Press, 1952.

"Asks End of International." *New York Times*, December 10, 1933, 27.

Athans, Mary Christine. *The Coughlin-Fahey Connection: Father Charles E. Coughlin, Father Denis Fahey, C.S.Sp., and Religious Anti-Semitism in the United States*. New York: Peter Lang, 1991.

Au, William A. *The Cross, the Flag, and the Bomb: An American Catholic Interpretation*. Westport, Conn.: Greenwood Press, 1985.

Aubert, Roger. *The Church in a Secularized Society*. New York: Paulist Press, 1978.

Avella, Steven M., and Elizabeth McKeown, eds. *Public Voices: Catholics in the American Context*. New York: Orbis Books, 1999.

Barnes, William, and John Heath Morgan. *The Foreign Service of the United States: Origins, Development and Functions*. Washington, D.C.: Government Printing Office, 1961.

Barry, Colman J., O.S.B., ed. *Readings in Church History*. Vol. 3: *The Modern Era: 1789 to the Present*. Westminster, Md.: Newman Press, 1965.

Bayor, Ronald H. "Klans, Coughlinites and Aryans Nations: Patterns of American Anti-Semitism in the Twentieth Century." *American Jewish History* 76 (December 1986): 181–96.

———. *Neighbors in Conflict: The Irish, Germans, Jews, and Italians of New York City, 1929–1941*. 2nd ed. Urbana: University of Illinois Press, 1988.

Bechhofer, C. E. *Through Starving Russia: Being the Record of a Journey to Moscow and the Volga Provinces in August and September 1921*. Westport, Conn.: Hyperion Press, 1977.

Belknap, Michael R. *Cold War Politics: The Smith Act, the Communist Party, and American Civil Liberties*. Westport, Conn.: Greenwood Press, 1977.

Bell, Daniel, ed. *The Radical Right*. Garden City, N.Y.: Anchor Books, 1964.

Bennett, Edward M. *Recognition of Russia: An American Foreign Policy Dilemma*. Waltham, Mass.: Blaisdell, 1970.

Bishop, Donald G. *The Roosevelt-Litvinov Agreements: The American View*. Syracuse, N.Y.: Syracuse University Press, 1965.

Blanshard, Paul. *Paul Blanshard on Vatican II*. Boston: Beacon Press, 1966.

Blantz, Thomas E., C.S.C. *George N. Shuster: On the Side of Truth*. Notre Dame, Ind.: University of Notre Dame Press, 1993.

―――. *A Priest in Public Service: Francis J. Haas and the New Deal*. Notre Dame, Ind.: University of Notre Dame Press, 1982.

Blet, Pierre, S.J. *Pius XII and the Second World War: According to the Archives of the Vatican*. Translated by Lawrence J. Johnson. New York: Paulist Press, 1997.

Blouet, Brian W. *Geopolitics and Globalization in the Twentieth Century*. London: Reaktion Books, 2001.

―――. *Halford Mackinder: A Biography*. College Station: Texas A and M University Press, 1987.

Bohn, Frank. *The Catholic Church and Socialism*. Chicago: Charles H. Kerr, 1912.

Bolloten, Burnett. *The Spanish Civil War: Revolution and Counter-Revolution*. Chapel Hill: University of North Carolina Press, 1991.

"Book Awards to Be Made." *New York Times*, January 28, 1952, 15.

"Books in Brief." *Nation*, August 5, 1931, 139.

Borah, William E. "The Argument for Diplomatic Relations." In *The American Image of Russia, 1917–1977*, edited by Benson Grayson, 83–87. New York: Frederick Ungar, 1977.

Boyer, Paul. *By the Bomb's Early Light: American Thought and Culture at the Dawn of the Atomic Age*. New York: Pantheon, 1985.

Brinkley, Alan. *Voices of Protest: Huey Long, Father Coughlin and the Great Depression*. New York: Vintage, 1983.

Broderick, Francis L. *Right Reverend New Dealer: John A. Ryan*. New York: Macmillan, 1963.

Browder, Robert Paul. *The Origins of Soviet-American Diplomacy*. Princeton, N.J.: Princeton University Press, 1953.

Buckley, Michael J., S.J. *The Catholic University as Promise and Project: Reflections in a Jesuit Idiom*. Washington, D.C.: Georgetown University Press, 1998.

Burner, David. *Herbert Hoover: A Public Life*. New York: Knopf, 1979.

Burns, James MacGregor. *Roosevelt: The Lion and the Fox*. New York: Harcourt Brace Jovanovich, 1956.

Carlen, Claudia. *Papal Pronouncements, A Guide: 1740–1978*. Vol. 1: *Benedict XV to Paul VI*. Ann Arbor, Mich.: Pierian Press, 1990.

Carroll, James. *Constantine's Sword: The Church and the Jews, A History*. Boston: Houghton Mifflin, 2001.

"Castle Backs Hull on Neutrality Aim." *New York Times*, July 9, 1939, 25.

"The Catholic Press." *Time*, May 28, 1956, 73.

"Catholic Relief Mission to Russia." In *Modern Encyclopedia of Russian and Soviet History*, 43 vols., edited by Joseph L. Wieczynski, 6: 138–140. Gulf Breeze, Fla.: Academic International Press, 1978.

"Catholics Launch Near East Drive." *New York Times*, December 16, 1926, 25.

"Catholic Veterans at Special Mass." *New York Times*, November 10, 1941, 11.

Caute, David. *The Great Fear: The Anti-Communist Purge under Truman and Eisenhower*. New York: Simon and Schuster, 1978.

Centola, Kathleen Gefell. "The American Catholic Church and Anti-Communism, 1945–1960: An Interpretive Framework and Case Studies." Ph.D. diss., State University of New York at Albany, 1984.

Chace, James. *Acheson: The Secretary of State Who Created the American World*. New York: Simon and Schuster, 1998.

Chomsky, Noam, et al., eds. *The Cold War and the University: Toward an Intellectual History of the Postwar Years*. New York: New Press, 1997.

"Church Group Backs Use of Atomic Bomb." *New York Times*, December 6, 1950, 18.

Clancy, William. *Catholicism and Socialism*. Bridgeport, Conn.: Advance, 1912.

Clarkson, J. D. "What Think Ye of Russia?" *New Republic*, September 16, 1928, 157.

Cohalan, Florence D. *A Popular History of the Archdiocese of New York*. Yonkers, N.Y.: U.S. Catholic Historical Society, 1983.

Cohn, Roy. *McCarthy*. New York: New American Library, 1968.

Cole, Wayne S. *Roosevelt and the Isolationists, 1932–1945.* Lincoln: University of Nebraska Press, 1983.

"Communism for World War, Says Fr. Walsh." *Tablet,* November 9, 1935, 1.

Cooke, Alistair. *A Generation on Trial: USA versus Alger Hiss.* New York: Knopf, 1951.

Corrigan, Raymond, S.J. *The Church and the Nineteenth Century.* Milwaukee: Bruce, 1938.

Crockatt, Richard. *The Fifty Years War: The United States and the Soviet Union in World Politics, 1941–1991.* London: Routledge, 1993.

Crosby, Donald F., S.J. *God, Church, and Flag: Senator Joseph R. McCarthy and the Catholic Church, 1950–1957.* Chapel Hill: University of North Carolina Press, 1978.

———. "The Politics of Religion: American Catholics and the Anti-Communist Impulse." In *The Specter: Original Essays on the Cold War and the Origins of McCarthyism,* edited by Athan Theoharis and Robert Griffith, 18–38. New York: New Viewpoints, 1974.

Cross, Robert D. *The Emergence of Liberal Catholicism in America.* Chicago: Quadrangle, 1958.

Cuddy, Edward. "'Are the Bolsheviks Any Worse Than the Irish?': Ethno-religious Conflict in America during the 1920's." *Eire-Ireland: A Journal of Irish Studies* 11, no. 3 (1976): 13–32.

Curran, Robert Emmett. "Georgetown's Self-Image at the Turn of the Century." In William C. McFadden, ed., *Georgetown at Two Hundred: Faculty Reflections on the University's Future,* 1–15. Washington, D.C.: Georgetown University Press, 1990.

———, ed. *American Jesuit Spirituality: The Maryland Tradition, 1634–1900.* New York: Paulist Press, 1988.

Curry, Lerond. *Protestant-Catholic Relations in America, World War I Through Vatican II.* Lexington: University Press of Kentucky, 1972.

Dallek, Robert. *Franklin D. Roosevelt and American Foreign Policy, 1932–1945.* New York: Oxford University Press, 1979.

———. *The American Style of Foreign Policy: Cultural Politics and Foreign Affairs.* New York: Knopf, 1983.

"'Dangerous' Views Charged to Envoy." *New York Times,* July 28, 1952, 3.

Davis, Donald E., and Eugene P. Trani. *The First Cold War: The Legacy of Woodrow Wilson in U.S.-Soviet Relations*. Columbia: University of Missouri Press, 2002.

Davis, Lynn Etheridge. *The Cold War Begins: Soviet-American Conflict Over Eastern Europe*. Princeton, N.J.: Princeton University Press, 1974.

De Balla, Valentine. "Review of *Total Power*." *Catholic World* 167 (August 1948): 469–70.

De Leon, Daniel. *Abolition of Poverty: Socialist versus Ultramontane Economics and Politics (Originally Published in Response to Public Address of Rev. Thomas I. Gasson, S.J., in Boston, 1911)*. Brooklyn: New York Labor News, 1969.

"Demands Roosevelt Give Soviet Stand." *New York Times*, October 5, 1932, 9.

DeSantis, Vincent P. "American Catholics and McCarthyism." *Catholic Historical Review* 51, no. 1 (April 1965): 1–30.

Diamond, Sigmund. *Compromised Campus: The Collaboration of Universities with the Intelligence Community, 1945–1955*. New York: Oxford University Press, 1992.

"Diocesan Confidential Questionnaire on Communism, Commissioned by the National Catholic Welfare Conference with Responses from the Diocese of St. Augustine, Florida, 1945." In *Public Voices: Catholics in the American Context*, edited by Steven M. Avella and Elizabeth McKeown, 237. New York: Orbis Books, 1999.

Dohen, Dorothy. *Nationalism and American Catholicism*. New York: Sheed and Ward, 1967.

Dollen, Charles. "Ambassador of Mercy," *Homiletic and Pastoral Review* 63 (March 1963): 536–37.

Donnelly, James Francis. "Catholic New Yorkers and New York Socialists, 1870–1920." Ph.D. diss., New York University, 1982.

Donovan, Robert J. *Conflict and Crisis: The Presidency of Harry S Truman, 1945–1948*. Columbia: University of Missouri Press, 1977.

———. *The Roots of American Communism*. New York: Viking Press, 1957.

Draper, Theodore. *American Communism and Soviet Russia: The Formative Period*. New York: Viking Press, 1960.

Drury, Betty. "Review of *The Last Stand.*" *Bookman* 73, no. 6 (August 1931): 658–59.

Duffy, Eamon. *Saints and Sinners: A History of the Popes.* New Haven: Yale University Press, 1997.

Dulles, Foster Rhea. "Back-Wash of the War." *Bookman* 67, no. 6 (August 1928): 697.

Dumenil, Lynn. "The Tribal Twenties: 'Assimiliated' Catholics' Response to Anti-Catholicism in the 1920s." *Journal of American Ethnic History,* Fall 1991, 21–49.

Dunn, Dennis J. *Caught Between Roosevelt and Stalin: America's Ambassadors to Moscow.* Lexington: University Press of Kentucky, 1998.

Duranty, Walter. *I Write As I Please.* New York: Simon and Schuster, 1935.

Durkin, Joseph T., S.J. *Georgetown University: First in the Nation's Capital.* New York: Doubleday, 1964.

Edmondson, Charles M. "An Enquiry into the Termination of Soviet Famine Relief Programmes and the Renewal of Grain Export, 1919–1923." *Soviet Studies* 33, no. 3 (1981): 370–85.

Ehler, Sidney Z., and John B. Morrall, eds. *Church and State through the Centuries: A Collection of Historic Documents with Commentaries.* Westminster, Md.: Newman Press, 1954.

Etzold, Thomas H., and John Lewis Gaddis, eds. *Containment: Documents on American Policy and Strategy, 1945–1950.* New York: Columbia University Press, 1978.

"Faiths at Capital Hit Persecutions," *New York Times,* December 6, 1938, 11.

Fariello, Griffin. *Red Scare: Memories of the American Inquisition, An Oral History.* New York: Norton, 1995.

"Father Walsh Answers Browder." *Informationes et Notitiae* 3, nos. 4–5 (May–June 1938): 3–4.

"Father Walsh Lauds Portes Gil Accord." *New York Times,* July 4, 1929, 3.

"Father Walsh on Russia." *America,* April 29, 1933, 74.

"Father Walsh on Russia." *Commonweal,* June 16, 1933, 187.

Fausold, Martin L. *The Presidency of Herbert C. Hoover.* Lawrence: University Press of Kansas, 1985.

"Fears War Menace in German Election." *New York Times,* September 17, 1930, 2.

"Federal Officials Accused As 'Reds.'" *New York Times*, February 12, 1935, 5.

"Fifty Years in Jesuit Order." *New York Times*, April 30, 1952, 10.

"Georgetown Aide Hailed." *New York Times*, May 5, 1952, 25.

Figes, Orlando. *A People's Tragedy: The Russian Revolution, 1891–1924*. New York: Viking, 1997.

"Fight against NRA Is Laid to Moscow." *New York Times*, August 30, 1934, 8.

Filene, Peter G. *Americans and the Soviet Experiment, 1917–1933*. Cambridge, Mass.: Harvard University Press, 1967.

Fisher, H. H. *The Famine in Soviet Russia, 1919–1923: The Operations of the American Relief Administration*. New York: Macmillan, 1927.

Fisher, James Terence. *The Catholic Counterculture in America, 1933–1962*. Chapel Hill: University of North Carolina Press, 1989.

———. *Dr. America: The Lives of Thomas A. Dooley, 1927–1961*. Amherst: University of Massachusetts Press, 1997.

Fleming, David L., S.J. *A Contemporary Reading of the Spiritual Exercises: A Companion to St. Ignatius' Text*. Saint Louis: Institute of Jesuit Sources, 1980.

Flint, James, O.S.B. "English Catholics and the Bolshevik Revolution: The Origins of Catholic Anti-Communism." *American Benedictine Review* 42, no. 1 (1991): 4–21.

Floridi, Alexis Ulysses, S.J. *Moscow and the Vatican*. Ann Arbor, Mich.: Ardis Publishers, 1986.

Flynn, George Q. *American Catholics and the Roosevelt Presidency, 1932–1936*. Lexington: University of Kentucky Press, 1968.

———. *The Draft, 1940–1973*. Lawrence: University Press of Kansas, 1993.

———. *Roosevelt and Romanism: Catholics and American Diplomacy, 1937–1945*. Westport, Conn.: Greenwood Press, 1976.

———. *The Vatican and the American Hierarchy from 1789 to 1965*. Collegeville, Minn.: Liturgical Press, 1985.

Fogarty, Gerald P., S.J. "Francis J. Spellman: American and Roman." In *Patterns of Episcopal Leadership*, edited by Gerald P. Fogarty, S.J., 216–34. New York: Macmillan, 1989.

Forbes, B. C. *Men Who Are Making America*. New York: Forbes, 1917.

Ford, John C., S.J. "The Hydrogen Bombing of Cities." In *The State of the Question: Morality and Modern Warfare*, edited by William J. Nagle, 98–103. Baltimore: Hebron Press, 1960.

————. "The Morality of Obliteration Bombing." *Theological Studies* 5, no. 3 (September 1944): 261–309.

"Four New Books on Russia." *New York Times Book Review*, April 19, 1931, 12

Frank, Robert L. "Prelude to Cold War: American Catholics and Communism." *Journal of Church and State* 34, no. 1 (Winter 1992): 39–56.

Freeman, Joshua B. *In Transit: The Transport Workers Union in New York City, 1933–1966.* New York: Oxford University Press, 1989.

Freeman, Joshua B., and Steve Rosswurm. "The Education of an Anti-Communist: Father John F. Cronin and the Baltimore Labor Movement." *Labor History* 33, no. 2 (Spring 1992): 217–47.

Freidel, Frank. *Franklin D. Roosevelt: A Rendezvous with Destiny.* Boston: Little, Brown, 1990.

Fried, Albert. *Communism in America: A History in Documents.* New York: Columbia University Press, 1997.

Fried, Richard M. *Men against McCarthy.* New York: Columbia University Press, 1967.

Fritschel, Heidi. "The School That Father Walsh Built." *Georgetown Magazine*, November–December 1984, 2–8.

Gaddis, John Lewis. *Russia, the Soviet Union, and the United States: An Interpretative Essay.* New York: Wiley, 1978.

————. *Strategies of Containment: A Critical Appraisal of Postwar American National Security Policy.* New York: Oxford University Press, 1982.

————. *The United States and the Origins of the Cold War, 1941–1947.* New York: Columbia University Press, 1972.

Gaffey, James P. *Francis Clement Kelley and the American Catholic Dream.* 2 vols. Bensenville, Ill.: Heritage Foundation, 1980.

Gallagher, J. F. "Biography." *America*, May 11, 1963, 684.

Gallagher, Louis J., S.J. *Edmund A. Walsh, S.J.: A Biography.* New York: Benziger Brothers, 1962.

————. "Father Edmund A. Walsh." *Woodstock Letters* 86, no. 1 (February 1957): 21–70.

————. "With the Papal Relief Mission in Russia." *Studies* 13 (March 1924): 46–48.

Gardner, Lloyd C. *Safe for Democracy: The Anglo-American Response to Revolution, 1913–1923.* New York: Oxford University Press, 1984.

Garthoff, Raymond L. *A Journey through the Cold War: A Memoir of Containment and Coexistence.* Washington, D.C.: Brookings Institution Press, 2001.

Georgetown University. *On the Hilltop: Reminiscences and Reflections on Their Campus Years by Georgetown Alumni.* Washington, D.C.: Georgetown University Press, 1966.

Georgetown University School of Foreign Service. *Announcement, 1921–1922.* Ser. 2, bull. 2, rev. Washington, D.C.: Georgetown University Press, 1921.

———. *Catalogue, 1925.* Winter ed. Washington, D.C.: Georgetown University Press, December 1924.

———. *Catalogue, 1925.* Winter 1924. Washington, D.C.: Georgetown University Press, 1925.

———. *Catalogue, 1926.* Washington, D.C.: Georgetown University Press, 1926.

———. *Catalogue, 1931–1932.* Washington, D.C.: Georgetown University Press, 1931.

———. *Catalogue, 1933–1934.* Washington, D.C.: Georgetown University Press, December 1933.

———. *Catalogue, 1937.* Washington, D.C.: Georgetown University Press, June 1937.

———. *Catalogue, 1938–1939.* Washington, D.C.: Georgetown University Press, March 1938.

———. *Catalogue, 1939–1940.* Washington, D.C.: Georgetown University Press, March 1939.

———. *Catalogue, 1940–1941.* Washington, D.C.: Georgetown University Press, February 1940.

———. *Fall Quarter (October 1–December 21, 1945).* Washington, D.C.: Georgetown University Press, August 1945.

———. *Undergraduate Course in Foreign Service Catalogue, 1941–1942.* Washington, D.C.: Georgetown University Press, February 1941.

———. *Undergraduate Courses in Foreign Service, Business and Public Administration (War Bulletin 1, 1942).* Washington, D.C.: Georgetown University Press, March 1942.

———. *Undergraduate Curriculum, 1945.* Washington, D.C.: Georgetown University Press, 1945.

———. *War Bulletin 3.* Washington, D.C.: Georgetown University Press, April 1943.

————. *War Bulletin 4*. Washington, D.C.: Georgetown University Press, May 1944.

————. *Yearbook, February 1919–February 1920, Including Report of the Foundation Exercises*. November 25, 1919, 2nd impression. Washington, D.C.: Georgetown University Press, 1920.

[Gillis, James M.] "Editorial Comment." *Catholic World* (May 1923): 258–60.

Gimbel, John. *The American Occupation of Germany: Politics and the Military, 1945–1949*. Stanford, Calif.: Stanford University Press, 1968.

Ginder, Richard. *With Ink and Crosier: The Story of Bishop Noll and His Work*. Huntington, Ind.: Our Sunday Visitor Press, 1953.

Girard, Jolyon P. *America and the World*. Westport, Conn.: Greenwood Press, 2001.

Glazer, Nathan. *The Social Basis of American Communism*. New York: Harcourt, Brace and World, 1961.

Gleason, Philip. *Contending with Modernity: Catholic Higher Education in the Twentieth Century*. New York: Oxford University Press, 1995.

————. *Keeping the Faith: American Catholicism Past and Present*. Notre Dame, Ind.: University of Notre Dame Press, 1987.

Graham, Robert A., S.J. "A 'Footnote' on Nuremberg." *America*, June 12, 1948, 252–53.

————. *Vatican Diplomacy: A Study of Church and State on the International Plane*. Princeton, N.J.: Princeton University Press, 1959.

Gribble, Richard, C.S.C. *Guardian of America: The Life of James Martin Gillis, C.S.P.* New York: Paulist Press, 1998.

Griffith, Robert. *The Politics of Fear: Joseph R. McCarthy and the Senate*. Amherst: University of Massachusetts Press, 1987.

Gruber, Carol S. *Mars and Minerva: World War I and the Uses of Higher Learning in America*. Baton Rouge: Louisiana State University Press, 1975.

Gundlach, Gustav, S.J. "Moral Estimate of the Nuremberg Trial." *America*, November 9, 1946, 149–51.

Gurian, Waldemar. "Review of *Total Power: A Footnote to History*." *Catholic Historical Review* 34, no. 4 (January 1949): 473–75.

Guttmann, Allen. *The Wound in the Heart: American Response to and Interpretation of the Spanish Civil War*. Glencoe, Ill.: Free Press of Glencoe, 1962.

Halsey, William M. *The Survival of American Innocence: Catholicism in an Era of Disillusionment, 1920–1940.* Notre Dame, Ind.: University of Notre Dame Press, 1980.

Handy, Robert T. *A Christian America: Protestant Hopes and Historical Realities.* 2nd ed., revised and enlarged. New York: Oxford University Press, 1984.

Hart, Scott. *Washington at War, 1941–1945.* Englewood Cliffs, N.J.: Prentice-Hall, 1970.

"Haskell, William Nafew." In *National Cyclopedia of American Biography,* 63 vols., 1: 516–17. Clifton, N.J.: James T. White, 1955.

Hauner, Milan. *What Is Asia to Us? Russia's Asian Heartland Yesterday and Today.* Boston: Unwin Hyman, 1990.

Heale, M. J. *American Anticommunism: Combating the Enemy Within, 1830–1970.* Baltimore: Johns Hopkins University Press, 1990.

Healey, Paul F. "Diplomat Priest." *Extension,* December 1946, 19–20, 56, 63.

Hearne, Maurice. "Father Walsh in the United States." *Foreign Service Courier* 5, no. 12 (1957): 19–22.

Heinrichs, Waldo H. "Bureaucracy and Professionalism in the Development of American Career Diplomacy." In *Twentieth Century American Foreign Policy,* edited by John Braeman, Robert H. Bremmer, and David Brody, 119–206. Athens: Ohio State University Press, 1971.

Hennesey, James, S.J. *American Catholics: A History of the Roman Catholic Community in the United States.* New York: Oxford University Press, 1981.

———. "American Jesuit in Wartime Rome: The Diary of Vincent A. McCormick, S.J." *Mid-America* 56 (1974): 32–55.

Herberg, Will. *Protestant-Catholic-Jew: An Essay in Religious Sociology.* 2nd ed. Chicago: University of Chicago Press, 1983.

Herman, Arthur. *Joseph McCarthy: Reexamining the Life and Legacy of America's Most Hated Senator.* New York: Free Press, 2000.

Heyden, Francis J., S.J. "A Record of the Controversy between Fr. Edmund A. Walsh and *Time.*" *Woodstock Letters* 59, no. 2 (June 1930): 222–33.

Higham, John. *Strangers in the Land: Patterns of American Nativism, 1860–1925.* 2nd ed. New York: Atheneum, 1963.

Hogan, Michael J. *A Cross of Iron: Harry S. Truman and the Origins of the National Security State, 1945–1954*. New York: Cambridge University Press, 1998.

Holmes, J. Derek. *The Papacy in the Modern World, 1914–1978*. New York: Crossroad, 1981.

Holmes, John Haynes. "Religion in Revolutionary Russia." *Nation*, May 9, 1923, 541–44.

Holsinger, M. Paul. "The Oregon School Bill Controversy, 1922–1925." *Pacific Historical Review* 37, no. 3 (August 1968): 327–41.

Hoover, Herbert. *An American Epic*. Vol. 3: *Famine in Forty-Five Nations, the Battle on the Front Line, 1914–1923*. Chicago: Regnery, 1961.

———. *Memoirs*. Vol. 2: *The Cabinet and the Presidency, 1920–1933*. New York: Macmillan, 1952.

Huber, Raphael M., ed. *Our Bishops Speak, 1919–1951*. Milwaukee: Bruce, 1952.

Hudson, Winthrop S. *Religion in America: An Historical Account of the Development of American Religious Life*. 3rd ed. New York: Scribner's, 1981.

"Hungary—The Red Terror and the Jewish Problem." *Woodstock Letters* 54, no. 2 (1925): 91–97.

Hull, Henry. "The Holy See and Soviet Russia, 1918–1930: A Study in Full-Circle Diplomacy." Ph.D. diss., Georgetown University, 1970.

Hunt, Michael H. *Ideology and U.S. Foreign Policy*. New Haven, Conn.: Yale University Press, 1987.

Husband, William B. *"Godless Communists": Atheism and Society in Soviet Russia, 1917–1932*. DeKalb: Northern Illinois University Press, 2000.

Husslein, Joseph C., S.J. *The Pastor and Socialism: A Paper Read Before the Ecclesiastical Round Table of the Priests of the Ohio Valley*. New York: America Press, 1911.

Hutton, Leon. "Catholicity and Civility: John Francis Noll and the Origins of *Our Sunday Visitor*." *U.S. Catholic Historian* 15, no. 3 (Summer 1997): 1–22.

Ilchman, Warren Frederick. *Professional Diplomacy in the United States: A Study in Administrative History*. Chicago: University of Chicago Press, 1961.

Ingalls, Robert P. *Point of Order: A Profile of Senator Joe McCarthy.* New York: Putnam's, 1981.

Ireland, John. *The Church and Modern Society: Lectures and Addresses.* New York: D. H. McBride, 1899.

Isserman, Maurice. "Three Generations: Historians View American Communism." *Labor History* 26, no. 4 (Fall 1985): 27–52.

Jackson, Kenneth T. *The Ku Klux Klan in the City, 1915–1930.* New York: Oxford University Press, 1967.

"Jackson Lauded for Nuremberg." *New York Times*, July 10, 1946, 10.

Jaskiewicz, Walter C., S.J. "The Institute of Contemporary Russian Studies." In *As I Remember Fordham: Selections from the Sesquicentennial Oral History Project*, 99–101. New York: Fordham University Press, 1991.

Jedin, Hubert, ed. *History of the Church.* Vol. 10: *The Church in the Modern Age.* New York: Crossroad, 1981.

"Jesuit Tries to Justify Use of A-Bomb." *Christian Century,* January 10, 1951, 35–36.

Johnston, Charles. "Russia's Revolution as an Episode in the Human Tragedy," *New York Times Book Review*, July 1, 1928, 3.

"Jottings from Innsbruck about Russia." *Woodstock Letters* 52, no. 2 (1923): 224–40.

Kane, Paula M. *Separatism and Subculture: Boston Catholicism, 1900–1920.* Chapel Hill: University of North Carolina Press, 1994.

Kauffman, Christopher J. *Faith and Fraternalism: The History of the Knights of Columbus.* Rev. ed. New York: Simon and Schuster, 1992.

———. *Patriotism and Fraternalism in the Knights of Columbus: A History of the Fourth Degree.* New York: Herder and Herder, 2001.

Kayser, Elmer Louis. *Bricks without Straw: The Evolution of George Washington University.* New York: Appleton-Century-Crofts, 1970.

Kellock, Harold. "The Innocence of Father Walsh." *Nation,* July 25, 1928, 91–92.

Kennan, George F. *American Diplomacy, 1900–1950.* Chicago: University of Chicago Press, 1951.

———. *Memoirs, 1925–1950.* New York: Pantheon, 1967.

[———]. [under pseudonym "X"] "The Sources of Soviet Conflict." *Foreign Affairs,* July 1947, 566–82.

Kennedy, David M. *Over Here: The First World War and American Society*. New York: Oxford University Press, 1980.

———. *Freedom from Fear: The American People in Depression and War, 1929–1945*. New York: Oxford University Press, 1999.

Kessner, Thomas. *Fiorello H. LaGuardia and the Making of Modern New York*. New York: McGraw-Hill, 1989.

Kirk, Grayson. *The Study of International Relations in American Colleges*. New York: Council on Foreign Relations, 1947.

Klehr, Harvey. *The Heyday of American Communism: The Depression Decade*. New York: Basic Books, 1984.

Klehr, Harvey, and John Earl Haynes. *The American Communist Movement: Storming Heaven Itself*. New York: Twayne, 1992.

Klehr, Harvey, John Earl Haynes, and Fridrikh Igorevich Fuisov. *The Secret World of American Communism*. New Haven, Conn.: Yale University Press, 1995.

Kohn, Hans. *American Nationalism: An Interpretive Essay*, New York: Knopf, 1957.

———. "Story of Haushofer." *New York Times*, June 27, 1948, 3, 18.

Koriakov, Mikhail. "'Who Rules the Heartland . . .'" *New York Times*, July 8, 1951, 8.

Kress, Rev. William Stephens. *The Red Peril*. Cleveland: Ohio Apostolate, 1912.

Kselman, Thomas A., and Steven Avella. "Marian Piety and Cold War in the United States." *Catholic Historical Review* 72 (July 1986): 403–24.

LaFeber, Walter. *The American Age: United States Foreign Policy at Home and Abroad since 1750*. New York: Norton, 1989.

———. *America, Russia and the Cold War, 1945–1992*. 7th ed. New York: McGraw-Hill, 1993.

Landis, Mark. *Joseph McCarthy: The Politics of Chaos*. Cranbury, N.J.: Associated University Presses, 1987.

Leahy, William P., S.J. *Adapting to America: Catholics, Jesuits and Higher Education in the Twentieth Century*. Washington, D.C.: Catholic University of America Press, 1991.

Ledochowski, Father General Wlodimir. "Letter of Very Rev. Fr. General to the Provincials of the American Assistancy and Canada," *Informationes et Notitiae* 1, no. 4 (June 1935): iv.

Leffler, Melvyn P. "The American Conception of National Security and the Beginnings of the Cold War, 1945–1948." In *American*

Foreign Policy: Theoretical Essays, 2nd ed., edited by G. John Ikenberry, 140–61. New York: HarperCollins, 1996.

———. "The Interpretive War over the Cold War, 1945–1960." In *American Foreign Relations Reconsidered, 1890–1993*, edited by Gordon Martel, 106–24. London: Routledge, 1994.

———. *A Preponderance of Power: National Security, the Truman Administration, and the Cold War*. Stanford, Calif.: Stanford University Press, 1992.

Leuchtenberg, William E. *Franklin D. Roosevelt and the New Deal, 1932–1940*. New York: Harper and Row, 1963.

———. *The Perils of Prosperity, 1914–1932*. 2nd ed. Chicago: University of Chicago Press, 1993.

Levenstein, Harvey A. *Communism, Anti-Communism, and the C. I. O.* Westport, Conn.: Greenwood Press, 1981.

Levine, David O. *The American College and the Culture of Aspiration, 1915–1940*. Ithaca, N.Y.: Cornell University Press, 1986.

Lewis, Lionel S. *Cold War on Campus: A Study of the Politics of Organizational Control*. New Brunswick, N.J.: Transaction Books, 1988.

Lockwood, G. H. *The Priest and the Billy Goat*. Kalamazoo, Mich.: Lockwood, 1913.

Maddox, Robert James. *William E. Borah and American Foreign Policy*. Baton Rouge: Louisiana State University Press, 1969.

Marcus, Sheldon. *Father Coughlin: The Tumultuous Life of the Priest of the Little Flower*. Boston: Little, Brown, 1973.

Margulies, Herbert F. "Anti-Catholicism in Wisconsin Politics, 1914–1920." *Mid-America* 4, no. 1 (January 1962): 51–56.

Mark, Eduard. "October or Thermidor? Interpretations of Stalinism and the Perception of Soviet Foreign Policy in the United States, 1927–1947." *American Historical Review* 94, no. 4 (October 1989): 937–62.

Marks, Frederick W., III. *Wind Over Sand: The Diplomacy of Franklin D. Roosevelt*. Athens: University of Georgia Press, 1988.

"Martyrs in Russia Estimated at 6,000." *New York Times*, March 18, 1930, 9.

Marx, Paul, O.S.B. *Virgil Michel and the Liturgical Movement*. Collegeville, Minn.: Liturgical Press, 1957.

Massa, Mark S., S.J. *Catholics and American Culture: Fulton Sheen, Dorothy Day, and the Notre Dame Football Team*. New York: Crossroad, 1999.

May, Henry F. *The End of American Innocence: A Study of the First Years of Our Own Time, 1912–1917*. Chicago: Quadrangle Books, 1964.

Mayer, Arno J. *The Furies: Violence and Terror in the French and Russian Revolutions*. Princeton, N.J.: Princeton University Press, 2000.

Mayers, David. *George Kennan and the Dilemmas of U.S. Foreign Policy*. New York: Oxford University Press, 1988.

McCaughey, Robert A. *International Studies and Academic Enterprise: A Chapter in the Enclosure of American Learning*. New York: Columbia University Press, 1984.

McConnell, Stuart. "Reading the Flag: A Reconsideration of the Patriotic Cults of the 1890's." In *Bonds of Affection: Americans Redefine Their Patriotism*, edited by John Bodnar, 87–108. Princeton, N.J.: Princeton University Press, 1996.

McCullagh, Captain Francis. *The Bolshevik Persecution of Christianity*. New York: Dutton, 1924.

McDonough, Peter. *Men Astutely Trained: The Jesuits in the American Century*. New York: Free Press, 1992.

McFadden, William C., ed. *Georgetown at Two Hundred: Faculty Reflections on the University's Future*. Washington, D.C.: Georgetown University Press, 1990.

McGreevy, John T. "Thinking on One's Own: Catholicism in the American Intellectual Imagination, 1928–1960." *Journal of American History* 84, no. 1 (June 1997): 97–131.

McGuiness, Margaret M. "The Call of the East: The Early Years of the Catholic Near East Welfare Association." *Records of the American Catholic Historical Society of Philadelphia* 103, nos. 3–4 (1992): 33–42.

McKeown, Elizabeth. *War and Welfare: American Catholics and World War I*. New York: Garland, 1988.

McKevitt, William G. *The Hilltop Remembered*. Washington, D.C.: Georgetown University Press, 1982.

McNamara, Patrick J. "A Study of the Editorial Policy of the Brooklyn *Tablet* under Patrick F. Scanlan, 1917–1968. " Master's thesis, Saint John's University, 1994.

McNeal, Patricia F. *The American Catholic Peace Movement, 1928–1972*. New York: Arno Press, 1978.

McShane, Joseph M., S.J. *"Sufficiently Radical": Catholicism, Progressivism, and the Bishops' Program of 1919.* Washington, D.C.: Catholic University of America Press, 1986.

"Mgr. Walsh Backs Moves." *New York Times,* October 4, 1941, 3.

Miller, William D. *Dorothy Day: A Biography.* San Francisco: Harper and Row, 1982.

————. *A Harsh and Dreadful Love: Dorothy Day and the Catholic Worker Movement.* New York: Liveright, 1973.

"Minutes of the Inter-Province Meeting on Communism and Atheism." *Informationes et Notitiae* 1, no. 4 (June 1935): iv.

Miscamble, Wilson D., C.S.C. *George F. Kennan and the Making of American Foreign Policy, 1947–1950.* Princeton, N.J.: Princeton University Press, 1992.

"Misleading the Public Again." Editorial. *America,* April 26, 1930, 57–58.

Moody, Joseph N., ed. *Church and Society: Catholic Social and Political Movements, 1789–1950.* New York: Arts, 1953.

"Moscow Statement on Religion Disappoints White House Circles." *New York Times,* October 6, 1941, 1, 4.

"Moscow's Reply to the Pope in Line with Expectations." *New York Times,* February 23, 1930, III, 5.

"Moves to End Jam on Neutrality Act." *New York Times,* May 4, 1939, 7.

"M.S.C. Class Told Civil War Is Here." *New York Times,* June 15, 1937, 9.

Murphy, David Thomas. *The Heroic Earth: Geopolitical Thought in Weimar Germany.* Kent, Ohio: Kent State University Press, 1997.

Murray, Robert K. *Red Scare: A Study in National Hysteria, 1919–1920.* Minneapolis: University of Minnesota Press, 1955.

Musicant, Ivan. *Empire by Default: The Spanish-American War and the Dawn of the American Century.* New York: Henry Holt, 1998.

Naison, Mark D. *Communists in Harlem during the Depression.* Urbana: University of Illinois Press, 1976.

Nevils, W. Coleman, S.J. *Miniatures of Georgetown, 1634–1934: Tercentennial Causeries.* Washington, D.C.: Georgetown University Press, 1934.

Ninkovich, Frank. *Germany and the United States: The Transformation of the German Question since 1945.* Boston: Twayne, 1988.

————. *The Wilsonian Century: U.S. Foreign Policy since 1900*. Chicago: University of Chicago Press, 1999.

Nolan, Hugh J., ed. *Pastoral Letters of the National Hierarchy, 1792–1970*. Huntington, Ind.: Our Sunday Visitor Press, 1971.

Nove, Alec. *An Economic History of the USSR*. New York: Penguin Books, 1992.

O'Brien, David J. *American Catholics and Social Reform: The New Deal Years*. New York: Oxford University Press, 1968.

————. *Isaac Hecker: An American Catholic*. New York: Paulist Press, 1992.

————. *Public Catholicism*. New York: Macmillan, 1989.

————. *The Renewal of American Catholicism*. New York: Oxford University Press, 1972.

O'Connell, Dan. "Father Walsh and Japan." *Foreign Service Courier* 5, no. 12 (1957): 12–25.

O'Connor, David L. "Defenders of the Faith: American Catholic Lay Organizations and Anticommunism, 1917–1975." Ph.D. diss., State University of New York at Stonybrook, 2000.

O'Connor, Thomas H. *Boston Catholics: A History of the Church and its People*. Boston: Northeastern University Press, 1999.

————. *South Boston: My Home Town: The Story of an Ethnic Neighborhood*. Boston: Quinlan Press, 1988.

O'Leary, Cecilia Elizabeth. *To Die For: The Paradox of American Patriotism*. Princeton, N.J.: Princeton University Press, 1999.

O'Malley, John W. *The First Jesuits*. Cambridge, Mass.: Harvard University Press, 1993.

O'Malley, William J., S.J. *The Fifth Week*. 2nd ed. Chicago: Loyola University Press, 1996.

O'Reilly, Kenneth. *Hoover and the Un-Americans: The FBI, HUAC, and the Red Menace*. Philadelphia: Temple University Press, 1983.

O'Sullivan, John, and Alan M. Meckler, eds. *The Draft and its Enemies: A Documentary History*. Urbana: University of Illinois Press, 1974.

Ogden, August Raymond, F.S.C. *The Dies Committee: A Study of the Special House Committee for the Investigation of Un-American Activities, 1938–1944*. Washington, D.C.: Catholic University of America Press, 1945.

Oshinsky, David M. *A Conspiracy So Immense: The World of Joe McCarthy*. New York: Free Press, 1983.

O'Toole, James M. *Militant and Triumphant: William Henry O'Connell and the Catholic Church in Boston, 1859–1944*. Notre Dame,
Ind.: University of Notre Dame Press, 1992.

Ottanelli, Fraser. *The Communist Party of the United States: From
the Depression to World War II*. New Brunswick, N.J.: Rutgers
University Press, 1991.

Ó Tuathail, Gearóid / Gerald Toal. "Spiritual Geopolitics: Father Edmund Walsh and Jesuit Anticommunism." In *Geopolitical Tradi-
tions: Critical Histories of A Century of Geopolitical Thought*,
edited by David Atkinson and Klaus Dodds, chap. 8. New York:
Routledge, 2000.

Overy, Richard J. *Interrogators: The Nazi Elite in Allied Hands, 1945*.
New York: Viking, 2001.

"Pan-Europe Called Aim of Nazi Drive." *New York Times*, February
17, 1940, 4.

Parker, Geoffrey. *Western Geopolitical Thought in the Twentieth Century*. New York: St. Martin's Press, 1985.

Parrish, Michael. *Anxious Decades: America in Prosperity and Depression, 1920–1941*. New York: Norton, 1992.

Patenaud, Bernard. *Herbert Hoover's Brush with Bolshevism*. Kennan Institute for Advanced Studies, Occasional Paper 248. Washington, D.C.: Woodrow Wilson Center, 1992.

Paterson, Thomas G. *Meeting the Communist Threat: Truman to
Reagan*. New York: Oxford University Press, 1988.

Patterson, James T. *Grand Expectations: The United States, 1945–
1974*. New York: Oxford University Press, 1990.

Peris, Daniel. *Storming the Heavens: The Soviet League of the Militant Godless*. Ithaca, N.Y.: Cornell University Press, 1998.

Perrett, Geoffrey. *America in the Twenties: A History*. New York:
Simon and Schuster, 1982.

Piehl, Mel. "The Catholic Worker and Peace in the Early Cold War
Era." In *American Catholic Pacifism: The Influence of Dorothy Day
and the Catholic Worker Movement*, edited by Anne Klejment and
Nancy L. Roberts, 77–90. Westport, Conn.: Praeger, 1996.

Pipes, Richard. *Communism: A History*. New York: Modern Library,
2002.

———. *A Concise History of the Russian Revolution*. New York: Vintage, 1995.

Pius XII. *Annus fere iam est. Acta Apostolicae Sedis* 14 (1922): 417–19.

"Pope Congratulated on Fifth Anniversary." *New York Times,* February 13, 1927, 22.

Power, Edward J. *A History of Catholic Higher Education in the United States.* Milwaukee: Bruce, 1958.

Powers, Richard Gid. *Not without Honor: The History of American Anticommunism.* New York: Free Press, 1995.

"President's Hands Free, Says Walsh." *New York Times,* October 22, 1933, 25.

"Priest Attacks Rule of the Soviet." *New York Times,* March 24, 1925, 13.

"Priest Justifies Use of Bomb for Defense." *New York Times,* December 25, 1950, 5.

Puhl, Louis J., S.J. *The Spiritual Exercises of St. Ignatius: Based on Studies in the Language of the Autograph.* Chicago: Loyola University Press, 1951.

Quigley, Carroll. "Constantine McGuire: Man of Mystery." *Foreign Service Courier* 14, no. 2 (December 1965): 12–16.

———. "Father Walsh as I Knew Him." *Protocol,* June 1959.

Quirk, Robert E. *The Mexican Revolution and the Catholic Church, 1910–1929.* Bloomington: Indiana University Press, 1973.

Rahner, Karl, S.J. *Spiritual Exercises.* Translated by Kenneth Baker, S.J. New York: Herder and Herder, 1965.

"Recovery or Disaster." *Commonweal,* October 13, 1933, 543–45.

"Reds Seen Backing Roosevelt." *New York Times,* March 7, 1936, 5.

Reeves, Thomas C. *America's Bishop: The Life and Times of Fulton J. Sheen.* San Francisco: Encounter Books, 2001.

———. *The Life and Times of Joe McCarthy: A Biography.* New York: Madison Books, 1997.

Reher, Margaret Mary. "Dougherty, Dennis Cardinal." In *Encyclopedia of American Catholic History,* edited by Michael Glazier and Thomas J. Shelley, 454. Collegeville, Minn.: Liturgical Press, 1997.

"Reverend Edmund A. Walsh, S.J., 1885–." In *Catholic Authors: Contemporary Biographical Sketches, 1930–1947,* edited by Matthew Hoehn, O.S.B., 758. Newark, N.J.: Saint Mary's Abbey, 1948.

"Review of *The Fall of the Russian Empire.*" *Catholic World* 128, no. 763 (October 1928): 113–14.

Rhodes, Benjamin D. "An Ohio Kitchen Inspector and the Soviet Famine of 1921–1922: The Russian Odyssey of Henry C. Wolfe." *Ohio History* 103 (Summer–Autumn 1994): 190–99.

Roberts, Roxanne. "Alsop's Faded Georgetown." *Washington Post*, August 2, 1996, A1.

Robins, Raymond. "United States Recognition of Russia Essential to World Peace and Stabilization." In *Selected Articles on Recognition of Soviet Russia*, edited by E. C. Buehler, B. W. Maxwell, and George R. R. Pflaum, 270–78. New York: H. W. Wilson, 1931.

Rorty, James. "More Truth about Russia." *New Republic*, July 8, 1931, 213.

Rose, Lisle A. *The Cold War Comes to Main Street: America in 1950.* Lawrence: University Press of Kansas, 1999.

Rossi, Joseph S., S.J. *American Catholics and the Formation of the United Nations*. Lanham, Md.: University Press of America, 1993.

Rosswurm, Steve. "Manhood, Communism, and Americanism: The Federal Bureau of Investigation and the American Jesuits, 1935–1960." Paper presented at the American Catholic Studies Seminar, University of Notre Dame, April 18, 1996.

Ruhan, Anthony, S.J. "The Origin of the Jesuit Tertianship: Meaning, Interpretation, Development." *Woodstock Letters* 94 (Fall 1965): 407–23.

"Russia." *America*, April 14, 1923, 604.

"Russia's Aid Seen Lagging." *New York Times*, December 14, 1944, 6.

Ryan, James H., Ph.D. *The Papal Relief Mission in Russia*. Washington, D.C.: National Catholic War Council, 1923.

Ryan, John A. *The Church and Socialism, and Other Essays*. Washington, D.C.: University Press, 1919.

———. *Social Reform on Catholic Lines*. New York: Columbus Press, 1913.

Sánchez, José M. "The Spanish Civil War and American Catholics." In *Encyclopedia of American Catholic History*, edited by Michael Glazier and Thomas J. Shelley, 1345–46. Collegeville, Minn.: Liturgical Press, 1997.

"Says Soviet Envoys Plot Revolutions." *New York Times*, April 16, 1930, 20.

[Scanlan, Patrick F.] "Bolshevism in Operation." Editorial. *Tablet*, April 7, 1923, 6.

Schaffer, Ronald. *America in the Great War: The Rise of the War Welfare State*. New York: Oxford University Press, 1991.

Schatz, Ronald W. "American Labor and the Catholic Church, 1919–1950." *U.S. Catholic Historian* 3, no. 3 (Fall–Winter 1983): 178–90.

Schlesinger, Arthur M., Jr. *The Age of Roosevelt*. Vol. 1: *The Crisis of the Old Order, 1919–1933*. Boston: Houghton Mifflin, 1957.

Schrecker, Ellen. *No Ivory Tower: McCarthyism and the Universities*. New York: Oxford University Press, 1986.

Schroth, Raymond A., S.J. *Fordham: A History and Memoir*. Chicago: Loyola University Press, 2002.

Schultenover, David G., S.J. *A View from Rome: On the Eve of the Modernist Crisis*. New York: Fordham University Press, 1994.

Schulzinger, Robert D. *The Making of the Diplomatic Mind: The Training, Outlook and Style of United States Foreign Service Officers, 1908–1931*. Middletown, Conn.: Wesleyan University Press, 1975.

Schwarz, Jordan A. "Hoover and Congress: Politics, Personality and Perspective in the Presidency." In *The Hoover Presidency: A Reappraisal*, edited by Martin L. Fausold and George Mazuzan, 87–100. Albany: State University of New York Press, 1974.

"Sees Bomb Secret Lost: Father Walsh Tells FBI Group Russia Has Blueprints." *New York Times*, October 4, 1947, 9.

Sheen, Fulton J. *Communism and the Conscience of the West*. New York: Bobbs-Merrill, 1948.

Sheerin, John B., C.S.P. *Never Look Back: The Career and Concerns of John J. Burke*. New York: Paulist Press, 1974.

Shelley, Thomas J. "The Oregon School Case and the National Catholic Welfare Conference." *Catholic Historical Review* 75, no. 3 (July 1989): 439–57.

Sirgiovanni, George. *An Undercurrent of Suspicion: Anti-Communism in America during World War II*. New Brunswick, N.J.: Transaction, 1990.

Sittser, Gerald L. *A Cautious Patriotism: The American Churches and the Second World War*. Chapel Hill: University of North Carolina Press, 1998.

Sivachev, Nikolai V., and Nikolai N. Yakovlev. *Russia and the United States: U.S.-Soviet Relations from the Soviet Point of View*. Translated by Olga Adler Titelbaum. Chicago: University of Chicago Press, 1979.

Slattery, Joseph A., S.J. "In Memoriam: Very Rev. Fr. Vladimir Ledochowski." *Woodstock Letters* 72, no. 1 (March 1943): 1–20.

Slawson, Douglas J. *The Foundation and First Decade of the National Catholic Welfare Council.* Washington, D.C.: Catholic University of America Press, 1992.

Smith, Richard Norton. *An Uncommon Man: The Triumph of Herbert Hoover.* New York: Simon and Schuster, 1984.

"Social Council Urged for Nation by Walsh." *New York Times,* June 8, 1936, 13.

Southern, David W. *John LaFarge and the Limits of Catholic Interracialism.* Baton Rouge: Louisiana State University Press, 1996.

"Soviet Assailed at D.A.R. Congress." *New York Times,* April 18, 1929, 30.

"Soviet is Assailed at D.A.R. Meeting." *New York Times,* April 21, 1933, 12.

"Soviet Russia's Conditions." *New York Times,* August 24, 1924, 20.

"Soviets Seen Having Atomic Bomb Soon." *New York Times,* June 19, 1947, 9.

Spalding, Thomas W. *The Premier See: A History of the Archdiocese of Baltimore.* Baltimore: Johns Hopkins University Press, 1989.

Steel, Ronald. "The Domestic Core of Foreign Policy." In *The Domestic Sources of American Foreign Policy: Insights and Evidence,* 3d ed., edited by Eugene R. Wittkopf and James M. McCormick, 23–32. New York: Rowman and Littlefield, 1999.

Stehle, Hansjakob. *Eastern Politics of the Vatican, 1917–1979.* Athens: Ohio University Press, 1981.

Steinberg, Peter L. *The Great "Red Menace": United States Prosecutions of American Communists, 1947–1952.* Westport, Conn.: Greenwood Press, 1984.

Stern, Robert L. "Catholic Near East Welfare Association." In *Encyclopedia of American Catholic History,* edited by Michael Glazier and Thomas J. Shelley, 280–81. Collegeville, Minn.: Liturgical Press, 1997.

Strakhovsky, Leonid I. *American Opinion about Russia, 1917–1920.* Toronto: University of Toronto Press, 1960.

"Studebaker Denies Facing Pressure." *New York Times,* June 28, 1938, 11.

Sullivan, Thomas. "Review of *Edmund A. Walsh, S.J.*" *Emmanuel* 70, no. 3 (March 1964): 136.

Szczesniak, Boleslaw, ed. *The Russian Revolution: A Collection of Documents Concerning the Suppression of Religion by the Communists, 1917–1925.* Notre Dame, Ind.: University of Notre Dame Press, 1959.

Taylor, F. Jay. *The United States and the Spanish Civil War.* New York: Octagon Books, 1971.

Taylor, Telford. *Grand Inquest: The Story of Congressional Investigations.* New York: Simon and Schuster, 1955.

Tentler, Leslie Woodcock. *Seasons of Grace: A History of the Catholic Archdiocese of Detroit.* Detroit: Wayne State University Press, 1990.

Theoharis, Athan, ed. *From the Secret Files of J. Edgar Hoover.* Chicago: Ivan R. Dee, 1991.

Thomas, Lately. *When Even Angels Wept: Senator Joseph McCarthy—A Story without a Hero.* New York: William Morrow, 1973.

"Three Faiths Join in Assailing Soviets." *New York Times,* March 10, 1930, 1, 7.

[Tierney, Richard H.] "Russia and Oregon." Editorial. *America,* April 14, 1923, 614.

Tillman, Seth P. *Georgetown University's School of Foreign Service: The First 75 Years.* Washington, D.C.: Edmund A. Walsh School of Foreign Service, 1994.

"'Time' Limps in Again." *America,* May 17, 1930, 126.

Touchet, Francis Henry. "The Social Gospel and Cold War: The Melish Case." Ph.D. diss., New York University, 1981.

Traina, Richard P. *American Diplomacy and the Spanish Civil War.* Bloomington: Indiana University Press, 1968.

Troncone, Anthony. "Hamilton Fish, Sr., and the Politics of American Nationalism, 1912–1945." Ph.D. diss., Rutgers University, 1993.

"Truman Picks Nine to Study Training, Offer Youth Plan." *New York Times,* December 20, 1946, 1, 26.

Tull, Charles J. *Father Coughlin and the New Deal.* Syracuse, N.Y.: Syracuse University Press, 1965.

Tyack, David B. "The Perils of Pluralism: The Background of the Pierce Case." *American Historical Review* 74, no. 1 (October 1968): 74–98.

"Two Views of Russia." *Commonweal,* July 13, 1932, 290–92.

"Union Sodality Convenes at Georgetown University; Delegates Discuss Communism." *Informationes et Notitiae* 2, no. 3 (January 1937): 19.

U.S. Department of State. *Foreign Relations of the United States,*
1922. Vol. 2. Washington, D.C.: Government Printing Office, 1938.
————. *Foreign Relations of the United States, 1952–1954.* Vol. 8:
Eastern Europe, Soviet Union, Eastern Mediterranean. Washington, D.C.: Government Printing Office, 1988.

U.S. Federal Bureau of Investigation. "Subject: Edmund A. Walsh."
File 62–32073, sec. 1.

U.S. House of Representatives. Special Committee to Investigate
Communist Activities in the United States. *Hearings.* 71st Cong.,
2nd sess. Part 1. Vol. 1, June 9 and 13, 1930, and vol. 4, November
10, 24, and 25, and December 5, 1930. Washington, D.C.: Government Printing Office, 1930.

————. Special Committee on Un-American Activities. *Investiga-*
tions of Nazi Propaganda Activities and Investigation of Certain
Other Propaganda Activities: Public Hearings. 73rd Cong., 2nd
sess., December 17 and 18, 1934. Washington, D.C.: Government
Printing Office, 1935.

U.S. Senate. Committee on Foreign Relations. *Neutrality, Peace Leg-*
islation and Our Foreign Policy: Hearings. 76th Cong., 1st sess.,
part 1, April 5, 1939. Washington, D.C.: Government Printing Office, 1939.

"University Unit is 21 Years Old." *New York Times,* February 4, 1940,
II, 8.

"Urges New Peace Tribunal." *New York Times,* November 18, 1929,
28.

Valaik, J. David. "American Catholic Dissenters and the Spanish
Civil War, 1936–1939." *Catholic Historical Review* 53, no. 4 (January 1968): 537–55.

Van Allen, Rodger. *The Commonweal and American Catholicism: The*
Magazine, the Movement, the Meaning. Philadelphia: Fortress
Press, 1974.

Van Hoogstrate, Dorothy Jane. *American Foreign Policy, Realists and*
Idealists: A Catholic Interpretation. Saint Louis: B. Herder, 1960.

Vinca, Robert H. "The American Catholic Reaction to the Persecution of the Church in Mexico, 1926–1936." *Records of the Ameri-*
can Catholic Historical Society of Philadelphia 79, no. 1 (March
1968): 3–38.

"Walsh, Edmund A., S.J., Total Power: A Footnote to History." *Li-*
brary Journal 73, no. 6 (March 15, 1948): 472.

Walsh, Edmund A., S.J. "America, Russia and George Bernard Shaw." *Catholic Mind* 29, no. 21 (November 8, 1931): 489–99.

———. "The Basic Issue in the Recognition of Soviet Russia." *Catholic Mind* 31, no. 10 (May 22, 1933): 192–200.

———. "The Catholic Church in Present-Day Russia." *Catholic Historical Review* 18, no. 2 (July 1932): 177–204.

———. "The Catholic Church in Present-Day Russia." In *The Catholic Church in Contemporary Europe, 1919–1931,* edited by Peter Guilday. Vol. 2: *Papers of the American Catholic Historical Association,* 212–69. New York: P. J. Kenedy and Sons, 1932.

———. "The Challenge to Religion in a Changing World." *Annals of the American Academy of Social and Political Science* 41 (July 1935): 183–91.

———. "Comments and Corollaries." *America* November 9, 1946: 151–54.

———. "Democracy's Answer to Communism." *Informationes et Notitiae* 2, no. 1 (November 1936): 28–32.

———. "Editorial." *Informationes et Notitiae* 2, no. 1 (November 1936): 2.

———. "Education and Freedom under Democracy." *National Catholic Educational Association* 33 (November 1936): 88–104.

———. "An Epistle to the Romans: *Modern Style*." *Atlantic Monthly* February 1938: 240–43.

———. "Ethical Standards in High School Instruction." *Catholic Mind* 36, no. 856 (August 22, 1938): 336–38.

———. "The Fall of the Russian Empire: 1. The Plot Played by a Woman." *Atlantic Monthly,* January 1928, 46–59.

———. "The Fall of the Russian Empire: 2. The End of the Monarchy." *Atlantic Monthly,* February 1928, 228–40.

———. *The Fall of the Russian Empire: The Story of the Last of the Romanovs and the Coming of the Bolsheviki.* New York: Blue Ribbon Books, 1928.

———. "Geopolitics and International Morals." In *Compass of the World: A Symposium on Political Geography,* edited by Hans W. Weigert and Viljhamur Stefanson, 12–39. New York: Macmillan, 1944.

———. "The Great Fallacy." *Informationes et Notitiae* 2, no. 2 (December 1936): 11–13.

————. *The History and Nature of International Relations.* New York: Macmillan, 1922.

[————]."Jottings from Innsbruck about Russia." *Woodstock Letters* 52, no. 2 (1923): 224–40.

————. *The Last Stand: An Interpretation of the Five-Year Plan.* Boston: Little, Brown, 1931.

————. "The Last Days of the Romanovs." *Atlantic Monthly,* March 1928, 339–54.

[————]. "The Martyrdom of the Russian Church." *Catholic World* 117, no. 698 (May 1923): 221–30.

————. "Misleading the Public." *America,* April 12, 1930, 15–16.

————. "Papal Relief in Russia." *Woodstock Letters* 52, no. 1 (1923): 32–41.

————. "Pius the Eleventh, Champion of Truth." *America,* February 18, 1939, 462–63.

————. "Religion and the Modern Mind." *Catholic Mind* 33, no. 20 (October 22, 1935): 381–87.

————. "Rights and Obligations of Citizenship under the Constitution." *National Republic* 17, no. 9 (January 1930): 28–29.

————. "A Roman Catholic Indictment." *Current History* 32 (April 1930): 36–38.

[————]. "Russia," *America,* April 14, 1923, 604.

————. "Some Observations of the Soviet Problem." *Annals of the American Academy of Social and Political Science* 132 (July 1927): 8–13.

————. "Soviet Russia's Foreign Policy Does Not Justify U.S. Recognition Yet." *Annals of the American Academy of Social and Political Science* 121 (July 1926): 105–9.

————. "The Spiritual Aspect of Foreign Policy." *Catholic Mind* 50, no. 1079 (November 1952): 641–46.

————."The Third American Crisis." *Nation's Business* 25 (June 1937): 66–67.

————. *Total Empire: The Roots and Progress of World Communism.* Milwaukee: Bruce, 1951.

————. *Total Power: A Footnote to History.* New York: Doubleday, 1948.

————. "The Two Standards in 1935." *Informationes et Notitiae* 1, no. 4 (June 1935): 114–17.

————. "What Recognition of Russia Means." *Catholic Mind* 32, no. 2 (January 22, 1934): 27–32.

————. *Why Pope Pius XI Asked Prayers for Russia on March 19, 1930: A Review of the Facts in the Case Together with Proofs of the International Program of the Soviet Government.* New York: Catholic Near East Welfare Association, 1930.

"Walsh Calls Accord Harbinger of Peace." *New York Times*, June 22, 1929, 2.

Wangler, Thomas E. "Myth, Worldviews and Late Nineteenth Century American Catholic Expansionism." In *Rising from History: U.S. Catholic Theology Looks to the Future*, edited by Robert J. Daly, 71–82. Lanham, Md.: University Press of America, 1987.

Warren, Donald. *Radio Priest: Charles Coughlin, the Father of Hate Radio.* New York: Free Press, 1996.

Watkins, Anna, ed. *Footnotes to History: Selected Writings and Speeches of Edmund A. Walsh, S.J.* Washington, D.C.: Georgetown University Press, 1990.

Wattenberg, Ben J., ed. *Historical Statistics of the United States: From Colonial Times to the Present.* New York: Basic Books, 1976.

"Way Seen as Laid for Lasting Peace." *New York Times*, June 23, 1939, 22.

Weinstein, Allen. *Perjury: The Hiss-Chambers Case.* New York: Knopf, 1978.

Weissman, Benjamin M. *Herbert Hoover and Famine Relief to Soviet Russia, 1921–1923.* Stanford, Calif.: Stanford University Press, 1974.

"Where Protestantism is Defaulting." *Christian Century*, May 21, 1952, 604.

Whitley, Edward J., C.S.P. "Father John J. Burke, C.S.P., and Mexican Church-State Relations, 1927–1929." Master's thesis, Saint Paul's College, 1951.

Wiggers, Richard D. "Creating International Humanitarian Law (IHL): World War II, the Allied Occupations, and the Treaties That Followed." Ph.D. diss., Georgetown University, 2000.

Will, Allen Sinclair. "Destroying Religion in Russia." *New York Times*, June 1, 1924, III, 1:1, 24.

Williams, Michael. *The Shadow of the Pope.* New York: McGraw-Hill, 1932.

Wilson, Joan Hoff. *Ideology and Economics: U.S. Relations with the Soviet Union, 1918–1933*. Columbia: University of Missouri Press, 1974.

Wolf, Maggie Reichard. "A Landmark at 50." *Georgetown Magazine*, Winter 1999, 26–29.

Yergin, Daniel. *Shattered Peace: The Origins of the Cold War and the National Security State*. Boston: Houghton Mifflin, 1977.

Zatko, James J. *Descent into Darkness: The Destruction of the Roman Catholic Church in Russia, 1917–1923*. Notre Dame, Ind.: University of Notre Dame Press, 1965.

Zerzan, John. "Understanding the Anticommunism of the National Civic Federation." *International Review of Social History* 19, no. 2 (1974): 194–210.

Zienike, Earl F. "The Formulation and Initial Implementation of U.S. Occupation Policy in Germany." In *U.S. Occupation in Europe After World War II*, edited by Hans A. Schmitt, 27–44. Lawrence: Regents Press of Kansas, 1978.

Zimmermann, Warren. *First Great Triumph: How Five Americans Made Their Country a World Power*. New York: Farrar, Straus and Giroux, 2002.

Zink, Harold. *The United States in Germany, 1944–1955*. Princeton, N.J.: Van Nostrand, 1957.

Zitron, Celia Lewis. *The New York City Teachers Union, 1916–1964: A Story of Educational and Social Commitment*. New York: Humanities Press, 1968.

Zugger, Christopher Lawrence. *The Forgotten: Catholics of the Soviet Empire from Lenin through Stalin*. Syracuse, N.Y.: Syracuse University Press, 2001.

INTERVIEWS

Durkin, Rev. Joseph T., S.J., at Georgetown University, September 27, 1999.

Morse, George P., Jr. at Georgetown University, August 21, 2002.

O'Brien, Dr. William V., at Georgetown University, January 31, 1999.

INDEX

viet-American alliance and, 104,
108–109; Haushofer and, 111–12,
125–26; Geopolitics courses at
SFS, 114–15; War Department
and, 115–17; Nazism and, 104,
105, 106, 117–18, 124; Holocaust
and, 124–25; Nuremberg and,
121–30; as promoter of geopolitics, xiv, 112, 116, 133; on Cold
War, 134, 137–38; on Yalta, 151;
enhanced prestige during Cold
War, 135; on United Nations,
130–31; on Truman Doctrine,
141; on Marshall Plan, 141; on
militarization of American foreign
policy, 151–52; on Korean Conflict, 151; on China, 228n50; CIA
and, 149; UMT commission and,
143–148; and Truman, 148; on
atomic warfare, 152–54; FBI and,
63–64, 91, 160, 232n79; Joseph
McCarthy and, 157–60; George
F. Kennan and, 160–62; Protestant reaction to, 163–64; reputation within the Society of Jesus,
193n79; stroke, 165; final years
and death, 165–66; legacy, 166–
67, 170–71; as public speaker,
54–55; flair for publicity, 15–16;
as writer, 59, 74; on Catholic
anticommunism, 91–94; on Christianity and Western civilization,
29, 36, 47, 90, 105; on Catholic
patriotism, 77, 105
Walsh, John, 7
War Communism, 24

Washington Post, 157, 160, 166
Washington Star, 152, 155, 166
Washington Times-Herald, 166
Webster, Daniel, 3–4
Webster, Nesta, 42–43
Weigel, Gustave, 16
White, Edward D., 8
Whittlesey, Derwent, 116
*Why Pope Pius XI Asked Prayers for
Russia* (1930), 66–67
Wickersham, C. W., 120
Wiesel, Henri, 13
Williams, John, 7
Williams, Roger, 77
Wilson, Charles E., 143
Wilson, Joan Hoff, 74
Wilson, Woodrow, 1, 49, 56, 74, 103
Wilsonianism, 60
Winfrey, Cassie Jane, 144
Winthrop, John, 4, 131
Wolf, Maggie Reichard, 149
Woodstock College, 10
Woodstock Letters, 39
Wright, Quincy, 117

Yakovlev, Nikolai, 70
Yale Institute of International Stud-
ies, 112
Yalta, 151, 156
Yergin, Daniel, 139, 150

Zahn, Gordon C., 154
Zatko, James J., 31
Zeitschrift für Geopolitik, 110, 111
Zelie, John, 38
Zugger, Christopher, 33, 35